Turbo C® Programming

Alan C. Plantz
William M. Brown
Michael Yester
Lee Atkinson

Turbo C® Programming

© 1989 by Que® Corporation

Library of Congress Catalog No.: 88-63863

ISBN No.: 0-88022-430-4

93 92 91 90 89   8 7 6 5 4 3 2 1

Interpretation of the printing code: the rightmost double-digit number is the year of the book's printing; the rightmost single-digit number, the number of the book's printing. For example, a printing code of 89-4 shows that the fourth printing of the book occurred in 1989.

Turbo C Programming is based on Version 2.0 of Turbo C.

ABOUT THE AUTHORS ▼

Alan C. Plantz

Alan Plantz is quality assurance manager at Dome Software Corporation, which develops distributed object-oriented data management systems. He develops operating procedures and is heavily involved in product testing. The author of *C Quick Reference* and technical editor of *C Programming Guide*, 3rd Edition, both published by Que Corporation, Mr. Plantz has worked for several years with Turbo C and Turbo Pascal; he finds their development environments outstanding.

William M. Brown

William M. Brown has worked in the computer industry for over 13 years, including positions with Prime Computer and Massachusetts Computer Corporation. He has spent six years writing C application software for government and industry. Currently, Mr. Brown is the manager of professional services for Dome Software Corporation.

Michael Yester

For the last ten years, Michael Yester has been involved in the design, development, and management of financial systems. He holds an M.B.A. in finance and an M.S. in computer science and has taught courses in both systems design and accounting. Currently, he is an independent consultant residing in Los Angeles, California.

Lee Atkinson

Lee Atkinson has worked in data processing since 1969, and has been employed in government, industry, insurance, and banking. Currently, he is MVS/ESA systems programmer for Deposit Guaranty National Bank in Jackson, Mississippi. Off the job, he enjoys golf and flying. Lee and Bonnie Atkinson's son Christopher was born while work on this book was in progress.

Publishing Manager
Allen L. Wyatt, Sr.

Product Development Specialist
Bill Nolan

Project Coordinator
Gail S. Burlakoff

Editing and Indexing
Brown Editorial Service

Editorial Assistant
Ann K. Taylor

Keyboarding
Lee Hubbard
Type Connection, Indianapolis, Indiana

Technical Editor
Robert Jeffrey Moore

Illustrator
Susan Moore

Cover and Book Design
Dan Armstrong

Production
David Kline
Jennifer Matthews
Joe Ramon
Dennis Sheehan
Peter Tocco

Composed in Garamond and Universal Monospace #1
by Que Corporation and Alexander Typesetting

CONTENT OVERVIEW

Introduction 1

Part I Defining, Designing, and Coding the Program

Chapter 1 Defining Requirements and Designing
the Program *(Alan Plantz)* 5
Chapter 2 Coding the Program *(Alan Plantz)* 33
Chapter 3 Choosing the Right Tools *(Alan Plantz)* 59
Chapter 4 Using Library Functions *(Alan Plantz)* 91
Chapter 5 Miscellaneous Programming Features
(William M. Brown) 127
Chapter 6 Working with Turbo Assembler
(Michael Yester) 149

Part II Compiling and Linking

Chapter 7 Compiling, Checking, and Linking the Program
(Alan Plantz) 199
Chapter 8 Using TCC, the Command-line Compiler
(Alan Plantz) 231

Part III Testing and Debugging

Chapter 9 Testing and Debugging Strategies
(Lee Atkinson) 245
Chapter 10 Logic, Branch, and Path Testing
(Lee Atkinson) 289
Chapter 11 Data Validation and Analysis *(Lee Atkinson)* 317

Part IV Programming Projects

Chapter 12 Producing Graphs and Graphics
(William M. Brown) 371
Chapter 13 Reading a Mail Merge File *(William M. Brown)* . . .391
Chapter 14 Reading and Processing a Binary File
(William M. Brown) 407
Appendix A ASCII Codes and the Extended Character Set 421
Index 431

TABLE OF CONTENTS ▼

Introduction 1

▼

I **Defining, Designing, and Coding the Program**

1 **Defining Requirements and Designing the Program** *(Alan Plantz)* **5**

Program Development of Today's Applications 6
Defining Requirements................................ 7
The Importance of Being Specific 8
 Using Prototypes to Define Requirements 10
 Goals for Development 10
Designing the Program.............................. 11
 How Do You Choose a Design Strategy? 12
  General Design Techniques....................... 13
   Top-down Technique........................... 13
   Bottom-Up Technique 14
 Designing the User Interface 15
  Modes 16
  On-line Help.................................. 16
  Data Security 17
 Portability 17
 Structured versus "Quick and Dirty" Design 18
 Single-File versus Multiple-File Programs 19
 "Write Your Own" versus Purchased
  Routine Libraries 20
 Data Structures.................................. 21
  Stacks.. 22
  Queues 23
  Linked Lists................................... 24
  Trees 25
 Necessary Functions.............................. 26
  Error Handling................................ 26
  Files and I/O 27
  Memory Model Considerations 29
  Code Size 29
  Data Size 30
  Data Access Time 30
  Function Use 30

        Graphic or Text Displays 31
        Performance Considerations. 31
    Summary. 32

2   **Coding the Program** (*Alan Plantz*) 33

    Using the Editor Effectively. 34
        Coding Style 34
            Comment Headers. 35
            Inline Code Comments. 36
            Identifier Names 37
            Indenting and Brace Placement. 38
            Other Style Considerations. 41
        Working with Function Prototypes. 42
        Pair Matching 43
        Setting Markers. 44
        Using On-Line Help 44
        Memory-resident C and Pascal Help for Any Program
           (THELP.COM) 45
    Placing Functions and Modules. 46
        Making Functions Restricted or More Visible 50
            Using the Static Storage Class 50
                Using Function Prototypes 50
                Using Scope to Your Advantage. 52
                Accessing Data in More Than One File. 52
    Making Good Use of Header Files 53
        Include Files 53
        Constants. 54
        Typedefs. 54
        Variables 56
        Preprocessor Statements. 56
    Summary. 57

3   **Choosing the Right Tools** (*Alan Plantz*) 59

    Determining the Right Set of Tools for the Job 59
        Knowing Which Header Files To Use. 60
        An Overview of the Header Files. 63
            Memory Management (*alloc.h*). 63
            Assert Debugging Macro (*assert.h*) 65
            DOS BIOS Function Calls (*bios.h*) 65
            Console I/O (*conio.h*). 66
            Character Conversion and Classification (*ctype.h*). . . . 67
            Directory Manipulation (*dir.h*) 68
            DOS-specific System Routines (*dos.h*) 69

Error Message Numbering (*errno.h*) 71
Low-level File Attributes (*fcntl.h*) 72
Floating-point Parameters (*float.h*) 72
Graphics Information (*graphics.h*) 73
Low-level I/O (*io.h*) 75
Type Sizes and Environmental Limits (*limits.h*) 77
Mathematics (*math.h*) 77
Memory/Buffer (*mem.h*) 78
DOS Process Management (*process.h*) 79
Nonlocal Jumps (*setjmp.h*) 82
File Sharing (*share.h*) 82
Special Error Handling (*signal.h*) 83
Variable Arguments (*stdargs.h*) 83
Standard Definitions (*stddef.h*) 84
Standard I/O (*stdio.h*) 85
Miscellaneous Standard Library (*stdlib.h*) 86
String Handling (*string.h*) 88
File-handling Constants (*sys\stat.h*) 88
Current Time Information (*sys\timeb.h*) 89
Time Type (*sys\types.h*) 89
Time Functions (*time.h*) 89
Machine-dependent Constants (*values.h*) 90
Summary 90

4   **Using Library Functions** *(Alan Plantz)* **91**
The *allocmem( )* Function 92
The *bioskey( )* Function 94
The *bsearch( )* and *lsearch( )* Functions 98
The *coreleft( )* Function 101
The *country( )* Function 104
The *detectgraph( )* Function 107
The *getc( )*, *getch( )*, *getchar( )*, and
    getche( ) Functions 109
The *harderr( )* Function 112
The *qsort( )* Function 116
The *rand( )*, *srand( )*, *random( )*, and
    randomize( ) Functions 118
The *strtok( )* Function 120
The *va_start( )*, *va_end( )*, *va_list( )*,
    and *va_arg( )* Functions 122
Summary 125

5   Miscellaneous Programming Features
      (William M. Brown)............................ 127

Pseudovariables....................................... 127
Predefined Global Variables 131
    Variables for Reading Command-line Arguments
      and DOS Variables............................... 131
    Variables for Time and Time Zones 133
    Variable for Writing Output....................... 134
    Variables for Detecting Coprocessors
      and Version Numbers 135
    Variables for Errors 137
    Variables for System Values 138
    Variables for Interrupts.......................... 140
Interrupts.. 141
Floating-point Libraries.............................. 145
Summary... 148

6   Working with Turbo Assembler
      (Michael Yester) 149

Using Inline Assembly Statements 149
    Compiling a Program Containing Inline
      Assembly Statements 150
    The Structure of an Inline Assembly Statement..... 152
      Semicolons in Inline Assembly Statements 153
      Comments in Inline Assembly Statements.......... 154
      Labels in Inline Assembly Statements............ 154
    Preserving Registers.............................. 155
    Referencing Data in Inline Assembly............... 156
      Specifying Variable Sizes....................... 157
      Calling Inline Functions with No Arguments 157
      Returning Function Values....................... 159
      Using Function Arguments Passed by Value........ 160
      Using Function Arguments Passed by Reference ... 162
      Accessing Function Arguments as
        Memory Locations.............................. 165
      Problems in Using Local Data 169
      Using a Variable Number of Function Arguments .. 171
    The Naming Conventions Used by Turbo C
      and the Turbo Assembler 174
      Referencing Turbo C Identifiers from Inline
        Assembly Code................................. 175
      Avoiding Case Conflicts 177

Using Stand-alone Assembly Language Routines........... 178
  Segments and Memory Models...................... 178
    The Tiny Memory Model 179
    The Small Memory Model 180
    The Medium Memory Model..................... 180
    The Compact Memory Model 180
    The Large Memory Model 181
    The Huge Memory Model 181
    Using the Turbo Assembler's Simplified
      Segment Directives 182
  Sharing Data Items among Multiple Modules.......... 183
    Declaring Symbols Public....................... 183
    Declaring Symbols External 183
  Producing Assembly Language Programs
    from Turbo C 184
  Similarities between Inline and Stand-alone
    Assembly Code................................. 189
    Using Inline Code.............................. 189
    Calling Assembly Language Routines from C........ 190
    Calling C Routines from Assembly Language........ 192
  Summary... 194

II   Compiling and Linking

7   Compiling, Checking, and Linking
the Program *(Alan Plantz)* 199

Compiling the Program 199
  Use Maximum Error Checking for the First Compile.... 200
  Using TC's Built-in Syntax Checking.................. 200
  Is the Compiler Telling the Truth? 201
  Using Compiler Options 201
    Optimization................................. 202
    Debugging Information......................... 203
    Memory Models.............................. 203
  Using the CPP Preprocessor Separately 203
Linking the Program............................... 204
  Symbol Tables................................... 205
Linking and .MAP Files............................. 206
Addressing Problems in Linking 209
Making the Program............................... 212
  Creating a Project File............................ 212
File Dependencies and the Autodependency Feature 213

Accessing .OBJ files, Vendor Routines, and Graphics.... 213
Blending in Modules from Other Languages 214
Using a Make File with the Turbo C Compiler 216
    Invoking MAKE 217
    Creating a Make File............................ 217
    Using Macros with MAKE........................ 220
    MAKE Directives 221
Building the Program 223
Testing and Debugging the Program as a Whole.......... 224
   Benefits of Testing Code............................ 224
   Examples of Testing and Debugging.................. 226
   Types of Bugs and Types of Tests 227
Configuration Management and Source Code Control 228
   Version Control Techniques 228
   Version Numbering................................. 229
The Final .EXE (.COM) File 230
Summary.. 230

8   Using TCC, the Command-line Compiler

(Alan Plantz) **231**

Environment Options..................................... 233
Compiler Options.. 234
   Code Generation Options........................... 234
   Error Message Options 235
      ANSI Violation Options 236
      Common Error Options 236
      Less Common Error Options..................... 237
      Portability Warning Options 238
   Macro Options 238
   Memory-Model Options............................. 238
   Optimization Options 239
   Naming Segment Options 239
Source Code Options.................................... 239
Linker Options... 240
Summary.. 241

III   Testing and Debugging

9   Testing and Debugging Strategies

(Lee Atkinson) **245**

The Difference between Testing and Debugging.......... 246
   When Do You Have a Bug? 246

Recognizing that a Bug Exists 246
Discovering the Type of Bug 247
Locating the Bug 248
Fixing the Bug 249
Types of Testing 250
Unit Testing 250
Integration Testing 251
System Testing 252
Regression Testing 254
Performance/Time Testing 255
Remote Debugging 262
Hardware Debugging 265
General Testing Strategies 265
Top-Down, Bottom-Up, or Topsy-Turvy 266
Automating Testing Procedures and Documentation 267
Tips for Simplifying the Debugging Process 273
Write for the Most General User Audience 273
Use a Top-Down Design and Bottom-up
Coding Strategy 274
Prototype Code To Make Testing Incremental 275
Use Only One Development Language 275
Formalize the Data Validation and
Analysis Process 276
Learn the Full Range of Function in the Debugger . . . 276
Use the Black Box Approach 276
Debugging Program Internals 277
Beta Testing Your New Code 277
Selecting the Most Useful Debugging Environment 277
Using the Basic Debugging Tools in the
Turbo Debugger 279
Getting Started with the Turbo Debugger 279
TD Menus 281
TD Windowing 281
Identifying Windows 283
The Module Window 283
TD Hot Keys 284
Writing TD Macros for Automation and Retesting 284
Automating an Audit Trail of Events during Testing 286
Summary 286

10   **Logic, Branch, and Path Testing**
      (Lee Atkinson) 289
Preliminary Definitions 289
Tracing 291

Tracing Machine Instructions. 297
Capturing the PSP Address 298
Locating the End of the DOS Segment 300
Stepping Over 302
Automating Program Analysis with Breakpoints. 306
Simple Breakpoints and the Log Window 306
Setting Conditional Breakpoints. 307
Breakpoint Locations and External Identifiers 309
Writing Expression True Conditions 312
Summary. 315

11   Data Validation and Analysis *(Lee Atkinson)*. . . . 317

Data Validation 317
How Data Drives Logic 317
Looking at Live Data 318
The Inspect Command 318
Details on Overriding Scope 320
Understanding Scope 320
Inspecting Variables in Another Scope 324
Using Scope-Override Syntax 325
Representation of Simple Variables 327
Representation of Compound Variables. 329
Evaluating Expressions during Debugging. 333
Changing Values Using Expressions
with Side Effects 333
Using a Watches Window 336
Using the Variables Window. 341
Using the CPU Window. 342
Using the Registers Window. 343
Boundary Value Analysis. 344
Determining the Possible Range of Values 345
Finding Upper and Lower Limits,
and One Beyond 346
Automated Validation of Data 347
What Turbo C Can Do. 347
I/O Functions 347
Process Control Functions 347
Classification Macros 348
Conversion Functions. 349
Manipulation Functions 350
Diagnostic Functions 351
What Turbo C Cannot Do 351
Data Range Checking 352

Hard-Coded Data versus
    Code-Independent Data 353
    Metadata Concepts and Techniques 353
Designing Test-Case Data 354
  How Much Is Enough? Too Much? 354
  Allowing for Boundary Value Extremes 355
Designing Manageable Data Structures 355
  Local versus Global Variable Definitions 355
  Field Structuring 356
    Data Fields 356
      Numeric Data 356
    Text Data 356
  Controlling Variable Proliferation 357
  Handling Large Amounts of Data 357
    Tables versus Files 357
    Designing File Layouts 358
    Record and Block Buffers 358
    Using Turbo Debugger with Files 359
    Large-scale Text Buffers 359
    Using the Memory Dump Window 360
  Analyzing Parameters Passed to Functions 361
    Details on Address and Value Parameters 361
Common Sources of Data Errors 362
  Failure to Initialize Automatic Variables 363
  Reference to Automatic Variables
    That No Longer Exist 363
  Confusion of Operators 363
  Confusion about Operator Precedence 363
  Pointer Problems 365
  Arithmetic Errors 365
    Signed and Unsigned Types 365
    Mixed Field Lengths 365
    Failure To Account for Mathematical Anomalies 366
  Scope Errors 366
Summary 366

IV   Programming Projects

12   Producing Graphs and Graphics

    (William M. Brown) 371
  Defining Requirements 371
  Designing the Program 372

Implementing the Program 373
   Make Files 373
      The *bar3d.exe* File 375
      The *ourgrap.lib* File 375
      Other Object Code Files 375
   Input File for Module Names 376
   The Source Code 376
   Program Structures 386
   Program Variables and Functions 387
   Program Output 388
   Summary 389

13   **Reading a Mail Merge File** *(William M. Brown)*   **391**
   Analyzing Requirements 391
   Designing the Program 392
   Implementing the Application 394
   Summary 406

14   **Reading and Processing a Binary File**
      (William M. Brown) **407**
   Designing the Program 408
   Implementing the Program 408
   Summary 419

A   **ASCII Codes and the Extended Character Set** **421**

   Index **431**

TRADEMARK ACKNOWLEDGMENTS

Que Corporation has made every attempt to supply trademark information about company names, products, and services mentioned in this book. Trademarks indicated below were derived from various sources. Que Corporation cannot attest to the accuracy of this information.

ANSI is a registered trademark of American National Standards Institute.

Codeview is a trademark of Microsoft Corporation.

ProKey is a trademark of RoseSoft, Inc.

SuperKey, Turbo C, Turbo Debugger, and Turbo Pascal are registered trademarks and Turbo Prolog is a trademark of Borland International, Inc.

UNIX System V is a registered trademark and UNIX is a trademark of AT&T.

Introduction

Programming with Turbo C Professional can be both a creative art and a measured science. Developing programs involves more than just writing code—development includes defining requirements, selecting designs to impart what the developer hopes is optimal program performance, testing the program to see that the customer's expectations are met, and putting documentation and product together for release. In a world where everything seems to be going faster, programmers also hope to piece programs together faster and have a better quality product than could be developed in the past. *Turbo C Programming* stresses making program development easier.

This book discusses how to develop a program from start to finish. *Turbo C Programming* assumes that you already are familiar with the basics of the C programming language, the MS-DOS operating system, and that you are at least somewhat familiar with Borland's Turbo C compilers.

Throughout the book, advanced topics in all areas are discussed. Some of these topics are double indirection and advanced pointer usage in C, installing and working with critical-error handlers and other DOS interrupts, using the debuggers for boundary value analysis, and hints on using the compilers to your advantage.

The Turbo C Professional package helps programmers to accelerate their development time over traditional command-line compilers. The addition of two versions of a debugger is a boost that can cut program development time by 20 to 25 percent. Turbo C Professional also includes an assembler. The assembler is necessary for optimizing those portions of a program that must run as fast as possible to perform well. Additional utilities include `TDSTRIP`, for stripping out debugging information from executables, and `BGIOBJ`, which converts .BGI graphics device drivers into linkable object modules. These utilities give the programmer capabilities that otherwise would take a long time to develop.

This book explains these tools and describes others, such as some of the more obscure C standard library routines. Familiarity with the functions and utilities that are part of the Turbo C Professional package will pay off. If a feature needed for your program is not there, outside sources like external routine libraries, linkers, error-checkers and the like can be obtained from vendors.

A major portion of the book focuses on the integrated and stand-alone debuggers. Once the major pieces of development software missing from Borland's products, these debuggers now are here. Both versions have plenty of features to make debugging and testing easy.

This book explains testing techniques you can use to ensure that your program operates correctly or to point out weak areas you can improve. Having a well-tested, feature-laden program will mean less maintenance work for you later and happier customers up front. Whether the "customer" is you or a client, the program should run as well as possible and be able to handle unexpected conditions without crashing or locking up. Customers expect a lot—a program must be able not only to recover from errors but also to suggest correct solutions or alternatives. A sophisticated user interface and error-trapping adds a great deal of code to a program, increases development and testing times, but provides a better program.

Software development life cycles and development strategies are popular topics in computer science today. Even with newer technologies such as object-oriented programming, you still need the basic parts of development: requirements, design, coding, and testing. Testing was (and unfortunately still is) underutilized in program development. Developers today are also striving for ideas to save time as far ahead in the development process as possible: rapid prototyping, code generators, and code reusability are part of the answer. Verifying that requirements are met in design and coding is also part of the answer to shortening development and simultaneously making it more correct.

Enjoy *Turbo C Programming*, and try to pick up some development ideas from the book. You should find suggestions to help you produce a quality program at any level, learn how to use your present resources more efficiently, and perhaps point you in directions you have not yet considered.

Part I

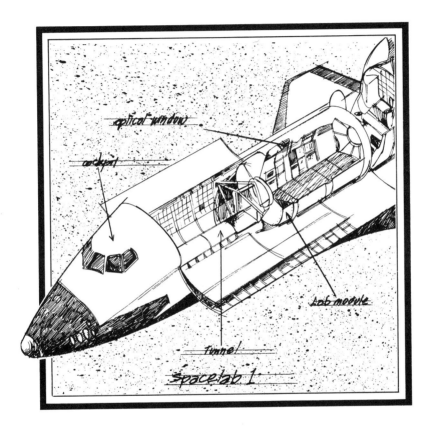

Defining, Designing, and
Coding the Program

Alan
Plantz

CHAPTER

1

Defining Requirements and Designing the Program

Writing a program is complicated. In this section of the book, which discusses the basics of authoring a computer application, you will learn the fundamental steps of development, along with shortcuts and pitfalls to watch out for. Because Turbo C Professional is geared toward a professional audience, professional development techniques are presented. This does not mean that your programs must be created for commercial gain; on the contrary, the methods demonstrated here can be used also for private or hobby applications.

In very general terms, this chapter covers the following:

❏ developing programs

❏ creating specific requirements

❏ choosing an appropriate design strategy

❏ design considerations such as modes, data structures, etc.

❏ portability

❏ using outside libraries

❏ trees, queues, stacks, and linked lists

❏ file considerations in creating a program

❏ memory model factors

❏ graphics

Program Development of Today's Applications

In computer science, the term *software engineering* has been assigned to the process of application development. The term indicates refinement of the development process into known steps and involves measurements to see whether goals are being met. In this chapter I discuss some aspects of software engineering that you can apply to your projects.

Writing a program involves many interrelated steps. In the past few years, the number of books, articles, and other resources describing the techniques of program development has skyrocketed. TSRs, screen compilers, animated graphics, McCabe's complexity measurement, lint, and other techniques and tools were once known to only a few. The main thing is to think carefully and thoroughly about what you want to do before doing it.

The days of programming "off the top of your head" are gone. Although this statement may offend some developers, they have no hope of tackling the complexity required in many programs without doing some planning. Spontaneous methodology suffices only for the shortest, most trivial programs. Anything more requires more thought.

Today's sophisticated programs usually require more features than those written five or more years ago. Increased error checking; a consistent, easy-to-use interface; flexible reports; and other attributes are now needed. Developers are already finding that 640K, once thought to be 10 times greater than the amount of memory that would ever be needed for development, is now far too little. Operating systems themselves are now well above this limit.

Because users have become more computer-savvy and have learned what computers and programmers are capable of doing, the characteristics users want in their applications have increased in number and complexity. Meeting these needs places an increased burden on the developer. It means cultivating new implementation techniques, improving on old algorithms, enhancing testing methods, and trying to keep track of myriad requirements.

As if that weren't enough, the time lines for all this activity are growing ever shorter. Projects always seem to be needed yesterday. The lack of development time puts extra pressure on developers, analysts, and other systems people.

Depending on the size of a program and on who will use it, you can either develop your own method of program development or choose one already in use. If you are looking for the "one and only true approach," don't waste your time—different projects involve different techniques. In the past year, journal articles have been published about prototyping, object-oriented design, the Jackson development method, and others. Try to become familiar with some of the program-development techniques and decide whether any will suit your needs.

The typical *software development life cycle* involves a series of steps:

1. determining user requirements

2. designing the program to fulfill these requirements

3. coding the design in one or more languages

4. testing the program to ensure not only that the requirements are met but also that errors are caught, unexpected events do not occur, and so on

This series of steps is an oversimplified version of the cycle(s) that occur in real life. Snags pop up along the way, originating perhaps even with user requirements, which may not be complete or mean the same thing to everyone. Design flaws may involve unforeseen hardware limitations, algorithms that are too slow to be effective, and so on. Testing may seem to take forever, and bugs may still exist in the program.

Defining Requirements

The "hurry-up bug" often seems to bite programmers—especially those who work independently. They fail to spend enough time determining requirements and designing the program, wanting to jump as soon as possible into coding and glide right on to project completion. Stepwise program development is usually a matter of discipline, and the developer must train himself or herself to reserve more time for these steps. Determining user requirements is especially important. According to some sources, anywhere from 40 percent to 80 percent of program failures stem from inadequate definitions of requirements.

Program development begins with identification of the user(s) of the program. This may be yourself or others at the workplace who need a certain utility. In the broadest commercial sense, *users* are the public—everyone from computer neophytes to advanced users who do programming themselves. Unfortunately, the term *user* sometimes has a negative connotation for programmers: the user is the person who makes life miserable for programmers by finding bugs, demanding additional features, complaining about deadlines, and so on. In this book, I refer to this group of people from now on as *customers*, since they buy or are the ultimate audience for the program. The customer does not make the program contain bugs—the responsibility lies with the programmer who did not accurately ascertain or meet the requirements, made a mistake in coding, or provided a faulty design. Sometimes the customer will set a deadline, but it may also be the programmer or company that sets a timeline and finds it impossible to comply with this limitation. Perhaps the programmer and customer need to discuss the development and both make concessions.

Once you have identified the customers for your program, find out what their specific needs are. Don't just *think* about these needs—write them all down so you won't overlook any. Interview the customers and ask them as many questions as you can. If *you* are the customer, think several times about the program requirements to make sure nothing has been overlooked.

There is nothing wrong in working with requirements in an iterative process. It is extremely difficult to think of everything the first time around. Determine whether you can fulfill each requirement within your program; you may leave some for later versions or omit them altogether.

The Importance of Being Specific

Application requirements include everything the program will be capable of doing. The customer's needs may include such broad issues as

❏ what the user interface should look like

❏ whether communication capabilities should be included

❏ whether information in the reports needs to be sorted

❏ whether customer input to the program should be one field at a time, or whether full-screen editing should be included

❏ how fast database record access should occur

The customer's desires may then be specified in greater detail:

1. All pop-up menus should have cyan borders with yellow text on a black background; highlighted items should be blue text on a magenta background.

2. The speed of communications transmissions should include 1200, 2400, and 9600 baud rates.

3. Accounting reports should include a subtotal for each division account and a subtotal for each division, with totals for all divisions. Include a blank line before and after the subtotal line. Totals should appear at the end of the report, separated from the body by a double blank line, with a double-underline appearing above the total. Accounts should be sorted by ascending account number.

4. Editing of fields should allow access to any field on the screen by means of the Tab or Enter key, or by using the arrow keys to move from field to field.

5. The database should allow manipulation of at least 5,000 records, with access to any record within 0.5 second.

If these definitions of requirements seem specific, they are meant to be. It is difficult to implement what you don't know or don't understand. Now examine each of the requirements listed and see what might have happened had requirements not been specified in adequate detail:

For the baud rate requirement, the customer could have said, "Varying communications rates are needed." What does that mean? That rates should vary from 300 to 19K baud? Should only 300 and 1200 baud rates be allowed? With this lack of exactness, the programmer could write code for performing communications at 19K baud for a customer who could use only 300 and 1200 baud levels. When the developer cannot pinpoint the requirement, producing an error-free program becomes geometrically more difficult.

For item 1, menu colors, the customer may have stated, "Pop-up menus should be colored consistently." Does this mean that pop-up menus can be the same color as on-screen text? Should the pop-ups use one color scheme in data entry mode and a different color scheme in edit mode? Too much is left to the imagination.

Vague wording for report formats (requirement 3) would be "Subtotals and totals should appear on each report." Should subtotals appear at the left end of a line, with totals on the right end of the same line? Should the subtotals appear immediately after the group to which they apply?

In item 4, the customer might have stated, "The program will allow access to any field on the screen." Does this mean by pressing Enter and going from one field to another, having to move through all fields in order to get back to the first field? Does it mean that the user can move back and forth among fields? Clearly, the more detailed specification is more useful.

For requirement 5, the record access standards could have been expressed as "Record access from the database should be acceptable." This requirement is ambiguous and does not give the developer a limit with which to work. Usually, the faster the access, the happier the customer. However, hardware and access algorithms can play a big role in fulfilling this customer need. Specifying a time limit could determine the type of access method needed for design, thus ruling out sequential record access and mandating a type of B^+ tree or hashing scheme.

A B^+ *tree* is a data structure that can form an index to a file to provide faster access to records. It is similar to an upside-down tree with the root at the top of the structure, rather than at the bottom. *Hashing* is a different method of indexing a file by providing direct access to records via keys made of parts of records. The number of records in the original requirement may also rule out a floppy-based system.

Stating requirements clearly helps you to hit the target. Requirements may also indicate a need for upgrading equipment if the present facilities cannot handle the customer's needs, or that you should use a particular communications protocol to handle data transmissions well at high speeds. Requirements also affect design. You, as the developer, may be given the freedom to choose a particular design or algorithm. In other cases, such as the database example, the customer's needs may narrow the range of methods allowable to implement his or her requests.

Using Prototypes To Define Requirements

No matter who determines requirements—you or the customer—the task certainly is not easy. More often than not, the customer may not know fully or exactly what he or she wants.

The *prototype method* is an increasingly popular way to help determine requirements. Under this system, the applications developer attempts to model the application using "fake" or real screens, reports, and so on to present a partial implementation of the customer's requirements. Automated tools, particularly those for designing screens and data-entry portions of a program, are especially useful. In other instances, the programmer's "bag of tricks" may consist of extensive routine libraries. The libraries should collect code previously tried and proven in another application. The tools and libraries provide a quick means of rapidly putting part of the program together to show customers. Some of the commercial prototyping programs available are Dan Bricklin's Demo Program, Matrix Layout from Matrix Software Technology Corporation, and ProtoGen from MacCulloh, Prymark Associates Limited.

Prototyping provides customer feedback and anticipates modification of requirements. Old, inadequate requirements can be changed, and new requirements added. Prototyping also can point out design flaws early on and can help you avoid later complications.

Goals for Development

When you start developing an application, set certain goals and keep them in mind. They will make your program more successful and your job easier. Your goals might include the following:

❑ Fulfill all customer requirements.

❑ Do the best possible job, eliminating as many errors as you can.

❑ Stay within time guidelines for development.

❑ Thoroughly test sections of the program—and the program as a whole—before giving them to the customer.

❑ Do not distribute an application you would not use yourself.

❑ Make the program as easy as possible for the customer to use, and provide adequate help facilities.

Designing the Program

Software design is the second "natural" step in program development. Design transforms requirements ("what" should be accomplished) into a program—"how" the task should be accomplished. The program's internal and external facets are determined in the design stage: the *algorithms* (a program's internal structure) are formulated; and data entry methods, program performance, memory requirement, graphics formats, and hardware considerations enter here in defining the program's external, physical aspects.

Design consists of models of what the program will look like and how it will act. The models convert concrete needs into abstract models. The C language itself does this transformation with devices—actual equipment is turned into abstract data structures that act the same no matter what equipment—disks, terminals, or printers—is involved. Then these models are examined or perhaps even programmed (as in a prototyping environment) to determine whether their logic and details are sound and perform efficiently enough to be part of the application.

Design involves levels of abstraction, structure, and modularization among programs. Care must be taken to place related routines in the same module, along with the data that will be used with the functions. For instance, you could place together in a module some memory-management routines and a buffer holding the data to be manipulated by the routines.

You might think of abstraction when you search for a particular algorithm to work with data structures such as binary trees, stacks, and queues. These data structures model—at least in some recognizable aspects—physical events such as apple trees in an orchard, piles of plates, or waiting in line at the store.

Another example of abstraction could be making a "chair" object for use in a CAD/CAM application, an interior design application, or perhaps for a furniture company examining material stress in order to build a stronger product. The chair could be turned into a C struct with the following form:

```
typedef struct chair
    {
    enum seatMaterial {wood, cloth, leather, plastic};
    enum frameMaterial {wood, metal, conduit};
    FASTENERTYPE fastener;
    int majorStressArea;
    double amtOfStress;
    } CHAIRTYPE;
```

This code defines an object type of CHAIRTYPE with fields for tracking the type of seat and frame material, the type of fastener for the frame, major area of stress, and the amount of stress at that point. You could declare two variables of the CHAIRTYPE to use in the program by adding the following line:

```
CHAIRTYPE testchair1, testchair2;
```

If you wanted to work with more than just a few chairs, you could make a "file of chairs" or an "array of chairs." The `struct chair` example also demonstrates a trait that seems to go hand-in-hand with abstraction. In this trait, called information hiding, the details may be a level or more deeper into the structure used. For instance, `fastener` is of type `FASTENERTYPE` about which you do not know the details. The actual description of this type may be hidden in a header file. Wherever it is located, you do not know now how it is implemented. Programmers should be able to work with such abstraction without knowing the minutiae of program components.

Design is one of the most creative parts of applications or systems development. The designer must be familiar with a number of system features: memory limitations and how memory is accessed; various sorting algorithms (to determine which will best fit the job); code portability, if the application will be moved from one machine to another, and so on. Perhaps the designer will think of an entirely new method or algorithm to use. (Maybe it will even be named after the designer, like the Boyer-Moore pattern-matching algorithm.)

The developer should spend considerable time thinking about design issues because the more time spent here, the more solid the implementation can be later. The cost of moving forward too hastily can be an algorithm too slow to handle the entire database or a line-drawing model that cannot accurately handle clipping outside of viewports. Lack of proper design can be even more disastrous, leading to database failure, an inability to handle different hardware, or logic that fails under certain conditions.

How Do You Choose a Design Strategy?

So many factors can affect design that it is hard to pinpoint them, even for a certain portion of a program. Literally *everything* can affect design.

As the first step in determining a design direction, you should examine customer requirements. The requirement *"All pop-up menus should have cyan borders with yellow text on a black background; highlighted items should be blue text on a magenta background"* tells a designer to forget about using a windows-management package that supports only monochrome or black-and-white monitors. Likewise, the screen package that implements only Lotus-style, pull-down menus is "out the door."

Another design consideration is just how intricate or complex the program needs to be. For example, there is probably no need to build in pop-up windows and a menuing system if the only inputs to the program are an input and an output file for converting data from one format to another. In this case, just asking for the name of the input file on one screen line and for that of the output file on another line would suffice, as would allowing them to be included on the command line of the program. A complicated user interface adds bulk to a program meant to be a simple utility. However, even a simple interface should provide adequate error checking in order to prevent such problems as searches for files that are not on the disk. Error checking keeps the application from crashing and may give the user another chance to enter the file name correctly.

Eliminating a user-friendly interface in this instance does not mean that such a shell does not have its place in other instances. As most programs become increasingly complicated, a user interface is necessary to help the customer operate the application. Consistent windowing, on-line help, "smart" menu choices, and other such features all can add greatly to the benefits of a program. Context-sensitive help is almost a necessity because programs have become so large and intricate that the customer gets lost trying to find his or her way around.

General Design Techniques

Design requires thought. The analyst must ponder what should happen in the program, be familiar with various methods and algorithms of execution, and know when to implement them. Performance measurements, the degree of difficulty involved in implementing and maintaining the design, the designer's personal experience, and other factors influence whether one strategy is preferable to another.

Top-down Technique

In the "top-down" design technique, you break down a program, a subprogram, or even a requirement into ever smaller pieces until the most elementary level is achieved. This technique is similar to writing an outline for a document. First, the main sections (I, II, and so on) are determined. Next come the sublevels (A, B, and so forth), with the breakdown continuing until small modules of basic ideas are created. The same happens with a program. For a program to convert data from one word-processing format to another, you might start like this:

I. Get input file
II. Get output file
III. Process file
IV. Close files

The next iteration of refinement might be

I. Get input file
    A. Check whether file exists
    B. If file does not exist, ask again for name
    C. Open file for input processing

II. Get output file
    A. Check whether file exists
    B. If file does not exist, ask again for name or create a file with that name
    C. Open file for input processing
III. Process file
    A. Read file
    B. If a character has a value of over ASCII 126, convert it
    C. Continue processing until end-of-file is reached
IV. Close files
    A. Close input file
    B. Close output file
    C. Exit the program

A partial expansion at the next level could be

I. Get input file
    A. Check whether file exists
        1. If a drive is given, check drive validity; if not valid, ask again for name
        2. If a path is given, attempt to find the path; if not valid, ask for name
        3. Attempt to find file; if not valid, ask for name

You can continue in this way until you reach the level of individual functions or simple data types such as `int`, `float`, and `char`.

Bottom-Up Technique

The "bottom-up" technique reverses the top-down scheme. The analyst starts with the fine details and works up toward the main level of the program. In this process, you first plan data structures, files, and so on, then develop algorithms to act on the data, and then perhaps create the menus to bind things together into a program. This method often is used in database applications if the existing functionality is mostly there. The analyst can start by creating record and file structures, then determine what additional functions need to be added to the system. You may need to include specific reports, sorting on multiple keys, or increased validation of data entered by the user. In reality, application design is often a combination of these two techniques.

Methods for stating the top-down or bottom-up strategies also vary. *Data flowcharts* are diagrams in which a variety of boxes and arrows are used to demonstrate the movement of data within a program. *Control flowcharts* are similar diagrams that display the movement of logic and execution within a system. *Pseudocode*, usually a "near-English" translation of the steps that must take place in the program, may help you understand the design. Even an *outline* like the one shown earlier can be used to document the design. *Data dictionaries* may be used with databases to provide a record of what is included in the database. Professionals may use techniques that involve various ways to draw flowcharts or implement structured design. These methodologies allow graphical representations in the form of flowcharts, hierarchies, and other diagrams showing relationships between functions (*HIPO charts*), data relationships (*Jackson structured methodologies*), and using truth tables (*Warnier-Orr diagrams*). Each of these design methods follows certain procedures to annotate the program design.

A popular, relatively new bottom-up method is called *object-oriented design*. Object-oriented design describes the world as "objects," which are units including both data and functions. A child object can inherit this information from a parent object, just as we inherit traits from our parents. The following sections address some of the design issues facing microcomputer programmers.

Designing the User Interface

The user interface, one of the most complicated parts of any program to develop, is increasingly important. Customers are demanding more (and friendlier) features to help them run applications more efficiently. Only the simplest programs provide only a command-driven approach.

Entire books have been written about user-interface traits, development, and problems. Some of the major considerations are

❏ Color

❏ Sound

❏ Wording

❏ Ease of manipulation

❏ Availability of help

❏ Consistency

❏ Security

User interface design can rely heavily on psychological aspects of customer-programmer interaction. Correct communication is paramount. Incorrect signals can confuse the customer and appear as a defect in the program. For example, ordinary messages should not be displayed in red and accompanied by computer chimes. Although you might use this treatment for the most fatal of warnings, using such a program is enough to raise the blood pressure of most people. The almost universal meanings of red for stop, yellow for caution, and green for go can be used to advantage in a program. Many customers strongly prefer to choose their own colors.

In addition to colors and sounds, wording also affects the customer's impressions of a program. The error message:

```
Primary key nonfunctional in quicksort algorithm
```

means nothing to the customer; a better message would be

```
Sort field value is too long. Please enter a shorter value.
```

Avoid computer jargon and examine all displayed program text, making sure that the customer will be able to understand it.

Modes

Customers want to be able to move around easily on-screen and to switch from one mode to another—from editing to deleting, for example. Full-screen editing is almost mandatory today. Designers rarely use the old-fashioned method of printing a prompt, getting user input, then displaying the next field prompt. The most widely used method of screen editing places all prompts on-screen and allows the customer to move from one field to another, up and down, left to right, and vice versa. Customers used to feel hemmed in also in the area of report generation—either users could generate reports only at certain points in a program, or only predefined reports were available. Report generators that give users flexibility in changing report formats are a great help.

Programs often work in *modes*. Edit modes often are different from view modes, in which data can be examined but not changed. Problems arise when keys are used inconsistently in different modes. For example, you can create a program in which the customer uses the Esc key to leave edit mode, but presses F10 to leave view mode. Consistency is important in computer applications.

Consistency eliminates guesswork and speeds up use because the customer knows what to expect when a certain key is pressed or a window appears. More precisely, be consistent in as many fundamental items as possible (for example, F1 always gives context-sensitive help). Although sometimes one keystroke in one mode will mean something else in another, this isn't necessarily bad. Look at Turbo Debugger for some examples of this.

On-line Help

Early microcomputer applications did not include any displays explaining the program. Messages may have appeared on-screen, but for an explanation of these messages and information about what to do, customers had to look in the user's manual (if one existed).

Today, help is considerably more sophisticated. *On-line help* is the capability of displaying help summaries while a customer uses the program. *Context-sensitive* help goes even further—it is tailored to a specific situation. For instance, when the customer places the cursor on a word and then presses a hot key, a help window appears with the relevant message. (A *hot key* is a specially designated key or set of keystrokes—F1 and Ctrl-Y, for example—that can be pressed at any time during program execution to perform certain actions.) In some cases, the help may be intelligent enough to suggest what to do next or to identify the problem. Such messages are typical of compiler syntax help; because the compiler knows what it expects, it can inform the customer of the proper syntax.

Data Security

Security is also a growing concern. Customers want to limit access to sensitive data. Security is especially prevalent in industry, where managers set different access levels for employees. Database applications and networks present additional problems. Customers usually cannot change a record's data while someone else is working with that record. In other cases, the customer can access the record only for viewing but cannot modify it. Unfortunately, security may also mean that the program must check itself for modification. Computer viruses and other infringements may introduce unseen dangers to applications.

Portability

As the marketplace fills with more types of hardware, languages, file formats, and other features, developers must stretch their skills to accommodate portability. One of the problems in dealing with so many different cases is a lack of standards. Programs that can handle many conditions are more likely to be accepted.

Portability has a certain meaning for the customer. It may mean that word-processing documents done on one machine can be transferred directly and used with a different program without having to be translated on another machine. Portability may also mean that the customer can expect the same response to the same keys on two different machines. For many customers, consistency and portability are synonymous. Customers who run consistent programs do not have to learn different sets of commands or different actions for different machines. Such customers may not even sacrifice program functionality.

For many Turbo C programmers, portability may mean adequate handling of various graphics adapters or disallowing hot-key assignment to certain keys on the extended keyboard. But to reach the widest market segment, you may need to consider other hardware environments. By keeping portability in mind when you design a program, you will have an easier job if you decide later to port your code. Spending some extra time up front can mean significant savings later—or even determine whether the port can be performed.

Portability has a different connotation for programmers and developers. In order to implement portability in code, more attention may have to be paid to detail and design, or the program's effectiveness may have to be expanded.

Luckily for Turbo C programmers, the ANSI C Standard exists. Written code that follows this standard should run the same when it is ported to another compiler or to another operating system, as long as the compiler in that environment also conforms to the standard. Although the guidelines are not yet finalized, many compiler vendors are already complying to a large extent with the Proposed Standard.

Nonstandard code, such as graphics routines, could be placed in separate modules or given generic interfaces. Take, for example, the graphics routine `ellipse()`, which takes six parameters in Turbo C: the X and Y coordinates of the center of the ellipse, the starting and ending angles, and the horizontal and vertical axes. Suppose that you are working with compiler X and a similar routine that uses the same coordinates, but in which the starting and ending angles and the horizontal and vertical axes are switched. You might address using the same graphics routine on two different machines or compilers by writing a separate routine and using conditional compilation:

```
void far drawEllipse(int x, int y, int startAngle,
                     int endAngle, int horizRadius,
                     int vertRadius)
    {
#ifdef COMPX
     ellipse(x, y, horizRadius, vertRadius, startAngle, endAngle);
#else
     ellipse(x, y, startAngle, endAngle, horizRadius,
          vertRadius);
#endif
    }
```

You can now use `drawEllipse()` consistently and get the same behavior whether you use compiler X or the Turbo C compiler. Compilers on the same machine under the same operating system may have routines that behave the same (although chances are they won't), but it is more a matter of chance to have similar routines for compilers on different machines. It is wise to isolate these types of portability issues or draw attention to them with appropriate comments. Isolation is the better method because it places the code sections within the conditional compilation statements apart from the rest of the code so that these code sections can be more easily accessed for updating, problem detection, and so on.

Structured versus "Quick and Dirty" Design

"Quick and dirty" or "shootin' from the hip" design, once the most common form of program design, was often the style of BASIC programmers and designers using other interpretive languages. This approach simply does not suffice for any but the simplest programs. There are far too many considerations in developing an application today to meet all the details and deal from memory with the complexity of the program. The graphics routine discussed in the preceding section demonstrates this complexity. If the designer does not consider the type of environment in which the application will run, many problems can occur—particularly incompatabilities between systems.

Whether you use top-down, bottom-up, or object-oriented structured design, a modular system forces you to put more thought into the program. This should eliminate some problems before you begin the coding and testing stages.

Single-File versus Multiple-File Programs

A prime consideration in design is how best to manipulate the data used by a program. Is it better to put all the information in one file? Or should you separate it into logical units to avoid redundancy and perhaps save storage space? Unless you are working with small amounts of data, the best move often is to plan to use and express relationships between multiple files.

Single-file as opposed to multiple-file programming deals with how you store and use information. Database applications benefit the most from clarification of this issue. Whether to use a single file or multiple files may relate to whether you are designing a *flat file* or *relational* database. Many programs for which all information can be placed in one file and manipulated use the common flat-file architecture. It may not be efficient when the size of a record becomes large and difficult to handle; then, storing parts of the information in different files and bringing it together in one may be more advantageous.

The relational database format links files so that information within them can be accessed and displayed even though the information is not stored in two files. This format saves space overall, because information does not have to be stored physically in both files. To access a record, a specific key is used to form a link. For example, a customer number could be the key for finding the customer name and address in one file, then for using that information in a second file that contains invoicing data.

Whether to use one or more than one file may depend also on other database issues. Even with a flat-file format, you may have to decide whether the key information for performing searches, sorts, and so on should be stored in a separate file or with the binary tree structure for the data file. The specific algorithm for implementing the binary or B^+ tree format may dictate placement of the key file and make the decision for you.

"Write Your Own" versus Purchased Routine Libraries

When starting or designing a project, the developer may not always have all the routines needed to implement the system fully. One option is to write any necessary functions; another is to obtain a commercial package in "ready-to-use" format. No matter which method you use, there are trade-offs.

Developing your own routines takes time. Finishing a project in time for a deadline may rule out writing all of your own routines. But if time is not a problem, you can design, implement, and test your own routines. If you develop the routines to be as generic as possible, the library of routines remains available for any future projects. Another advantage is that source code is available and can be modified.

Using a commercial set of routines also has advantages and disadvantages. One definite advantage is time savings. Commercial routines usually are ready to be used straight from the package—but check them out before you use them. The routines may be so complex or numerous that a good deal of study will be necessary to use them properly. Once learned, however, they can provide time savings.

Another advantage, depending on the quality of the package, is that the routines may have been thoroughly debugged and tested and may already have survived well in the field. On the other hand, a new package (or one of dubious quality) may introduce errors that are hard to track down and even harder to correct. Correction is especially difficult in packages that do not include source code. The alternative here is that when an error is found, the vendor of a commercial package may issue a patch or a new version of the routines. For shareware packages, the developer frequently is on his or her own.

One of the disadvantages of commercial routines is their cost. Some packages may be prohibitively expensive for a specific project, and their cost may not be justified for "one-time only" use. This may be especially true if you are developing only public-domain or shareware packages. Again, the more professional your application, the greater its chances for survival among the hundreds of other packages on the market. For other packages of routine collections, the cost of obtaining the source code (if it can be purchased at all) may be prohibitive.

You should consider also the level of support and documentation for commercial packages. Lack of support may mean error problems and delays in implementation. Documentation should be thorough and easily understood. Some packages do not provide adequate documentation and thus may not be worth using even if they are adequate functionally.

Also, the total functionality you need may not be present in the commercial package. If the package contains, say, 85 percent of the functions you need, you may need to decide whether to use it or whether to develop a set of routines that includes all the functions but takes time to create. The degree of functionality will have a direct bearing on what your program will and will not be able to do. For example, if you use a windowing and data entry package, it may lack functionality for user-defined data validation or checking data entry for certain conditions, ranges, and so on. You may rule against using the package or, if user-defined data validation is not absolutely necessary, you may decide that the package is still worthwhile. In other cases, you may deal with overkill; some packages of routines are so extensive that only a portion of the routines will ever be used. In this case, it will pay to look for a simple, less expensive set of routines.

Table 1.1 summarizes some of the factors to consider when you examine routine libraries.

Table 1.1. *Design Considerations of Routine Libraries*

Factor	Commercial	Custom
High cost	X	
Long time for implementation		X
Abundant features	X	
Source code availability	X	
Known errors	X	X
Documentation and Support	X	

Data Structures

Data structures are complex and wide-ranging. They embody a form of abstraction—making something concrete and physical into a more flexible form. Abstraction also can involve information hiding, in which some details are enveloped in types or in some other manner. Arrays in C can hold more than one data element, but each element must be of the same type. With data structures such as linked lists and queues, the elements can vary.

In C, abstraction and information hiding are implemented in terms of `structs`, `unions`, and `typedefs` (all of which are C keywords). These features allow data structures to be composed of various C-language types such as arrays, integers, or strings, all of which can be contained within the same unit. The structure may or may not include functions by means of using function pointers or arrays of pointers to functions.

Putting the data and functions together is a beginning step to object-oriented programming. The variables made from the data structure will exhibit the same behavior when an accompanying function is performed on them. An example of such a data object is a menu, which exhibits characteristics: it may be pull-down, pop-up, or Lotus-style. It also contains choices to be displayed and might even include function pointers. The function pointer points to an action carried out by a specific menu item. Actually, the menu choices and actions would probably already have been specified in an initialization statement. Such an object might appear as

```
typedef struct aMenuChoice
    {
    char *choice;
    int action(void);
    } menuChoice;

typedef struct aMenu
    {
    enum menuType {pulldown, popup, lotusStyle, relocatable};
    menuChoice  choices[15];
    } menu;
```

To declare a variable, you would use code such as

```
menu editMenu;
```

and to access parts of the variable you might include

```
editMenu.menuType = pulldown;
strcpy(editMenu.choices[3].choice, "New File");
editMenu.choices[3].action() = openNewFile();
```

Over the years, structures (stacks, queues, linked lists, binary trees, B$^+$ trees, hash tables, directed graphs, forests, and sets, among others) have been developed. Each of these structures deals with a certain type of problem.

If you want to learn more about actual implementation and other issues concerning data structures, you may want to examine one or more books about data structures (such as *Data Structures and Algorithms* and *File Structures, A Conceptual Toolkit*, both published by Addison-Wesley). Some of these books are language-generic, others specific to a language. Table 1.2 points out the major design considerations for various data structures.

Stacks

Stacks are LIFO (last-in, first-out) structures that can be applied to a variety of situations. The compiler uses this sort of structure to handle function arguments and recursion. Tracing features can use stacks, obtaining and working with the top item on the stack, then getting the next item, and so forth. By moving backwards through the stack, the user can stop at any point or work all the way back to the point of origin. Stacks can be used also for deletions, as in a word processor. (A program can remember various levels of deletions if the deletions are placed on the stack; any level of deletion can be accessed by moving back through the stack.)

A stack accepts access to its data in one kind of order only. Access cannot be random or start at either end. Because of this access limitation, the stack is not suitable for modeling random file access, for example.

Table 1.2. *Data Structures and Design*

Structure	Type	Considerations
Stack	LIFO	Once accessed, element is deleted. All operation done from one end. Acccessed in one direction only.
Queue	FIFO	Once accessed, element is deleted. Elements added at one end and deleted from the other. Accessed in one direction only.
Linked List	Element	May be added at any point. Element can be accessed without deletion. Does not require a contiguous area of memory for implementation. May be accessed in more than one direction.
Tree	Element	May be added at any point. Element can be accessed without deletion. Does not require a contiguous area of memory for implementation. May be accessed in more than one direction. Fewer steps required to find an element than to find lists. Multiway trees have advantages over B-trees but are harder to implement.

Two actions usually associated with a stack are *pushing*, or placing an item onto the stack, and *popping*, which removes an item from the stack. By using multiple pops, you can access elements more than one level deep. You must then store the elements in a buffer and replace them when necessary.

Queues

Queues, unlike stacks, are FIFO (first-in, first-out) structures. Instead of all data being manipulated from one end, as with the stack, a user adds elements at one end of the queue and deletes them from the other. This is an important distinction: Once an item is removed from one end of the list (unless it is put back at the other end), that item is no longer accessible unless the programmer stores it elsewhere. Queues are handy for batch processing. Communications and device drivers (printers, keyboard buffers, serial port protocols) often use queues, because data coming in at one end does not disrupt data obtained from the other end of the structure. Printers, for example, use queues to line up and take out jobs from one end; the user can add new jobs at the other end without disrupting printing. A queue is useful whenever data must be obtained from a program at the same time it may also be added to the program.

A variation of a queue, called a *circular queue*, has adjacent beginning and ending points and is used effectively in some implementations of keyboard buffers. By keeping track of the ending point, the program can tell whether the queue is full. (It is full when the ending point equals the beginning point.)

Linked Lists

Linked lists come in different flavors. Singly linked lists allow travel through the list in only one direction. Doubly linked lists have two pointers that allow travel in either direction. As the name implies, a linked list is like a chain. Links can be added or deleted at any point along the structure, unlike queues and stacks, in which data is added or deleted only at the ends. Another major difference between stacks or queues and linked lists is that linked lists do not necessarily delete an element once it is accessed; a specific delete operation is required. And queues and stacks usually require a contiguous area of memory, like the area devoted to an array, to be set aside for their use. Because they use pointers to connect the elements, linked lists can be scattered throughout memory, intermingled with other data. New links can be added or deleted by changing the address of the pointers or using a temporary pointer when you add or delete elements. Another pointer acts as the scanning point to travel up or down the list. This scanner, which is used for performing comparisons or searches on list members, stops when the appropriate member is found.

You can also create and maintain linked lists of linked lists if doing so is appropriate for a specific application. Linked lists of linked lists are somewhat similar to an array of strings, in which each element of the array holds a string and each string, in turn, consists of a "list" of characters.

Linked lists also allow data to be added in sorted order. Elements can be added or deleted from any point in the list; the list can be searched (by using an index, or key) for the correct location at which to insert a new element. Once the location is found, new links are established to tie the new element into the linked list without moving other list elements.

Linked lists can be used when the amount of data is limited but access should be flexible. Usually, because access is not fast enough, they are not adequate for handling large databases, but for small files you can use linked lists instead of other structures, such as trees. After the linked list is built from the database, new elements can be added or deleted without affecting the order of the physical database—elements can be accessed in order while they are added at the end of the physical database.

Linked lists can be widely applied because of their flexibility. They can be used for lists of items, word-processing documents, database items, and other programming categories.

Trees

Trees are composed of a root, branches, nodes, and leaves. The *root* is a single element from which one or more *branches* extend. *Nodes* are elements in the individual data items contained in a tree. The root is a node, as are the elements contained at the "crotch," or point of branching. In a strict binary tree, no more than two branches are possible at a node. In multiway trees, more than two branches may extend from a node. When the end of a branch is reached, the element found there is called a *leaf*. Like linked lists, trees allow data to be inserted and deleted at any point. Trees are well suited for ordering data. Depending on the method of tree traversal (moving through the branches and leaves), data can be accessed in ascending or descending order without any rearrangement.

The main advantage of trees over linked lists is that fewer operations or accesses are required to find a particular data item. In a worst-case situation, if you wanted to get the last element of a list, you would probably have to travel the entire length of the list (visiting each element on the way) before reaching it. In a correctly balanced tree, you probably could find the last element by examining fewer than half the elements.

A tree is *balanced* if the length of the shortest path from a branch node to a leaf node does not exceed more than one level more than the length of the longest path from a branch node to a leaf node. Levels are determined by the distance from a node. For example, nodes one path away from the root node are on the same level. Unbalanced trees look more like a straight line than a branching tree. There are special algorithms to ascertain when a tree is unbalanced and also what should be done to balance the tree. Trees offer extremely efficient access, an even more pronounced benefit when large numbers of data elements must be handled.

Because trees are efficient, they often are used with databases. At the program design stage, you determine whether to construct the tree whenever the program is started, updated, and then deleted from memory, or whether to store the tree on disk. In many cases, the tree is stored as an index in a special file. Because more than one index file can be used for different keys, customers can sort data files on last name as well as ZIP-code fields.

Binary trees are the simplest form of tree structures. Other types are B^+ trees, B^* trees, and AVL trees. A B^+ *tree* has an index associated with it; a B^* *tree* has records divided into pages (each at least two-thirds full of data) that are stored on disk; and an *AVL tree* uses special node insertion to maintain a balanced condition.

Necessary Functions

After you finish the top-level design for a program (and perhaps some of the lower-level design), make a list of functions you may need for the program. Some of the advantages to doing this now instead of waiting until the coding stage follow:

- ❏ By studying them beforehand, you can familiarize yourself with the functions.

- ❏ You can determine whether the functions in the standard library will do or whether you need to get an outside collection or write your own.

- ❏ You can determine whether the functions are what you need or whether you need to develop others.

- ❏ You can get an idea of how the pieces fit together, so that you can better plan the layout of modules, data, and functions.

By doing a little more planning up front, you can avoid possible problems (such as lack of functionality or missed deadlines) later, during implementation.

Error Handling

Notifying the user of errors and uncertain operating conditions and recovering from these conditions is an important aspect of a program. All too often a program "chokes," "goes West," or "goes to La-la Land." Program crashes are never the customer's fault. Programs crash because they cannot properly handle a condition, such as division by zero or improper input. The program should handle whatever input is given to it and provide a meaningful error message instead of crashing, even if the data is wrong or unexpected.

Just as allowing crashes and abnormal program exits or lockups is undesirable, so is leaving the customer in the dark about what is happening. Vague error messages should be avoided. It is equally important to avoid giving the customer the impression that something may be wrong with the program. When pauses occur during program execution, as they do during sorts or long disk accesses, the application should explain what is happening and reassure the customer that everything is working as it should.

The degree of expediency with which an error is handled depends on what is taking place. A probable program crash must be handled immediately, but an incorrect number typed in a database field may not have to be checked immediately, depending on the type of constraint placed on the field. If a correct value has a bearing on the next field to be entered, checking should be immediate. If this sort of validation is not required, the application can wait until the entire screen is done, perform validation, and then continue.

Error handling should be extensive enough to notify the customer which part of the program is affected. The severity of the error can be part of the message. Error information is standard in a compiler—the message status can be informational only, a warning, an error, or a fatal error. Whereas line numbers mean nothing to most application users, the name of the module or menu item will help clarify the location of the error. Knowing where the error occurs helps when the customer or maintenance programmer must re-create the condition to determine the cause of the error.

If your program is going to be used overseas or in areas in which English is not common, you may want to consider another factor. Messages placed in a separate file are much easier to modify or translate into another language. More often than not, error messages are hard-coded into the program and cannot be modified without changing the source code and recompiling. And if error messages are placed in a separate text file, a message that is misspelled or does not match the proper error is much easier to correct.

Files and I/O

Use of files and other forms of input/output is a big subject. The need for data files can be triggered by data that changes or by having more data to handle than can be stored in the program. Arrays are often initialized and used as part of the program, for example. But large arrays can take up precious space needed for other variables and may not be changed as easily as those variables. Files allow the storage area to contract and expand. Much more information can be stored in secondary storage (such as disks) than in the program's limited RAM. In some cases, the use of files means that data can be moved more easily or that others can access it. Other considerations include

- ❏ ASCII or binary storage format
- ❏ fixed-length or variable-length records
- ❏ sequential or random access
- ❏ buffered or unbuffered data entry
- ❏ sorted or random record order
- ❏ indexed or not indexed
- ❏ immediate deletion of records or marking them for later deletion

Programs may work more efficiently with binary file formats and will take up less disk space than if all information is stored in ASCII format. The ASCII format, on the other hand, enables the customer to modify the data more easily, because almost any editor or word processor can be used for the task. This also makes the data readable by anyone, because ASCII uses the standard character set and binary files have an "encrypted" form. ASCII files are often used to store readable text or for printer definitions that the customer can change.

Whether to use fixed-length or variable-length records is also a matter of space availability. With a fixed-length file format, all records are exactly the same size and must be large enough to hold the maximum amount of information. When records do not normally contain this much data, unused space is lost. The loss of unused space is eliminated with variable-length records, but they are more difficult to program. More calculation is necessary to find an individual record, and the risk of errors is greater. Access to records is also slower than with a fixed-length format. If saving space is the primary factor, variable-length records can be efficient.

Today, sequential access usually is used on small data files or when reading input files for format conversion or some other form or processing. In *sequential access*, the file pointer moves along in order from the beginning of the file to each record. The pointer cannot move randomly among records, and searching always starts either from the beginning of the file or from the file pointer's current position. With *random access*, sometimes called *direct access*, the file pointer can go immediately to any individual record without having to scan linearly over the others. Access thus is much faster than with sequential methods. Text files usually are accessed sequentially, but most other database files are random access. If your files contain fewer than 200 records and are not accessed often, sequential access may work fine. Under other conditions, random access is preferable.

Buffers are temporary data-storage areas. Many files speed up operation by placing several records in a memory buffer for access by the program. This increases the speed of operation, because disk reads and writes are not done as often. If buffers are used, changes may also take place more easily—the changes occur first to data in the buffer, then are saved to the data file. Uunbuffered I/O, usually reserved for low-level operations involving direct calls to the operating system, is much slower than buffered methods. The ANSI C Standard supports buffered I/O but does not contain routines for unbuffered access, because such routines decrease code portability. Turbo C, on the other hand, does include the more machine-specific, unbuffered access routines if you do need them.

You may need to consider also whether to store your database in sorted order, such as alphabetically by client's last name, or in random, "as-entered," format. Although keeping a file in sorted order may mean easier access, it also means more difficult insertion and deletion of records. If a record must be added or removed from the middle of the file, all the records from that point to the end must be rewritten (consuming time and computer resources). Adding and deleting records is much easier if records are placed in the file as they are entered by the user. A means of accessing any record in a particular order must be provided, however—often through indexing, with a B^+ tree or another method.

Deciding whether to use sorted or random-access order is related to whether you decide to use indexing. If records must be accessed in an ordered format, such as from the oldest date to the most current, or in alphabetical order by one of the fields, and so on, then a form of indexing must be provided. Indexes provide faster, more efficient record access. Customers almost always want the capability of sorted access. Indexes are much easier to change or rebuild than the file itself.

Yet another factor is how to delete records. As mentioned earlier, deleting records from a sorted file can be cumbersome. In some cases, a special *flag field*, whose value determines whether a record is deleted, is used. A deleted record is marked "true"; "false" indicates that it is not deleted. This method saves the time needed to actually delete the record, and the customer can change his or her mind and get the record back. The customer should be asked whether the intent is to actually delete the record. Either your code should provide a special method for this, or the program must be made intelligent enough to detect when to remove records that are marked for deletion. Database programs may delete records at the end of a session, provide a specific command to perform the file compression at any time, or erase deleted records whenever the customer switches from one mode to the next. If records are not deleted, the file may eventually take up too much space.

Methods of working with files and I/O can be important in terms of program efficiency and user needs. Measure their effectiveness carefully.

Memory Model Considerations

You may wonder how to determine which memory model to use when you develop a program. Memory models belong to two classes: one includes the Tiny, Small, and Medium memory models and uses near pointers for most data and code access; the other class includes the Compact, Large, and Huge memory models and uses far pointers for data and code. The Medium and Compact models work somewhat differently. The Medium model allows more than 64K of code but only 64K of data (far code pointers and near data pointers), whereas the Compact model allows only 64K of code but more than 64K of data (near code pointers and far data pointers). Factors that can help you decide which model to use include the following:

- ❏ Size of code used
- ❏ Size of data used
- ❏ Data access times
- ❏ Function use

Code Size

If you know your program will provide many features and may well surpass 64K of code, you may need to use the Medium, Large, or Huge memory model. The amount of code includes not only your source files, but also any libraries you may use.

You should start working with the smallest memory model you think will fit, then work up. If there is any doubt about which class of model to use for program code, the linker will tell you. If it issues an `out of memory` message, you must use a larger memory model. Working with the smallest model required will reduce program size. A program compiled under the Large model may be almost twice the size of the same program compiled under the Small model. Execution speed may also be a consideration. Using a large memory model and larger pointers can slow down execution, but compared to other compilers, the Turbo C compiler is very efficient in using far and huge pointers.

Data Size

For most data needs you will use a 64K data segment. The data segment contains variables that are global (static) in nature—local (auto) variables and function arguments are in the stack segment. The Tiny, Small, or Medium models can be applied if data amounts to 64K or less. You need a large data model only if you will handle data that totals more than 64K. If a single data item (such as an individual record or array) will be larger than 64K, you must use the Huge memory model. In many cases, one of the small class of memory models is adequate for holding data.

Data Access Time

As a general rule, the larger the pointer, the slower the access. Clearly, although Turbo C's implementation of huge pointers is efficient, you should use huge pointers only when absolutely necessary. Use near pointers whenever possible (when using less than 64K of data) and far pointers otherwise.

Function Use

For the uninitiated, mixing memory models is not a wise idea. Problems can arise, especially when you use packages of routines you have not developed yourself. Turbo C requires that you use far pointers regardless of the memory model used in the rest of the program. You must remember to use the `graphics.h` include file in order to use the graphics routines successfully. Such routines are often written for a specific memory model and may not be readily adaptable to other models unless the source code can be accessed.

Modules compiled with small memory models use and expect to receive near pointers; modules compiled with large memory models use and expect to receive far pointers. Mixing modules compiled with different memory models confuses the issue and will usually cause crashes.

The solution is to use function prototypes that specifically state the type of memory model required. In other words, the type of pointer expected, near or far, is stated explicitly. Then, regardless of the memory model used, the compiler can handle the proper code generation by creating the proper pointer type or function return type. Strange bugs and erratic behavior may appear if the model type is not handled correctly.

The correct use of memory models affects the amount of code and data your program can work with. You can avoid problems if you understand which model to use.

Graphics or Text Displays

Many applications use text only—others make effective use of graphics. Graphics add interest to a program but also require more work, and text is sometimes more difficult to handle in graphics modes. As operating systems become more graphics-oriented, it will be easier to develop applications that take advantage of the graphics. At present, adequate tools for making graphics programming easier than using text in most cases have not been created but are under development. Graphics operating systems like the Presentation Manager require all text to be expressed graphically.

Hardware enhancements, such as the higher-resolution cards and their built-in capabilities, also make working with graphics easier. These cards are capable of many more functions (like panning and scrolling) than their predecessors, and sometimes problems (like the "snow" from CGA cards) are remedied. The EGA and VGA boards are much better suited than the older boards for graphics.

Performance Considerations

Program performance can involve many factors, including the following:

❏ Type of memory model and pointer used

❏ Algorithm used

❏ Data held in memory rather than stored on disk

❏ Compiler options

You won't know whether you need to improve performance unless you measure it. *Profilers*, programs that measure the amount of time spent in each function or even on each line of code, are especially good at measuring performance. Programmers can also create timing routines by obtaining a start and end time from the system, placing a call at the beginning and end of a function or line of code, and then finding the difference after execution.

The algorithm used can often have dramatic effects on time and efficiency. Many sources compare sorting routines, for example, noting which of them work better than others. Searching routines can vary widely also. The programmer can also make headway by carefully examining routines after they work correctly to see whether they can be optimized. Sometimes optimization may simply be a matter of setting a particular switch of a compiler option. In other cases, steps can be combined or eliminated, register variables can be used, etc.

Working with information in memory is always faster than working with it from disk. The questions of memory or disk use consider the amount of memory that must be manipulated and the amount of memory available to hold the data.

Summary

Program design involves converting customer requirements into a program. The "how" rather than the "what" is stressed. Because many factors influence design, programmers must be familiar with a wide range of programming concerns before they can make efficient programs. Time spent in the design stage can reduce errors later in the program.

The design phase can also encourage creation of new algorithms or improvement of existing ones. Your work may broaden the scope of computer science by adding new paradigms and methods to this growing field.

Alan
Plantz

2

Coding the Program

As you saw in Chapter 1, coding the program—turning ideas and customer needs into a physical entity—is only one part of the development process. Coding is the programmer's "bread and butter." This chapter addresses some of the physical aspects of coding, focusing on the following topics:

❑ How to use the integrated Turbo C Editor more effectively to check delimiter pairs, create function prototypes, and so on

❑ Factors in developing a coding style

❑ Using on-line help

❑ How to work with functions and source modules when developing programs larger than one module

❑ The basics of header files

In this chapter, which dovetails with others that discuss such coding concerns as how to select the correct function to implement a concept, which header file to use, and so on, you will learn ways to make your coding more efficient.

Coding translates design into instructions the computer can understand. In the development process, designers should check that user requirements are met. When they have finished coding, good designers verify that the implementation fulfills both the design and the requirements. Coding is actually a small portion of the development process, usually well under 30 percent of the total time spent. Typically, in environments in which the designer is not disciplined or is a "home computerist," coding is a much larger concern than the requirements and design phases.

The implementation of a program allows the programmer to show his or her stuff—low-level hardware access, interrupts, complex algorithms, and flexible data structures may all be included in this phase. Although the design should still be followed, the programmer will more than likely find at least one spot where the design is shaky, or where he or she thinks of a better solution to a requirement than the one presented in the design document.

People who have difficulty thinking of a program in a structured way will have problems, especially when programs become large and complex. But there is hope—the techniques for structured design and following design through to coding can be learned.

In most instances you will be using C, but you may also try to optimize certain portions of code by using assembly language, or you may prefer to work in Pascal or Prolog to reduce the amount of recoding of routines already written in these languages.

Debugging (finding and removing program bugs) is also part of programming. Both the integrated and stand-alone debuggers for Turbo C Professional are discussed in Chapter 9. Ideally, debugging should be done on individual routines or small sections of the program, then applied in increasingly large chunks until operation of the entire program has been verified.

As you program, the editor becomes a necessary tool. The following section explains some of the finer points of how Turbo C's Editor can be used to produce code efficiently.

Using the Editor Effectively

The Turbo C Editor serves for most editing purposes. Although it does not allow multiple windows on-screen at the same time or accept keyboard macros, the Editor has advantages because it is part of the Turbo C integrated development environment (IDE). The Editor also provides context-sensitive on-line help, which can save you hours that would otherwise be spent looking up references. This section discusses some of the ways you can use the Editor more effectively in your programming.

Coding Style

Style tends to be a religious issue for some people— designers are either for it or against it. By developing a coding style, you can make code easier to read, especially if more than one person will work on it. A distinct style can simplify maintenance and can even help in error detection or prevention. Just being consistent is not enough; you should develop good style habits and then use them consistently.

Comment Headers

Comment headers are comment blocks placed at the beginning of each routine; a similar block is placed at the beginning of each module. Headers separate functions and make them easier to distinguish. As you can see from figure 2.1, the function comment block explains each function in terms of

❏ its prototype

❏ what each argument is and does

❏ its return type

❏ what the function does

Fig. 2.1. *A function comment block.*

```
/*************************************************************
 *   Function:         void sortFile(FILE filename);         *
 *                                                           *
 *   Use:              sortFile() sorts the data file based on the *
 *                     name key.  Sorting is done alphabetically. *
 *                                                           *
 *   Arguments:        The only argument is filename, which is the *
 *                     name of the file to be sorted.        *
 *                                                           *
 *   Returns:          None                                  *
 *                                                           *
 *   Date:             8/19/88                               *
 *************************************************************/
```

The function comment header should contain at least this information, but can include more. You also may want to consider adding a change history section to keep track of changes—who made them, when they were made, and what they were. This section, properly updated, is an excellent maintenance tool.

You can make a template of this header (without explanations) and save it as a separate file. Then, while editing, you can retrieve the file containing the header by pressing the Retrieve Block keys (Ctrl-K, Ctrl-R), or you can enter the name of another source code or text file into the window containing the default file name to retrieve. This is quick and eliminates much typing.

The format of a module comment header (see fig. 2.2) can be similar to that of your function comment header. The module comment header explains the purpose of the entire source code module and includes any special notes, such as the types of routines used in the module and how this module interacts with others. It should state also the name of header files used within the module.

Fig. 2.2. *A module comment block.*

```
/*************************************************************
 *  Module:          fileio.c                                *
 *                                                           *
 *  Header file:     fileio.h                                *
 *                                                           *
 *  Use:             Contains routines for buffered file I/O *
 *                   using variable-length records.  Routines*
 *                   include addRec, delRec, getRec, appendRec*
 *                   flushBuf, and recCount.                 *
 *                                                           *
 *  Date:            8/19/88                                 *
 *************************************************************/
```

If you include in the module comment block a brief description of each function, you will not have to scan the entire file to find out what a function does. Both function and module headers can also contain the name of the author, which is especially important if more than one person works on a program.

Inline Code Comments

Comments are as important as the code itself. Proper use of comments helps make source code more understandable and easier to maintain. This does not mean that every line needs a comment, but code—like text—can be separated into "paragraphs." Too many comments can reduce the readability of your code. A good habit is to place a comment before each paragraph, as well as for any lines that do something out-of-the-ordinary. You should add comments, for instance, for system-specific features, programming "tricks" such as strange pointer references, or notes on why you used one algorithm instead of another. Too many comments are preferable to too few.

If you change a piece of code, and the meaning of the comment changes, be sure to modify the comment to correlate with the code change. A frequent sore spot among people who must maintain code is that the comments are not an accurate reflection of what the code does; thus, they defeat the purpose of adding remarks.

Some programmers develop the habit of first writing comments as pseudocode that explains, in general terms, what the program will do. This process may point out errors in the program's logic or design. Then, with the comments in place, the designer writes the code.

Frequently, programmers do not comment code until after it is written. This approach can cause problems. Either the programmer is assigned to a different project before comments are complete, or time does not allow the programmer to even begin adding comments. In other instances, if the programmer does not add the comments until weeks or months after the code was originally written, he or she may not recall exactly what the routines are or what they do. Try to establish the habit of commenting as you write the code, not after.

Another good use of comments is to explain #defines, as well as the variables, typedefs, complex declarations, and other elements used in a program. Explaining variables can greatly increase the clarity of the code without making a programmer guess the purpose of the variable.

Although Turbo C understands *nested comments*—comment(s) inside other comments—nesting is not recommended. Because many compilers do not yet support this feature, code written in this way lacks portability. A better method than using nested comments is to use conditional compilation statements before and after blocks of code you want to "comment out." These conditional compilation statements will not have to be removed (even for a final compilation).

Identifier Names

Type, variable, and constant names are important. Variable names often start with lowercase letters and may contain underscores to separate "words" in the name (get_file or rkt_fuel_amt, for example); in others, a "word" may begin with an uppercase letter, as in getFile or rocketFuelAmount. Although some older compilers allow only 8 letters in an identifier, most compilers now support the ANSI C Standard feature of allowing at least 31. Check this limit if you are porting code to other compiler environments. Unless dictated by some standard at work, whether to use underscores or uppercase letters is usually a matter of personal preference. Also, try to make identifiers meaningful. Meaningful identifiers add a great deal of built-in documentation to the program without requiring additional comments. C programmers, who once loved being terse (especially with variable names), developed names such as wfil and rktfamt instead of workFile or rocketFuelAmount. Which are easier to understand?

The main thing is to choose a method and stick with it. Be consistent and use meaningful identifier names.

In the past, style dictated that non-function identifiers used with #define were all uppercase, as with

```
#define TRUE 1
```

This made it easy to spot the difference between a variable and a macro. Common style for functions defined as macros has always been lowercase letters. In some cases, identifiers may begin with an underscore to denote that they are functions.

You may want to develop also a method for distinguishing typedefs from other variables, as well as whether a variable is global, static, or auto in scope. Again, be consistent. You could even develop a method for classifying identifiers as to type, such as adding the prefix *i* for an int, *f* for a float, *c* for a char, etc. Perhaps a second prefix or suffix (like *p* or *ptr*) could be used to designate a pointer. Using this method could eliminate guesswork or having to find the declaration of an identifier to find out what type it is.

Indenting and Brace Placement

Proper indentation not only makes source code much easier to read but also, when used correctly, can help point out the error when a step is out of place. In Turbo C 2.0, a tab, which can be used to provide indentation of source code, can use up to 16 spaces but can be set to less under Options or with TCINST. Optimum fill can be used when you are working with tabs and indenting in Turbo C. Tabs usually take from two to five spaces. If more spaces per tab are used, several levels of indentation will shove your program off the right side of the page. A good lint program will point out errors in indentation.

Brace placement can rouse programmers' emotions. The typical Kernighan and Ritchie (K&R) style was

```
...
if (!done){
    doaction1();
    count++;
}
else {
    doaction2();
    total += count;
}
```

A better approach might be to place braces on a line by themselves, so that they are easily seen, and then to line them up. The eye must move back-and-forth when, as in the K&R example, the braces are not lined up. Furthermore, a brace is more easily overlooked in a complex, multilevel nested structure. You should scrutinize any piece of code that contains many levels of nested statements because they not only cause confusion but also may signal a design problem. If you place braces on their own lines, the process of discovering what code belongs inside each brace is less confusing. Two sample brace-placement styles follow:

```
...                          or        ...
if (!done)                             if (!done)
    {                                  {
    doaction1();                           doaction1();
    count++;                               count++;
    }                                  }
else                                   else
    {                                  {
    doaction2();                           doaction2();
    total += count;                        total += count;
    }                                  }
```

Either of these methods of brace placement is easier to read and examine for problems than the nonaligned K&R style. Placing a statement in the wrong block, leaving out a statement, or forgetting a brace is easy to do. The real benefits of aligning braces one above the other are evident when you work with more complex examples of blocks, loops, `if` statements, etc., especially when you use multiple `if..then..else` statements. Try drawing lines between matching pairs of braces in both listings 2.1 and 2.2—you will see which style is easier to read and find problems in. Listing 2.2 should be clearer to interpret than listing 2.1.

Increasingly, programmers are using the "brace by itself" style to mark both functions and blocks. Try to figure out what is going on in the convoluted code in listing 2.1.

Listing 2.1

```
...
if ( ! done && cnt <= total ) {
    if ( inEdtMd ) {
        gobcktofil ( filnm, spot ) ;
        cnt++;                       }
    else {
        savfil ( filnm, dsk, ".DOC" ) ;
        if ( wantfrmt ( ascii ) ) {
            usefrmt ( );
            emptybuf (wrkbuf);
            }
    else {
        savoldfrmt(filnm);
        if (ok) {
            finish ( );
            done=TRUE;
            }
        }
    }
}
```

By the way, when I created listing 2.1 I left off a brace at the end and didn't catch the error until I lined up the braces (see listing 2.2). Notice also the mistake in the indentation of the last `else` clause. This error will be perceived correctly by the compiler, but not usually by the human.

Listing 2.2 is just like listing 2.1, except that the brace placement has been changed.

Listing 2.2

```
...
if ( ! done && cnt <= total )
    {
    if ( inEdtMd )
        {
        gobcktofil ( filnm, spot ) ;
        cnt++;
        }
    else
        {
        savfil ( filnm, dsk, ".DOC" ) ;
        if ( wantfrmt ( ascii ) )
            {
            usefrmt ( );
            emptybuf (wrkbuf);
            }
        else
            {
            savoldfrmt(filnm);
            if (ok)
                {
                finish ( );
                done=TRUE;
                }
            }
        }
    }
```

In listing 2.3, other style factors have been corrected, and I have used better variable names, comments, and so on. Wouldn't you rather read and maintain this version?

Listing 2.3

```
...
/* start processing file for saving */
if (!done && errorCount <= totalErrors)
    {
    /* go back to editing the file if in edit mode */
    if (inEditMode)
        {
        goBackToFile(fileName, spot);
        errorCount++;
        }
```

```
    else
            /* save as formatted file otherwise */
            {
            saveFile(fileName, disk, ".DOC");
            if (wantFormat(ascii))
                    {
                    useFormat();
                    emptyBuffer(workBuffer);
                    }
            else
                    /* or save in old format if no ASCII */
                    {
                    savOldFormat(fileName);
                    if (ok)
                            {
                            finish();
                            done = TRUE;
                            }    /* end of if OK */
                    }    /* end of else */
            }    /* end of else */
    }    /* end of if !done */
```

Other Style Considerations

Some of the smaller points you can use to set up a standard style follow:

1. Do not use a space between the name of a function and the opening parenthesis.

   Use `getFile()`   **Not** `getFile ()`

2. Use only one statement per line. (Note: This is also a prerequisite for some profilers and other program checkers that cannot report accurately the results of multiple-statement lines.)

   Use `count++;`
   `getNextRec(workFile);`

   Not `count++; getNextRec(workFile);`

3. Do not use a space between a unary operator and the operand. This is especially important when you work with pointers.

   Use `*intPtr = 1;` **Not** `* intPtr = 1;`

   and

   Use `if (!done)`   **Not** `if (! done)`

4. When you work with binary operators, use a space on both sides of the operator.

   Use `total = number * subTotal + shipping;`

   Not `total = number *subTotal + shipping;`

   or `total = number*subTotal+shipping;`

5. Place all debugging statements at the far left margin. They stand out better this way.

```
        getRec(firstRec);
#ifdef DEBUG
        printf("Error in file I/O module");
#endif
    if (!OK)
            closeFile();
```

6. If a loop statement has a null body, place the semicolon and the loop on separate lines.

   Use `for (x = 0; reverseData(x) < 12; x++)`
   `        ;`

   Not `for (x = 0; reverseData(x) < 12; x++);`

7. Use white space wherever needed. In other words, use blank lines, as well as proper spacing, to separate "paragraphs" of code.

Working with Function Prototypes

ANSI C accepts function prototypes. Prototypes can greatly reduce the chances of errors, because the compiler knows the type and number of parameters and the return type of the function before the functions are actually used. When you use a function that has already been prototyped, the compiler can check the function calls and report any mismatches between the call, the prototype, and the actual function definition. This eliminates errors that otherwise would go unnoticed by the programmer and the compiler—such errors as omitting a parameter, using a parameter of the wrong type without a cast, or not having enough parameters in the function call. Mixing the new function prototyping with the older K&R function declaration styles is not a good idea.

Function prototypes have another benefit. In older versions of C, you must declare a function, especially one that does not return an `int`, inside every function where it is used. But you need to specify a prototype just once—at the beginning of the module—instead of inside each function in which that routine is used.

It is wise to place prototypes together near the beginning of a file, usually before the `main()` routine. Another method—placing the prototypes in header files—is especially useful when you work with multiple source files.

An underused facility of the Turbo C Editor can help you gather the prototypes. Use the Set Place Marker command (Ctrl-K0, Ctrl-K1, Ctrl-K2, Ctrl-K3) to set the location of your prototype collection, as well as to mark the last place you found a prototype. Then use the Find Place Marker command (Ctrl-Q0, Ctrl-Q1, Ctrl-Q2, Ctrl-Q3) to move from one location to the next. For example:

1. Go to a place in the source file just before the `main()` function.

2. Press Ctrl-K0 to set the first marker.

3. Go to the beginning of the first user-defined function in the source file (including the return type).

4. Press Ctrl-K1 to mark this location.

5. Using the Mark block-begin command (Ctrl-KB), mark the beginning of the block.

6. Move to the closing parenthesis of the argument list for the function.

7. Press Mark block-end (Ctrl-KK) to mark the end of the block.

8. Now press Find Place Marker (Ctrl-Q0). This takes you to the first marker—the location at which you want to place the collection of function prototypes.

9. Press Copy block (Ctrl-KC) to copy the function information from the buffer to the file.

10. Don't forget to go to the end of the prototype and add a semicolon.

11. Now repeat the process. Press Find Place Marker, but this time use (Ctrl-Q1) to go to the first user-defined function (refer to Step 3).

12. Move to the next function in the file, press Set Place Marker (Ctrl-Q1), and repeat the process until all the functions have prototypes in the file.

This procedure cuts down on the time and keystrokes needed to get where you need to go. Granted, it would be easier if the Editor supported keyboard macros, but this at least partially automates the process of gathering prototypes. If you want to use keyboard macros inside the Editor, you can use products such as Superkey or Prokey.

Pair Matching

Turbo C's Editor has a relatively new feature—the capability of finding the following matching delimiters:

‹› ( ) /* */ ' ' { } " " [ ]

The matching procedure is simple—if you are looking for any delimiters besides the apostrophe (') or quotation marks ("), you can place the cursor on either the opening or closing brace and press Ctrl-Q along with either a [or] bracket. The Editor is smart enough to know in which direction to go. To find the quotation marks, use the following procedure:

1. Place the cursor on either the opening or closing delimiter for which you want to find the mate.

2. If the cursor is on the opening delimiter, press Ctrl-Q[to find the closing delimiter; if on the closing delimiter, press Ctrl-Q] to search backward for the opening mate.

3. You receive a message if the matching delimiter cannot be found.

This feature is useful for long comment blocks, large blocks of code, and argument lists. It is particularly useful for initialization of complex variables using arrays, structs, or unions in which braces are used to an extreme. Multiple-level nested if statements and loops also can be readily checked by using pair matching. And you can use this feature to check statements with complex conditions and locate sources of errors.

Setting Markers

As I have already mentioned, you can use markers for finding and gathering function prototypes. Markers can be extremely useful in the general scheme of work also—you can use them to keep track of one location while you go to another to view the code there, see what a variable declaration is, and so forth. If you want to use the Editor efficiently, learn to use markers.

Using On-Line Help

Turbo C provides excellent on-line Help that can save you significant amounts of time. Many programmers became familiar with this feature by using it to determine available editing functions. Help does much more. Not only does using the Help facility greatly increase time savings, it also enhances your efficiency and productivity.

To get to the Help feature at any time, press F1. The first screen displays Editor commands and their meaning. Pressing F1 a second time brings up the index of available Help. Press F1 again if you want to place the cursor on the highlighted words and go to another screen with more highlighted words or the information you need. To go backward, press Alt-F1, which enables you to move back through as many as 20 help screens. Pressing Alt-F1 after you have exited Help will return you to the location from which you exited Help.

One of the handiest Help features is the capability of looking up function information. If the function is one of those included in the Turbo C package, you can get context-sensitive help by simply placing the cursor on the function and pressing Ctrl-F1. A window appears (if the function is spelled correctly) with the function declaration, information about its prototype (including which header file contains its prototype for the `#include` statement), the arguments, return value, and so on. The window may include highlighted references to related routines or information. The help obtained is terse but nevertheless convenient—it beats trying to look up the routine in the reference manual.

The same feature is available for C keywords such as `if`, `struct`, `while`, etc., and for most other features of the C language, including operator precedence.

The Help facility can even be accessed after you begin compiling, as well as while the cursor is in the Message window. Simply highlight any warning or error by placing the cursor on it, and then press F1 (not Ctrl-F1). A window displays an explanation of that message, perhaps giving a hint as to why it occurred and how the situation can be fixed. Handy—you don't have to look up the error or warning message in the manual.

Memory-resident C and Pascal Help for Any Program (THELP.COM)

A new feature in Turbo C 2.0 and Turbo C Professional is THELP.COM and its accompanying files. (The file THELP.DOC explains how THELP.COM operates.) With this small program (it uses about 8K of memory) you can access Turbo's help within another editor, a word processor—actually any other program. THELP.COM is especially useful in the Turbo debugger. The program provides help for both Turbo Pascal and Turbo C, but not for Turbo Assembler.

The hot key that activates the program (normally 5 on the numeric keypad) can be changed. To change the default hot key, use a command-line option of /K followed by a four-digit number. The first two digits signify the left or right Shift key, the Ctrl key, or the Alt key. The last two digits are from the second part of the combination, usually an alphanumeric key. For example, you could specify /K0816 to represent Alt-U as the hot key. You may want to avoid using hot-key combinations such as Ctrl-F1, which are used also in Turbo C.

The handy feature here is that THELP.COM not only works with other programs in addition to the compiler/linker and the debugger, but that this help program also has a cut-and-paste capability. Although this capability is not very flexible, it does enable you to paste a highlighted keyword or the entire help screen into the application running at the time. By pasting the entire screen, you get the prototype, explanation, header file, and so on, which perhaps isn't all that bad. Although you cannot trim the insertion to just the section you really want (the function prototype, for example), you can use what you need and delete the rest of the text.

Additionally, the help screen can be saved to a disk file called THELP.SAV. Additional stored screens are appended to THELP.SAV if it exists. There is no chance of overwriting any information. Being able to save the help screens to a file facilitates creating program documentation for future development and maintenance purposes.

One of the drawbacks of Turbo C's help is that unless you use the cut-and-paste feature, as soon as a key is pressed, the help window disappears instead of remaining on-screen to provide assistance.

Placing Functions and Modules

When you work on large projects, the placement of functions, modules, variables, and other elements is crucial if you want to create a program that executes correctly and avoid conflicts with compiling, linking, and scope.

Part of your design should include a *map* —a detailed description of the routines and how they will be distributed among modules. Basically, the criteria for deciding where functions will be placed depend on the following factors:

❏ Are the functions related in use?

❏ Do the functions manipulate the same data?

The first factor is fairly obvious. For example, you would want to group graphics-handling functions in one module, file-handling functions in another module, matrix-inversion routines in yet another source module, data-validation functions in a separate module, and so on. This distribution of files resembles the logical scheme of the C compiler's header files. Each source module you write can have its own header file containing global variables for that module, function prototypes, type definitions, macros, and so forth. The `main()` function should go in a module by itself, along with a list of header files the program will use. Even global data and types could be placed in a separate header file rather than in the same module with `main()`.

In addition to forming the function prototype, you must use it properly. One of C's strengths is information hiding and handling separate source modules well. Information hiding can be accomplished by using the `static` storage class modifier before the function prototype in order to restrict its visibility to the module in which the function is declared. A second method of controlling visibility is to place the function prototypes inside the source module where the corresponding functions are declared.

The sample program in listing 2.4 demonstrates prototypes, information hiding, using separate and multiple source files, as well as how to use storage class modifiers.

Along with some of the standard C library routines, this sample program includes three user-defined functions: getInt(), validInt(), and getStr(). getInt() obtains an integer from the user, validInt() checks to see whether the integer is in the range of 1 to 100, and getStr() gets a string from the user. Because getInt() and validInt() both work with integers, they are placed in the same module; getStr() is located in a module by itself.

The integer-handling module, GETINT.C, is shown in listing 2.4.

Listing 2.4.

strmod.h contains:

```
/***** routines for manipulating strings*****/
char *getStr(void);
```

intmod.h contains:

```
/***** routines for handling integers *****/
int getInt(void);
static int validInt(int anyInt);

#include <stdio.h>
#include <ctype.h>
#include <conio.h>
#include <string.h>
#include <stdlib.h>
#include "intmod.h"

int getInt(void)
   {
   char answer[80];     /* holds answer given by the user */
   int value;

   gotoxy(10,10);
   clreol();
   printf("%s:  ", "Enter an integer");
   do
      {
      gets(answer);
      value = atoi(answer);
      } while ((strlen(answer) >= 80) || (!validInt(value)));
   return(atoi(answer));
   }

static int validInt(int anyInt)
   {
   if (anyInt >= 1 && anyInt <= 100)
      {
      gotoxy(0,24);
      clreol();
      puts("Integer is valid.");
      return(1);
      }
```

Listing 2.4 continues

Listing 2.4 continued

```
    else
      {
      puts("Invalid integer, please try again.");
      return(0);
      }
   }
```

Listing 2.5 shows the module containing the string-handling routine GETSTR.C.

Listing 2.5

```
#include <stdio.h>
#include <string.h>
#include <conio.h>
#include "strmod.h"

char *getStr(void)
   {
   char answer[80];     /* holds answer given by user */

   gotoxy(10,10);
   clreol();
   printf("%s:  ","Enter a string");
   do
     {
     gets(answer);
       } while (strlen(answer) >= 80);

       return(answer);
   }
```

The program's main module (MODTEST.C) is shown in listing 2.6.

Listing 2.6

```
#include <stdio.h>
#include <string.h>
#include "intmod.h"
#include "strmod.h"

#define MAXNO   4   /* maximum number of array members allowed */

void main(void)
   {
   int x;   char strValues[MAXNO][80];
   int  intValues[MAXNO];

   for(x = 0; x < MAXNO; x++)
      {
      intValues[x] = getInt();
      strcpy(strValues[x][0], getStr());
      }
   }
```

To compile the program correctly, you must build the following three-line project file (MODTEST.PRJ):

```
modtest
getint
getstr
```

for use with the IDE version of the Turbo C compiler, or use a make file with TCC, the command-line version of the compiler. If files in the .PRJ file are not in the current directory, include before each name the correct path for finding the files.

If the project file were not used, Turbo C would display a message stating that getInt() and getStr()—both names preceded by an underscore—could not be found when link was used (unresolved references). You solve this problem by using the project file.

Examine the contents of the five source files to see how they fit together. One file, GETINT.C, will contain any integer-handling routines. Notice how the function prototype for validInt() is placed near the beginning of GETINT.C. Since validInt() is static in scope and unknown outside of the module that contains it, there is no need to put its prototype in a header file to be included in another source file. The function getInt(), which is in the header file as a prototype, can be accessed from other files. GETSTR.C contains the routine getStr(); its prototype is found in STRMOD.H.

Structuring the source files in this manner makes a good framework for further additions of variables and functions. For example, other functions that work with integers can be placed in GETINT.C and, if needed, variables common to any of these functions can be shared by placing them in the same file. Likewise, any variables that should be used globally (that is, by the functions within GETINT.C and by other source modules or the main program) can be put into INTMOD.H. Additionally, these variables might be placed inside conditional compilation statements within INTMOD.H to ensure that memory is allocated only once. For example, you could use

```
#ifdef MAIN
    int startInt, endInt;
#else
    extern int startInt, endInt;
#end
```

along with defining MAIN in the module containing main(). These conditional statements tell the compiler to allocate memory only if MAIN is defined; otherwise, the variables are declared as extern, meaning that the compiler should look elsewhere for the actual variable definition.

Note that both header files are placed in MODTEST.C so that getInt() and getStr() can be used and the compiler will see their prototypes.

Making Functions Restricted or More Visible

You can use information hiding to create functions that can be used by other programmers, but the internals of the functions cannot be altered.

The programmer can control the visibility not only of data, but also of functionality within a program. This can lead to powerful methods of allowing access to, and displaying only those functions that should be seen by, other users. For instance, to create a special routine for sorting file names, you can hide from the outside world the underlying functions of reading directory information from disk and the quicksort—qsort()—or another type of sort. Users need see only the function to actually sort the file name; they never need to know its internals. This is the so-called *black box* concept of computer science: the user can see what goes in and what comes out, but what happens inside remains a mystery.

In C, by using the storage modifier, static, and function prototypes you can either hide functions from other parts of the program or expose them for all to understand and use.

Using the Static Storage Class

As you can see from GETINT.C (refer to listing 2.4), I have declared validInt() as static. This means that it will be known only in the module in which is it located and that it is not accessible by other modules. validInt() can be used only by getInt() in this example.

Using Function Prototypes

Another way to restrict the knowledge of functions is the placement of function prototypes. If a function should be accessible from more than one module, the prototype for that function can be placed in a header file and the header file included in each module that calls the function. As long as the compiler uses the proper level of error checking, it catches the use of a function without a prototype.

On the other hand, you can restrict knowledge of a function to a particular source module by placing the prototype only at the beginning of that module (instead of in a header file). For instance, in the previous example using getInt() and validInt(), the source code file (GETINT.C) that contains the two functions (refer to listing 2.4) would also contain the function prototype for validInt(). However, the prototype for getInt() would be placed only in the header file (INTMOD.H) to be accessed not only by the source file containing the function definitions but also by the module containing main().

Listing 2.7 shows the modified GETINT.C source file.

Listing 2.7

```c
#include <stdio.h>
#include <ctype.h>
#include <conio.h>
#include <string.h>
#include <stdlib.h>
#include "intmod.h"

/* function prototype placed here to restrict access */
static int validInt(int anyInt);

int getInt(void)
  {
  char answer[80];    /* holds answer given by the user */
  int value;

  gotoxy(10,10);
  clreol();
  printf("%s:  ", "Enter an integer");
  do
    {
    gets(answer);
    value = atoi(answer);
    } while ((strlen(answer) >= 80) || (!validInt(value)));

  return(atoi(answer));
  }

static int validInt(int anyInt)
  {
  if (anyInt >= 1 && anyInt <= 100)
    {
    gotoxy(0,24);
    clreol();
    puts("Integer is valid.");
    return(1);      }
  else
    {
    puts("Invalid integer, please try again.");
    return(0);
    }
  }
```

Notice that the original INTMOD.H file:

```c
int getInt(void);
static int validInt(int anyInt);
```

has been modified to the following single line:

```c
int getInt(void);
```

None of the modules in the example shares any common variables with other modules, although they could be common if the code included more extensive routines. Different storage classes in C affect the lifetime of a variable.

Using Scope to Your Advantage

When you consider data and where it should be stored, one important factor is how the data will be used by the functions and the rest of the program. Another consideration is information hiding, or protecting the data, variables, and types from general view. Information hiding is also helpful in debugging your program. The more global data you use, the harder it is to trace changes made to a particular variable. With C you can restrict data access by using storage class modifiers and by placing data in modules not global to the entire program. This "hiding" could even involve placing a variable definition inside a function and attaching the static modifier to the variable. The definition will last throughout the rest of the program, but only certain functions will know about the definition; other functions will be ignorant of the definition.

If you try to make data global or static to one module and then try to access it in another, you will run into difficulties working with multidimensional arrays that do not specify a size for the first dimension, as in

```
char menuItems[][40] = {
            "Open File",
            "Edit File",
            "Save File",
            "Exit"};
```

The compiler can resolve the size in the source module where this definition and initialization of menuItems occur, but if you try to access this variable in another source module by using

```
extern char menuItems[][40];
```

you will get an error message from the compiler if you actually try to use this data item. The message will refer to an undefined variable.

Accessing Data in More Than One File

As an example of accessing data in more than one file, I will use two files. File 1 contains the main() function, as well as some global data. One piece of global data is the string:

```
char catalogItem[50];
```

The string is defined in the preceding statement, and storage is set aside for it. If I want to use the string catalogItem in File 2, which contains a function that gets the value for the string, the compiler will tell me that catalogItem is undefined in File 2. To remedy the situation, I place the keyword extern before a declaration (not definition) for catalogItem.

To illustrate, let's say that the contents of File 1 include the following code:

```
char catalogItem[50];
void main(void)
    {
    ...
    }
```

and that File 2 includes:

```
char *getItem(void)
    {
    char answer[50];
    ...
    strcpy(catalogItem, answer);
    }
```

To solve the problem, simply change File 2 to the following:

```
extern char catalogItem[];

char *getItem(void)
    {
    char answer[50];
    ...
    strcpy(catalogItem, answer);
    }
```

Note the declaration for `catalogItem` at the beginning of File 2. Note also that no size has been given for the character array. Because the size was specified in the definition in File 1, it does not have to be stated again. Storage for the variable also was allocated in file 1 and should not be repeated in File 2.

To further restrict the view of `catalogItem` so that only certain functions within the module File 2 have access to it, the declaration can be moved from the top of the file and placed inside the first routine that needs to access `catalogItem`.

Making Good Use of Header Files

Header files are an important element of C source code. They contain information about type definitions, variables, constants, macros, function prototypes, and other data that the program needs. The compiler builds a cross-reference table on identifiers from all the modules to ensure that no duplications of identifiers for data and functions occur.

Include Files

To access header files in a program, you use the `#include` statement followed by the file name, as in:

```
#include <stdio.h>
```

The brackets signify that the compiler should look in a directory other than the current directory to find the header file. If a programmer encloses the file name in double quotation marks, the compiler first searches the current directory for that file. If the file is not found in the current directory, the compiler searches the specified standard directory. In some instances, you may want to include the path along with the file name to specify where the compiler should look.

Constants

This discussion covers two varieties of *constants*. The most common form—also called a *macro*—is formed by using the preprocessor statement `#define` along with a name and value:

```
#define MAXARRAYSIZE 100
```

The `#define`'d identifier is replaced by the value or text following it at each occurrence of the identifier in the source code.

Remember that the ANSI C Standard supports the `enum` data type, which can take the place of some of the `#define` statements for defining screen colors or values in a series.

The second type of constant is now formed using the type modifier `const` before an integer variable to form a constant value:

```
const int noOfPages = 30;
```

Here the integer variable, `noOfPages`, is defined, allocated storage, and initialized in the same step. The `const` modifier means that the value of `noOfPages` cannot be changed in the program except in the original definition/initialization statement.

Placing constants in header files is good practice, not only so that they can be readily accessed and used by more than one source file, but also so that they are easier to find. Placing them in one place near the top of a file is much handier than searching for them through many kilobytes of code.

Typedefs

Type definitions are an underused feature of C. The older practice was to use the `#define` statement to provide a substitution for a "new" variable type. But because the preprocessor substitutes text only, it cannot properly handle some complicated function declarations.

You can use C's `typedef` feature to create a new type for further use (actually, `typedef` just creates a new name for the type). With `typedef` you can make your own varible types, function types, and so on, then use the newly formed `typedef` to create new variables and functions that have the same properties throughout your program.

typedefs aid portability. When you port code to a new machine, you need to change only the typedef—you do not have to change each definition of the variable. Using typedefs centralizes information, and this centralization is an important aspect of maintaining large programs.

typedefs also make reading code easier and aid in abstraction. Using a variable type called CHAIR is much easier than using the entire structure whenever a variable must be declared (and it's easier to understand). For example, if you enter the following:

```
typedef struct chairs
    {
    int seatType;
    float age;
    colors fabricColor
    } CHAIR;
```

you can use CHAIR when you declare variables, use casting, and so on. Your code would follow this format:

```
CHAIR rocker, sofa, recliner;
```

A typedef is particularly useful when an otherwise complicated cast would be required. For example, you might use the qsort() routine from the standard C library; qsort() takes as its last parameter a pointer to a function that returns an int and which needs two arguments that are const void pointers:

```
int (*compare)(const void *, const void *)
```

which can be turned into a typedef of the following:

```
typedef QsortFunc int (*compare)(const void *, const void *);
```

Now, in the call to qsort(), if the function used for providing comparisons returns a double instead of an int, we could use a cast to change the return type into the int expected by qsort().

```
qsort(strArray, sizeof(strArray), sizeof(strArray[0]),
      (int (*compare)(const void *, const void *))fcmp);
```

Using the typedef in the cast would make it much simpler:

```
qsort(strArray, sizeof(strArray), sizeof(strArray[0]),
      (QsortFunc)fcmp);
```

Some other typedef examples are

```
typedef enum{CGA, EGA, VGA} graficsBoard;
typedef struct decimal
    {
    int intPart;
    float fractionPart;
    }DECIMALNO;
typedef int *startingPoint;
```

which can be used to define and declare variables as

```
graficsBoard      myBoard;
DECIMALNO         noOfOunces;
startingPoint     start;
```

You should get into the habit of using `typedefs`—they have many advantages.

Variables

Global (`extern`) variables should be placed in header files along with other data to be shared between modules. One caution: *make sure that the variables are defined only once.*

There is a difference between defining and declaring a variable:

❑ *Defining* notifies the compiler of the variable's name and sets aside storage for the variable.

❑ *Declaring* a variable just notifies the compiler of its name; no storage is allocated.

One common way to ensure that a variable has storage set aside only once is to use the `#if` or `#ifdef` preprocessor statements to define the variables in one section, then declare them as `externs` in the `#else` section of the preprocessor statement, as shown in the following example:

```
#ifdef MAIN
     int pageNo;
     char title[80];
     float cost;
#else
     extern int pageNo;
     extern char title[80];
     extern float cost;
#endif
```

If the `#define` constant of `MAIN` is turned on (defined) in the module containing `main()`, storage will be allocated to the variables there. Otherwise, all other modules will only find the declaration of the variables. As I mentioned earlier, you can declare a variable for use in a module using the storage modifier extern when that variable has actually been defined in a different module.

Preprocessor Statements

As I have shown in the previous example, preprocessor statements have some uses in header files. Other preprocessor statements, such as conditional compilation for various machine environments and memory models, should also go into header files if at all possible. Again, placing preprocessor statements into header files centralizes these program elements so that they are easier to locate and change if needed.

Conditional compilation statements are particularly common in header files because they set up the environment needed for the program. In the preceding example (in the "Variables" section), conditional compilation decides whether storage will be established for variables. There is almost no limit to the types of situations conditional compilation can handle.

Summary

Coding a program is not always simple. Along the way you face many hazards, such as misinterpreting the design, leaving out requirements or necessary information, using incorrect syntax, etc. The larger the program, the greater the chance for error. The intertwining of modules becomes increasingly important also in large programs. Good tools—good editors, for instance—can make the programmer's job easier by offering special indenting and unindenting features along with matching delimiters. On-line help speeds up development.

Following a consistent coding style can reduce coding errors and make the source code easier to read.

Knowing how to structure code to provide easy access, information hiding, and yet take advantage of separate module compilation is not difficult and can strengthen your program. Using header files properly causes fewer errors and aids information retrieval. This isn't all there is to coding, however, and using the best tools available will help your program. I talk about these tools of the standard C library in the next chapter.

SUMMARY

Alan
Plantz

CHAPTER 3

Choosing the Right Tools

E very C programmer's toolkit includes the functions of the standard C library. This collection of functions comes with the compiler and provides an extensive means of dealing with a variety of problems: sorting, string manipulation, file I/O, math operations, and more. More compiler-specific collections include graphics libraries, system constants and definitions, windows, and system interface functions.

It pays to have a thorough knowledge of what is in the library and how to use it effectively. Through use and research, you can learn the "tricks" of the routines. You will learn, for example, which string-manipulation routines deal with the terminating null character at the end of a string and which work up to, but do not include, the null character.

Knowledge of related functionality also increases your efficiency. If you can remember a routine that does a certain function but is not quite what you want, there may well be a related function that will do the task.

This chapter discusses the bodies of related functions, which are grouped into the *header* files that appear at the beginning of source files. The header files and related libraries of functions are like buying a car and getting a toolchest as part of the bargain—or perhaps even more like a small factory you can use to build more cars. Each header file in this chapter is summarized, and a list of the functions in each file is given.

Determining the Right Set of Tools for the Job

Just as carpenters, plumbers, and engineers have various tools at their disposal, programmers also have a set of "tools." These tools, which may be supplied with the original compiler package, purchased from a third party, or created by the programmer, help the programmer code faster and more efficiently. These routines can be among the most important items a programmer learns to use, because he or she does not have to reinvent the wheel whenever common routines are needed. Reliable and (hopefully) error-free, the sets of routines can be used over and over; they rarely break and generally are portable. Remember that there are different degrees of portability, ranging from programs that work under a different compiler on the same machine and under the same operating system all the way to the program working on an entirely different processor under a different operating system and different compiler.

The standard C library, defined by the proposed ANSI C standard, has well over 130 functions defined and implemented. In Turbo C, the entire standard compiler library contains over 400 routines. Almost all of the ANSI C routines are implemented in the Turbo C libraries, except those dealing with foreign languages that use multibyte characters and those dealing with locale-specific information. There is also an extensive graphics library for handling drawing, animation, business graphics, graphics-oriented text, and other features. The graphics library is not defined in the ANSI standard as part of the standard C compiler library—it is too implementation-specific to be of use among all the C compilers.

The functions in the C run-time library are grouped by functionality. Similar functions have their function prototypes—along with required type definitions, global variables, and so on—in a header file. By including this header file in your source module, you can access those routines correctly.

If you forget to include a header file needed by the compiler, you will receive error messages ranging from `Unknown type` to `Function declaration mismatches`. When a function declaration or prototype is not found by the compiler, the type checking performed by the compiler will produce errors due to not finding the function information needed. Macros will not work because they have not been "defined." Functions returning `int`s may not show a problem because the `int` return type is the default used by the compiler when no prototype or other declaration exist.

The function prototypes relay to the compiler information about

❑ the return type of a function.

❑ the number of arguments of the function.

❑ the type of each argument.

By tracking down errors from function calls and incorrect return specifications, the prototypes can save you hours of work.

Knowing Which Header Files To Use

Programmers, especially beginning C programmers, wonder how to determine the correct header file to use in a program. Deciding which header file to use is usually the last part of several steps:

1. The programmer decides what must be done.

2. The programmer then decides which routine might accomplish the task.

3. The programmer calls the routine and looks for the correct header file for passing along to the compiler prototype information for that routine or a piece of data used by the function such as a type, constant, or variable.

4. The programmer then places an #include statement near the beginning of the file to tell the compiler the name of the header file. Once you become familiar with the functions of the library, you could include the header file name in the source module before actually calling the function. You can almost always #include the header file of stdio.h in your source modules because stdio.h's routines are used so often in programs. The compiler compiles header files as well as other source code modules.

The header files, also called *include files,* contain functions of related usage (reflected in the name of the header file) as well as constants, type definitions, and global variables which may be needed by the functions. Table 3.1 shows the header files that are part of the C standard library as defined by the ANSI C standard.

Table 3.1. *ANSI C Header Files Found in Turbo C 2.0*

File Name	Functions Supported
assert.h	Contains macro for assert()
ctype.h	Type checking and character conversion
errno.h	Contains system-error numbers
float.h	Constants and prototypes for floating-point math
limits.h	System limits for variable types
math.h	Prototypes for math routines
setjmp.h	Jump routine information
signal.h	Error-detection and reporting routines
stdarg.h	Allows use of variable-length argument lists
stddef.h	Contains standard system definitions
stdio.h	Holds general I/O functions
stdlib.h	Miscellaneous functions
string.h	String-manipulation routines
time.h	Time-manipulation information and routines

The header files found in table 3.2 are specific to Turbo C and not part of the ANSI C library.

Table 3.2. *Turbo C-specific Header Files (2.0)*

File Name	Functions Supported
alloc.h	Memory-management functions
bios.h	Routines for access to DOS BIOS
conio.h	Console I/O routines
dir.h	Directory-handling information
dos.h	DOS functions and interrupts
fcntl.h	Low-level file routines
graphics.h	BGI graphics routines and other data
io.h	General input and output
mem.h	High-speed memory functions
process.h	Parent- and child-process handling
share.h	File-sharing information
sys\stat.h	Low-level file I/O attributes
sys\timeb.h	Time information
sys\types.h	General types used by compiler/programmer
values.h	Limits of system data types

You should become familiar with the contents of each file and learn how you can apply it to your project. Tucked away in the C standard library are many gems—one may be just what you need to accomplish your task.

By examining or printing the header files, you can understand much more of what is going on "behind the scenes" when you use the functions. If you use one particular group of functions, such as the graphics routines, it definitely pays to inspect the file closely and keep it on hand so that you can use it to refer to constants and data definitions. Header files also can add to your understanding of

❏ how macro functions differ from normal C functions.

❏ how various C types, such as struct, union, and enum, can be used.

❏ function prototypes.

❏ conditional compilation.

❏ data abstraction.

❏ scope and information hiding.

The Turbo C documentation contains an order form that you can use to purchase the Turbo C run-time library source code from Borland International. Owning the source code has a number of advantages.

The library source code is an instructional example of professionally written code. It is tight and fast, and you can learn some coding tricks from it. The source code also enables you to clone a function and change it—slightly, or as much as you like—to meet your own needs. These changed, cloned functions should be given different names from the standard library routines so that the compiler (and perhaps the programmer) will not be confused. You can also recompile the source code using various options, such as Underbars Off, to make a library version more compatible with outside routine libraries. By recompiling the functions in this way, you will not get error messages when you try to use commercial libraries.

An Overview of the Header Files

This section describes each of the header files and briefly explains their contents.

Memory Management (*alloc.h*)

The alloc.h header file contains the function prototypes for memory allocation and deallocation routines found in table 3.3.

Table 3.3. Comparison of Memory-Management Routines

Name	"Far" Functions	DOS System Functions
malloc()	farmalloc()	allocmem()
calloc()	farcalloc()	—
realloc()	—	setblock()
free()	farfree()	freemem()

These memory routines use an area of computer memory called the *heap*. The far memory-management routines access the far heap, which is found in all the memory models except tiny (see table 3.4). The *far heap*, which consists of memory remaining above the stack, is used for the creation, manipulation, and removal of dynamic variables which are accessed through pointers. In the small and medium memory models, you find the *near heap*—the remainder of the data segment (DS) above the global and static data used in your program. The routines from this header file should be examined when you are using pointer variables for which you must allocate space, as in linked lists, trees, and so on. The various data structures are discussed in Chapter 1.

Table 3.4. *Heap/Memory Model Information*

Model	Type of Heap Available
Tiny	Near only
Small	Near or far (or both)
Medium	Near or far (or both)
Compact	Far only
Large	Far only
Huge	Far only

Note that `alloc.h` is the normal location in which Turbo C keeps the information for memory-management routines; ANSI C keeps its versions of the routines (which do not include the specialized `far...` versions) in `stdlib.h`. Thus, if your memory allotments work only with the near memory models, you could include `stdlib.h` instead of `alloc.h`.

The header file also contains several type definitions: `ptrdiff_t` holds the difference between two pointers; `size_t` holds the value of the `sizeof` operator; and NULL, which is also used by the memory routines, is defined also. Remember always to check the return of a memory allocation routine for NULL to see whether there was space for performing the allocation:

```
float *grandtotalptr;

if ((grandtotalptr = calloc(1,sizeof(float))==NULL)
    printf("Unable to allocate memory.");
```

The DOS system routines listed in table 3.3 are found in the `dos.h` file rather than in this header file. These nonportable routines are the low-level equivalents of `malloc()` and other such routines. Unless you have a specific need to work close to DOS, use the `malloc()` routines to create more portable code. Memory-management functions are found in table 3.5.

Table 3.5. *Memory-Management Functions*

Name	Purpose
brk()	Set new address for first byte after memory used within data segment
calloc()	Allocate memory and clear each byte to 0
coreleft()	Find amount of memory left in heap
farcalloc()	Allocate memory on far heap and set to 0
farcoreleft()	Find amount of memory in far heap
farfree()	Free memory in far heap
farmalloc()	Allocate memory in far heap
farrealloc()	Resize memory block in far heap

Name	Purpose
free()	Free memory block
malloc()	Allocate block of memory
realloc()	Resize a block of memory
sbrk()	Change value of brk address (In other words, readjust end of memory used within data segment by an incremented amount)

Assert Debugging Macro (*assert.h*)

The sole routine in the assert.h header file is a macro used for debugging programs:

assert   Perform debugging test

It is used, along with a preprocessor "constant" (NDEBUG), to turn on or off the action of assert(). Use of this ANSI-compatible header file is limited.

The assert() macro, which takes the place of an if statement, tests a condition. If the condition is true, the program is halted and an error message is printed.

DOS BIOS Function Calls (*bios.h*)

This file, which is not part of the ANSI C standard, contains more low-level access routines for DOS. Routines specified in this file deal with I/O functions such as serial communications, equipment checking, low-level printing capabilities, and time access (see table 3.6). When you go through the BIOS to do a task or get information, using these functions is handier than having to write your own (using interrupts, pseudovariables, and so on). These functions already include the necessary interrupts and setup needed to do the job. No other information is contained in this header file.

Table 3.6. *The bios.h Functions*

Name	Purpose
bioscom	Communications (serial) port manipulation
biosdisk	Disk manipulation
biosequip	Determine current hardware
bioskey	Keyboard manipulation
biosmemory	Low-level memory handling
biosprint	Check printer status
biostime	Get system clock count

The seven `bios.h` routines often are used in conjunction with those from `dos.h`. You can use these functions, for example, if you are writing a specialized diskette-handling program, such as one that does fast backups, or a program that accesses the keyboard buffer so that you can create keyboard macros or extend the typing buffer. The `biosprint()` function checks printer status and other print settings. Some of the functionality is simple—for instance, `biosmemory()` simply reports the amount of free memory in the system.

Console I/O (*conio.h*)

The non-ANSI header file, `conio.h`, contains routines used specifically for working (under DOS) with the screen, using text only. This file contains setup information such as color attributes. These attributes are defined as a variable of `enum` type; a structure containing text information about attributes, locations, and so on is also defined as an `enum` type and is part of the setup information. Another variable, `directvideo`, stores your response to whether screen writing should take place directly to video memory or through BIOS routines. The routines in this file contain such screen-handling functions as `clreol()`, `clrscr()`, and `lowvideo()`. Text-manipulating routines—`textbackground()`, `textcolor()`, `textmode()`, and so on—also are here, as are windowing functions like `window()` and `gotoxy()`. If you want to use color to display text, you can use this file's `cputs()` and `cprintf()` functions rather than the usual `puts()` and `printf()` functions.

These functions have a wide variety of applications but (like most screen-handling functions) are not portable out of a DOS environment. Although you would include this header file whenever you want to work with windows, the windowing capabilities here are small. You probably will prefer working with a library of routines you have developed yourself, obtained through public domain or shareware, or purchased commercially.

The `conio.h` file provides text-handling routines, especially those for moving the cursor and changing foreground or background colors. Because these routines mimic those in Turbo Pascal, translating programs to that language is easier if you include `confio.h` in your source file. And if you plan to include even one call to `clrscr()`, be sure to include the `conio.h` file in your source file.

Table 3.7 lists the `conio.h` functions.

Table 3.7. *The conio.h Functions*

Name	Purpose
clreol	Clear to the end of a line
clrscr	Clear the screen
delline	Delete a line
gettext	Get text from a window
gettextinfo	Get text information such as colors
gotoxy	Go to a specific screen location

Name	Purpose
highvideo	Turn on highlighted video attributes
insline	Insert a line
lowvideo	Turn on low intensity
movetext	Move text from one coordinate to another
normvideo	Go to normal video intensity
puttext	Display text at the given coordinates
textattr	Change foreground and background text colors
textbackground	Change background text color
textcolor	Change foreground text color
wherex	Determine X coordinate of cursor
wherey	Determine Y coordinate of cursor
window	Make a window at the coordinates
cgets	Get a string on the terminal
cprintf	Print on the terminal
cputs	Place a string on the terminal
cscanf	Get input from terminal
getch	Get a character without displaying it
getche	Get a character and display (echo) it
getpass	Get a password
kbhit	Check whether a key has been pressed
putch	Display a character on the screen
ungetch	Reinsert a character in the buffer

Character Conversion and Classification (*ctype.h*)

This frequently used ANSI-compatible header file is quite portable. You can use its set of functions to determine the type of data you are working with (number, string, punctuation, and so on). The ctype.h file includes such is... functions as isdigit(), ispunct(), isupper(), isalpha(), and isspace(). The file also has two functions—toupper() and tolower()—and corresponding macros—_toupper() and _tolower()—for converting characters from upper- to lower-case and vice versa. The toascii() function, which changes an integer value to its ASCII equivalent, is not ANSI-compatible.

These routines are useful for data validation. For instance, if you want to enter a number in a field that accepts text, you can use one (or a combination) of the routines to see whether your entry meets the criteria. The isdigit() function, for example, checks whether a character is in the range of 0 to 9. To see whether a string contains any punctuation, you can use ispunct() to check the string character-by-character for signs or a decimal. Because these routines are simple, you may need to build on them in your own library of data-validation routines (unless you use a package designed for that purpose).

These functions are useful also for parsing data, such as languages you create yourself, although file `string.h` contains other routines that are better-suited to parsing.

To find some good, concise examples of bit manipulation, such as bitwise AND-ing and ORing, examine the definitions of the macro routines in `ctype.h` (see table 3.8). You must `#include` the `ctype.h` file to use the macros correctly. Note that `toupper` and `tolower` are *functions*—everything else in this table is a macro.

Table 3.8. *The ctype.h Functions*

Name	Purpose
isalnum	Test whether character is alphanumeric
isalpha	Test whether character is alphabetic only
isascii	Test whether character is in the ASCII set
iscntrl	Test whether character is a control character macro
isdigit	Test whether character is a digit (0 to 9)
isgraph	Test whether character is a graphics char
islower	Test whether character is lowercase
isprint	Test whether character is a printable character
ispunct	Test whether character is a punctuation character
isspace	Test whether character is a whitespace character
isupper	Test whether character is uppercase
isxdigit	Test whether character is a hexadecimal character
_toupper	Change character to uppercase
_tolower	Change character to lowercase
toascii	Convert character to ASCII character
tolower	Function to convert character to lowercase
toupper	Function to convert character to uppercase

Directory Manipulation (*dir.h*)

The `dir.h` header file contains the structural definition for a file block; macro constants for directory and file limits; and functions for working with drives, paths, directories, and files. This DOS-specific file is not portable to other machines.

These routines are useful when you work with disks and files. Almost all programs that display a list of files or that provide file menus use some of these functions, as do programs that enable users to change directories or drives. The functions `getcurdir()`, `getcwd()`, `mkdir()`, `rmdir()`, and `chdir()` operate on directories. They help you find the current directory, create and delete directories, and switch between directories. For file manipulation, use `findfirst()` and `findnext()` to find files, and `mktemp()` to create a unique file name. The `getdisk()` and `setdisk()` functions get the current drive and change the drive. To combine names and portions of paths into one path; parse a path, including the PATH environment variable; and search the path string for a name, use `fnmerge()`, `fnsplit()`, and `searchpath()`.

Applications such as diskette catalogers, duplicate file-name finders, and related programs all use the functions in `dir.h`. Almost any program that deals with disk I/O will use at least one of these routines. For instance, `findfirst()` and `findnext()` are invaluable when you want to manipulate files, choose one file out of all files, or establish a file list for display. The functions found in `dir.h` are listed in table 3.9.

Table 3.9. *The dir.h Functions*

Name	Purpose
chdir	Change directory
findfirst	Find first matching file
findnext	Find next matching file
fnmerge	Merge file names, path
fnsplit	Split (parse) file names, path
getcurdir	Get current directory for specified drive
getcwd	Get current working directory including drive
getdisk	Get current disk drive
mkdir	Make a directory
mktemp	Make a unique temporary file name
rmdir	Remove (delete) a directory
searchpath	Search environment or file path for a file
setdisk	Select a new drive

DOS-specific System Routines (*dos.h*)

If you need to access DOS for anything, the first place to look is the header file `dos.h`. This non-ANSI file contains routines for working at the DOS level. You can use these routines to do the following, and more:

❏ hardware functions

❏ low-level port I/O

❏ low-level disk access

❏ system calls

❏ byte-by-byte memory access through `peek()` and `poke()`

❏ far pointer and memory manipulation

Many structures for items such as file allocation tables (FATs), file control blocks (FCBs), country information, device drivers, software registers, and the date and time are stored in this header file. The `dos.h` file also provides global variables for holding pointers to the command-line arguments, version numbers, and so on. It contains the necessary details for implementing many features that interface directly with DOS.

Important Note: The `getswitchar()` function is listed in the header file but is not explained in the reference manual. It gets the character (/ or -) before a command-line option. Because this Turbo C function accesses an *undocumented* DOS function call (37h), and because the underlying DOS is subject to change without notice in a future version of DOS, its use is not recommended to ensure portability.

A portion of the file allows special manipulation of memory at a very low level by using the `peek()` and `poke()` macros; also included are macros for far pointers and memory addressing. You can use these routines to access any portion of DOS memory.

You can use the contents of this header file in almost any application: music and sound generation; real-time programming by means of system calls and interrupts to instruments; creating new device drivers for printers, scanners, video equipment, or other apparatus; using new storage media, such as tape drives or CD-ROM applications, and so on. A great deal of work goes into building up systems, because the routines themselves operate at such an elementary level that each one does only one specific task.

Functions from the header file `dos.h` are listed in table 3.10.

Table 3.10. *The dos.h Functions*

Name	Purpose
absread	Perform absolute disk read
abswrite	Perform absolute disk write
allocmem	Allocate DOS memory (in paragraphs)
bdos	Perform BDOS call with `int` argument
bdosptr	Perform BDOS call with pointer argument
country	Country-specific information
ctrlbrk	Set Ctrl-Break handler
delay	Set delay in milliseconds
disable	Disable interrupts
dosexterr	Get DOS extended error information
dostounix	Convert time and date to UNIX format
enable	Enable interrupts
fp_off	Extract offset portion of a far pointer (macro)
fp_seg	Extract segment portion of a far pointer (macro)
freemem	Free DOS-allocated memory
geninterrupt	Generate interrupts
getcbrk	Test whether Ctrl-Break flag is on or off
getdate	Get system date
getdta	Get DTA address
getdfree	Get free disk space
getfat	Get drive FAT information
getfatd	Get default disk FAT information
getpsp	Get Program Segment Prefix (PSP)

Name	Purpose
getswitchar	Get the character before command-line arguments
gettime	Get current system time
getverify	Get verification setting of disk
harderr	Create a hardware error handler
hardretn	Return for hardware error handler
inport	Get word from port
inportb	Get byte from port
int86	Perform software interrupt
int86x	Perform software interrupt using DS, ES and segment registers
intdos	Execute DOS interrupt 21
intdosx	Execute DOS interrupt 21 using DS and ES registers
intr	Perform software interrupt (Turbo C specific)
keep	Make program memory-resident
mk_fp	Construct far pointer from specified segment and offset components (macro)
outport	Send word to port
outportb	Send byte to port
parsfnm	Parse file name and path
peek	Examine word in memory
peekb	Examine byte in memory
poke	Place a word into memory
pokeb	Place a byte into memory
randbrd	Read random block to disk
randbwr	Write random block to disk
segread	Get segment register values
setblock	Change size of allocated memory
setcbrk	Set value of Ctrl-Break flag
setdate	Set system date
setdta	Set DTA address
setswitchar	Specify command-line switch character
settime	Set system time
setvect	Create new interrupt for function 25
setverify	Set verify status for disk
sleep	Pause a number of seconds
sound	Turn on sound
unixtodos	Convert UNIX-style date and time to DOS
unlink	Delete a file

Error Message Numbering (*errno.h*)

The errno.h include file contains system error numbers and two variables that hold the number of an error when that number is returned by DOS. This ANSI-compatible file includes UNIX-type errors also. There are no functions in this file.

Not only can the numbers in `errno.h` be used to identify errors; they also can be the basis of developing an error handler that displays a user-friendly message along with the error number when an error occurs. The last system error that occurred is returned in the `_doserrno` or `errno` variables.

Low-level File Attributes (*fcntl.h*)

The `fcntl.h` header file contains the attributes used for setting and working on other files with the low-level system routines—such as `open()`, `read()`, `write()`—that do not provide buffering or other specific formatting. Use the `fcntl.h` file in conjunction with the header file `io.h` to explain in which mode (read, write, append, or a combination of these) the file should be opened. Other attributes declare whether the file is to be manipulated in binary or text mode and can be used in combination with the attributes for setting and working on files. The three functions, `open()`, `read()`, and `write()`, are found in `io.h`.

You use the `fcntl.h` file only with nonstandard file-access routines. These nonstandard file-access routines are present in many compilers; because they differ from one operating system to another, they are not part of the ANSI C standard. If portability is a concern, using `fopen()`, `fread()`, `fwrite()`, and related routines is much better than using these system routines. Also, most new software is expected to use the portable ANSI versions.

There are no function prototypes in this file.

Floating-point Parameters (*float.h*)

This file contains everything you need to work with floating-point numbers and emulation according to Institute of Electrical and Electronic Engineers (IEEE) floating-point standards. A part of the ANSI C standard language definition, this header file contains definitions of ranges for different classes of floating-point numbers (float, double, long double); routines for working with the 80x87 math chip; and error messages. Parts of the floating-point number—*exponent, mantissa,* and *precision*—are defined by their upper limits. The file includes error numbers for conditions such as division by zero, loss of precision, overflow and underflow, and rounding errors. You can use the `signal()` function to detect floating-point errors and then call a user-defined error-condition handler to take whatever action the user deems necessary.

You need to include this file in any applications that involve business math, scientific calculations, or floating-point numbers so that their mathematical operations function properly. If your programs do not work correctly at first, make sure that your source code contains an `#include` for this header file. Table 3.11 contains the functions from `float.h`.

Table 3.11. *The float.h Functions*

Name	Purpose
_clear87	Clear floating-point status
_control87	Set new floating-point status
_fpreset	Reset floating-point status
_status87	Read floating-point status

Graphics Information (*graphics.h*)

The graphics.h header file contains all the basic information needed for working with the Borland Graphics Interface (BGI) functions and graphics constants. This file, which is not at all a part of the ANSI standard routines, is compiler-specific—so much so, in fact, that its functions are likely not to be compatible even with other DOS C compilers.

One section of this file contains the numbers for graphics-system error messages. Another section contains values for colors, even defined for the CGA and EGA/VGA systems. Various graphics hardware operating modes are defined as enumerated (enum) types, along with line and pattern styles. If you are not familiar with the enum type in C, you can examine this file to better understand how it can be used. Structures also are defined for line, text, and arc information. The file also contains the function prototypes for all graphics functions.

This file includes all graphics functionality, such as functions for setting up graphics hardware, registering fonts, drawing shapes, changing colors, generating business graphics, animation, and saving graphics.

Whenever you want to use the graphics routines—for drawing or text in graphics mode, font access, and so on—you must use this header file in your source code and remember to link in the graphics library, GRAPHICS.LIB. The list of functions from graphics.h is found in table 3.12. Note that all pointers used in graphics.h are far pointers, no matter what memory model is being used. All of Turbo C's library functions except graphics have six different varieties, one for each memory model.

Table 3.12. *The graphics.h Functions*

Name	Purpose
arc	Draw an arc of given size
bar	Create a rectangle filled with a pattern
bar3d	Create a 3-D rectangle filled with a pattern
circle	Draw a circle of given size
cleardevice	Clear the graphics screen
clearviewport	Clear the active graphics "window"
closegraph	Close the graphics system

Table 3.12 continues

Table 3.12 *continued*

Name	Purpose
detectgraph	Determine the graphics-environment hardware
drawpoly	Draw a polygon
ellipse	Draw an ellipse
fillellipse	Draw an ellipse filled with a pattern
fillpoly	Draw a polygon filled with a pattern
floodfill	Paint an enclosed area with a pattern and color
getarccoords	Get the endpoints of an arc
getaspectratio	Get the aspect ratio
getbkcolor	Determine the background color
getdefaultpallette	Get the default color palette
getdrivername	Find the name of the current graphics driver
getfillpattern	Find the current pattern for filling
getfillsettings	Find the current settings for filling
getgraphmode	Get the current graphics mode
getimage	Save the current image in a buffer
getlinesettings	Find the current line thickness and style
getmaxcolor	Find the maximum color allowed
getmaxmode	Find the maximum graphics mode allowed
getmaxx	Find the maximum X coordinate allowed
getmaxy	Find the maximum Y coordinate allowed
getmodename	Get name of current graphics mode
getmoderange	Get current range of this mode
getpixel	Save a screen pixel's information
getpalette	Get a palette's information
getpalettesize	Find the current number of palette colors
gettextsettings	Find the current text values
getviewsettings	Find the current viewport settings
getx	Get current X coordinate
gety	Get current Y coordinate
graphdefaults	Get current graphics default values
grapherrormsg	Match an error message with an error code
graphfreemem	Free memory the user previously defined
graphgetmem	Set aside memory for graphics use
graphresult	Get result of last graphics operation
imagesize	Determine bytes needed to save an image
initgraph	Initialize the graphics system
installuserdriver	Install a user-defined graphics driver
installuserfont	Install a user-defined font for text
line	Draw a line between two coordinates
linerel	Draw a line using an offset from a point
lineto	Draw a line from current position to another point
moverel	Move to an offset that is another point
moveto	Move to a new X-Y location

Name	Purpose
outtext	Display a string with the current font
outtextxy	Display a string at X-Y location
pieslice	Draw a filled pie slice for a graph
putimage	Place a saved image on the screen
putpixel	Set a pixel's colors
rectangle	Draw a rectangle of a given size
registerbgidriver	Register a driver already loaded
registerfarbgidriver	Register a far driver already loaded
registerbgifont	Register a font already loaded
registerfarbgifont	Register a far font already loaded
restorecrtmode	Restore text mode after using graphics
sector	Make a filled sector as part of an ellipse
setactivepage	Set the active graphics-display page
setallpalette	Set all palettes to these colors
setaspectratio	Set the aspect ratio to these values
setbkcolor	Set background color
setcolor	Set foreground color
setfillpattern	Set fill pattern for painting
setfillstyle	Set fill style for painting
setgraphbufsize	Set size of graphics buffer
setgraphmode	Set the graphics mode
setlinestyle	Set style for line drawing
setpalette	Set the palette
setrgbpalette	Set colors of the palette
settextjustify	Set style of text justification
settextstyle	Set style of text
setusercharsize	Set size of user-defined characters
setviewport	Determine the current viewport size
setvisualpage	Set current graphics page for display
setwritemode	Set write mode for drawing
textheight	Set text height
textwidth	Set width of text

Low-level I/O (*io.h*)

This file contains prototypes and other information useful when you work with low-level, unbuffered input and output. The io.h file is used in conjunction with fcntl.h, which contains values of attributes used with the functions in io.h.

With unbuffered I/O, no storage space is set aside to hold the data coming from or going to the file. Thus, disk accesses are more frequent than when you use buffered routines such as fopen() or fread(). The functions also work better with binary files than with text files because no formatting is necessary to work with binary files. Another difference is that these functions access a file by using a handle instead of the FILE * associated with the higher-level routines. Except for these differences, the low-level routines operate much like their higher-level counterparts, keeping track of the file pointer's current location within a file, opening and closing a file, performing read and write operations, and so on. Do not mix functions using buffered I/O with those using unbuffered I/O.

Some functions listed in table 3.13 provide access to files. These functions are access(), close(), filelength(), open(), creat(), and tell(). Others, such as setftime(), lock(), unlock(), and setmode(), provide miscellaneous functionality. Part of this functionality includes the ability to lock and unlock files, which can be useful in a networking or database application.

Table 3.13. *The io.h Functions*

Name	Purpose
access	Examine file permission status
_chmod	Change file permission status
chmod	Change file permission status
chsize	Change file size
_close	Close a file (DOS specific)
close	Close a file (from UNIX)
_creat	Create a file (DOS specific)
creat	Create a file (from UNIX)
creatnew	Create a new file
creattemp	Create a temporary file
dup	Duplicate a file handle
dup2	Duplicate the old handle to a new handle
eof	Check for an end-of-file condition
filelength	Determine length of file in bytes
getftime	Get file time and date information
ioctl	Perform I/O through DOS function 44
isatty	Check device to see whether it can handle text
lock	Lock a file
lseek	Perform a long seek on a file
_open	Open a file (DOS specific)
open	Open a file (from UNIX)
_read	Read contents of a file (DOS specific)
read	Read contents of a file (from UNIX)
setftime	Set file time and date
setmode	Set file mode attribute
sopen	Open a shared file on a network
tell	Return current file pointer position
umask	Change permission mask for all further files

Name	Purpose
unlink	Delete a file
unlock	Unlock a file on a network
_write	Write to a file (DOS specific)
write	Write to a file (from UNIX)

The I/O functions listed in table 3.13 are system-dependent and not part of the ANSI C standard. You may not need them unless you are working with code from another system in which these functions were used.

Type Sizes and Environmental Limits (*limits.h*)

This file, which conforms to the ANSI standard, contains the ranges of values for integral types such as the signed and unsigned counterparts of char, short, int, and long. These definitions may be present also in the header file stddef.h.

By checking the specific contents of this file in your program, you can verify whether an integer is within its minimum or maximum value. Because these values are placed in a header file, they also can be tailored to a specific host environment in which integer sizes vary depending on the hardware.

The limits.h file can be used when, because of portability concerns, you need to control the upper and lower value limits of character and integer variables.

There are no functions in this file; it contains only constants.

Mathematics (*math.h*)

The math.h header file is compatible with ANSI C. The file contains necessary information for using the math functions, determining math errors, and supplying constants used in math calculations.

Because the constants include values to over 20 places of precision for pi, logs, the square root of pi, etc., execution of these routines can be quite slow on systems without an 8087 or 80x87 (for instance, when floating-point emulation must be used). The constants are used in the functions for calculating sines, cosines, arcs, powers of 10, logs, and for other math operations. One routine, atof(), changes a number specified as a string into a floating-point number. This file must be included whenever you perform math functions in your program. The math.h functions are listed in table 3.14.

Table 3.14. *The math.h Functions*

Name	Purpose
acos	Calculate arccosine
asin	Calculate arcsine
atan	Calculate arctangent
atan2	Calculate arctangent (full quadrant version)
atof	Convert decimal number in ASCII form to floating-point number
cabs	Calculate absolute complex number value
ceil	Get smallest integer
cos	Calculate cosine
cosh	Calculate hyperbolic cosine
exp	Calculate exponential function
fabs	Get absolute value of floating-point number
floor	Calculate largest integer less than specified value
fmod	Calculate modulus (remainder)
frexp	Separate number into mantissa and exponent components
hypot	Calculate hypotenuse
ldexp	Construct number from mantissa and exponent components
log	Calculate natural log (base e)
log10	Calculate log (base 10)
matherr	Hold value of math error
modf	Separate number into integer and fraction
poly	Create polynomial number
pow	Calculate power of a number
pow10	Calculate powers of 10 of a number
sin	Calculate sine
sinh	Calculate hyperbolic sine value
sqrt	Calculate square root
tan	Calculate tangent
tanh	Calculate hyperbolic tangent

Memory/Buffer (*mem.h*)

The functions and other information needed to work with buffers and memory are located in this file, which is not ANSI-C compatible. Most of the routines start with mem... and are high-speed, optimized functions for accessing or changing memory. The routines work by manipulating a specific number of bytes and are similar to the functions in string.h; in fact, because most of the mem... routines are included also in string.h, you may need to #include in your source file only one or the other of these header files.

You can use the mem.h routines to initialize, move, copy, compare, search, and swap memory. Because they have no regard for data types, these routines can be used to advantage for moving data to and from video buffers, strings, file buffers, or just about any other type of data within memory.

Because the information they move is done strictly as a block of bytes, you may lose some information if you don't specify the correct size, starting point, or destination. This may or may not be a problem, depending on what the programmer is doing and how well he or she understands what is happening. You can use a mixture of the string and `mem...` routines, for example, but you must ensure that the null terminator at the end of a string is handled correctly. If an error occurs, the null character most likely has been omitted or an overlap of information has occurred in memory.

The memory-management functions (see table 3.15) are underutilized by some programmers. These functions have many advantages and are worth becoming familiar with.

Table 3.15. *The mem.h Functions*

Name	Purpose
memccpy	Copy one buffer to another (non-ANSI)
memchr	Search for byte in buffer (ANSI)
memcmp	Compare two bytes in buffer (ANSI)
memcpy	Copy one buffer into another (ANSI)
memicmp	Do case-insensitive comparison (non-ANSI)
memmove	Perform high-speed move on memory (ANSI)
memset	Set all bytes to one character (ANSI)
movedata	Move data between buffers (non-ANSI)
setmem	Set buffer to one character (non-ANSI)
unmovmem	Move a specified number of bytes from buffer to buffer (non-ANSI)

DOS Process Management (*process.h*)

The `process.h` file is not part of the ANSI C standard. This header file contains the prototypes for functions that perform such tasks as spawning child processes, executing other programs, exiting, and the `system()` function prototype. It also includes some information about the program segment prefix (PSP), which is used in conjunction with these functions.

A *parent process* is the originating (starting) program of a system. If a routine within the parent program runs another program, this new program is called a *child*, or *child process*. While the child process is running, the parent process's execution is suspended because current and previous DOS versions are capable of handling only one task (except printing). A child process can, in turn, become a parent process and initiate the execution of other subprocesses. COMMAND.COM is the original process in DOS. Basically, a child process can do one of two things:

❏ It can overlay (and delete) the parent process and then run.

❏ It can be located in memory so that both the parent and the child process coexist. (The parent is either terminated or suspended until the child process terminates.)

The exec() and spawn() functions have different flavors because they allow options when you set up the child process. These variations depend on how the command-line arguments are accessed, how the path is examined and manipulated, and how other environment variables are handled. The variations of exec() and spawn() are indicated by a one- to three-character suffix in the function name. Table 3.16 shows these function variations.

Table 3.16. *Variations of exec() and spawn() Functions*

Suffix	Meaning
e	Pointer to environment strings passes along file-location information.
l	Statement calling function spawn() or exec() contains command-line arguments.
_p	DOS PATH is used to locate files.
_v	Command-line arguments are in form of pointer to string array.
none	Parent information is inherited.

A call to the exec() function overlays the child where the parent used to be and, when the child finishes processing, program control goes to DOS. spawn() can act just like exec(), or it can place the child elsewhere in memory; and, when the child finishes processing, spawn() can pass control back to the parent instead of restoring control to DOS. These functions can therefore create overlays, but there is no actual overlay manager as there is in Turbo Pascal.

While you work with parent and child processes, you can use the signal() function to trap errors, and the abort() or exit() functions to end execution. The system() call can perform DOS commands as though they were typed at the DOS command prompt.

system() looks for the value of the environment variable COMSPEC, which usually holds the value of COMMAND.COM. A second copy of COMMAND.COM is loaded by system() if memory is available, and a second DOS prompt appears.

These process-management functions give added capabilities to systems. You can use these functions in at least three areas:

❏ They can be used ideally in a menuing or shell system. A *shell* can be explained as either of two concepts: 1) leaving a program and entering DOS to perform system-level commands, or 2) a user-friendly system that allows users to perform DOS commands and more without actually being in DOS, and with some protection from errors. In such an application, the menu or shell can reside in memory and—using `spawn()`—a program specified as a menu choice can be executed. When the menu choice finishes executing, control comes back to the menu for another selection. DOS commands can be performed through the menu by using the `system()` function.

❏ From your program you can access an existing application, such as an editor or special graphics program, provided that enough free memory exists to load the application. Creating and running a child process enables you to access that program without having its source code.

❏ When your program gets too big for memory, you can use `spawn()` or `exec()` to break it into chunks and execute the pieces one at a time, setting up buffers or files for sharing common data between the processes, if necessary.

The functions governing process control are listed in table 3.17.

Table 3.17. *The process.b Functions*

Name	Purpose
abort	Terminate a program
execl	Execute a child process, command-line args in statement
execle	Execute a child process, command-line args in statement and environment pointer passed
execlp	Execute a child process, command-line args in statement and PATH variable used
execlpe	Execute a child process, command-line args in statement with both PATH and environment pointer
execv	Execute a child process, pointer to command-line args
execve	Execute a child process, pointer to command-line args with environment pointer
execvp	Execute a child process, pointer to command-line args and PATH variable used
execvpe	Execute a child process, pointer to command-line args with both PATH and environment pointer
_exit	Terminate a program
exit	Terminate a program
spawnl	Execute a child process, command-line args in statement
spawnle	Execute a child process, command-line args in statement with environment pointer
spawnlp	Execute a child process, command-line args in statement and PATH variable used
spawnlpe	Execute a child process, command-line args in statement with both PATH and environment pointer
spawnv	Execute a child process, pointer to command-line args

Table 3.17 continues

Table 3.17 *continued*

Name	Purpose
spawnve	Execute a child process, pointer to command-line args and environment pointer passed
spawnvp	Execute a child process, pointer to command-line args and PATH variable used
spawnvpe	Execute a child process, pointer to command-line args with both PATH and environment pointer
system	Perform a system command

Nonlocal Jumps (*setjmp.h*)

This small header file contains the ANSI C compatible setjmp() and longjmp() functions, as well as a structure, called jmp_buf, that holds information from them. The setjmp.h file is related to the process.h file in that the setjmp.h functions are used also in process control, along with others from stdlib.h.

The setjmp() and longjmp() functions allow jumps between functions instead of strictly within a function. First, the environment at the time the jump occurs is saved in a buffer of type jmp_buf. Then program flow transfers to the position of longjmp(), which is inside a different function from setjmp(). When longjmp() finishes executing, control is returned to the statement following setjmp(), and the environment conditions are restored (the stack is returned to its proper state so that return addresses and parameters are the same as before the jump was performed). A mixed-up stack can lead to a program crash.

These functions were developed to provide a means of getting to error conditions or other conditions from anywhere in the program. Due to their inherent nature of spreading control over the program, they are used only when absolutely necessary. The functions for setjmp.h are

Name	Purpose
longjmp	Perform jump back to line after setjmp
setjmp	Perform jump across functions

File Sharing (*share.h*)

This non-ANSI C compatible file provides for file-sharing capabilities within DOS. It is used with the sopen() routine along with the #include files of io.h, fcntl.h, and sys\stat.h, which are all related to low-level file I/O.

The small share.h file holds only attributes that dictate the modes for file sharing, together with other file attributes from fcntl.h. These features are originally from UNIX systems, where file sharing is a common occurrence.

Under DOS, file sharing is used only on networks. This header file can be used with the low-level routines for developing file systems with file-sharing and file-locking capabilities.

This header file does not contain any functions.

Special Error Handling (*signal.h*)

The `signal.h` file contains the prototypes for the `signal()` and `raise()` functions. It also includes numbers of various error conditions that can be identified and handled by `signal()`. These functions and the errors are ANSI-compatible.

The `raise()` function creates an error condition that can then be handled by `signal()`, provided that an exception handler has been developed for this error.

The errors produced by the `raise()` and `signal()` functions can include abnormal terminations, floating-point problems, Ctrl-C program breaks and recovery, and other abnormal conditions. The `signal()` and `raise()` routines are for that "extra measure" of error control to help prevent a program crash, such as avoiding division by zero in floating-point math or catching a Ctrl-C to ask the customer if he or she really wants to stop the program or prefers to continue. Using `signal()` instead of the `setcbrk()` and `getcbrk()` functions makes trapping a Ctrl-C or Ctrl-Break more portable between environments. Allowing Ctrl-C to be entered means that the program does not get a chance to clean up, close files, etc. The error-handling functions in `signal.h` are

Name	Purpose
raise	Create an error condition
signal	Execute error-condition handler

Variable Arguments (*stdargs.h*)

This ANSI-standard file contains the macros and functions for dealing with variable-length argument lists in C functions. Functions such as `printf()`, `spawn()`, and `scanf()` do not take a specific number of parameters; the number can vary. The minimum requirement is that there be at least one "fixed" or known parameter at the front of the list. In the `printf()` or `scanf()` families, this fixed parameter corresponds to the format string that defines what to expect for the arguments that follow.

The routines included are `va_start()`, `va_end()`, and `va_arg()`, all of which are macros. The type `va_list`, which is also part of the `stdargs.h` file, is used for defining a varying number of argument-list variables.

Variable arguments are very useful in C. How do you know when you need to use these functions? If you do not know the exact number of arguments, or if the number of arguments will change from one call of the function to the next call, you probably need to use these functions to manipulate arguments. The va... functions allow a degree of flexibility in defining functions, which is especially useful when data must be printed. In another example, an equation could use a varying number of variables, ranging from summing only a couple of numbers to many numbers. Using these routines rather than self-defined macros or functions that "climb the stack" searching for the arguments can ensure a greater degree of code portability.

Functions such as vprintf(), vsprintf(), and others in the stdio.h header file will also work with a variable number of arguments, but differently from va_start and others in stdargs.h. The vprintf() group uses only a pointer to an argument list rather than arguments themselves. The vprintf(), vsprintf(), and related functions can act as templates when you develop your own routines for printing, data entry (from files, for example), or output to the screen. These usages require an unknown number of arguments in each call of the v... functions, as well as in your own user-defined routine. The functions in stdargs.h appear in table 3.18.

Table 3.18. *The stdargs.h Functions*

Name	Purpose
va_start	Find start of argument list
va_arg	Get next argument in list
va_end	Clean up at end of argument list

Standard Definitions (*stddef.h*)

This short file, which does not contain any function prototypes, contains three type definitions and a declaration for one variable that holds the system error number. This ANSI C-compatible file also contains the definitions for ptrdiff_t, which holds the difference between two pointers and is adjusted for either the large or small memory models. The second type definition is size_t, which holds the value returned by the sizeof operator. The final definition, for NULL, takes into account the large or small memory models.

This file is used by other C library routines when they need to access these types. The programmer can use it also to help provide standard, portable definitions for variables needed in a program. These definitions may also be repeated in other files, such as stdio.h, stdlib.h, and alloc.h.

Standard I/O (*stdio.h*)

This large ANSI C standard file definitely is used more than any library file. It appears in almost every program. The file contains routines for such input and output tasks as text on the terminal, printer, files, etc. A major portion of the file allows output to various devices, including predefined streams, `stdin` (standard input), `stdout` (standard output), `stdprn` (standard printer), and `stderr` (standard error).

The `stdio.h` file also includes definitions and constants for working with files, or streams, as well as buffered I/O functions. *Streams* are device-independent, continuous collections of bytes. `stdio.h` includes the `struct` for files, file mode attributes, buffer constants, and so on. This header file also includes system limits for files, such as the maximum number of files open at one time.

Also included in this header file are function prototypes and macros for working (on character, word, or text levels) with files and devices—both for getting data from the devices and for sending data to them. Table 3.19 lists functions found in the `stdio.h` file.

Table 3.19. *The stdio.h Functions*

Name	Purpose
clearerr	Clear an error for new one
fclose	Close a file
fcloseall	Close all files
fdopen	Open a file using a file handle
feof	Check for end-of-file
fflush	Flush file buffers
fgetc	Get a character from stream
fgetchar	Get a character from `stdin`
fgetpos	Get the position of a file pointer
fgets	Get string from file
fileno	Return handle of file
flushall	Flush all buffers
fopen	Open a file
fprintf	Print to a file or stream
fputc	Write a character to the stream
fputchar	Write a character to `stdout`
fputs	Write a string to the stream
fread	Read a file
freopen	Change the file pointer to point to a different file
fscanf	Get formatted input from a stream
fseek	Go to a new file location with file pointer
fsetpos	Set a new position in the file
ftell	Determine the current file pointer location
fwrite	Write to a file

Table 3.19 *continues*

Table 3.19 *continued*

Name	Purpose
getc	Get a character
getchar	Get a character from stdin
gets	Get a string
getw	Get an integer
perror	Print an error message
printf	Print to stdin
putc	Write a character
putchar	Write a character to stdin
puts	Write a string
putw	Write an integer
remove	Delete a file
rename	Rename a file
rewind	Set the file pointer to the beginning of a stream
scanf	Get formatted input from stdin
setbuf	Set buffer size for file I/O
setvbuf	Establish buffering for a file
sprintf	Write to a string (like strcat)
sscanf	Get formatted input from a string
_strerror	Get an error string
strerror	Get an error string
tmpfile	Open a temporary file
tmpnam	Get a temporary file name
ungetc	Put a character back into the buffer
unlink	Delete a file
vfprintf	Perform a write with variable arguments to a stream
vfscanf	Perform input with variable arguments from a stream
vprintf	Perform a write with variable arguments to stdout
vscanf	Perform input with variable arguments from stdin
vsprintf	Perform a write with varargs from a string
vsscanf	Perform input with varargs from a string

Miscellaneous Standard Library (stdlib.h)

This ANSI C-compatible #include file contains many functions for different purposes: memory allocation, data conversions, sorting and searching, program aborts and exits, and random number generation. This file is a "catchall" for functions that do not belong in other header files—if you can't find a routine anywhere else, look for it here. Table 3.20 contains a brief description of all the functions in stdlib.h.

Table 3.20. *The stdlib.h Functions*

Name	Purpose
abort	Terminate a program
abs	Find absolute value of a number
atexit	Stack up conditions for exiting
atof	Convert ASCII character to floating-point number
atoi	Convert ASCII character to integer
atol	Convert ASCII character to a long
bsearch	Perform a binary search
calloc	Allocate memory and clear it with 0s
div	Perform integer division
ecvt	Convert floating-point number to a string
exit	Exit program
fcvt	Convert floating-point number to a string with rounding
free	Free block of memory
gcvt	Convert floating-point number to a string and return string
getenv	Get environment information
itoa	Convert integer to string
labs	Calculate absolute of a long
lfind	Do linear search on an array
ldiv	Perform long integer division
_lrotl	Rotate long integer left
_lrotr	Rotate long integer right
lsearch	Do linear search on an array
ltoa	Convert long integer to string
malloc	Allocate a block of memory
max	Find maximum of range
min	Find minimum of range
putenv	Write information to the environment
qsort	Perform a quicksort
rand	Get a random number
random	Get a random number between 0 and $num - 1$
randomize	Seed the random-number generator
realloc	Change size of an allocated memory block
_rotl	Rotate long integer left
_rotr	Rotate long integer right
srand	Seed the random-number generator
strtod	Convert string to a double
strtol	Convert string to a long
strtoul	Convert string to an unsigned long
swab	Swap two bytes
system	Do a DOS system call
ultoa	Convert unsigned long to string

String Handling (*string.h*)

The string.h file contains almost all the routines for working with strings and buffers in memory. The routines copy, search, parse, duplicate, convert, and delete strings or portions of strings. The buffer-manipulation routines are found also in mem.h, which is not part of the ANSI C standard string.h. To learn about the mem... routines, refer to the earlier section about the header file mem.h. The string.h functions are listed in table 3.21.

Table 3.21. *The string.h Functions*

Name	Purpose
stpcpy	Copy a string into another string
strcat	Append one string onto another string
strchr	Search for a character in a string
strcmp	Compare two strings
strcmpi	Do case-insensitive comparison of a string
strcpy	Copy a string into another string
strdup	Duplicate a string
_strerror	Get an error message string
strerror	Get an error message string
stricmp	Do a case-insensitive comparison
strlen	Find the length of a string
strlwr	Convert a string to lowercase
strncat	Append *n* characters onto a string
strncmp	Compare *n* characters of a string
strncmpi	Do case-insensitive comparison of *n* chars
strncpy	Copy *n* characters from one string to another
strnicmp	Do case-insensitive comparison of *n* chars
strnset	Set *n* chars of string to given value
strpbrk	Find occurrence of any character in string
strrchr	Find last occurrence of a character
strrev	Reverse the order of a string
strset	Set characters of a string to a given value
strspn	Find character of one string not in second string
strstr	Search for a string inside another string
strtok	· Parse a string into tokens
strupr	Convert a string to uppercase

File-handling Constants (*sys\stat.h*)

This file, which is not ANSI C compatible, contains the definitions for file-handling constants. These definitions are used with the fstat() and stat() routines, which are also inside this file, to determine the file's present drive, file mode, time of last modification, and so on. This information is kept in a variable of the type struct stat, which is defined also in the stat.h file. Determination of the file mode is done by checking certain bits in the variable `st_mode`, whose value should correspond to a value of one of the constants. The modes indicate whether the file is used for reading, writing, etc. The two functions found in `stat.h` are

Name   *Purpose*

`fstat`   Determine file status of unbuffered file using handle

`stat`   Determine file status using path's name

Current Time Information (*sys\timeb.h*)

This small file holds a struct, `timeb`, which stores time information. This structure is used by the `ftime()` function, also found in this non-ANSI header file. `ftime()` gets the current time, which can then be printed. Even time-zone information is included, along with whether daylight saving time is in effect. The `timeb.h` header file contains only one function—`ftimeGet`. Its purpose is to get current time information.

Time Type (*sys\types.h*)

This small header file contains only the type definition of `time_t`, which is used to declare variables for storing time information. It is not compatible with the ANSI C standard. There are no functions in this file.

Time Functions (*time.h*)

The `time.h` file, which is ANSI C compatible, contains function prototypes for two kinds of routines: those used for obtaining and manipulating time information—`ctime()`, `difftime()`, `stime()`, and so on—and those used for converting time—`asctime()`, `localtime()`, and `gmtime()`. The appropriate structure for holding the time data, `tm`, is also part of the file. This structure holds seconds, minutes, hours, day of the month, year, and other information. The `time()` function returns the time expressed as the number of seconds since January 1, 1970.

The header file also contains a constant that defines the number of hardware timer interrupts as returned by Int 9h, expressed as "ticks per second" (18.2).

These routines are useful whenever time is a factor, as in profilers, file manipulation, time-zone maps, appointment calendars, and project schedulers, to name a few. The functions for `time.h` are presented in table 3.22.

Table 3.22. *The time.h Functions*

Name	Purpose
`asctime`	Convert time struct to a string
`ctime`	Convert binary time to a string
`difftime`	Find difference in time
`gmtime`	Get Greenwich mean time

Table 3.22 *continues*

***Table 3.22** continued*

Name	Purpose
localtime	Get local time
time	Get seconds since January 1, 1970
clock	Get program execution time in clock ticks
stime	Set system time
tzset	Set variables from the environment

Machine-dependent Constants (*values.h*)

This header file, which is not ANSI- or DOS-compatible, contains no function prototypes. It contains constants that are basically machine-dependent and supplied so that the compiler is compatible with UNIX V. These constants, which include ranges for floating types, integers, and other types, are useful when you write code for UNIX applications and need to know system constants and values.

Summary

Header files are a necessary part of programming in C. They contain information that is vital to the correct operation of the compiler and linker by containing information about what to expect of function calls and identifiers. Header files can be examined by the programmer to see what the compiler needs and how the features contained in the header files can best be implemented.

By defining constants, types, and global variables in standard locations, header files also provide a way to increase code portability. And these include files are necessary in order for certain systems (such as the graphics system) to work properly, because the information on types and memory models is essential for the compiler to generate the correct code.

If you learn to use header files efficiently, they will make your programming much easier.

Alan
Plantz

CHAPTER

4

Using Library Functions

Turbo C provides standard library functions so powerful that they handle your ordinary programming needs without supplemental routines. The standard library for most C compilers now follows the ANSI C standard library, which comprises over 130 routines. Using these routines helps to ensure your code's portability.

Turbo C has more than 300 routines that are not part of the ANSI standard library, however. These nonstandard routines deal with DOS calls and interrupts, file and directory manipulation, DOS process control, text windows, and graphics. Although such functions and features are not necessarily portable among compilers, they are fairly standard among versions of Turbo C; thus, one upgrade does not outdate past work. Some functions, such as those in the graphics library, are similar to those of Microsoft C, which helps you port applications from one C environment to another.

Knowing which routines to use for a task in your program is similar to having the right tool for a repair job. Familiarity with the available functions also means that you can use a specialized tool for a specific task, such as using the country() function to establish the proper environment for computing in a foreign country. By becoming familiar with the routines in the compiler's run-time library, you won't have to "reinvent the wheel."

This chapter explores the finer points of some of the library functions and explains some of the more obscure functions. You may find that they are just what you need!

The functions chosen generally are obscure or not used often. Some, such as the get...() character functions and the random-number functions are simple to use, but often misused. For example, some programmers may tend to reseed the random number generator before each individual call to it—and then wonder why their numbers are not random.

During development of the examples in this chapter, the debuggers provided in Turbo C Professional, especially the integrated debugger, proved invaluable. The debugger's watch feature was used on every example in order to observe how each variable changed during program execution. Even simple errors like reversing the arguments in a cell to strcpy() jump out at you in the Watch window. Using the debugger reduced development time by about 20 to 30 percent. The expanded view of data afforded in the stand-alone debugger is even more revealing, but not as handy for simpler data structures like those in this chapter. For complex structures like linked lists, structs within structs within arrays, etc., the stand-alone debugger cannot be beat.

The *allocmem()* Function

Function Prototype

```
int allocmem(unsigned size, unsigned *segp);
```

Header File

```
#include <dos.h>
```

Parameter List

unsigned size   The number of paragraphs to set aside

unsigned *segp   The variable to hold the address of the block after it is set aside

The allocmem() function provides an alternative to using the standard library routine malloc(); however, allocmem() is nonstandard and nonportable.

The purpose of allocmem() is to set aside memory in 16-byte blocks from the DOS memory pool. These blocks are referred to as *paragraphs*. A − 1 is returned if the memory request is successful. Any other number indicates the number of paragraphs left in memory for allocation. A subsequent call to allocmem() using the previously returned value (or a smaller value) for the size parameter will then be successful. The function that frees this memory is freemem(), which should be used after all work with the block is finished. Function freemem() takes the address in segp as its argument. This function directly invokes DOS function 49h. You are asking for trouble (a system crash is likely) if you try to free memory with freemem() when it wasn't obtained by way of a previous call to allocmem().

The function allocmem(), like malloc(), can be used to obtain memory. Whereas malloc does not relay information about the amount of memory left for allocation, allocmem() does return the amount of free memory. You could use this value to warn the user if free memory is getting low. Also, malloc() will allocate memory in any size, but allocmem() sets aside memory in paragraph-sized chunks only, so you may not need all the memory allocated.

If an error occurs as you use `allocmem()`, the value of the error is placed in Turbo C's predefined global variable _doserrno. This value can then be used with the function `strerror()` to obtain an error message for a DOS error. Such a message uses a call with the format `strerror(_doserrno)`. These messages, however, are not always the most understandable, and you may want to build your own lookup table to translate them into more understandable language for your customers. Listing 4.1 gives an example of using `allocmem()`.

Listing 4.1

```
#include <dos.h>
#include <stdlib.h>         /* need this .h file for exit() */
#include <stdio.h>

#define  SUCCESS       -1   /* whether allocation is successful */
#define  NOOFBLOCKS    100  /* no. of 16-byte blocks to allocate */

int result;
unsigned segmentPtr;

void main(void);

void main(void)
  {
  if ((result = allocmem(NOOFBLOCKS, &segmentPtr)) != SUCCESS)
    {
    printf("Allocation %s", strerror(_doserrno));
    printf("allocmem() could not allocate needed memory.\n");
    printf("Only %u bytes are available\n", result * 16);
    exit(1);
    }
  /* print out allocation information for the user */
  printf("%u bytes of memory allocated starting at segment 0x%X\n",
         NOOFBLOCKS * 16, segmentPtr);
  /*  free memory when finished */
  freemem(segmentPtr);
  }
```

This simple code fragment uses `allocmem()` to attempt allocation of a certain number (here, 100) of memory blocks. If the allocation is unsuccessful, the code calls the `strerror()` function to display the error message that corresponds to the special global variable, _doserrno, which was set by `allocmem()`. Another message prints out to explain that `allocmem()` was not successful.

The *bioskey()* Function

Function Prototype

```
int bioskey(int command);
```

Header File

```
#include <bios.h>
```

Parameter List

int command   BIOS keyboard function to perform (for values, see table 4.1)

This simple routine can perform any of three separate functions; the choice is determined by the value of the command parameter. The bioskey() function uses IBM BIOS Int 16h and returns an integer value that could be a character read, the status of a key, or a true or false value if the keyboard buffer holds a keypress. Note that the function kbhit() also performs the last function and is more convenient to use than bioskey(). Table 4.1 shows the basic functions of bioskey() and other routines you can substitute for them.

Table 4.1. *Functions of bioskey()*

Value	Function	Turbo C Library Routine
0	Get the next character from the buffer or wait for a character (unbuffered)	getc()
1	See whether a keypress is waiting in the keyboard buffer. (Doesn't work if no keypress is in buffer.)	kbhit()
2	Return status of the "lock" keys: Scroll Lock, Num Lock, Caps Lock; return status of the Ctrl, Alt, and Shift keys.	none

As you can see from table 4.1, instead of using a bioskey() function you may prefer to use getc() or an equivalent routine, or kbhit(). The real usefulness of bioskey() is in the third function (value = 2): reporting the condition of the special keys. Normally, finding the status of the Shift keys or the Scroll Lock key is fairly difficult and of great use in many programs that use menus and special keystroke operations or that substitute a custom value for a key. The memory location must be accessed at 0x00400017 to get the special key status unless `bioskey()` or an interrupt is used. Programmers familiar with BIOS functions may prefer to use `bioskey()` instead of assembly language routines.

Because the status of the key is represented by a single bit, the result of `bioskey()` must be masked or shifted to determine the value of the individual bit. The bits to check for a particular key status are shown in table 4.2. When the bit is on or has a value of 1 or TRUE, the meaning is applicable. Otherwise, the meaning is not true if the bit is off or has a value of 0. Note that this does *not* mean that the function waits for you to press the Caps Lock or Alt key. The `bioskey()` function merely reports the key's current status. If you try running the sample program, you will be able to press various keys as it runs and see correct results for the special keys.

Table 4.2. *Special Key Status from bioskey()*

Meaning When Bit Is On	Bit
Right Shift key is pressed	0
Left Shift key is pressed	1
Ctrl key is pressed	2
Alt key is pressed	3
Scroll Lock is on	4
Num Lock is on	5
Caps Lock is on	6
Ins (insert) state is on	7

Some applications, such as terminate-and-stay-resident programs, use a combination of the special keys (with or without regular keys) as a hot-key combination that triggers the application. Other programs, such as editors, word processors, or data-entry applications, toggle the Ins key to switch between insert and overwrite modes.

Note that newer keyboards may have a problem in Alt-key detection, because there are two Alt keys and each has a separate scan code. There may be a difference also in codes for 101-key keyboards that have both a numeric keypad and a separate pad for the cursor-movement keys.

A possible solution to keyboards with two Alt keys is to check the scan code as each key is pressed. By ORing the choices together you can effectively make both Alt keys behave the same:

```
key = loByte(key);
if (key = RIGHTALT || key = LEFTALT)
    ...
```

The scan codes can be obtained by using the character as an integer value and performing a bitwise AND (&) with the character and the value 0xff, or 255. This manipulation obtains the low-order byte of a 2-byte `int` value. The operation can be turned into a macro:

```
#define loByte(b)    ((b)&0xff)
```

Use `bioskey()` with a parameter of "0" to get the keystroke, or use an interrupt routine or other method.

The sample program in listing 4.2 checks the current keyboard status and reports the condition of the special keys such as Ctrl and Caps Lock. Whatever key is pressed at the time of execution or whose LED is "on" generates a message to print its status. No other messages appear. The program uses function 2 of `bioskey()`; then each bit is checked from most to least significant to see if it is 0 or 1. If any keys are pressed or have activated LEDs, a message is reported.

Listing 4.2

```
#include <stdio.h>
#include <bios.h>

#define TRUE    1
#define FALSE   0

/***************** function prototypes  *****************/

int odd(int value);
int checkBit(int *target, int bitNo);
void specKey(void);
void main(void);

/***************** main program  *****************/
void main(void)
   {
   specKey();
   }

/***************** functions  *****************/
void specKey(void)
   {
   #define READKEY     0      /*  reads a char from kbd */
   #define KEYBRDFREE  1      /*  checks if char is waiting */
   #define SPECKEY     2      /*  used to get special keys */
   /* use the values other than SPECKEY to perform the other features
      of the bioskey() function */

   int newChar = 0;
   int shiftCount, temp;
```

Listing 4.2 continues

Listing 4.2 continued

```
printf("Calling bioskey(int service) with service = %u\n", SPECKEY);
printf("(Gets shift states and status)\n\n");

newChar = bioskey(SPECKEY);
temp = newChar;
for (shiftCount = 7; shiftCount >= 0; shiftCount--)
   {
   newChar = temp;
   switch (shiftCount)    /* check each bit */
      {
      case 7 : printf("Insert mode is  %s\n", (checkBit(&newChar,
                     shiftCount) ? "ON" : "OFF"));
               break;
      case 6 : printf("Caps Lock is    %s\n", (checkBit(&newChar,
                     shiftCount) ? "ON" : "OFF"));
               break;
      case 5 : printf("Num Lock is     %s\n", (checkBit(&newChar,
                     shiftCount) ? "ON" : "OFF"));
               break;
      case 4 : printf("Scroll Lock is  %s\n", (checkBit(&newChar,
                     shiftCount) ? "ON" : "OFF"));
               break;
      case 3 : printf("ALT key was     %s\n", (checkBit(&newChar,
                     shiftCount) ? "pressed" : "not pressed"));
               break;
      case 2 : printf("CTRL key was    %s\n", (checkBit(&newChar,
                     shiftCount) ? "pressed" : "not pressed"));
               break;
      case 1 : printf("Left Shift was  %s\n", (checkBit(&newChar,
                     shiftCount) ? "pressed" : "not pressed"));
               break;
      case 0 : printf("Right Shift was %s\n", (checkBit(&newChar,
                     shiftCount) ? "pressed" : "not pressed"));
               break;
      }  /* end of switch */
   }  /* end of for */
}  /* end of specKey */

int checkBit(int *target, int bitNo)
   {
   int tempInt;
   tempInt = *target;
   tempInt >>= bitNo;         /* shift right bitNo times */
   /* if the value is odd, then return true */
   return(odd(tempInt) ? TRUE : FALSE);
   }

int odd(int value)
   {
   return(value % 2);   /* use modulus to check for remainder */
   }
```

Notice the strange form of the printf() statement in the example. The print statements use the *ternary* operator in C. Using this operator is like using an if...else statement. In the first printf() using the ternary operator, for example, the statement prints out *Insert mode is*. The value returned by checkBit() determines whether *ON* or *OFF* is printed—if checkBit() is TRUE, the word *ON* is printed; if checkBit() returns a value of FALSE, the word *OFF* is printed.

The bits are checked by shifting them to the right. To check bit 6, shift right by 6. The bit's value is then checked to see whether it is odd or even, and TRUE is returned if the value is odd, meaning that bit is on.

In another brief example, you could use the following code:

```
newChar = bioskey(SPECKEY);
if (checkBit(&newChar, 4))
    printf("Caps Lock is on--all text uppercase.\n");
```

to display a message on-screen if a certain condition were true. Try the other values (READKEY and KEYBRDFREE) with bioskey() to see how the results differ from using SPECKEY.

The *bsearch()* and *lsearch()* Functions

Function Prototypes

```
void *bsearch(const void *key, const void *base, size_t nelem,
size_t width, int (*fcmp)(const void *element1, const void *element2));

void *lsearch(const void *key, const void *base, size_t *nelem,
size_t width, int (*fcmp)(const void *element1, const void *element2));
```

Note the difference in the parameters for the lsearch() routine. It needs a pointer for the number of elements (nelem) whereas bsearch() does not need a pointer. The help screens also present this incorrectly. The correct form was found by looking at the prototypes in the header files for each routine.

Header File

```
#include <stdlib.h>
```

Parameter List

const void *key	The key or item searched for
const void *base	The address of the array or table searched by the routine
size_t nelem	The number of items in the array
size_t width	The size of each item in the array

int (*fcmp)(const void *, const void *))

A function pointer that points to an integer function. The function uses two arguments to compare array elements (element1 and element2).

When you search an area of memory—in particular, an array—the `bsearch()` and `lsearch()` routines are handy. Although they look basically the same, `bsearch()` performs a binary search on a presorted array, and `lsearch()` performs a linear search on a sorted or unsorted array. The arrays may contain such data as file names, part numbers, or conversion factors. Both functions have advantages. When applied to the same data, and with the array sorted, `bsearch()` should be faster than `lsearch()`. The `lsearch()` routine can add the element searched for to the end of the array if it cannot be found in the array. This is not always preferable, because you may want only a "table lookup" function that restricts the user to a certain group of responses. Adding one to the end of this list would effectively allow the user to do whatever he or she desired. On the other hand, you can use this feature to your advantage, such as in a database application in which `lsearch()` could add an array element to the list if it was not already included. The application could then sort the list and use the `bsearch()` function to obtain the elements without adding additional items, thereby enabling users to pick from a restricted list.

The `bsearch/lsearch` example contains another C construct that may be strange to you: *double indirection*. Double indirection is caused by the use of two asterisks before a pointer variable, as in the comparison routine, `compareNames()`. The array holding the names is actually an array of pointers to strings. Remember that the list of command-line parameters used by `main()` in a C program is the same data type—`char *argv[]`. You can use also the notation `char **argv` to work with the command-line parameters. To access a string in the array, use `*argv`; use `**argv` to work inside a string.

Double indirection has a multitude of uses in areas as diverse as sorting, string manipulation, working with objects on the heap, or in object-oriented environments, and so on.

Another instance in which array-searching routines are used is in the implementation of parsers and compilers, where a table is searched for keywords or other identifiers. The `bsearch()` or `lsearch()` routine could make this work more easily.

These routines return a `NULL` if the item cannot be found in the array, or else the address of the item as an offset from the beginning of the array, or a subscript could be returned.

Two related routines are useful but beyond the scope of this discussion. The `lfind()` function performs a linear search on an array without adding an element to the end, and `qsort()` provides a fast way to sort an array or other group of variables. The `qsort()` function is handy when you must sort an array before you use `bsearch()`.

Listing 4.3 is an example of how both `bsearch()` and `lsearch()` can be used in the same context.

Listing 4.3

```c
#include <stdio.h>
#include <stdlib.h>
#include <string.h>

/***** function prototypes *****/
int compareNames(const char **fstName, const char **sndName);
void main(void);

/*****  external (global) variables *****/
char entry[100];            /* holds user entry for key */
char **choice;              /* points to entry */
char *nameList[15] =        /* name list for manipulation */
  {"Jake", "Frank", "Zeke", "Alexander",
   "Martha", "Cathie", "Barbara"};

void main(void)
{
  char answer[3];       /* answer to questions */
  char **result;        /* pointer to searching results */
  char **tablePtr;      /* pointer for name list */
  size_t elementSize;   /* size of an array element */
  size_t count;         /* number of array elements */

  *choice = entry;      /* ptr choice will point to entry */
  elementSize = sizeof(nameList[0]);
  /* change all names in list to uppercase for better */
  /* comparison and return the number of members in the  */
  /* array via count note the display difference with */
  /* the similar for loop near the end of this program -- */
  /* pointers are much faster than using a regular loop */
  for (count = 0, tablePtr = nameList;
       *tablePtr != NULL;
       count++, tablePtr++)
    printf("%s\n", strupr(*tablePtr));

  printf("Enter item to search for:  ");
  strupr(gets(*choice));
  printf("Add element to the list if not already there? (Y/N) ");
  strupr(gets(answer));
  /* use lsearch if we want to add the item to the list; otherwise, */
  /* just use binary search */
  if (answer[0] == 'Y')
  {
    /* remember 'count' must be an address */
    result = lsearch(choice, nameList, &count,
                     elementSize, compareNames);
    if (result == NULL)
    {
      printf("%s was not found in the list\n", *result);
      printf("Now %d elements in the table\n", count);
    }
    else
      printf("%s was placed in the array\n", *choice);
```

```
      }
      else
      {
         /* don't forget array must be sorted for binary searching */
         qsort(nameList, count, elementSize, compareNames);
         result = bsearch(*choice, nameList, count,
                          elementSize, compareNames);
         if (result == NULL)
         {
            printf("%s was not found in the list\n", *choice);
         }
         else
            printf("The answer is:  %s\n", *result);
      }  /* end of if..else */

      printf("Now %d elements in the table\n", count);

      /* now print out the final list */
      for (tablePtr = nameList; *tablePtr != NULL; tablePtr++)
         printf("%s\n", *tablePtr);

   }  /* end of main */

   /******* comparison function for lsearch and qsort *******/
   int compareNames(const char **fstName, const char **sndName)
   {
      return(strncmp(*fstName, *sndName, strlen(*fstName)));
   }
```

This code segment assumes that a list (array) of names already exists. The user is asked whether to add a name to the list; if the name is not found, the user types it. The list of names is searched by the appropriate method, and then added to the list if it does not exist, or the name list is left untouched.

This code example assumes that a list (array) of names already exists. After searching for the name in the list, the program does one of two things: 1) If the name is not found in the list and the user answers *Y* to the query, the name is added to the end of the list; or 2) if the name is not found in the list and the user answers *N* to the query, the name is *not* added to the list.

The *coreleft()* Function

Function Prototype

```
   unsigned long coreleft(void);
```

or

```
   unsigned       coreleft(void);
```

and

```
unsigned long farcoreleft(void);
```

Header File

```
#include <alloc.h>
```

The return type of `coreleft()` varies, depending on which memory model is used. The unsigned long version of `coreleft()` is used in the large-memory models (huge, large, and compact). The unsigned version is applied in the small-memory models (tiny, small, and medium). With the large models, you can also use `farcoreleft()`.

This function returns the amount of memory available for DOS to allocate for functions such as `malloc()` and `allocmem()`. The amount of memory reported depends on what is measured. In small-memory models, `coreleft()` measures space left in the near heap. In large-memory models, the function returns the total amount of memory available, which comes from the far heap. Actually, for compilations with a large model, `coreleft()` and `farcoreleft()` return the same results.

The `coreleft()` function returns the available memory for operations such as manipulating records in a database, building data structures like linked lists, and setting aside buffers. The sample program shown in listing 4.4 uses the routine. This example highlights the following features related to Turbo C:

❏ conditional compilation

❏ declaration of variables within blocks

❏ use of `printf()` to display `longs`

Listing 4.4

```
#include <stdio.h>
#include <alloc.h>
#include <conio.h>

/***** function prototypes *****/
void main(void);
void printMemoryModel(void);

void main(void)
  {
  unsigned long memoryLeft;

#if defined(__TINY__) || defined(__SMALL__)||defined(__MEDIUM__)
  unsigned int coreMemory;

  printMemoryModel();
```

```
   #if !defined __TINY__
     printf("Both near and far heaps are available.\n");
   #else
     printf("Near heap available.\n");
     printf("(Far heap not initially owned by the program.\n");
   #endif

   memoryLeft = farcoreleft();
   coreMemory = coreleft();

   printf("   %blu bytes far  heap available\n", memoryLeft);
   printf("   %bu bytes near heap available\n", coreMemory);

 #else
   unsigned long coreMemory;

   printMemoryModel();
   memoryLeft = coreleft();
   coreMemory = farcoreleft();

   printf("Far heap only available, no near heap.\n");
   printf("   %blu bytes far  heap available\n", memoryLeft);
   printf("   %blu bytes total heap available\n", coreMemory);
 #endif
   }

void printMemoryModel(void)
   {
   printf("\n\n");
#if defined __TINY__
   printf("Tiny");
#elif defined __SMALL__
   printf("Small");
#elif defined __MEDIUM__
   printf("Medium");
#elif defined __COMPACT__
   printf("Compact");
#elif defined __LARGE__
   printf("Large");
#elif defined __HUGE__
   printf("Huge");
#endif
   printf(" Memory Model\n");
   printf("---------------------------------\n");
   }
```

Depending on the memory model used for compilation, the program defines unsigned int or unsigned long variables with which it will work. The calls to the two versions of the coreleft() routine are basically the same. A cast is applied in the small-memory models, however, to avoid compiler problems. The printf() calls use %lu in the case of the longs, where the l is inserted just

to print `longs` correctly. You should get different values in the small models, because the function examines the space left on the near heap and the far heap. In the
large models, both values should be the same because only the far heap is
measured.

The *country()* Function

Function Prototype

```
struct country *country(int xcode, struct country *cp);
```

Header File

```
#include <dos.h>
```

Parameter List

`int xcode`	Code for the country
`struct country *cp`	Pointer to structure containing country information

This function to get country information has been included in Turbo C releases
since DOS V2.0, but only with DOS V3.0 and later versions could you set the information also. By using `country()` you can make your programs more suitable for
international use. Features such as decimals, date and time display, and currency
symbols can be modified.

The information for the current country is stored in a structure that contains
fields for various time, date, and currency formats that vary from country to country. Note that the *Turbo C Reference Manual* refers incorrectly to the type of three
fields. The `co_currstyle`, `co_digits`, and `co_time` fields are actually integer
(`int`) fields instead of `char` fields as shown in the *Turbo C Reference Manual*.
Table 4.3 shows country structures and their possible values.

Table 4.3. Country Structures

Structure	Value
`co_date`	Three types of dates
	0 = USA
	1 = European
	2 = Japanese
`co_curr`	Currency symbol
`co_thsep`	Thousands separator for numbers
`co_desep`	Decimal separator for numbers

Structure	Value
co_dtsep	Date separator
co_tmsep	Time separator
co_currstyle	Location of currency symbol relative to the amount
	0 = before amount with no gap
	1 = after amount with no gap
	2 = before amount with gap
	3 = after amount with gap
co_digits	Number of significant currency digits
co_time	Time format
	0 = 12-hour clock
	1 = 24-hour clock
co_case	Address of the case map routine, which can be used for specifying sorting sequences.
co_dasep	Data separator
co_fill	Reserved

These settings are especially useful when you customize data-display and data-entry routines for various countries. For example, West German values are listed in table 4.4.

Table 4.4. *West German Country Structure Values*

Structure	Value
co_date	1
co_curr	DM
co_thsep	.
co_desep	,
co_dtsep	.
co_tmsep	.
co_currstyle	0
co_digits	2
co_time	1
co_case	02BC:1696
co_dasep	;
co_fill	Reserved (empty)

You can select a country by using the international telephone prefix as the value for xcode in the function call. Listing 4.5 shows a small sample of code that uses the function call.

Listing 4.5

```
#include <stdio.h>
#include <dos.h>

typedef struct country COUNTRYSTRUCT;
COUNTRYSTRUCT countryData, *ctryDataPtr;

void main(void)
    {
    ctryDataPtr = &countryData;
    #define CD(val)  (ctryDataPtr->val

    country(49, ctryDataPtr);
       /* use international phone code for West Germany */
    printf("\nWest Germany processed\n\n");
    printf("Date format:           %d\n",  CD(co_date));
    printf("Currency symbol:       %s\n",  CD(co_curr));
    printf("Thous. sep:            %s\n",  CD(co_thsep));
    printf("Decimal sep:           %s\n",  CD(co_desep));
    printf("Date sep:              %s\n",  CD(co_dtsep));
    printf("Time sep:              %s\n",  CD(co_tmsep));
    printf("Currency style:        %d\n",  CD(co_currstyle));
    printf("Signif. digits ($):    %d\n",  CD(co_digits));
    printf("0-12 hr, 1-24 hr time: %d\n",  CD(co_time));
    printf("Case map:              %Fp\n", CD(co_case));
    printf("Data sep:              %s\n",  CD(co_dasep));
    printf("Reserved:              %s\n",  CD(co_fill));
    }
```

As an excercise, change the program to allow user input of any country code.

This example simply calls country(), using the international telephone code for West Germany, and then reports the values in the appropriate country structure after that call. More than likely, existing values would have been different. Because a global structure was used, the structure would show blanks or values of zero before a call to country(), since external variables are initialized to 0 in C. If the structure were auto (defined inside of main()), it would contain garbage values unless explicitly initialized. After a call to country(), the global structure would contain the values from the previous call to the country() function. Remember that auto variables in C retain values between function calls only if declared as static. Notice that you can refer to structure members using #define to make the syntax seem much shorter. Because the identifier is "parameterized," a portion can vary from one occurrence to another. Because C's preprocessor uses substitution in these cases, val is appended to the end of the pointer ctryDataPtr-> as though it had been written that way originally. Using this sort of technique correctly leads to appropriate information hiding—or may hide too much!

The *detectgraph()* Function

Function Prototype

```
void far detectgraph(int far *graphdriver, int far *graphmode);
```

Header File

```
#include <graphics.h>
```

Parameter List

`int far *graphdriver`	Far pointer to the integer value for the graphics driver
`int far *graphmode`	Far pointer to the integer value for the hardware graphics mode

With the `detectgraph()` function, your program can check for existing graphics hardware and use the maximum resolution and colors possible in the system. The function selects the correct graphics driver for the hardware, and the graphics mode with the highest resolution. If the hardware does not support graphics, a negative value (namely, −2) is returned by `detectgraph()`.

By specifying a graphics mode via `graphmode`, you can override previous information returned by a call to another graphics system function, `initgraph()`. The `initgraph()` function is similar to `detectgraph()`, and it actually calls `detectgraph()`. Another option is to set `graphdriver`'s value to the constant, `DETECT` (defined in `graphics.h`), which provides automatic graphics hardware detection. Using `DETECT` also causes `graphmode` to choose the highest possible resolution (maximum X and Y coordinates) and the maximum number of colors available on the hardware detected.

The function `initgraph()` goes beyond what `detectgraph()` does—it loads the graphics driver into memory by first allocating memory (using the `_graphgetmem()` function) and then reading from disk the .BGI file that matches the hardware configuration. Instead of loading the .BGI driver from a separate file, you can make the .BGI file or files into one or more .OBJ files that can then be linked into your program. The advantage of this conversion method is that, because the .BGI files are part of the program, the user does not have to have them somewhere on the system.

Always check the values returned by `detectgraph` and the other graphics functions to ensure that the operation was performed correctly. If you miss an error in values here, you could end up attempting to perform graphics on a system that supports nothing but text windows.

Listing 4.6 contains a brief example of `detectgraph()`. The code determines the current configuration of the graphics board. If the system includes a certain combination of driver and mode, the routine selects a different mode and sets the hardware to that value.

Listing 4.6

```
#include <stdlib.h>        /* need for exit() */
#include <stdio.h>
#include <graphics.h>      /* must use for proper graphics */

/***** function prototypes *****/
void main(void);
void checkGrError(void);

/***** main program *****/
void main(void)
{
  int gDriver = DETECT;   /* set to autodetect */
  int gMode;              /* graphics mode */

  printf("This example requires use of an EGA as written\n");
  printf("Change variables to use your equipment.\n");

  /* find what kind of graphics hardware is present */
  detectgraph(&gDriver, &gMode);
  checkGrError();

  if (gDriver == EGA)
  {
    if (gMode != EGAHI)
      printf("Not operating properly, check program or board.\n");

    /*  now we'll set the mode to low resolution */
    gMode = EGALO;

    /* reset to higher resolution */
    /* this line intentionally has an error in the path so */
    /* the program finds a graphics error condition */
    /* put in your own path and see the results */
    initgraph(&gDriver, &gMode, "C:/TC2/BI/");
    checkGrError();

    printf("Now in EGALO mode\n\nPress Enter to exit...'');
    getchar();
    closegraph();

  }  /* end of if */
}  /* end of main */

/* this function prints out error numbers and messages and */
/* should be called after every graphics function */
void checkGrError(void)
  {
  int gErrorCode;

    /* check error code against OK macro from graphics.h */
    if ((gErrorCode = graphresult()) == grOk)
      printf("Graphics system OK to proceed.\n");
```

```
    else
    {
      printf("Graphics Error %3d:  %s\n", gErrorCode,
             grapherrormsg(gErrorCode));
      exit(1);
    }  /* end of if */
  } /* end of checkError */
```

The graphics example also has a simple error-handling routine that can be called after every graphics routine. The handler checks the value of `graphresult()` and prints a message with the corresponding error number and appropriate text so that there is no need to look up the meaning of a particular error code.

Previous examples called `detectgraph()` using the value of `DETECT` to force automatic detection of the graphics hardware. This function checks also to see whether an EGA system is present. If the mode was previously low resolution, `detectgraph()` sets it to high resolution.

The *getc()*, *getch()*, *getchar()*, and *getche()* Functions

Function Prototypes and Header Files

```
int getc(FILE *stream);          #include <stdio.h>

int getch(void);                 #include <conio.h>

int getchar(void);               #include <stdio.h>

int getche(void);                #include <conio.h>
```

Parameter List

FILE *stream   A pointer to a file or device from which a character will be read

These four functions obtain characters from the keyboard for further processing. Each is slightly different. Knowing how to use each of them effectively is important.

Output for the keyboard is either buffered or unbuffered. The `getc()` and `getchar()` functions provide buffered I/O, meaning that the user presses Enter to signal the end of the input. The `getche()` and `getch()` functions, on the other hand, provide unbuffered I/O and do not require the carriage return—entering a single character will cause input to halt and program execution to continue. The `getc()` function obtains a character from the stream you specify, including the predefined `stdin` stream. Once a character is read from the file, the file pointer moves to the next position to enable a further read. `EOF` indicates that the end of the file has been reached or an error has occurred.

The `getch()` function is unbuffered and does not echo the character just read to the screen. When your application calls for a single keystroke to be entered and then used immediately, usc this routine.

Because the `getchar()` function provides buffered input, use a carriage return to terminate input. This function is actually a macro, defined in terms of the stream function `getc()` for the specific stream `stdin`. It gets its values only from the keyboard, the `stdin` device.

Because the `getche()` function echoes the character typed to the screen, it is unsuitable for creating passwords. The function gets characters from the keyboard device.

> Turbo C 2.0 does not always correctly flag an error involving a function call. For example, calling function `kbhit()` using `if(kbhit)` without parentheses after `kbhit` does not result in an error. Using a macro as a function, such as `getc()`, without parentheses will result in an error message, however.

Try these routines to see clearly how they differ, especially during input and when the `getc()` function encounters the end-of-file character. Listing 4.7 shows an example of these functions in typical situations. Try running it to see your results.

Listing 4.7

```
#include <dos.h>
#include <conio.h>
#include <stdio.h>

/***** function prototypes *****/
int flushKbdBuffer(void);
void main(void);

void main(void)
{
  int result;

  clrscr();
  result = flushKbdBuffer();
  printf("Enter a character for getc(stdin):    ");
  printf("Character entered has a value of %4d\n", getc(stdin));

  printf("Enter a character for getchar():     ");
  printf("Character entered has a value of %4d\n", getchar());
```

```
    printf("Enter a character for getch():        ");
    printf("Character entered has a value of %4d\n", getch());

    printf("Enter a character for getche():       ");
    printf("Character entered has a value of %4d\n", getche());
    result = flushKbdBuffer();
    printf("Keyboard buffer:  %d\n", result);
}
/*  getc    echoes         char and            requires a CR */
/*  getch   does not echo char and does not require  a CR */
/*  getche  echoes         char and does not require  a CR */
/*  getchar echoes         char and            requires a CR */
/* function to clear to keyboard buffer -- nonportable */
int flushKbdBuffer(void)
    {
    union REGS inRegs, outRegs;  /* REGS defined in dos.h */

    /* load with 0C to flush buffer */
    inRegs.h.ah = 0x0C;
    intdos(&inRegs, &outRegs);
    return(outRegs.h.al);
    }
```

For a quick comparison of the getc... functions and macros, see table 4.5.

Table 4.5. getc... *Comparison*

Name	Function or Macro	Carriage Return Required	Echo	Buffered
getc()	M	yes	yes	yes
getch()	F	no	no	no
getche()	F	no	yes	no
getchar()	M	yes	yes	yes

It is best to use these getc...() routines one at a time to observe their true behavior. To use these routines, a prompt is displayed and a character is requested. Depending on the routine you use, pressing Enter may seem to create strange behavior. For example, your program may display the next request and continue suddenly without waiting for a character to be entered. A quirk like this occurs if a character is already waiting in the keyboard buffer from the previous call; the functions using buffered entry will look in this buffer instead of allowing the user to continue with the program.

A small routine is provided that uses a DOS interrupt to do nothing more than flush the keyboard buffer.

The *harderr()* Function

Function Prototype

```
void harderr(int (*handler)());
```

Header File

```
#include <dos.h>
```

Parameter List

```
int (*handler)()
```

The function `harderr()` uses the much-touted DOS "critical-error handler," which is accessed through Int 24h. This interrupt is usually associated with some form of hardware mishap, such as when the drive door remains open during a diskette read or when the printer is not operating properly, which can lead to the infamous DOS message `Abort, Retry, Ignore`. When these types of errors occur, the application usually "crashes," either terminating or exiting to DOS, leaving the user not knowing exactly what happened. When the program executes the `harderr()` function, the `handler()` function is called, which usually notifies the user of the error and may activate some other condition such as a subprogram.

This handler contains the information necessary to obtain device information for rectifying the error condition. The actual prototype for the error-handling routine is

```
int handler(int errval, int ax, int bp, int si);
```

The first argument of `handler()` is to an error number, `int errval`, which holds a value representing the error. This error number explains the general type of error. By checking bit 15 of the `ax` argument—the second parameter of `handler()`—the program can detect other error information about the disk. When such an error occurs, you may use either of two routines to process the error condition correctly. The `hardresume()` and `hardreturn()` functions either return to DOS after the error or return to the program at the point at which the error occurred. The third and fourth arguments (`int bp` and `int si`) check the base pointer (BP) and source index (SI) register, respectively. These two parameters act as a pointer to header information for the device accessed. In this way `int bp` and `int si` obtain error information that the function relays to the rest of the program.

A variety of messages can be returned from the error-handling routine. As you can see from the nested `if` statements, some messages appear only if certain bit patterns appear. Do not be surprised if you see at least two identical sets of output. DOS will try at least twice to rectify a critical situation such as writing to a write-protected disk or trying to print on a printer that is out of paper. Also, the error handler has been created with a "tell everything" attitude about the errors; you may want to omit some of the error messages.

Notice that the checkBit() and odd() routines, which are very handy for low-level work, have been reused here.

As with other interrupt handlers, this function is "installed," or called, before it performs any action that might trigger the critical-error interrupt. If an error does occur, the new handler you have provided takes over. When the new handler completes all actions affecting the interrupt, the old interrupt handler is reinstalled automatically when the program terminates.

The primary advantages of these routines are not merely that they provide an interface to the critical-error handler, but also that the interface can be built and implemented entirely in C without reliance on assembly language. A portion of the code in listing 4.8 shows how the harderr()function could be used.

Listing 4.8

```c
#include <dos.h>
#include <string.h>
#include <stdio.h>

#define PROBLEM   -1    /* if there's a problem */
#define SUCCESS    0    /* here's the go-ahead */
#define TRUE       1
#define FALSE      0

/***** function prototypes *****/
int criticalErrorHandler(int errorValue, int ax, int bp, int si);
int checkBit(int *target, int bitNo);
int odd(int value);
void main(void);

/***** main program *****/
void main(void)
{
  FILE *workFile;
  char workFileName[80];

  /* install the error handler */
  /* before performing any disk I/O */
  /* easy to install, isn't it? */
  harderr(criticalErrorHandler);

  /* ask for any drive and file name for testing */
  printf("Enter drive:file to write:  ");
  gets(workFileName);

  /*  leave drive A: door open before trying to read the file */
  workFile = fopen(workFileName, "w+");
  if (workFile == NULL)
    printf("This test file is not working.\n");
  else
    fclose(workFile);
```

Listing 4.8 continues

Listing 4.8 *continued*

```
}

int criticalErrorHandler(int errorValue, int ax, int bp, int si)
   unsigned far *deviceInfo;
   int nonDiskError;

   /* create a far pointer to the device header info */
   deviceInfo = MK_FP((unsigned)bp, (unsigned)si);
   nonDiskError = *(deviceInfo + 4);

   /* code to handle errors - check low byte of error value */
   switch (errorValue & 0xff)
   {
      case 0  :  printf("Disk is write protected.\n");
                 break;
      case 1  :  printf("Error unknown\n");
                 break;
      case 2  :  printf("Disk drive not ready\n");
                 if (checkBit(&ax, 15) == 0)
                 {
                    /* check which of the 3 choices are allowed */
                    if (checkBit(&ax, 13) != 0)
                      printf("Ignore, ");
                    if (checkBit(&ax, 12) != 0)
                      printf("Retry, ");
                    if (checkBit(&ax, 11) != 0)
                      printf("Abort");
                    printf(" possible\n");
                    switch(checkBit(&ax, 10) || checkBit(&ax, 9))
                    {
                       case 00 : printf("MSDOS error has occurred\n");
                                 break;
                       case 01 : printf("FAT error has occurred\n");
                                 break;
                       case 10 : printf("Directory problem\n");
                                 break;
                       case 11 : printf("Problem with data\n");
                                 break;
                       default : printf("Unknown drive error\n");
                                 break;
                    } /* end of switch */
                    if (checkBit(&ax, 8) == 0)
                      printf("Disk read error\n");
                    else
                      printf("Disk write error\n");
                 }
                 else  /* error not disk I/O related */
                 {
                    if (checkBit(&nonDiskError, 15) == 0)
                      printf("Bad FAT image in memory\n");
                    else
                      printf("Error in a character device\n");
```

```
                     }
                     break;
      case 3   :  printf("Command not recognized\n");
                     break;
      case 4   :  printf("Bad CRC check on data\n");
                     break;
      case 5   :  printf("Problem requesting drive info\n");
                     break;
      case 6   :  printf("Error finding records in file\n");
                     break;
      case 7   :  printf("Disk media unknown\n");
                     break;
      case 8   :  printf("Unable to find sector on disk\n");
                     break;
      case 9   :  printf("Check paper in printer\n");
                     break;
      case 'A' :  printf("Error in writing to disk\n");
                     break;
      case 'B' :  printf("Error in reading from disk\n");
                     break;
      case 'C' :  printf("General failure of nonspecific type\n");
                     break;
                     /* default essential to catch anything else */
      default  :  printf("Error condition unexpected!!\n");
                     break;
   }

   /*  return to the program after detecting error */
   hardretn(PROBLEM);
   return(PROBLEM);
}

int checkBit(int *target, int bitNo)
   {
   int tempInt;

   tempInt = *target;
   tempInt >>= bitNo;          /* shift right bitNo times */
   /* if the value is odd, then return true */
   return(odd(tempInt) ? TRUE : FALSE);
   }

int odd(int value)
   {
   return(value % 2);   /* use modulus to check for remainder */
   }
```

Here, the program installs the error handler before taking any action, such as reading a disk file. In this way, any problems are caught. If the drive door is left ajar while the program tries to read the file, you normally get the Abort, Retry, Ignore message; if the door is left open, you eventually have to use Abort to exit.

This terminates the program prematurely, leaving you at the DOS prompt. The error handler helps your code recover gracefully from the error and return to the program, where the code can suggest an appropriate action.

The *qsort()* Function

Function Prototype

```
void qsort(void *base, size_t nmemb, size_t size, int
(*compar)(const void *, const void *));
```

Header File

```
#include <stdlib.h>
```

Parameter List

void *base	The address of the array to be sorted
size_t nmemb	The number of members in the array
size_t size	The size of an individual member

int (*compar)(const void *, const void *)
A pointer to a function; the pointer returns an integer and takes two arguments, both of which are constant void pointers.

The qsort() function is the only sorting algorithm represented in the standard C library, which says something about its power and flexibility. This is one of the fastest, most efficient overall sorting methods around, and this generic implementation fits a wide variety of uses. The qsort() function is best implemented on arrays that hold more than 10 members; it works better with more members. It is also more efficient if the original array is in unsorted, almost random order, rather than close to being sorted.

This function requires the use of void pointers, as do bsearch(), lsearch(), and other functions. With void pointers, any type of pointer data may be passed to the routine, making it more truly generic. Although they may be added for clarity and documentation, casts are not required when you use void pointers, because void pointers are compatible with all other pointer types. Using casts might be a good idea if the application will be ported, especially to a compiler that does not support void pointers. As in the searching routines, you write the compar() function to be compatible with the types of information used in the application, or use a standard library function if it applies. The output of the compar() function helps determine the sort order (ascending or descending) for qsort(). The outcome value of the compar() function is one of the following three values:

compar( ) Argument Relationships	compar( ) Result
1st arg ‹ 2nd arg	Negative
1st arg = 2nd arg	Zero
1st arg › 2nd arg	Positive

Switching the negative and positive values in the preceding table changes the sort order from ascending to descending. In order to obtain these return values, you may have to write your own code to differentiate among data, or you simply may need to use another built-in C function, such as strcmp( ).

Listing 4.9 shows an example of a small program using qsort( ) to sort an array alphabetically. Notice that double indirection is used in the string comparison routine as it was in the lsearch/bsearch( ) example. The code can be modified easily for your other sorting needs.

Listing 4.9

```
#include <stdio.h>
#include <string.h>
#include <stdlib.h>

/***** function prototypes *****/
int compareStrings(const char **string1, const char **string2);
void main(void);

static char *stringArr[] =
        {
        "Jacqueline",
        "Steve",
        "Frank",
        "Jack ",
        "Bob  ",
        "Arnold"
        };

void main(void)
   {
   register int count;
   size_t noOfElements;

   noOfElements = sizeof(stringArr) / sizeof(stringArr[0]);
   /* sort the array using qsort */
   qsort(stringArr, noOfElements, sizeof(stringArr[0]),
        compareStrings);

   printf("The sorted list:\n\n");
   for (count = 0; count < noOfElements; ++count)
     printf("%s\n", stringArr[count]);

   }
```

Listing 4.9 continues

Listing 4.9 continued

```
/* function to compare two strings for use in qsort */
int compareStrings(const char **string1, const char **string2)
   {
   return(strcmp(*string1, *string2));
   }
```

This example uses qsort() to sort a very small array of names; here a simple exchange sort would probably be more efficient. A function is created to compare two strings and return the result. This listing assumes ascending alphabetical order. The qsort() function is called by passing it the starting address of the name array, the size of the array, and the size of one member of the array. A pointer (function name only) is passed, which points to the sorting routine and thereby executes it. The program prints the sorted list.

The *rand(), srand(), random(),* and *randomize()* Functions

Function Prototypes

```
int rand(void);

void srand(unsigned seed);

int random(int num);

void randomize(void);
```

Header File

```
#include <stdlib.h>
```

Parameter List

unsigned seed	The beginning value for a series of pseudorandom numbers
int num	The upper range (actually num −1) of random numbers supplied by the function; these numbers lie in the range of 0 to num −1.

These functions generate a pseudorandom number of sequence of numbers. They are not truly random; hence their name. The rand() and srand() functions are ANSI C compatible functions; random() and randomize() mimic two functions from Turbo Pascal. If portability is a concern, remember to be careful playing "mix 'n' match" with your program's functions.

The first step in obtaining a random number is to provide a value to *seed*, or start, the *random-number generator*, which is a special number-generator algorithm. The random-number generator can use a value such as the system time to produce an entire series of numbers. If the same seed is used again, the same series of numbers is generated. Using the system time as a seed value provides a way of generating different series of numbers. Some programmers make the mistake of seeding the random-number generator in each loop that requires a number. This is not always reliable, and it is perhaps better to seed the generator only once before calling `rand()` or `random()`. The reseeding causes the numbers to be less random, just like using the same seed. The same numbers can result; if the loop is tight (short) enough, the same seed value could be used, leading to a repeat of the number sequence. The `randomize()` function, which is actually a macro, makes a call to `time()` to seed the generator. Because a call to the `time()` function is made, you should also include `<time.h>` in your source module.

Two functions obtain and return a random number. The `rand()` function returns a value between 0 and 2^{32}. The `random()` function returns a value between 0 and 1 less than the number given to it as an argument. For example, to pick a number between 1 and 100, you can use `random(101)` and check to see whether the number returned was greater than or equal to 1; if not, `random()` is called again. You can use `random(100)` also to obtain a value between 0 and 99; use `random(100)+1` to obtain values between 1 and 100. The `rand()` function may have a different range from compiler to compiler, or from machine to machine.

Programmers may believe that each number generated is different; that is, if you obtain values between 0 and 10, that you obtain only one 1, one 2, one 3, and so on. This is not so—eventually, numbers will repeat themselves. Only by building a table (array) and checking it can you ensure that a number is not repeated. Using `random(10)` to make sure that each number from 0 to 9 appears at least once, for example, may take more than 10 calls to `random()` because some numbers may repeat in the sequence. By comparing the numbers to array values, you will know how long to run the generator to obtain the full sequence. Listing 4.10 shows how to use a pair of randomizing functions.

Listing 4.10

```
#include <stdio.h>
#include <stdlib.h>
#include <time.h>

void main(void)
    {
    register int count;
    int value;
    time_t genSeed;
```

Listing 4.10 continues

Listing 4.10 *continued*

```
/*  seed the generator  */
genSeed = time(NULL);
srand((unsigned)genSeed);

/*  generate 5 random numbers  */
for(count = 0; count < 5; count++)
    {
    value = rand();
    printf("Random value #%2d = %6d\n", count + 1, value);
    }
}
```

The applications for random numbers are varied and numerous. Randomization can be used in "gambling" and other games, real-world simulations, statistics, probability, mathematics, graphics, and other applications.

The brief example in listing 4.10 seeds the random-number generator once and then obtains and displays five random numbers. If you use the same seed to run the program a second time, you get the same set of "random" numbers. Using a different seed generates different numbers.

The *strtok()* Function

Function Prototype

```
char *strtok(char *string1, const char *string2);
```

Header File

```
#include <string.h>
```

Parameter List

`char *string1`	Argument is string on which process of tokenizing is done.
`const char *string2`	A constant pointer to a string that contains all the characters to delineate the tokens.

This function's name is an abbreviation of its mission: to tokenize strings. In other words, `strtok()` splits a string into substrings, each of which is separated by punctuation or another character.

The process begins by looking for any one of the characters in the string `string2` that acts as a delimiter to separate parts of `string1`. The delimiter list consists of one or more characters. On the first call using `strtok()`, if a delimiter is found, the portion of `string1` to the left of the delimiter is returned by strtok(). A null pointer is returned if none of the delimiters is found. After the first call using strtok(), use NULL as the first parameter to strtok() instead of the string variable. Because even new delimiters may be specified in subsequent calls, you do not have to use the same set time after time.

If you need to retain the value of string1, make a copy of the string before submitting it to strtok() the first time, because the function alters string1 by replacing the characters from a token with NULL characters (\0). This replacement "shortens" the string after finding a token because C uses the null character as the end of a string.

You can include strtok() in many applications. It can parse almost any string, line, or paragraph. Other uses include translating files, building parsers for commands or languages, or separating strings such as dates and file names. Listing 4.11 shows how to use strtok() for finding tokens in a sentence.

Listing 4.11

```
#include <stdlib.h>
#include <stdio.h>
#include <string.h>

/***** function prototypes *****/
void main(void);

void main(void)
  {
  char delimiters[] = "-/ +,.";
  char input[256];                /* holds input string */
  char *part;                     /* points to token */
  register count = 0;

  printf("Please enter the string to parse:  \n");

  /* as long as the string contains something, parse it */
  if (gets(input) != NULL)
    printf("Token #%2d = %s\n", ++count, strtok(input, delimiters));
  else
  {
    printf("A parsing error has occurred.\n");
    exit(1);
  }
  /* keep parsing until the end of input is reached */
  while ((part = strtok(NULL, delimiters)) != NULL)
    printf("Token #%2d = %s\n", ++count, part);
  }
```

This sample code enables the user to enter characters from the keyboard. A string such as This is a test, a good+ test, and !one/that should fail would separate into these tokens after successive calls to strtok():

```
This    is    a      test    a         good
test    and   !one   that    should    fail
```

Note that the exclamation mark remains as part of the token. Even though the exclamation point is punctuation, `strtok()` does not recognize it in this case because it was not specified as a delimiter in the list. Because a space is included in the delimiter list, regular words can be processed easily.

The *va_start()*, *va_end()*, *va_list()*, and *va_arg()* Functions

Function Prototypes

```
void va_start(va_list arg_ptr, prev_param);

void va_end(va_list arg_ptr);

<type> va_arg(va_list arg_ptr, <type>);
```

Header File

```
#include <stdarg.h>
```

Parameter List

`va_list arg_ptr`	A pointer to the argument list kept on the stack
`prev_param`	A pointer to the first known argument

A major advantage of C is that you can create user-defined functions in which the number of arguments varies from one call of a certain function to the next. The manner in which the arguments are accessed on the stack facilitates this feature, which is lacking in languages such as Pascal. You should be aware that C passes parameters from right to left (the opposite of Pascal). This means that functions similar to `printf()`, `scanf()`, and others can be programmed. The only requirement is that you must signal the end of the argument list by using a null, special value, or delimiter.

To write a routine that accepts a variable number of arguments, perform the following steps after making sure to include the header file `stdarg.h`:

1. Supply at least one fixed parameter to the argument list. You cannot have zero arguments—you must use at least one.

2. Declare a varying number of arguments using the ellipsis (...) in the argument list of the function definition and prototype after one or more fixed arguments have been declared, for example, `int func(int go, ...)`.

3. Define a variable to be of type `va_list`, which travels along the argument list.

4. Define a variable or constant value to signal the end of the portion of the argument list that contains a variable number of arguments—such as a large negative integer number (-32767) for `int`s or a null value. The programmer can use any value he or she wants.

5. To start accessing the arguments, call `va_start` to set up stack pointers and other conditions. Use the argument pointer as the first parameter to this function and the name of the first known argument from the function definition, as in the following line:

   ```
   va_start(argPointer, char *guide);
   ```

   where `argPointer` has previously been declared of type `va_list`.

6. Travel along the argument list via some form of loop. Use `va_arg` to access successive arguments in the list:

   ```
   pic = va_arg(argPointer, char *);
   ```

   The second parameter of `va_arg` must match the type of the argument you are trying to obtain. The type can vary from one call of `va_arg()` to a second call.

7. When the end of the list has been reached and all arguments have been processed, use `va_end()` to return the stack to its proper form. An example is

   ```
   va_end(argPointer);
   ```

   `va_end()` sets `argPointer` to `NULL`. Do not set `argPointer` to `NULL` yourself when you finish processing the argument list, or you may miss other altered conditions. Because restoring conditions to the state prior to accessing the argument list may vary from compiler to compiler, setting `argPointer` to `NULL` instead of using `va_end()` could reduce portability or pass over other conditions that might be restored.

If you do not restore the stack as in Step 7, you may cause an improper stack access for the next function called, causing the program to crash.

The `va_arg()` function returns a value of the same type as that used by the second argument `va_arg()`. If the second argument is a string, `va_arg()` returns a string; if the second argument is a long double, `va_arg()` returns a long double. This enables you to "switch" types when you access the arguments, where the type of the argument corresponds to a format option. For example, using a string with `%s %d` creates a character array, or string, as the first argument; an integer is needed as the second argument. Learn to anticipate and properly handle any type of variable needed.

A similar set of functions—vprintf(), vfprintf(), and vsprintf()—also accepts a variable number of arguments, but processes them in the same way as the printf() group of functions. The vprintf(), vfprintf(), and vsprintf() functions enable you to build customized routines for displaying values, printing values to a stream, and so on, for a variable number of arguments.

The example in listing 4.12 shows how to use the va_... functions in a custom function that calculates the difference between two numbers and sums the differences. The function sumDiff() performs the calculations. It finds the first argument, then the second, and calculates the difference. The sumDiff() function then makes the second argument the first for the next calculation, and continues switching argument positions to the end of the list. Notice that va_start() gets the beginning of the argument list, and va_arg() gets each argument. The va_end() function restores order. What will happen if there is only one valid argument to the list? Will the function operate properly?

Listing 4.12

```
#include <stdio.h>
#include <stdarg.h>
#include <string.h>

#define TRUE        1
#define FALSE       0
#define ENDARG     -32767

/***** function prototypes *****/
void sumDiff(int answer, ...);
void main(void);

void main(void)
{
    int result = 0;

    printf("\n\nThis example calculates the sum of\n");
    printf("the difference of successive integers.\n");
    printf("%d is used to designate the end of the list\n", ENDARG);
    printf("Numbers are:  %s\n", "33, 22, 54, 7, 19");
    sumDiff(result, 33, 22, 54, 7, 19, ENDARG);
    printf("Numbers are:  %s\n", "18, 39, 3");
    sumDiff(result, 18, 39, 3, ENDARG);
    printf("Numbers are:  %s\n", "3, 14, 829, 63, 71, 1004, 55, 91");
    sumDiff(result, 3, 14, 829, 63, 71, 1004, 55, 91, ENDARG);
}
void sumDiff(int answer, ...)
{
    va_list arglist;        /* argument list of the function */
    int *nextArg;           /* next argument in the list */
    int *fstNumber;         /* first number for calculation */
    int *sndNumber;         /* second number for calculation */
    int temp;               /* holds temporary value */
```

```
   /* get the start of the argument list */
   va_start(arglist, answer);

   /* continue getting arguments until hit the end marker */
   /* use pointers to advantage */
   for (nextArg = arglist, fstNumber = nextArg, sndNumber = nextArg + 1;
        (*nextArg = va_arg(arglist, int)) > ENDARG;
        fstNumber++, sndNumber++)
   {
     /* subtract the second argument from the first */
     /* stop before we use the value of ENDARG */
     if (*sndNumber > ENDARG)
     {
       temp = *fstNumber - *sndNumber;
       /* print out the equation */
       printf("fstNumber - sndNumber = %6.0d - %6.0d = %6.0d\n",
               *fstNumber, *sndNumber, temp);
       answer += temp;
     } /* end of if (*sndNumber) */
   } /* end of for */

   /* clean up the stack for exiting the function */
   va_end(arglist);

   printf("The answer is:   %6.0d\n\n", answer);
}  /* end of sumDiff */
```

Summary

This chapter covered some standard C library functions that are difficult to use or usually not well-explained. Some, like the critical-error handling routine, provide fundamental routines to prevent program crashes and increase user friendliness. Other routines, like country( ), allow you to easily broaden the scope of your program's usefulness to other nations and cultures. You must become familiar with the contents of the Turbo C standard library in order to work with it effectively.

Also discussed in this chapter were such advanced programming features as bit-checking, double indirection, the ternary operator, interrupts, and variable-argument lists. Using pointers also makes data and function manipulation easier and faster. Get into the habit of using the Turbo C debuggers—they will help you to quickly spot problems you've never seen before.

William M.
Brown

CHAPTER

5

Miscellaneous Programming Features

This chapter explores some other Turbo C features you can use as you write programs. These features, which provide a wealth of information about the current operating environment and increase program performance, are not portable among all compilers or systems; take care when you use them.

Pseudovariables

Three types of registers are available in Turbo C: general-purpose, segment-address, and special-purpose. With Turbo C you can access these registers directly by using pseudovariables. A *pseudovariable* is an identifier you use to access a corresponding register. You can use the pseudovariable just like any other identifier. The only difference is that these variables are already declared for you with a specific type and have several rules you must follow:

1. Pseudovariables reference registers; because registers do not have an address, you cannot use the address-of operator (`&_AX` is invalid).

2. Just about every function in Turbo C and in the CPU uses these variables. Therefore, you have no guarantee that what you store in a pseudovariable will stay there. This is especially true when your program calls other functions.

3. Be very careful when you use some of the segment-address and special-purpose registers. Turbo C uses these registers; changing them causes sudden and unexpected program failures (your code will "go to La-la Land"). In Turbo C the BP register serves as a secondary stack pointer, the CS register points to your code segment, the SP register points to an offset into your stack segment, and SS points to the stack segment. Do not change any of these register values via corresponding pseudovariables. The 16-bit general-purpose registers/pseudovariables hold and manipulate data. In addition to being general-

127

purpose, these registers perform special functions (for example, the _AX variable is the Accumulator). The 8-bit general-purpose registers/pseudovariables access either the upper (high) or lower (low) bytes of their corresponding 16-bit registers. Tables 5.1 and 5.2 identify these registers and their purposes.

Table 5.1. *General-Purpose Registers/Pseudovariables (16-bit)*

Type: unsigned int

Register Name	Pseudo-variable Name	Purpose
AX	_AX	This register, known also as the Accumulator, is used in math operations, I/O operations, and some string operations.
BX	_BX	The BX (Base) register is used frequently in operations that address memory.
CX	_CX	This register serves as a Count register in some LOOP instructions.
DX	_DX	Many Turbo C instructions use the DX (Data) register to store data, multiply and divide data and port numbers in I/O operators.

Table 5.2. *General-Purpose Registers/Pseudovariables (8-bit)*

Type: unsigned int

Register Name	Pseudo-variable Name	Purpose
AH	_AH	This register is masked to the upper byte of the AX register.
AL	_AL	The AL register is masked to the lower byte of AX.
BH	_BH	The BH register is masked to the upper byte of the BX register.
BL	_BL	This register is masked to the lower byte of BX.
CH	_CH	This register is masked to the upper byte of the CX register.

Register Name	Psuedo-Variable Name	Purpose
CL	_CL	The CL register is masked to the lower byte of CX.
DH	_DH	The DH register is masked to the upper byte of the DX register.
DL	_DL	This register is masked to the lower byte of DX.

The 16-bit segment-address registers/pseudovariables hold segment base values. Table 5.3 identifies these registers.

Table 5.3. *Segment Address Registers/Pseudovariables (16-bit)*

Type: unsigned int

Register Name	Pseudo-variable Name	Purpose
CS	_CS	This register contains the segment address of the code currently being executed.
DS	_DS	The DS register contains the segment address of the current data segment.
SS	_SS	The SS register contains the segment address of the current stack segment.
ES	_ES	The ES register contains the segment address of an "extra" segment. Sometimes used to define an auxiliary data segment.

Turbo C uses the 16-bit special-purpose registers/pseudovariables to perform special functions; however, the pseudovariables also can perform general-purpose functions. Table 5.4 identifies these registers.

Table 5.4. *Pointer and Index Registers/Pseudovariables (16-bit)*

Type: unsigned int

Register Name	Pseudo-variable Name	Purpose
SP	_SP	This pseudovariable indexes into the _SS (stack segment) pseudovariable.
BP	_BP	This pseudovariable also indexes into the _SS.
DI SI	_DI _SI	Use the _DI and _SI pseudovariables just like one of the general-purpose registers. Turbo C uses _DI and _SI as register variables.

The sample program in listing 5.1 shows how you can use pseudovariables to check the status of the printer.

Listing 5.1

```
/* Pseudovariable example. */
#include <stdio.h>
#include <dos.h>

/* Macros used to determine printer status. */
#define TIMEOUT  (1 << 0) /* Printer timed-out. */
#define NOTUSED1 (1 << 1) /* Not used. */
#define NOTUSED2 (1 << 2) /* Not used. */
#define IOERROR  (1 << 3) /* I/O error. */
#define SELECTED (1 << 4) /* Printer selected. */
#define NOPAPER  (1 << 5) /* Out of paper. */
#define ACK      (1 << 6) /* Printer acknowledge. */
#define NOTBUSY  (1 << 7) /* Printer not busy. */
#define PRTINT   0x17     /* Printer interrupt #. */
#define PRTFUNC  0x02     /* Get status function. */
#define LPT1     0        /* 0=LPT1, 1=LPT2, 2=LPT3. */

/* Function to display the printer's status. */
void main(void)
{
    unsigned char saveAH;
    /* Generate interrupt to check status of printer. */
    _AH = PRTFUNC;
    _DX = LPT1;
    geninterrupt(PRTINT);

    /* Save the AH; printf will try to use it. */
    saveAH = _AH;
```

```
    /* Check status. */
    printf("Your PRINTER is ");

    if((saveAH & (NOTBUSY | SELECTED)) ==
        (NOTBUSY | SELECTED))
        printf("ready.\n");

    else if((saveAH & (NOPAPER | SELECTED)) == (NOPAPER |
        SELECTED))
        printf("disconnected or powered-off.\n");

    else if(saveAH & NOPAPER)
        printf("out of paper.\n");

    else if(~saveAH & SELECTED)
        printf("off-line.\n");

    else
        printf("sending a status that is not supported.\n");

    exit(0);
}
```

In listing 5.1, pseudovariables are used to communicate with the printer interrupt. This interrupt (0X17) returns the status of the printer. The _AH pseudovariable tells the interrupt which function to call, and the _DX pseudovariable indicates which printer port to check. Notice that after calling the interrupt function, the _AH pseudovariable is saved. It must be saved because the function printf() uses the _AH pseudovariable as does the printer interrupt. If it is not saved, printf will destroy the printer status.

Predefined Global Variables

Some variables are *predefined global variables*. The compiler declares and uses these variables, and allows your programs to examine them. These variables are compiler specific and may not be portable. Some of the common variables are discussed in the following sections.

Variables for Reading Command-line Arguments and DOS Variables

The following variables are used for reading command-line arguments and DOS-environment variables:

_argc   This variable contains the number of command-line arguments. Note that the name of the command itself is included in the count. The same information is passed to the variable argc in the argument list of main ( ).

_argv This is an array of pointers to command-line arguments. The same information is passed to your main program if you include an argv variable in the argument list of main ( ).

environ This is an array of pointers to a copy of the DOS-environment variables. The same information is passed to your main program if you include an env variable argument list of main ( ).

Listing 5.2 shows how to use _argc, _argv, and environ.

Listing 5.2

```
/* _argc, _argv, and environ example */
#include <stdio.h>
#include <stdlib.h>
#include <dos.h>

/* Allow access to global variables declared in dos.h. */
/* Function to access and display arguments. */
void dispArgs(void)
{
int   i; /* Index variable. */
printf("The number of arguments is %d\n", _argc);
printf("The arguments are \n");
for(i = 0; i < _argc; i++)
printf("%d\n", _argv[i]);
}

/* Function to access and display the environment. */
void dispEnv(void)
{
    int   i; /* Index variable. */
    printf("The environment strings are \n");
    for(i = 0; environ[i] != NULL; i++)
    printf("%d\n", environ[i]);
}

/* Main function that calls dispArgs. */
void main(void)
{
    dispArgs();
    dispEnv();
    exit(0);
}
```

This sample program allows a function to read the command-line arguments and DOS-environment variables without having to pass them from the main program to the function.

The input of this program is passed to it on the command line. The command-line arguments were

```
arg1 arg2 "arg3 and arg4"
```

The output of this program displays in the following format:

```
The number of arguments is 4

The arguments are

C:\BOOK\EX6_1.EXE
arg1
arg2
arg3 and arg4

The environment strings are

COMSPEC=C:\COMMAND.COM
PATH=c:\;c:\dos
```

Note that in the line `C:\BOOK\EX6_1.EXE`, the command name is available only in DOS V3.X (and will be a null string in DOS V2.X).

Variables for Time and Time Zones

When your code involves time, use the following variables:

`daylight`   This variable indicates whether daylight saving time is in effect. The variable will be set to a 1 to indicate daylight saving time, to a 0 for standard time.

`timezone`   This variable contains the difference (in seconds) between local time and Greenwich mean time (GMT).

`tzname`   This variable contains two pointers to character strings containing abbreviations for the time zones. The `TZ` environment variable must be properly set and the `tzset` function called, or both of these strings will contain a NULL. You can set this environment variable by executing the following command:
        SET TZ=PST8PDT
where *PST* is Pacific Standard Time, *8* is the 8-hour difference between PST and GMT, and *PDT* is Pacific Daylight Time. (If daylight saving time is not currently in effect, don't specify this.)

`_StartTime`   This variable stores the current BIOS time in ticks for the `clock()` function when your program is invoked.

An example of code using these global variables is presented in listing 5.3.

Listing 5.3

```
/* daylight, timezone, and tzname example. */
#include <stdio.h>
#include <stdlib.h>
#include <time.h>

/* Allow access to global variables declared in time.h
   (e.g.  daylight, timezone). */
extern   char  *tzname[2];

/* Main function that displays current time. */
void main(void)
{
    time_t  ttVal;

    /* Set up the tzname variable. */
    putenv("TZ=EST5EDT");
    tzset();

    /* Display what is in the global variables. */
    printf("The variable  daylight contains %d\n", daylight);
    printf("              timezone contains %ld\n", timezone);
    printf("              tzname[0] contains %s\n", tzname[0]);
    printf("              tzname[1] contains %s\n", tzname[1]);

    /* Show how this information might be used. */
    time(&ttVal); /* Get current time. */
    printf("Time = %24.24s %s\n",
        asctime(localtime(&ttVal)),
        tzname[daylight]);
    exit(0);
}
```

This sample program prints the time zone abbreviation, along with the local time. Notice how the new-line character was removed with the `printf` format `%24.24s`.

The output of this program displays in the following format:

```
The variable  daylight contains 1
              timezone contains 18000
              tzname[0] contains EST
              tzname{1} contains EDT
Time = Tue Jan 17 19:40:02 1989 EDT
```

Variable for Writing Output

The variable that selects whether output should go to random access memory (RAM) or to the Basic Input/Output Services (BIOS) is

directvideo   This variable determines how the output for your monitor
              is written. If the value of directvideo is 1, output is

written directly to the video portion of RAM. Setting `directvideo` to 1 speeds up output; the caveat here is that your graphics adapter must be 100 percent IBM compatible (most are, these days). Note that the default value is 1.

If the value of `directvideo` is 0, output is written using the BIOS. This method works on machines that are 100 percent IBM BIOS-compatible, but is slower than writing directly to the video RAM.

Variables for Detecting Coprocessors and Version Numbers

The following variables are useful when your code runs on different configurations.

`_8087`   This variable indicates whether a math coprocessor chip is installed in your computer. The value is 1, 2, or 3 when the startup code detects either an 8087, 80287, or 80387, respectively. Otherwise, the variable contains a 0, indicating that no math coprocessor is installed.

Note: Even if a math coprocessor is installed by the environment variable 87 and has a value of N0 (done by entering SET 87=N0 at the DOS prompt), `_8087` will have a value of 0 only if Options/Compiler/Code Generation/Floating Point/Emulation (O/C/C/F/Emulation) is set. `_8087` will not be affected by the 87 environment variable if O/C/C/F/8087/ 80287 is set. Furthermore, `_8087` may not be set properly if your program has no floating-point code.

`_version`   This variable contains the DOS version number—the major version number in the low byte and the minor in the high byte.

`_osmajor`   This variable contains the major DOS version number, which can be found also in the low byte of `_version`.

`_osminor`   This variable contains the minor DOS version number.

Listing 5.4 shows how these global variables are used.

Listing 5.4

```
/* directvideo, _8087, _version, _osmajor and _osminor
   example. */
#include <stdio.h>
#include <stdlib.h>
#include <dos.h>
#include <conio.h>

/* Byte macros. */
#define LOBYTE(w)    ((unsigned char)(w))
#define HIBYTE(w)    (((unsigned int)(w) >> 8) & 0xff)

/* Main function that displays current time. */
void main(void)
{

    /* Indicate operating system version. */
    printf("DOS version %d.%d [%d.%d]\n",
        LOBYTE(_version), HIBYTE(_version),
        _osmajor, _osminor);

    /* Indicate what type of math coprocessor is present. */
    switch(_8087)
        {
        case  0:
            printf("   No");
            break;
        case  1:
            printf(" 8087");
            break;
        case  2:
            printf("80287");
            break;
        case  3:
            printf("80387");
            break;
        }
    printf(" math coprocessor detected\n");
    exit(0);
    }
```

This sample program prints the DOS version number two ways. It also determines what type of math coprocessor (if any) you have installed. All output is written using the "f-a-s-t" directvideo mode of 1, which writes directly to video from random access memory (RAM).

The output of this program displays in the following format:

```
DOS version 3.30 [3.30]
   No math coprocessor detected
```

Variables for Errors

The following global variables handle error conditions:

errno   When a system error occurs, this variable contains the error number. You can use this variable to index into the _sys_errlist table and display the proper error message.

_doserrno   This variable contains the actual DOS error code when a DOS system call results in an error. The variables errno and _doserrno may or may not contain the same value.

_sys_errlist   This array consists of pointers to error-message strings. If no error message is available for an error number, a NULL occurs in that position.

sys_nerr   This variable contains the number of error-message strings currently in the variable _sys_errlist.

Listing 5.5 provides an example of code in which these global variables are used.

Listing 5.5

```
/* errno, _doserrno, _sys_errlist and sys_nerr example. */
#include <stdio.h>
#include <stdlib.h>
#include <dos.h>
#include <errno.h>

/* Main function that displays the error variables. */
void main(void)
{
   int i;

   /* Print the error-message list. */
   printf("Total number of error messages is %d\n",
      sys_nerr);
   for(i = 0; i < sys_nerr; i++)
      printf("Error #: %02d  Msg: %s\n",
         i, sys_errlist[i]);

   /* Print the error-message variables. */
   printf("_doserrno is %d and errno is %d\n",
      _doserrno, errno);
   exit(0);
}
```

This sample program prints the error-message strings contained in the variable _sys_errlist. It also prints the contents of the two error number variables, but because the program did not generate any errors, these variables contain 0.

The output of this program displays in the following format:

```
Total number of error messages is 36
Error #: 00  Msg: Error 0
Error #: 01  Msg: Invalid function number
Error #: 02  Msg: No such file or directory
Error #: 03  Msg: Path not found
Error #: 04  Msg: Too many open files
Error #: 05  Msg: Permission denied
Error #: 06  Msg: Bad file number
Error #: 07  Msg: Memory arena trashed
Error #: 08  Msg: Not enough memory
Error #: 09  Msg: Invalid memory block address
Error #: 10  Msg: Invalid environment
Error #: 11  Msg: Invalid format
Error #: 12  Msg: Invalid access code
Error #: 13  Msg: Invalid data
Error #: 14  Msg: (null)
Error #: 15  Msg: No such device
Error #: 16  Msg: Attempted to remove current directory
Error #: 17  Msg: Not same device
Error #: 18  Msg: No more files
Error #: 19  Msg: Invalid argument
Error #: 20  Msg: Arg list too big
Error #: 21  Msg: Exec format error
Error #: 22  Msg: Cross-device link
Error #: 23  Msg: (null)
Error #: 24  Msg: (null)
Error #: 25  Msg: (null)
Error #: 26  Msg: (null)
Error #: 27  Msg: (null)
Error #: 28  Msg: (null)
Error #: 29  Msg: (null)
Error #: 30  Msg: (null)
Error #: 31  Msg: (null)
Error #: 32  Msg: (null)
Error #: 33  Msg: Math argument
Error #: 34  Msg: Result too large
Error #: 35  Msg: File already exists
_doserrno is 0 and errno is 0
```

Variables for System Values

The following variables check the file-translation mode, near heap length, stack size, and the segment address of the program segment prefix (PSP):

_fmode   This variable contains the default file-translation mode. If its value is 0X4000 (in hex, which is the default), the file-translation mode is text. If the value is 0X8000, the mode is binary. You can set this value to the mode of your choice; most file routines enable you to override this value.

Note: You usually deal with these values in symbolic terms—O_TEXT for text mode and O_BINARY for binary mode (defined in FCNTL.H with values 0x4000 and 0x8000).

_heaplen   If you are using the tiny-, small-, or medium-memory models, this variable contains the length of the near heap. (The _heaplen variable doesn't exist in large, compact and huge models, which don't have a near heap.) The default value for this variable is 0, which causes the data-segment size to be calculated according to the following algorithms:

Tiny-memory model

256 bytes PSP
+ code area
+ global data area
+ heap area
+ stack area
_____

64K bytes (everything, including code)

Small- and Medium-memory models

global data area
+ heap area
+ stack area
_____

64K bytes (data segment)

_stklen   This variable holds the size of the stack. The default stack size is 4K; the minimum is 128 words. If you plan to use write-recursive functions or pass large structures using the stack, you may need to increase the stack size.

_psp   This variable contains the segment address of the PSP structure. This structure contains information that MS-DOS passes to any TSRs as well as to any transient programs when they are loaded, regardless of whether the program requires it.

Listing 5.6 is an example of code that uses these global variables.

Listing 5.6

```
/* _fmode, _heaplen, _stklen and _psp example. */
#include <stdio.h>ts
#include <stdlib.h>
#include <dos.h>
#include <fcntl.h>

/* Main function that displays content of variables. */
void main(void)
{
    char far *pspPtr;
```

Listing 5.6 continues

Listing 5.6 continued

```
    /* Display address of PSP. */
    pspPtr = MK_FP(_psp, 0x0000);
    printf("The Program Segment Prefix structure is at %Fp\n", pspPtr);

    /* Determine default file mode. */
    switch(_fmode)
      {
      case O_BINARY:
         printf("Default file mode is BINARY\n");
         break;
      case O_TEXT:
         printf("Default file mode is TEXT\n");
         break;
      }

    /* Report the sizes of the stack and heap. */
    printf("The heap length is %d\n", _heaplen);
    printf("The stack length is %d\n", _stklen);
    exit(0);
}
```

This sample program prints the address of the PSP. Notice that the offset for the PSP is 0. This program also prints the default file-translation mode, heap length (medium-memory model), and the reduced stack length.

The output of this program displays in the following format:

```
The Program Segment Prefix structure is at 114A:0000
Default file mode is TEXT
The heap length is 0
The stack length is 8192
```

Variables for Interrupts

Now let's look at some other (not-so-common) variables. Turbo C saves various interrupt vectors when your program is invoked and restores them when your program terminates. This is done because functions in Turbo C may use these vectors at runtime. Keep this system process in mind if you decide to replace these interrupts. The following interrupts are saved and used:

_Int0Vector   This divide-by-zero interrupt service routine is called automatically at the end of a DIV or IDIV operation that results in an error or overflow. Turbo C installs a default divide-by-zero handler that displays the message Divide error.

_Int4Vector   This interrupt traps arithmetic errors generated by the INTO instruction if the OF flag is set. You can install a handler for this interrupt by setting a signal for SIGFPE.

_Int5Vector   This interrupt traps BOUND instructions. It is available only on processors that support it (80186, 80286, 80386, and NEC V series). Turbo C does not generate this interrupt in the code it generates directly, but user-written INLINE assembly code or assembly language routines linked in *could* contain this interrupt.

_Int6Vector   This interrupt traps invalid opcodes. It is available only on processors that support it (80186, 80286, 80386, NEC V40 and V50).

Interrupts

Interrupts suspend the current action of the computer's central processing unit (CPU) and transfer control to a program called the *interrupt handler*. Most interrupt handlers determine what caused the interrupt, take any necessary action, and then return control to the suspended program. This is not necessarily true with all interrupts. For example, the keyboard interrupt handler typically won't bother to check what caused the interrupt; it already knows that a key was pressed.

The sample programs listed here show how to install a custom interrupt handler that allows several programs to share memory. Why would you want to share memory? One instance would be when you use the spawn() function—you can pass arguments to child processes, but the only thing the child process can pass back to its parent is an exit code. If this custom interrupt handler is installed, the child process can communicate directly to the parent's memory. Commands can be sent to the child process, and the child process can pass commands or results directly back to the parent's memory.

After you define the interrupt handler, you use the setvect function to set your interrupt handler in the interrupt-handler table. It is wise to use _getvect to obtain the previous interrupt handler so that you can restore the old interrupt handler after you exit the program. The custom handler is not dependent on an external hardware event; when you want to invoke your interrupt handler, use the function geninterrupt().

The sample program in listing 5.7 consists of a parent process and a child process. The parent process installs an interrupt handler; after getting a memory address from the interrupt handler, the child process communicates with the parent's memory. The parent and child processes are separate executable (.EXE) files.

Listing 5.7

```
/* Interrupt example, parent process. */
#include <stdio.h>
#include <stdlib.h>
#include <conio.h>
#include <dos.h>
#include <process.h>

/* Macros used. */
#define  INT60     0x60      /* User interrupt. */
#define  BUFSIZE   128
#define  PUT       0x0001
#define  GET       0x0002

/* Store old interrupt address. */
void interrupt (*oldInt)();

/* Global buffer used for communications. */
char buffer[128];

/* This program's memory manager interrupt. Note: In order
   to access the 3 registers (passed as variables on the
   stack), we had to define 9 variables. This is the order
   in which the variables are passed on the stack. The
   compiler will complain that the other 8 variables have
   been defined but never used. Alternatively, the
   pseudovariables _ES, _BX, and _AX could have been used,
   removing the need to pass variables on the stack. */
void interrupt newInt(unsigned bp, unsigned di, unsigned si,
        unsigned ds, unsigned es, unsigned dx,
        unsigned cx, unsigned bx, unsigned ax)
{

    /* Pointer to global array. */
    static char far *localArray;

    /* Turn interrupts back on to avoid crippling other
       device interrupts or accuracy of system clock. */
    enable();

    /* Check AX register for mode. If mode = 1, install a
       pointer to an array into the local pointer. */
    if(ax == PUT)
        {

        /* The local array is set to the client array
           using ES:BX as its address. */
        localArray = MK_FP(es, bx);
        }

    /* If AX register mode = 2, return the address
       of the client array. */
```

```
    else if(ax == GET)
        {
        es = FP_SEG(localArray);
        bx = FP_OFF(localArray);
        }
}

/* Main function that "spawns" child process. */
void main(void)
{

    /* Install the interprocess memory manager. */
    oldInt = getvect(INT60);
    setvect(INT60, newInt);

    /* Install the local array as the global memory pointer. */
    _ES = FP_SEG(buffer);
    _BX = FP_OFF(buffer);
    _AX = PUT;
    geninterrupt(INT60);
    printf("global buffer installed at %Fp\n",
    MK_FP(FP_SEG(buffer), FP_OFF(buffer)));

    /* Invoke another program (must be in the current
       directory and called INTER2.EXE) to communicate with
       user through the pseudoshared memory via user-defined
       interrupt 60H. If spawnl is changed to spawnlp, the
       program INTER2.EXE could be anywhere in the DOS path
       environment variable. */
    strcpy(buffer, "Hello child process, this is your parent!");
    spawnl(P_WAIT, "inter2", "inter2", NULL);

    /* Check to see if any messages from JR. */
    printf("The child says: %s\n", buffer);

    /* Restore the old interrupt vector and exit. */
    setvect(INT60, oldInt);
    exit(0);
}

/* Interrupt example, child process. Resulting executable
   file must be named INTER2.EXE (to match the spawnl
   argument in the parent process) and be in the default
   directory. In this program, the library function
   strcpy() is used to communicate messages. In this
   example, strcpy() is being used to copy into a far
   pointer; you must use a large memory model (LARGE,
   COMPACT, OR HUGE); otherwise, strcpy() will be forced to
   a near pointer and the program will fail. If you do not
   want to use a large memory model, don't use strcpy().
   Instead_copy directly. The following table lists some
   memory models and and indicates whether these programs
   fail: */
```

Listing 5.7 continues

Listing 5.7 continued

```
        PROGRAM            Models used

        Parent Process   S   C   C   C   L
        Child Process    S   S   C   L   L

        Examples work?   N   N   Y   Y   Y

*/
#include <stdio.h>
#include <stdlib.h>
#include <conio.h>
#include <dos.h>

/* Macros used. */
#define  INT60      0x60      /* User interrupt. */
#define  GET        0x0002

/* Main function of the child process. */
void main(void)
{
    char far *parentMemory;

    /* Obtain the global memory pointer from Int 60H. */
    _AX = GET;
    geninterrupt(INT60);

    /* Make a far pointer from ES:BX, so program can access
       the parent process's memory, just as though it were
       the program's own memory. */
    parentMemory = MK_FP(_ES, _BX);
    printf("parent memory is at %Fp\n", parentMemory);
    if(parentMemory == NULL)
        exit(1);
    printf("The parent says: %s\n", parentMemory);

    /* Now communicate a message back to the parent. */
    strcpy(parentMemory, "Gee, thanks Mom.");
    exit(0);
}
```

The output of this program displays in the following format:

```
global buffer installed at 1410:040C
parent memory is at 1410:040C
The parent says: Hello child process, this is your parent!
The child says: Gee, thanks Mom.
```

In this sample program, the custom interrupt handler (called newInt) communicates to other programs by using the AX, ES, and BX registers. Once this interrupt handler is installed, any program can invoke it by generating Int 0x60 (interrupts 0x60–0x67 are reserved specifically for user-written interrupts). The parent process installs the interrupt handler, and then invokes it by loading an address in the interrupt handler's local address pointer. Now, if anyone invokes this handler and requests the address of the pointer, the segment is returned in the ES register and the offset in the BX register.

The main problem with programming interrupt handlers is trying to debug them. Interrupts can occur asynchronously because they are caused by external events. Bugs in interrupt handlers can cause your system to behave strangely. If possible, write your interrupt function just as you would any other program; then test it before you install it as an interrupt handler.

Floating-point Libraries

Using the floating-point library functions is simple: Use them as you would any other function. Whether these functions are emulated by software or executed on the 8087/80287/80387 math coprocessor does not matter to the programmer. If the functions are executed on the math coprocessor, however, expect to see anywhere from 10 to 100 times the performance of their software-emulated counterparts.

Some functions in this library enable you to access the math coprocessor directly. To make effective use of these functions, you need to be very familiar with the architecture of the math coprocessor; if you aren't, don't modify any of the following functions:

`_control87` This function accesses advanced features of the math coprocessor. You can modify the precision control, rounding control, infinity control, and exception masks.

`_clear87` This function clears the math coprocessor's status word. The status word reflects the overall status of the math coprocessor.

`_status87` This function returns the contents of the math coprocessor's status word. You use the status word to determine the state of the math coprocessor.

Suppose that you want to calculate several polar-coordinate curves and then display them on the graphics monitor. The program in listing 5.8 does just that.

Listing 5.8

```
/* Floating-point libraries example. */
#include <stdio.h>
#include <stdlib.h>
#include <math.h>
#include <dos.h>
```

Listing 5.8 *continues*

Listing 5.8 continued

```c
#include <float.h>
#include <graphics.h>
#include <conio.h>          /* For goto xy() call I added*/

/* Macros used. */
#define  OFFSET     6.3
#define  INCREMENT  0.001
#define  SIZEVAL    20.0

/* Function to determine whether math coprocessor is
   installed. */
void MathProcIs(void)
{

   /* Print type of coprocessor installed. */
   printf("Math coprocessor installed is: ");
   switch(_8087)
      {

      case 0:
         printf("None");
         break;

      case 1:
         printf("8087");
         break;

      case 2:
         printf("80287");
         break;

      case 3:
         printf("80387");
         break;
      }
}

/* Main function that displays a pretty flower. */
void main(void)
{      int      GraphDriver;
   int      GraphMode;
   double   i;
   double   Radius;
   double   PosX;
   double   PosY;
   double   FromX;
   double   FromY;

   /* Perform Auto detection of graphics driver. */
   GraphDriver = DETECT;
```

```
/* Note: the "" argument in the function initgraph() is
   used to inform the function that the *.BGI files are
   in the current directory. Alternatively, you could
   specify a path (e.g. "C:\\TURBOC\\BGI") */
initgraph(&GraphDriver, &GraphMode, "");

/* Display current math coprocessor. */
MathProcIs();

/* Generate a series of polar coordinate curves using
   the COS and SIN floating-point library functions. */
for(i = 0.0; i < OFFSET; i += INCREMENT)
    {

    /* Calculate line position. */
    Radius = 4 * cos(2 * i);
    PosX   = (OFFSET + (Radius * cos(i))) * SIZEVAL;
    PosY   = (OFFSET + (Radius * sin(i))) * SIZEVAL;

    /* Draw line. */
    if(i != 0.0)
        line(PosX, PosY, FromX, FromY);

    /* Save old position. */
    FromX = PosX;
    FromY = PosY;
    }

/* Wait for user to hit a key before closing the graphics
   device. */
gotoxy(1,25);
printf ("Press Any Key to exit...");
getch();
cleardevice();
closegraph();
exit(0);
}
```

Listing 5.8 uses the global variable _8087 to tell the user which math coprocessor has been detected by the start-up code. If None is printed, *all* floating-point math is emulated in software (if the program is compiled with Emulation mode turned on). This program uses the floating-point library functions cos and sin to calculate polar-coordinate curves, and then uses the graphics library functions initgraph, line, cleardevice, and closegraph to display the curves.

The output of this program displays in the following format:

`Math co-processor installed is: None`

Whenever your program uses floating-point library functions, you must compile with either emulation or 8087/80287 mode. Specifying None will cause link errors. If you compile your program with emulation mode turned on, the start-up code checks for a math coprocessor and, if one exists, uses it. If no math coprocessor is found, floating-point emulation software is installed. If you specify 8087/80287 mode and no math coprocessor is found, the system will crash.

Summary

In this chapter you learned how to do the following:

- ❏ Use pseudovariables and interrupts to check the printer status
- ❏ Read the command-line arguments and environment by examining global variables
- ❏ Change the time zone and display the time
- ❏ Get the DOS version number
- ❏ Change the stack size
- ❏ Display the error-message table
- ❏ Communicate to other processes, using pseudoshared memory

These sample programs give you a taste of Turbo C's other programming features. These features provide a rich and powerful extension to an already extensive run-time library. With so many functions and global variables available, you can do the same task several ways—choose the way that works best for you.

Michael
Yester

CHAPTER

6

Working with
Turbo Assembler

Although every computer language has its own set of fanatically devoted follow-
ers, no single language is perfect. Every language arose to solve a particular
programming challenge; consequently, each language has its own unique strengths
and weaknesses.

For example, if you compare a program written in C with a functionally identical
program written in assembly language, you probably will find that whereas the C
version was developed more quickly and is easier to maintain, the assembly language version executes faster and has a smaller .EXE file.

Fortunately, a single executable program can be created from source statements
written in several different programming languages. This process—called *mixed-
language programming*—enables you to combine the best features of each
product.

This chapter presents two ways of combining assembly language routines with
Turbo C. The first method, called *inline assembly*, uses Turbo C's asm instruction
to insert assembly language statements directly into a C program. The second (and
more traditional) method involves linking separate object modules produced by
the Turbo Assembler with those produced by the Turbo C compiler.

Using Inline Assembly Statements

Writing a program in assembly language is as close as you can get (and, probably,
as close as you will ever *want* to get) to writing a program with the ones and zeros
of machine code. Consequently, an assembly language program can fully exploit the
power of your PC; if it can be done on your computer, it can be programmed in
assembly language.

149

Not surprisingly, then, one of the reasons given for the popularity of C is its proximity to assembly language. Although C functions offer the convenience and structure of a high-level language, some C keywords and operators (for example: ++, --, >>, &, etc.) correspond closely to individual assembly statements. In other words, C offers an optimal balance between the convenience of a high-level language and the power of assembly language.

Nevertheless, not even Turbo C can consistently produce code that is as compact or as fast as a well-written assembly language routine. Most of the time, a C program is larger and slower than its assembly language counterpart. Even small discrepancies, however, become significant if the function is called frequently.

Turbo C's inline assembly feature solves this problem. With very few exceptions, any assembly language statement—or set of statements—can be inserted *inline* into any Turbo C program, enabling you to optimize your program to any extent your application requires.

Compiling a Program Containing Inline Assembly Statements

Turbo C programs containing inline assembly statements can be compiled only with the tcc.exe command-line compiler. You can, of course, still use the tc.exe integrated compiler to enter and edit your program. However, the integrated compiler generates error messages when it encounters asm statements.

By default, Turbo C generates an .OBJ object module. When Turbo C compiles a program containing inline assembly statements, however, it first generates assembly language source text for the entire module, uses it as input to the TASM.EXE Turbo Assembler, and then links the object modules to produce an executable program. This process is shown schematically in figure 6.1.

An .ASM assembly language source file will be created under one of the following conditions:

❏ When the tcc.exe command-line compiler is invoked with the –B (compile via assembly) option, as follows:

```
TCC -B PROGNAME
```

the complete assembly and linkage process is selected.

❏ When the tcc.exe command-line compiler is invoked without the B option, as follows:

```
TCC PROGNAME
```

an .OBJ file is produced until the first asm statement is detected. At that point, the compiler erases the partially created object file, issues a warning, then automatically restarts the compilation with the B option enabled.

Fig. 6.1. Compilation of a Turbo C program.

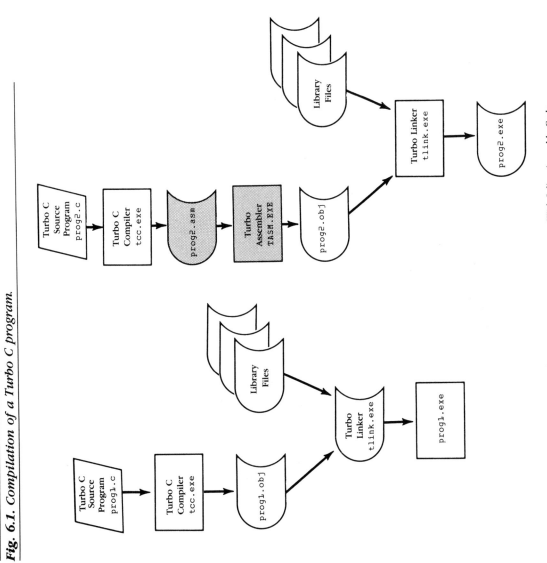

❑ The `#pragma` statement

```
#pragma inline
```

informs the compiler that `asm` statements appear in the module. When the `#pragma` statement is detected at the beginning of the source text, compilation proceeds just as if the B option were selected.

Technically, all three methods produce the same results. However, the use of the `#pragma` statement provides the best program documentation and, consequently, is the preferred method to use.

The Structure of an Inline Assembly Statement

To convert an assembly language statement to inline format, simply preface the statement with the keyword `asm`. Few other changes are required. The complete syntax of the inline assembly statement is as follows:

```
asm   [<label>]   <opcode/directive>   <operands>   <; or newline>
```

where

❑ The `asm` keyword begins every inline assembly statement.

❑ `[<label>]` is an optional data label.

❑ `<opcode/directive>` is either an assembly language opcode or directive.

❑ `<operands>` is the list of operands (if any) for the opcode or directive.

❑ `<; or newline>` is the end of the statement—either a semicolon or a newline.

When the Turbo C compiler encounters an inline assembly statement, it removes the `asm` keyword and passes the statement to the assembly language text file. The syntax of the statement itself is left unchecked.

For example, BIOS interrupt 12h returns, in the AX register, the number of contiguous 1K memory blocks in your PC's motherboard. In assembly language, the call is invoked with the statement

```
int    12h
```

In Turbo C, the same call is invoked with

```
asm    int    12h;
```

or

```
asm    int    12h
```

Immediately after this statement has been executed, the amount of memory can be accessed through the Turbo C pseudovariable `_AX`. The `memsize.c` program in listing 6.1 uses this `asm` statement to create a simple utility that displays the size of your machine's memory.

Listing 6.1

```
/* MEMSIZE--display memory available on motherboard */

#pragma inline

main()
{
    asm    int    12h;
    printf( "This PC has %3dK bytes of internal memory", _AX );
}
```

Because the #pragma statement is used, the program must be compiled with the command

TCC MEMSIZE

Note that if turboc.cfg exists, the options in that file will be used.

Figure 6.2 shows the resulting display for the compilation, assembly, and linkage process, and also shows the output produced when the program is executed.

Fig. 6.2. Compilation and execution of the memsize.c *program.*

```
C>tcc memsize
Turbo C Version 2.0  Copyright (c) 1987, 1988 Borland International
memsize.c:
Turbo Assembler  Version 1.0  Copyright (c) 1988 by Borland International

Assembling file:    MEMSIZE.ASM
Error messages:     None
Warning messages:   None
Remaining memory:   167k

Turbo Link  Version 2.0  Copyright (c) 1987, 1988 Borland International

        Available memory 298502

C>memsize
This PC has 640K bytes of internal memory
C>
```

Notice that the one command invoked three separate programs: the tcc.exe compiler, the TASM.EXE assembler, and the tlink.exe linker.

Semicolons in Inline Assembly Statements

In assembly language, only one instruction or directive can be placed on each line of source text. Inline assembly statements are just like other C statements—several of them can be entered on the same line, provided that each pair is separated by a semicolon.

If only one inline statement appears on a line, a semicolon *can* be used (but is not required) to terminate an inline assembly statement. For example, in the following `if` statement,

```
if ( Variable_A < Variable_B )
    asm   inc   WORD PTR Variable_A
else
    printf( "The two variables are equal!" );
```

the inline assembly statement does not have to end in a semicolon.

Conversely, because a newline is always assumed to terminate an inline assembly statement, no inline assembly statement can continue to another line.

Comments in Inline Assembly Statements

In assembly language, a semicolon marks the beginning of a comment field. All characters following the semicolon on the program line are ignored.

Because inline assembly statements must be read by the same preprocessor that handles ordinary Turbo C statements, the syntactic rules of C must be applied consistently. Consequently, any comments that appear in inline assembly statements *must* be written like ordinary C comments. In other words, a comment must begin with the character pair /* and must terminate with the characters */, as follows:

```
asm int 12h                    /* BIOS interrupt 12h */
asm mov ax,6                   /* load 6 into the AX register */
asm push WORD PTR i;           /* this semicolon is valid */
asm mov ax,3; asm mov bx,4;    /* two statements in one line! */
```

Labels in Inline Assembly Statements

In C, the `goto` instruction enables you to jump to another statement within the current function.

```
x = 0;                          /* initialize the x variable */
TopOfLoop:                      /* mark a place in the code */
    x++;                        /* increment the x variable */
    if ( x < 10 ) goto TopOfLoop;  /* jump back to start of loop */
```

The target location is identified with a label, consisting of a valid identifier followed by a colon.

The following set of assembly language instructions is functionally similar to the preceding C instruction:

```
        mov ax,0        ; initialize the AX register
loop:   inc ax          ; increment the AX register
        cmp ax,10       ; compare AX with 10
        jl loop         ; jump to "loop" if (AX < 10)
```

Here again, a label marks a code location referenced by a `jump` statement. However, inline assembly code statements may *not* include statement labels. Hence, the following inline code is illegal:

```
asm         mov ax,0        /* initialize the AX register */
asm   loop: inc ax          /* increment the AX register */
asm         cmp ax,10       /* compare AX with 10 */
asm         jl loop         /* jump to "loop" if (AX < 10) */
```

Instead, code labels must be written in standard C format. Consequently, the previous statements must be rewritten in the following form:

```
      asm   mov ax,0        /* initialize the AX register */
loop:                       /* standard C label */
      asm   inc ax          /* increment the AX register */
      asm   cmp ax,10       /* compare AX with 10 */
      asm   jl loop         /* jump to "loop" if (AX < 10) */
```

On the other hand, the label for any inline data declaration *must* be written as part of the inline statement itself. For example, the following code is illegal:

```
Info:

      asm   db   13
        :
        :
      asm   mov ax,Info
```

Here, the label `Info` references data; consequently, it must be included *within* the inline statement, as follows:

```
asm   Info  db   13
  :
  :
asm         mov ax,Info
```

Preserving Registers

The 8086-family processor is designed to reference memory locations through the combination of specific segment:offset register pairs. For example, the address of the next executable statement is CS:IP; the data currently being used by the program is located at DS:SI and, possibly, also at DS:DI; similarly, the top of the stack is located at SS:SP. In addition, programs frequently use the BP register to store important stack offset values.

When a Turbo C function executes, it has complete control of the PC—and, as a result, complete control of these registers. (This is why a function is commonly called a *subprogram*.) Consequently, for the main program to regain control smoothly when the function terminates, any modified registers must be reset to the values they had before the function call was made.

Except for the instruction pointer (IP), your Turbo C program can directly access and modify all of these registers (SI, DI, BP, SP, CS, DS, or SS). As a result, whenever a function includes an instruction that modifies one of these registers, the function *must* also include code to save and restore that register. Formally, this rule is termed the *calling convention* of the Turbo C language.

All of the remaining registers in the PC (specifically, the general-purpose registers AX, BX, CX, DX; the extra segment register, ES; and the flags register) may be freely used and modified by your inline code; their values don't need to be restored when the function terminates.

Normally, the compiler handles all of this automatically. If you modify any register using an inline assembly language statement, however, it becomes *your* responsibility to push the register on to the stack at the beginning of the function and to pop the register at the end of the function to restore it to its original value. For example, to include the statement

```
asm    mov    ds,newseg;
```

your function must save the value of the DS register before the inline statement is encountered, and must restore that value when the function terminates, as follows:

```
{
:
asm    push ds;            /* save the initial value of DS on the stack */
:
:
asm    mov  ds,newseg;  /* modify the DS register */
:
:
asm    pop  ds;            /* restore DS to its original value */
:
}
```

The only exceptions to this rule are the SI and DI registers, which normally are used by the compiler to store word-sized local data and variables declared as type `register`. If Turbo C discovers either SI or DI in an inline assembly statement, their use for storing local data and `register` variables is suspended, and `push` and `pop` assembly instructions are generated automatically.

Referencing Data in Inline Assembly

You can use C language identifiers within your inline code statements wherever comparable assembly language identifiers would be allowed. The Turbo C compiler automatically converts every identifier to its appropriate memory location.

Nevertheless, remember that C is more helpful and protective than assembly language. As you will see later in this chapter, many features involving the use of identifiers—features offered automatically by the Turbo C compiler—are lost when you create the .ASM file and must specifically be taken into account when you develop inline assembly code.

Specifying Variable Sizes

The bumpup.c program in listing 6.2 demonstrates how an inline assembly statement can reference a C language identifier. The int variable TestValue is incremented with the assembly language inc opcode.

Listing 6.2

```
/* BUMPUP--increment a variable using inline assembly */

#pragma inline

main()
{
   int  TestValue;                       /* define a local variable */
   TestValue = 35;                       /* initialize the variable */
   printf( "%2d + 1 = ", TestValue );    /* print the initial value */

   asm  inc  WORD PTR TestValue;         /* increment the value */

   printf( "%2d\n", TestValue );         /* print the new value */
}
```

The bumpup.c program displays the following line when it executes:

```
35 + 1 = 36
```

When the Turbo C compiler processes a source program, it stores each variable in a symbol table, along with such information as the size of the data the variable can hold. After that, whenever the variable appears in the program, the compiler can reference the information in the symbol table to generate appropriate code. For example, if you declare a variable (such as TestValue) as an int, any C statement that uses the variable will produce word-sized instructions in the object file.

When you use an inline assembly statement in your C program, however, only the assembly language source file is passed to the assembler. All symbol table entries—including variable sizes—are lost. Consequently, such fundamental characteristics as the size of a data item must be made clear to the assembler within the context of the inline statement itself—in this case, with the WORD PTR size override.

Calling Inline Functions with No Arguments

Every inline assembly statement is regarded as an extension to the Turbo C language. The statements simply are passed along to the .ASM file to await subsequent processing by the assembler. Hence, to the C program itself, the overall structure and operation of a function is unaffected by the presence of any inline code the function may contain.

Similarly, the process of calling a function that contains inline assembly code is indistinguishable from calling a function that contains only standard C statements.

The `blink.c` program in listing 6.3 demonstrates the use of two functions—`blank()` and `restore()`—that consist almost entirely of inline assembly code. After `blank()` is called, the PC's display adapter card continues to receive data from video memory, but no image is forwarded to the monitor. Five seconds later, `restore()` reestablishes the connection and the original screen image returns.

This process—known as *screen blanking*—is the program's equivalent of temporarily turning the monitor off and on. Blanking is not the same as erasing a screen. Because screen output can be performed while blanking is in effect, you can use these routines to obtain the illusion of "instantaneous" screen updates.

Listing 6.3

```
/* BLINK--disable the screen for 5 seconds */

#pragma inline

void blank()
{
asm             int     11h             /* invoke BIOS interrupt 11h */
asm             and     al,30h          /* examine monochrome flag */
asm             cmp     al,30h          /* is monochrome flag set? */
asm             jne     color           /* no, so go to "color" */
asm             mov     ax,21h          /* mono, so: Send 21h to... */
asm             mov     dx,3B8h         /*             ...port 3B8h */
                goto    sendcode;       /* C goto statement */
        color:
asm             mov     ax,25h          /* color, so: Send 25h to... */
asm             mov     dx,3D8h         /*             ...port 3D8h */
        sendcode:
asm             out     dx,ax           /* blank the screen */
}

void restore()
{
asm             int     11h             /* invoke BIOS interrupt 11h */
asm             and     al,30h          /* examine monochrome flag */
asm             cmp     al,30h          /* is monochrome flag set? */
asm             jne     color           /* no, so go to "color" */
asm             mov     ax,29h          /* mono, so: Send 29h to... */
asm             mov     dx,3B8h         /*             ...port 3B8h */
                goto    sendcode;       /* C goto statement */
        color:
asm             mov     ax,2Dh          /* color, so: Send 2Dh to... */
asm             mov     dx,3D8h         /*             ...port 3D8h */
        sendcode:
asm             out     dx,ax           /* restore the screen */
}

main()
{
    blank();                            /* disable video controller */
    delay( 5000 );                      /* wait 5 seconds */
    restore();                          /* enable video controller */
}
```

Note that the `blink.c` program is designed to work only on PCs equipped with color graphics adapter (CGA) or monochrome display adapter (MDA) cards.

Blanking is achieved by modifying the CRT controller's mode-control register, which is located at port 3B8h for the monochrome adapter card and port 3D8h for the color graphics card. BIOS interrupt 11h returns equipment status information in the AX register that can be used to determine which card is installed—if bits 4 and 5 are set, the PC is configured for monochrome. (Note that the codes shown for the color adapter—25h and 2Dh—apply to text mode only. Consult the *IBM Technical Reference Manual* for additional options.)

Returning Function Values

Turbo C uses registers to hold values returned by a function.

A word-sized value is returned in the AX register. Four-byte return values use DX for the high-order word and AX for the low-order word. Larger return values are handled in two steps: the value itself is placed in a static storage location; the function then returns a pointer to the value. When the return value is a pointer, the offset is placed in AX and a segment value (if necessary) is placed in DX. Table 6.1 summarizes these rules.

Table 6.1. *Registers Used To Return a Function Value in Turbo C*

Data Type	Register Used
char	AX
short	AX
signed char	AX
signed short	AX
unsigned char	AX
unsigned short	AX
int	AX
signed int	AX
unsigned int	AX
long	Low-order word in AX High-order word in DX
unsigned long	Low-order word in AX High-order word in DX

Table 6.1 continues

Table 6.1 *continued*

Data Type	Registered Used
`float`	Low-order word in AX High-order word in DX
`double`	Return on 8087 stack or top of stack ST(0) or *emulator* top of stack register if not 80x87
`long double`	Return on 8087 stack or top of stack in emulator
`struct`	Address to value: offset in AX, segment in DX
`near pointer`	Address to value: offset in AX
`far pointer`	Address to value: offset in AX, segment in DX

If a function written principally with inline assembly statements uses AX and DX for its work fields, no `return` statement is explicitly required when the function terminates. For example, the `Combination()` function is designed to return the sum of its two arguments.

```
int Combination( int Argument1, int Argument2 )
{
    asm    mov    ax,Argument1    /* set AX to Argument1 */
    asm    add    ax,Argument2    /* add Argument2 to AX */
                                  /* no "return _AX" needed */
}
```

Because AX is used as the work field for calculating the total, the statement

```
return   _AX
```

is unnecessary.

Using Function Arguments Passed by Value

By default, when a function is passed an argument other than an array, the argument is passed by value. This means that a *copy* of the argument is placed on the stack. The function can then access and manipulate the copied value without modifying the original variable.

An identifier used to declare a function argument is, therefore, actually a reference to the location of the data on the stack. Turbo C allows argument identifiers to be used as operands within inline assembly statements wherever memory operands would normally be allowed.

Because a function argument refers to a memory location, and because memory-to-memory operations are not allowed, every argument should be assigned to a register before any further processing is performed.

```
int IntTotal( int First, int Second, int Third )
{
   asm      mov      ax,First     /* initialize AX with First */
   asm      add      ax,Second    /* increment AX with Second */
   asm      add      ax,Third     /* increment AX with Third */
                                  /* no "return" is required */

}
```

The `diskswap.c` program in listing 6.4 demonstrates two functions: `CurrentDrive()`, which takes no arguments but returns an integer indicating the current disk drive; and `SelectDrive()`, a void function that resets the current drive based on its integer-sized argument. Both functions make extensive use of inline assembly statements.

Listing 6.4

```
/* DISKSWAP--detect the current drive and select a new drive */

#pragma inline

/* the CurrentDrive() function returns the current drive. A value of 0
is returned for drive A:, 1 for B:, 2 for C:, and so on */

int CurrentDrive( void )
{
asm      mov      ah,19h    /* request DOS function 19h */
asm      int      21h       /* invoke the DOS interrupt */
asm      mov      ah,0      /* because only AL is affected */
                           /* no "return" is required */

}

/* the SelectDrive() function sets the current drive. Use an argument of 0
to select drive A:, 1 to select drive B:, 2 to select drive C:, and so on */

void SelectDrive( int Drive )
{
asm      mov      ah,0Eh    /* request DOS function 0Eh */
asm      mov      dl,Drive  /* desired drive goes in DL */
asm      int      21h       /* invoke the DOS interrupt */
}

main()
{
   printf( "The current drive is%2d\n", CurrentDrive() );
   printf( "Now changing to A:\n" );
   SelectDrive( 0 );        /* 0 is used for Drive A:     */
   printf( "The current drive is%2d\n", CurrentDrive() );
}
```

The displays during compilation and execution of the `diskswap.c` program are shown in figure 6.3.

Fig. 6.3. Compilation and execution of the `diskswap.c` *program.*

```
C>tcc diskswap
Turbo C  Version 2.0  Copyright (c) 1987, 1988 Borland International
diskswap.c:
Turbo Assembler  Version 1.0  Copyright (c) 1988 by Borland International

Assembling file:    DISKSWAP.ASM
Error messages:     None
Warning messages:   None
Remaining memory:   166k

Turbo Link  Version 2.0  Copyright (c) 1987, 1988 Borland International

        Available memory 298214

C>diskswap
The current drive is 2
Now changing to A:
The current drive is 0

A>
```

Using Function Arguments Passed by Reference

When a Turbo C function is passed an argument declared as an array, the argument is passed by reference. This means that the *address* of the argument is copied on the stack. The function can use the address to directly access and modify the original variable.

In C, a string is an array of characters (that is, an array of type `char`) terminated by a null character. The compiler treats a string identifier as a pointer to the first character in the array. The constant pointer assignment

```
char alphabet[] = "ABCDEFGHIJKLMNOPQRSTUVWXYZ";
```

and the variable pointer assignment

```
char *alphabet  = "ABCDEFGHIJKLMNOPQRSTUVWXYZ";
```

both assign a pointer to the first character (the letter A) to the identifier `alphabet`.

In the `dropdown.c` program in listing 6.5, the `demote()` function increases the ASCII value of each string element by 32. When applied to a string containing all uppercase characters, `demote()` has the effect of changing the string to lowercase.

Because the argument passed to `demote()` is a string (actually, an array of `char`), the inline assembly statements automatically treat the argument as an address; the address operator `&` is not needed when the function is invoked. The first line of the function assigns the parameter directly to the BX register.

Listing 6.5

```
/* DROPDOWN--change uppercase alphabetic characters to lowercase */

#pragma inline

void demote( char * Letters )
{
            asm     mov     bx,Letters              /* move address of arg to BX */
                                                    /* start of loop */
        Start:
            asm     cmp     BYTE PTR [bx],0         /* test for terminating null */
            asm     jz      Finish                  /* end the routine */
            asm     add     BYTE PTR [bx],32        /* add 32 to the character */
            asm     inc     bx                      /* go to next byte */
            asm     jmp     Start                   /* return to start of loop */
        Finish:  ;                                  /* end of the loop */
}

main()
{
    char alphabet[] = "ABCDEFGHIJKLMNOPQRSTUVWXYZ";

    puts( alphabet );                               /* show initial characters */
    demote( alphabet );                             /* change to lowercase */
    puts( alphabet );                               /* show revised characters */
}
```

Figure 6.4 shows the displays for the resulting compilation, assembly, and linkage process. The figure also shows the output produced when the program is executed.

Fig. 6.4. *Compilation, assembly, and execution of the* dropdown.c *program.*

```
C>tcc dropdown
Turbo C  Version 2.0  Copyright (c) 1987, 1988 Borland International
dropdown.c:
Turbo Assembler  Version 1.0  Copyright (c) 1988 by Borland International

Assembling file:    DROPDOWN.ASM
Error messages:     None
Warning messages:   None
Remaining memory:   165k

Turbo Link  Version 2.0  Copyright (c) 1987, 1988 Borland International

        Available memory 298942

C>dropdown
ABCDEFGHIJKLMNOPQRSTUVWXYZ
abcdefghijklmnopqrstuvwxyz

C>
```

Pointers to data objects other than structures and arrays are handled similarly within the function itself. The `flipover.c` program in listing 6.6 demonstrates the `swap()` function, which uses pointers to exchange the values of two integer variables. Note that the address operator & must be used when the function is invoked.

Listing 6.6

```
/* FLIPOVER--exchange the values of two integer variables */

#pragma inline

void swap( int * Arg1, int * Arg2 )
{
                          /*****************************************/
                          /* step 1: CX = *Arg1                  */
                          /*-------------------------------------*/
    asm   mov   bx,Arg1;  /* move address of Arg1 to BX          */
    asm   mov   cx,[bx];  /* move value of Arg1 to CX            */
                          /*****************************************/

                          /*****************************************/
                          /* step 2: DX = *Arg2                  */
                          /*-------------------------------------*/
    asm   mov   bx,Arg2;  /* move address of Arg2 to BX          */
    asm   mov   dx,[bx];  /* move value of Arg1 to DX            */
                          /*****************************************/

                          /*****************************************/
                          /* step 3: *Arg1 = DX                  */
                          /*-------------------------------------*/
    asm   mov   bx,Arg1;  /* move address of Arg1 to BX          */
    asm   mov   [bx],dx;  /* move DX (Arg2's value) to location of Arg1 */
                          /*****************************************/

                          /*****************************************/
                          /* step 4: *Arg2 = CX                  */
                          /*-------------------------------------*/
    asm   mov   bx,Arg2;  /* move address of Arg2 to BX          */
    asm   mov   [bx],cx;  /* move CX (Arg1's value) to location of Arg2 */
                          /*****************************************/
}

main()
{
    int A = 120;
    int B = 65;

    printf( "Original values: %4d and %4d.\n", A, B );
    swap( &A, &B );
    printf( "Swapped values:  %4d and %4d.\n", A, B );
    swap( &A, &B );
    printf( "Swapped again:   %4d and %4d.\n", A, B );
}
```

Figure 6.5 shows the displays for the resulting compilation, assembly, and linkage process for `flipover`. The figure also shows the output produced when the program is executed.

Fig. 6.5. *Compilation, assembly, and execution of the* `flipover.c` *program.*

```
C>tcc flipover
Turbo C  Version 2.0  Copyright (c) 1987, 1988 Borland International
flipover.c:
Turbo Assembler  Version 1.0  Copyright (c) 1988 by Borland International

Assembling file:    FLIPOVER.ASM
Error messages:     None
Warning messages:   None
Remaining memory:   166k

Turbo Link  Version 2.0  Copyright (c) 1987, 1988 Borland International

        Available memory 298252

C>flipover
Original values:  120 and   65.
Swapped values:    65 and  120.
Swapped again:    120 and   65.

C>
```

Accessing Function Arguments as Memory Locations

Although accessing function arguments by their identifiers is convenient, referencing arguments by their locations in memory is occasionally more desirable. To do so, however, you should understand how Turbo C uses the stack.

Before a function is called, its parameters are pushed on the stack in the reverse from the order in which they appear in the function declaration—namely, from right to left. For example, the function call

```
triple( a, b, c );
```

first pushes c on the stack, then b, and finally a. Figure 6.6 shows how the stack looks at this point.

The actual number of bytes pushed on the stack for any given data type is listed in table 6.2. Notice that the 8086-family processor can push only word-sized data; consequently, even a char variable requires two bytes of storage.

Fig. 6.6. The parameter-passing sequence of the function call `triple(a,b,c)`.

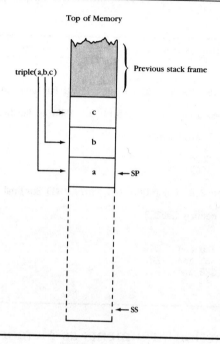

Table 6.2. Bytes Pushed on Stack for Different Data Types

Data Type	Number of Bytes
char	2
short	2
signed char	2
signed short	2
unsigned char	2
unsigned short	2
int	2
short int	2
signed int	2
unsigned int	2
long	4
unsigned long	4
float	4
double	8
near pointer	2
far pointer	4

The CS:IP register pair contains the segment and offset address of the next executable program statement. When the Turbo C function is invoked, the contents of these registers change to the address of the first line of the function. In order for a function in a small model program to return to the calling routine when done, the original value of the IP register must be saved by being pushed on the stack. If the function is outside the current code segment (technically, a far call), the CS register is saved also. The stack now appears as shown in figure 6.7.

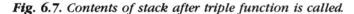

Fig. 6.7. *Contents of stack after triple function is called.*

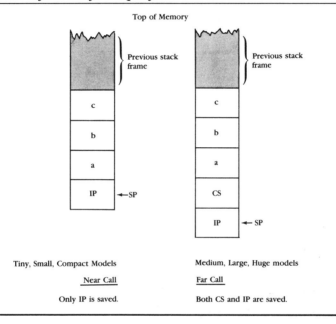

In a program that uses a tiny, small, or compact memory model, all code references are near; consequently, only the value of the IP register is saved. On the other hand, a program that uses a medium, large, or huge memory model regards all code references as far; consequently, both the IP and the CS registers are saved. Of course, a program also can perform a near call with the larger models and a far call with the smaller models if the *near* and *far* qualifiers are used.

The function begins by pushing the current base pointer on the stack. The BP register is then set to the value of the stack pointer. This new value provides a fixed reference—the memory above the BP (accessed with positive offsets) contains the function's parameters, whereas the region below the BP (accessed with negative offsets) is available for use as a work area. The stack now appears as shown in figure 6.8.

Fig. 6.8. Contents of stack after the base pointer is reset.

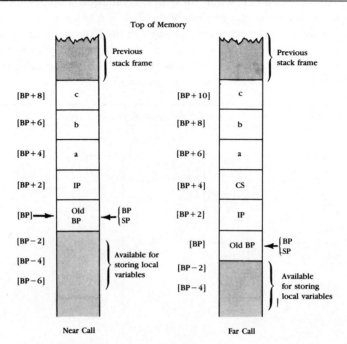

The memory region shown in figure 6.8 is called a `stack frame`, and the BP register itself is called the `frame pointer`.

Because value parameters are passed on the stack, function arguments actually are pseudonyms for memory references. For example, in

```
int funcA( int arg_A, int arg_B, int arg_C )
{
    int local_A;
    int local_B;
    int local_C;
    :
    :
}
```

all arguments and local data are memory locations that can be specified relative to the base pointer register (after the initial SP value is copied into BP), as shown in figure 6.9.

***Fig. 6.9.** The stack frame during function execution.*

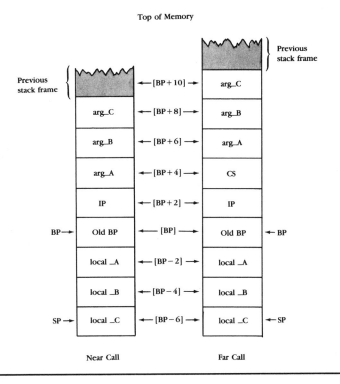

Top of Memory

Problems in Using Local Data

Because register access is much faster than memory access, Turbo C normally uses the SI and DI registers whenever possible to hold word-sized local variables. In contrast, most assembly language programs handle word-sized local variables as memory locations on the stack. When inline assembly statements are used in a function, the compiler is forced to follow the assembly language convention.

Figure 6.10 shows a side-by-side comparison of two functions, `nexthigher1()` and `nexthigher2()`, that both appear to use identical code to return integer values one unit larger than their arguments.

Fig. 6.10. *A comparison of standard C with inline assembly.*

Standard C Statements	*Inline Assembly Statements*

```
int nexthigher1( int basevalue1 )      int nexthigher2( int basevalue2 )
{                                       {
   int workfield1;                         int workfield2;
   workfield1 = basevalue1;                asm mov workfield2,basevalue2;
   workfield1++;                           asm inc workfield2;
   return workfield1;                      asm mov ax,workfield2;
}                                       }
```

The assembly language produced by the compiler for the nexthigher1() function uses the SI register to hold the local variable workfield1.

```
_nexthigher1    proc    near
                push    bp              ; save the BP register
                mov     bp,sp           ; use BP as frame reference
                push    si              ; save the SI register
                mov     si,word ptr [bp+4]  ; move basevalue1 to SI
                inc     si              ; increment SI
                mov     ax,si           ; move SI to AX for return
                pop     si              ; restore SI
                pop     bp              ; restore BP
                ret
_nexthigher1    endp
```

However, the assembly language produced for the nexthigher2() function uses stack space (specifically, the two bytes located at [BP − 2]) to store the local variable workfield2.

```
_nexthigher2    proc    near
                push    bp              ; save the BP register
                mov     bp,sp           ; use BP as frame reference
                sub     sp,2            ; reserve 2 bytes on stack for
                                        ; local variable
                mov     [bp-2],[bp+4]   ; move basevalue2 to local variable
                inc     [bp-2]          ; increment local variable
                mov     ax,[bp-2]       ; move local variable to AX
                mov     sp,bp           ; restore the SP register
                pop     bp              ; restore the BP register
                ret
_nexthigher2    endp
```

Unfortunately, the statement

```
mov     [bp-2],[bp+4]
```

is an illegal memory-to-memory operation. Further, the statement

```
inc     [bp-2]
```

requires the WORD PTR type override and will consequently cause a fatal assembly error.

The moral of this story is that you should follow several safety rules whenever you work with local data:

☐ Use the general-purpose registers (AX, BX, CX, and DX) wherever possible before you rely on local data defined in memory.

☐ Use registers to exchange data between function arguments and local variables. For example, rather than a single (and possibly illegal) statement such as

```
asm    mov    Local_Data_Field,Argument_Identifier
```

your function must use something like the following two-step approach:

```
asm    mov    dx,Argument_Identifier
asm    mov    Local_Data_Field,dx
```

☐ Whenever possible, local data should be placed in registers for subsequent processing. The stack should be used only for storing the original register values.

Using a Variable Number of Function Arguments

As a result of Turbo C's parameter-passing sequence, an individual function can handle a variable number of parameters. Because the first parameter passed is the last one pushed, it can always be found on the top of the stack, as shown in figure 6.11.

You can use the va_start, va_arg, and va_end macros and the va_list data type to access a variable argument list. The only restriction is that you must adopt a technique for clearly specifying the end of the series—usually, this is achieved by passing a separate parameter containing the number of arguments or by terminating the series with a specific value such as a null character or a numeric zero.

The varyorig.c program in listing 6.7 demonstrates how an arbitrarily long sequence of integers can be processed by a Turbo C function. Notice that whereas the number of parameters is unimportant, the series must be terminated with a numeric zero (the specific terminator used in this example).

Listing 6.7

```
/* VARYORIG--calculate the total of a series of integers */

#include <stdarg.h>

int SumUp( int FirstItem, ... )
{
    int Accumulator, Transfer;
    va_list argptr;
```

Listing 6.7 continues

Listing 6.7 continued

```
    va_start( argptr, FirstItem );
    Accumulator = FirstItem;
    while( (Transfer = va_arg( argptr, int )) != 0){
       Accumulator += Transfer;
    }
    va_end( argptr );
    return Accumulator;
}

main()
{
    printf( "Total is:%d\n", SumUp( 10, 20, 30, 0 ) );
}
```

When `varyorig` executes, it correctly computes and displays the total of the parameters passed to the `SumUp()` function.

A more straightforward (and, significantly, a more understandable) approach is to use inline assembly statements to access directly parameters passed on the stack.

Fig. 6.11. Accessing the first parameter of a C function.

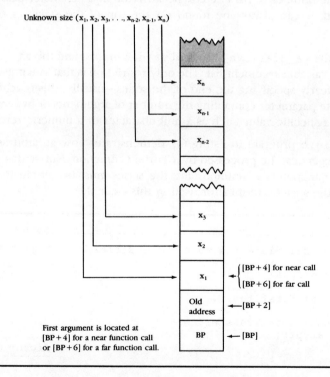

Unknown size ($x_1, x_2, x_3, \ldots, x_{n-2}, x_{n-1}, x_n$)

x_n

x_{n-1}

x_{n-2}

x_3

x_2

x_1 — $\begin{cases} [BP+4] \text{ for near call} \\ [BP+6] \text{ for far call} \end{cases}$

Old address — [BP+2]

BP — [BP]

First argument is located at [BP+4] for a near function call or [BP+6] for a far function call.

The `varyasm.c` program in listing 6.8 contains a revised version of the `SumUp()` function. No parameters are specified, but the code within the function sequentially processes each integer on the stack—beginning with the word located at [BP + 4] (or [BP + 6] for a large memory model) and ending with the first word discovered to contain a numeric zero.

Listing 6.8

```
/* VARYASM--calculate the total of a series of integers */

#pragma inline

int SumUp()
{
asm          push     bp                /* save base pointer */
asm          mov      bp,sp             /* create frame pointer */
asm          mov      ax,0              /* initialize AX to 0 */
asm          mov      bx,bp             /* stack pointer to BX */
asm          add      bx,4              /* skip BP and address */
      Tloop:
asm          cmp      WORD PTR [bx],0   /* is there another arg? */
asm          je       EndUp             /*    no, so terminate */
asm          add      ax,[bx]           /* add next value to AX */
asm          add      bx,2              /* get next value */
asm          jmp      Tloop             /* loop back */
      EndUp:
asm          pop      bp                /* restore base pointer */
}

main()
{
    printf( "The total of the first test is:  %6d\n",
            SumUp( 600, 700, 800, 0 ) );

    printf( "The total of the second test is: %6d\n",
            SumUp( 2, 2, 2, 2, 2, 2, 2, 2, 2, 2, 2, 2, 2, 0 ) );

    printf( "The total of the third test is:  %6d\n",
            SumUp( 10000, 2000, 300, 40, 5, 0 ) );

    printf( "The total of the fourth test is: %6d\n",
            SumUp( 0 ) );
}
```

Figure 6.12, which shows the resulting displays during the compilation, assembly, and linkage process, also shows the output produced when the program is executed.

Fig. 6.12. *Compilation, assembly, and execution of the* `varyasm.c` *program.*

```
C>tcc varying
Turbo C  Version 2.0  Copyright (c) 1987, 1988 Borland International
varying.c:
Turbo Assembler  Version 1.0  Copyright (c) 1988 by Borland International

Assembling file:   VARYING.ASM
Error messages:    None
Warning messages:  None
Remaining memory:  165k

Turbo Link  Version 2.0  Copyright (c) 1987, 1988 Borland International

       Available memory 297040

C>varying
The total of the first test is:    2100
The total of the second test is:     26
The total of the third test is:   12345
The total of the fourth test is:      0

C>
```

At first glance, the use of a terminating zero might seem sloppy—especially because functions such as `printf()` appear to allow any number of parameters in an almost free-form order. Consider, though, that because `printf()` is passed a format string as its first parameter, the function can scan the string and determine exactly how many additional parameters of each type should have been passed. Every standard Turbo C function that accepts a variable argument list has some built-in means of determining parameter count and type.

The Naming Conventions Used by Turbo C and the Turbo Assembler

A *naming convention* is the set of rules used by a compiler or assembler to compare identifiers.

For example, by default, the Turbo Assembler converts to uppercase all letters that appear in an identifier. Hence, the identifiers `xyz`, `XYZ`, and `Xyz` all are converted to `XYZ` and, consequently, are considered to be identical. The Turbo Assembler is said to be *case independent*.

Unlike the Turbo Assembler, Turbo C makes no case changes; however, it always adds an underscore (_) to the beginning of each identifier. As a result, Turbo C converts the identifiers `xyz`, `XYZ`, and `Xyz` to `_xyz`, `_XYZ`, and `_Xyz`, respectively, and—because Turbo C is *case sensitive*—considers these identifiers to be different.

When you write a program entirely in Turbo C, you must allow for the case sensitivity of the identifiers you select. You can pretty much ignore the use of the leading underscore—after all, the compiler applies it consistently.

The linker, however, uses the converted Turbo C identifier—the one that includes the leading underscore—to compare names referenced by modules created by both the Turbo C compiler and the Turbo Assembler.

Referencing Turbo C Identifiers from Inline Assembly Code

All Turbo C identifiers must be preceded by an underscore when you reference them in assembly code. For example, if your Turbo C program contains a function defined as OpenMasterFile(), any assembly language statement must reference it as _OpenMasterFile.

Conversely, to reference an assembly language identifier from Turbo C, its name *must* begin with an underscore, and the underscore *must* be omitted in the Turbo C program. For example, the assembly variable _abc is referenced as abc in a Turbo C module—the leading underscore is supplied automatically by the Turbo C compiler before the identifier is forwarded to the linker. An assembly language variable that does not have a leading underscore is inaccessible from Turbo C.

The song.c program in listing 6.9 is designed to play the first few notes of "Mary Had a Little Lamb." (Only three notes are actually played in this example, but a full seven-note range is available for you to use with other tunes.) Notice that the inline assembly statements need to access the three standard Turbo C functions sound(), delay(), and nosound(). Because inline assembly statements are passed directly to the .ASM file, no conversion is performed on the function names; consequently, the leading underscores are explicitly included.

Listing 6.9

```
/* SONG--play first line of "Mary had a little lamb." */

#pragma  inline

    asm   extrn  _sound:PROC          /* sound generation */
    asm   extrn  _delay:PROC          /* system delay */
    asm   extrn  _nosound:PROC        /* disable speaker */

void note( int Key )
{
    asm   jmp   NoiseMaker            /* bypass frequency table */

    asm   FrequencyTable  label  word;
    asm   dw    523                   /* C --- called as note( 1 ) */
    asm   dw    587                   /* D --- called as note( 2 ) */
```

Listing 6.9 continues

Listing 6.9 continued

```
        asm   dw    659             /* E --- called as note( 3 ) */
        asm   dw    699             /* F --- called as note( 4 ) */
        asm   dw    784             /* G --- called as note( 5 ) */
        asm   dw    880             /* A --- called as note( 6 ) */
        asm   dw    988             /* B --- called as note( 7 ) */

NoiseMaker:
                                    /* ======================== */
        asm   mov   bx,Key          /* get the key              */
        asm   dec   bx              /* change the offset by 1   */
        asm   shl   bx,1            /* multiply by 2 to look up  */
                                    /*    word in frequency table */
        asm   push  WORD PTR [FrequencyTable+bx] /* push frequency onto stack */
        asm   call  _sound          /* call the sound function  */
        asm   add   sp,2            /* clear frequency off stack */
                                    /* ======================== */
        asm   mov   ax,300          /* choose 300ms for delay   */
        asm   push  ax              /* push delay time on stack */
        asm   call  _delay          /* call the delay function  */
        asm   add   sp,2            /* take delay time off stack */
                                    /* ======================== */
        asm   call  _nosound        /* disable the speaker      */
                                    /* ======================== */
}

main()
{
    note( 3 );    note( 2 );        /*          Ma-ry           */
    note( 1 );                      /*          had             */
    note( 2 );                      /*          a               */
    note( 3 );    note( 3 );        /*          lit-tle         */
    note( 3 );                      /*          lamb...         */
}
```

As you may recall, the sound() and delay() functions both expect a single word-sized parameter. Before one of the functions is called, its parameter is pushed onto the stack. When the function terminates, the stack pointer is adjusted back to its original value. Because the argument on the stack does not need to be saved, a pop is not required—the value simply is overwritten with the next function call.

Figure 6.13 shows how the stack frame changes as this process occurs. Remember that because song.c is a small model program, the CS register will not be saved.

As you can see (a), before the function call begins, SP points to the most recently used memory location at the top of the stack. BP acts as frame pointer for the calling function.

First, the argument for the function to be called is pushed on the stack; SP now points to the location of the argument (b).

Fig. 6.13. *Stack activity during a function call.*

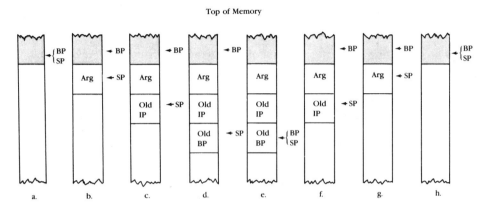

The CALL _FUNC command causes the current value of the IP register to be pushed on the stack (c).

The called function begins by pushing the current value of BP onto the stack (d). Next, with a mov bp,sp instruction, the called function sets BP equal to SP; the BP register is now the pointer for the new stack frame (e). When the called function terminates, it executes a POP BP instruction to restore BP to its original value (f).

As a result of the RET return instruction, the original value of the instruction pointer is popped off the stack, and the IP register is reset (g).

The C calling function executes ADD SP,2 to reset SP to the value it had before the argument was pushed on the stack (h).

Avoiding Case Conflicts

Because the linker used by the tc.exe integrated environment is case sensitive by default, no case conflicts can arise. However, when invoked directly from the command line, the tlink.exe linker defaults to being case independent—that is, it converts all identifiers to uppercase. Consequently, unintentional case conflicts can occur in mixed-language programming.

If a problem arises that appears to be related to a case conflict, you can take the following measures:

1. Run the Turbo Assembler with the /MX option in effect. Remember that the assembler has three options related to case sensitivity:

   a. /ML forces the assembler to treat all symbol names as case sensitive.

   b. /MU is the default option. It tells the assembler to convert all symbol names to uppercase.

    c. `/MX` causes public and external symbol names to be treated as case sensitive.

2. Run the `tlink.exe` linker with the `/c` option in effect to force lowercase characters to be treated as significant.

Of course, the simplest approach of all is to avoid the use of potentially conflicting names in the original code.

Using Stand-Alone Assembly Language Routines

The traditional way for C programs to use assembly language is to link object modules produced by an assembler with those produced by the C compiler. Unlike the inline method, which focuses on individual assembly instructions, linking makes entire assembly and C routines available to one another.

Compilers and assemblers translate program statements from a source language into instructions that can be understood by the PC's microprocessor. Some compilers and assemblers (which, not surprisingly, are collectively called *translators*) directly generate machine-language code. For example, the early releases of Borland's Turbo Pascal compiler produced an executable .COM file from a single pass of a source program. In contrast, most language translators—including both Turbo C and the Turbo Assembler—perform the intermediate step of producing object modules.

In a very real sense, the records composing an object module represent a specialized language that must itself be translated by the linker to produce the final machine-readable code. Hence, as long as all of these object records have compatible formats, the original source language is irrelevant.

Object files created by different compilers and assemblers must follow certain rules so that the modules can be linked successfully. These rules are presented in the following sections.

You should note, however, that this discussion assumes that you already are familiar with developing stand-alone assembly language programs. You may want to review the relevant sections of Borland's *Turbo Assembler User's Guide* before proceeding.

Segments and Memory Models

In an assembly language program, a *segment* is a collection of instructions or data whose addresses are all relative to the same segment register. Logical segments are defined with `SEGMENT` directives and are associated with segment registers through the use of the `ASSUME` directive.

A *group* is a collection of contiguous logical segments that can all be accessed from a single, common segment register during program execution. The `GROUP` directive specifies which logical segments are to be combined. The total size of the logical segments cannot exceed 64K.

To interface to code compiled by Turbo C, an assembly language module must use segments and groups that conform to the memory model of the final program.

Turbo C programs are composed of the three segments, shown in table 6.3. Both the `_BSS` uninitialized data segment and the `_DATA` segment contain program data. The `_BSS` and `_DATA` segments are combined in a group called `DGROUP`. The `_TEXT` segment contains the actual program code.

Table 6.3. *Segment Names Used by Turbo C*

Segment Name	Contents
`_BSS`	Uninitialized static data
`_DATA`	Initialized static data and all global data
`_TEXT`	Program code

An individual program may use any memory model that comfortably contains its code and data, although you should use the smallest model possible to avoid unnecessary loss of operating efficiency.

The various memory models use slightly different conventions for the segment name, and for the segment align, combine, and class types.

The Tiny Memory Model

In the *tiny* model, all program data and code must fit in a single segment; consequently, all segment registers are set to the same value. All code and data are *near*. Tiny models are the only memory models that can be transformed into .COM files. Segment types are shown in table 6.4.

Table 6.4. *Segments and Types Used by the Tiny Memory Model*

Name	Align	Combine	Class
`_TEXT`	byte	public	'CODE'
`_DATA`	word	public	'DATA'
`_BSS`	word	public	'BSS'

In addition, the following `group` and `assume` directives must be included:

```
DGROUP   group     _DATA,_BSS
         assume    cs:_TEXT,ds:DGROUP,ss:DGROUP
```

The Small Memory Model

In the *small* model, both code and data must be contained within single, although separate, segments. All code and data are *near*. Segment types are shown in table 6.5.

Table 6.5. *Segments and Types Used by the Small Memory Model*

Name	Align	Combine	Class
_TEXT	byte	public	'CODE'
_DATA	word	public	'DATA'
_BSS	word	public	'BSS'

In addition, the following `group` and `assume` directives must be included:

```
DGROUP    group    _DATA,_BSS
          assume   cs:_TEXT,ds:DGROUP,ss:DGROUP
```

The Medium Memory Model

In the *medium* model, all data must fit within a single 64K segment, but program code may occupy more than one segment. Data is near, but code is far. Segment types are shown in table 6.6. In the table, `fname` refers to the name of the program source file; this ensures that a segment named `fname_TEXT` is unique.

Table 6.6. *Segments and Types Used by the Medium Memory Model*

Name	Align	Combine	Class
fname_TEXT	byte	public	'CODE'
_DATA	word	public	'DATA'
_BSS	word	public	'BSS'

In addition, the following `group` and `assume` directives must be included:

```
DGROUP    group    _DATA,_BSS
          assume   cs:fname_TEXT,ds:DGROUP,ss:DGROUP
```

The Compact Memory Model

In the *compact* model, all code must fit within a single 64K segment, but program data may require more than one segment. In addition, no single array of data may exceed 64K in size. Code is *near*, but data is *far*. Segment types are shown in table 6.7.

Table 6.7. Segments and Types Used by the Compact Memory Model

Name	Align	Combine	Class
_TEXT	byte	public	'CODE'
_DATA	word	public	'DATA'
_BSS	word	public	'BSS'

In addition, the following `group` and `assume` directives must be included:

```
DGROUP    group      _DATA,_BSS
          assume     cs:_TEXT,ds:DGROUP
```

The Large Memory Model

In the *large* model, code and data may each exceed 64K, although no single array of data may exceed 64K in size. Both code and data are *far*. Segment types are shown in table 6.8. Just as in the medium model, `fname` refers to the name of the program source file.

Table 6.8. Segments and Types Used by the Large Memory Model

Name	Align	Combine	Class
fname_TEXT	byte	public	'CODE'
_DATA	word	public	'DATA'
_BSS	word	public	'BSS'

In addition, the following `group` and `assume` directives must be included:

```
DGROUP    group      _DATA,_BSS
          assume     cs:fname_TEXT,ds:DGROUP
```

The Huge Memory Model

In the *huge* model, code, data, and individual data arrays may each exceed 64K. Both code and data are *far*. Segment types are shown in table 6.9. Again, `fname` refers to the name of the program source file. Notice that no `_BSS` segment is used.

Table 6.9. Segments and Types Used by the Huge Memory Model

Name	Align	Combine	Class
fname_TEXT	byte	public	'CODE'
fname_DATA	word	public	'DATA'

In addition, the following `group` and `assume` directives must be included:

```
assume    cs:fname_TEXT,ds:fname_DATA
```

Using the Turbo Assembler's Simplified Segment Directives

Fortunately, Turbo Assembler provides simplified segment directives that alleviate a great deal of the pain involved in structuring an assembly language program.

The `DOSSEG` directive, usually the first line of a program, specifies that all segments should be grouped according to the Microsoft segment-ordering conventions which Turbo C follows.

The `.MODEL` directive specifies the memory model. One of the parameters `TINY`, `SMALL`, `MEDIUM`, `COMPACT`, `LARGE`, or `HUGE` is specified, as in `.MODEL SMALL`.

The `.CODE` and `.DATA` directives specify the start of your program's code and data segments, respectively. The `.DATA?` directive specifies the beginning of the _BSS segment containing uninitialized data.

Listing 6.10 contains the traditional skeleton for a small-model assembly language program that can interface with modules compiled by Turbo C.

Listing 6.10

```
_TEXT    SEGMENT  BYTE PUBLIC 'CODE'
DGROUP   GROUP    _DATA, _BSS
         ASSUME   CS:_TEXT, DS:_DATA
         :
         : Program code statements
         :
_TEXT    ENDS

_DATA    SEGMENT  WORD PUBLIC 'DATA'
         :
         : Initialized data declarations
         :
_DATA    ENDS

_BSS     SEGMENT  WORD PUBLIC 'BSS'
         :
         : Uninitialized data declarations
         :
_BSS     ENDS

         END
```

Modified to use simplified segment directives, the same program skeleton now appears as shown in listing 6.11.

Listing 6.11

```
DOSSEG
MODEL SMALL
.CODE
:
: Program code statements
:

.DATA
:
: Initialized data declarations
:

.DATA?
:
: Uninitialized data declarations
:

END
```

Clearly, you will want to use the simplified segment directives wherever possible.

Sharing Data Items among Multiple Modules

When a program is produced from several source files or modules, special consideration must be paid to commonly accessed symbol names.

In assembly language, symbols such as labels and variable names normally have meaning only within the source file in which they are defined. For a symbol in one module to be used by code in another module it must be declared *public* in the module in which it was created, and declared *external* in any module that accesses it.

Declaring Symbols Public

The PUBLIC directive is used to declare symbols public. (In other words, the PUBLIC directive makes a symbol visible to the linker.) A *public symbol* is any variable, procedure, or function defined within the current module that can be referenced by other modules. The syntax of the directive is as follows:

```
PUBLIC name[,name]...
```

PUBLIC directives can be placed anywhere in the source file.

Declaring Symbols External

The EXTRN directive tells the linker that an identifier is an external symbol that needs to reference a public symbol declared in another module. *External symbols* are the identifiers that a module uses but does not define. The linker gives each external symbol the characteristics of the *public* symbol it references.

The syntax of the directive is as follows:

```
EXTRN name:type[,name:type]...
```

When `EXTRN` is applied to an external function, the type included in the code can be `near`, `far`, or `proc`. For variables, labels, or symbols, the type must specify one of the following sizes: `byte`, `word`, `dword`, `qword`, or `tbyte`.

For example, if your small-model assembly language routine needs to access the global 16-byte variable `totalvalue` and the function `addup()`, the following directives would appear near the beginning of the source text:

```
extrn    _totalvalue:word
extrn    _addup:near
```

Remember that the Turbo C compiler always attaches a leading underscore to an identifier before forwarding it to the object file.

Producing Assembly Language Programs from Turbo C

You can use the Turbo C command-line compiler's −S option to generate an assembly language program directly from a file of C language source text.

Perhaps the simplest program presented in this chapter is `memsize.c` (refer to listing 6.1). An assembly language version of this program can be obtained by entering the following command at the DOS prompt:

```
TCC  −S MEMSIZE
```

The contents of the MEMSIZE.ASM program can be found in listing 6.12.

Listing 6.12

```
         ifndef ??version
?debug    macro
         endm
         endif
         ?debug S "\tc\memsize.c"
_TEXT     segment   byte public 'CODE'
DGROUP    group     _DATA,_BSS
         assume cs:_TEXT,ds:DGROUP,ss:DGROUP
_TEXT     ends
_DATA     segment word public 'DATA'
da label       byte
daw label      word
_DATA     ends
```

```
_BSS segment word public 'BSS'
b@    label    byte
b@w   label    word
         ?debug C E91D624A12135C7175655C746578745C6D656D73697A652E63
_BSS ends
_TEXT      segment   byte public 'CODE'
;          ?debug L 3
_main      proc near
;          ?debug L 5
      int      12h
;          ?debug L 7
         push  ax
         mov   ax,offset DGROUP:s@
         push  ax
         call  near ptr _printf
         pop   cx
         pop   cx
@1:
;          ?debug L 8
         ret
_main      endp
_TEXT      ends
         ?debug C E9
_DATA      segment word public 'DATA'
s@    label    byte
         db       84
         db       104
         db       105
         db       115
         db       32
         db       80
         db       67
         db       32
         db       104
         db       97
         db       115
         db       32
         db       37
         db       51
         db       100
         db       75
         db       32
         db       98
         db       121
         db       116
         db       101
         db       115
         db       32
         db       111
         db       102
         db       32
         db       105
         db       110
```

Listing 6.12 continues

Listing 6.12 *continued*

```
          db      116
          db      101
          db      114
          db      110
          db      97
          db      108
          db      32
          db      109
          db      101
          db      109
          db      111
          db      114
          db      121
          db      0
_DATA     ends
_TEXT     segment    byte public 'CODE'
          extrn  _printf:near
_TEXT     ends
          public _main
          end
```

Notice that the file contains several debugging statements which do not relate to the program operation itself. Note also that the _DATA segment stores strings in the form of individual ASCII characters. With a minimal amount of editing, the program can be simplified to a new version, MEMSIZE2.ASM, as shown in listing 6.13.

Listing 6.13

```
_TEXT     segment byte public 'CODE'
          extrn   _printf:near
          assume  cs:_TEXT,ds:_DATA,ss:_DATA

_main     proc    near
          int     12h
          push    ax
          mov     ax,offset _DATA:s@
          push    ax
          call    near ptr _printf
          pop     cx
          pop     cx
@1:
          ret
_main     endp
_TEXT     ends

_DATA     segment word public 'DATA'
s@        label byte
          db      'This PC has %3dK bytes of internal memory', 0
_DATA     ends

          public  _main
          end
```

This feature is extremely useful (and sometimes even essential) for discovering how you can implement a particular Turbo C construct in assembly language. In fact, the best way to learn how to develop assembly language interface modules is to write a short section of C code that has the same structure as the problem you want to solve, run the code through `tcc.exe` with the S option, and examine the resulting assembly listing.

For example, the `demo.c` program in listing 6.14 does absolutely nothing. However, it contains a variety of data declarations and function calls.

Listing 6.14

```
int aGlobal;                            /*****************************/
int bGlobal;                            /* define global variables   */
int cGlobal;                            /*****************************/

extern int aExternal;                   /*****************************/
extern int bExternal;                   /* define external variables */
extern int cExternal;                   /*****************************/

int FunctionDemo( int aParam, int bParam, int cParam )
{
    int aLocal;                         /*****************************/
    int bLocal;                         /* define local variables    */
    int cLocal;                         /*****************************/

    Func1( aParam, bParam, cParam );    /* call Func1 with parameters */

    aGlobal = aParam;                   /*****************************/
    bGlobal = bParam;                   /* move parameters to globals */
    cGlobal = cParam;                   /*****************************/

    Func2( aGlobal, bGlobal, cGlobal ); /* call Func2 with globals    */

    aLocal = aParam;                    /*****************************/
    bLocal = bParam;                    /* move parameters to locals  */
    cLocal = cParam;                    /*****************************/

    Func3( aLocal, bLocal, cLocal );    /* call Func3 with locals     */

    aLocal = aExternal;                 /*****************************/
    bLocal = bExternal;                 /* move externals to locals   */
    cLocal = cExternal;                 /*****************************/
}
```

The assembly language equivalent of `demo.c` is the DEMO.ASM program in listing 6.15. Such details as segment usage and function calls become clearly evident.

Listing 6.15. *The DEMO.ASM Program.*

```
_TEXT        segment     byte public 'CODE'
DGROUP       group       _DATA,_BSS
             assume      cs:_TEXT,ds:DGROUP,ss:DGROUP
_TEXT        ends

_TEXT        segment     byte public 'CODE'
_FunctionDemo            proc   near
             push        bp
             mov         bp,sp
             sub         sp,2
             push        si
             push        di

             push        word ptr [bp+8]
             push        word ptr [bp+6]
             push        word ptr [bp+4]
             call        near ptr _Func1
             add         sp,6

             mov         ax,word ptr [bp+4]
             mov         word ptr DGROUP:_aGlobal,ax
             mov         ax,word ptr [bp+6]
             mov         word ptr DGROUP:_bGlobal,ax
             mov         ax,word ptr [bp+8]
             mov         word ptr DGROUP:_cGlobal,ax

             push        word ptr DGROUP:_cGlobal
             push        word ptr DGROUP:_bGlobal
             push        word ptr DGROUP:_aGlobal
             call        near ptr _Func2
             add         sp,6

             mov         si,word ptr [bp+4]
             mov         di,word ptr [bp+6]
             mov         ax,word ptr [bp+8]
             mov         word ptr [bp-2],ax

             push        word ptr [bp-2]
             push        di
             push        si
             call        near ptr _Func3
             add         sp,6

             mov         si,word ptr DGROUP:_aExternal
             mov         di,word ptr DGROUP:_bExternal
             mov         ax,word ptr DGROUP:_cExternal
             mov         word ptr [bp-2],ax
@1:
             pop         di
             pop         si
             mov         sp,bp
             pop         bp
             ret
```

```
_FunctionDemo    endp
_TEXT       ends

_BSS        segment word public 'BSS'
_aGlobal    label    word
            db       2 dup (?)
_bGlobal    label    word
            db       2 dup (?)
_cGlobal    label    word
            db       2 dup (?)
_BSS        ends

_DATA       segment word public 'DATA'
s@          label    byte
_DATA       ends

            extrn    _cExternal:word
            extrn    _bExternal:word
            extrn    _aExternal:word

_TEXT       segment  byte public 'CODE'
            extrn    _Func3:near
            extrn    _Func2:near
            extrn    _Func1:near
_TEXT       ends

            public   _FunctionDemo
            public   _cGlobal
            public   _bGlobal
            public   _aGlobal
            end
```

Similarities between Inline and Stand-Alone Assembly Code

The following sections demonstrate how an inline assembly routine can be converted to a stand-alone assembly module.

Using Inline Code

In the c_avg0.c program in listing 6.16, the mean() function uses inline assembly statements to compute an integer average for all of the elements in a structure. The parameters passed to the mean() function consist of the address of the structure and the number of values it contains.

Listing 6.16

```
/* C_AVG0--calculate an integer average */

#pragma inline

#define  TEST_1  4
int TestValues_1[ TEST_1 ] = { 15, 25, 35, 45 };

#define  TEST_2  20
int TestValues_2[ TEST_2 ] = { 1, 9, 2, 8, 3, 7, 4, 6,  5, 5,
                                6, 4, 7, 3, 8, 2, 9, 1, 10, 0 };

int mean( int far * ValuePtr, int NumberOfValues )
{
asm       les     bx,[ValuePtr]          /* ES:BX points to input values */
asm       mov     cx,NumberOfValues      /* number of values */
asm       mov     ax,0                   /* initialize AX to 0 */
          MLoop:                         /* note that "asm" isn't used */
asm       add     ax,es:[bx]             /* add next value to AX */
asm       add     bx,2                   /* move to next value in array */
asm       loop    MLoop                  /* loop CX times */
asm       mov     dx,0                   /* clear DX */
asm       mov     bx,NumberOfValues      /* set BX to number of values */
asm       div     bx                     /* divide by number of values */
                                         /*    AX contains the quotient */
}

main()
{
   printf( "The average value of the first test is:  %2d\n",
           mean( TestValues_1, TEST_1 ) );

   printf( "The average value of the second test is: %2d\n",
           mean( TestValues_2, TEST_2 ) );
}
```

The displays during compilation and execution of the c_avg0.c program are shown in figure 6.14.

Calling Assembly Language Routines from C

The A_AVG1.ASM program in listing 6.17 contains the stand-alone assembly language equivalent for the mean() function in listing 6.16. Note the similarity between the code statements.

Listing 6.17

```
        DOSSEG
        .MODEL  SMALL
        .CODE
        PUBLIC  _mean
```

```
_mean    PROC
         push    bp               ; save BP
         mov     bp,sp            ; set BP to SP
         les     bx,[bp+4]        ; point ES:BX to input values
         mov     cx,[bp+8]        ; load number of values into CX
         mov     ax,0             ; initialize AX to 0

MLoop:   add     ax,es:[bx]       ; add next value to AX
         add     bx,2             ; move to next value in array
         lolop   MLoop            ; loop CX times

         mov     dx,0             ; clear the DX register
         mov     bx,[bp+8]        ; set BX to number of values
         div     bx               ; divide AX (total) by BX (number of values)
                                  ;    AX is now equal to quotient
         pop     bp               ; restore original BP
         ret                      ; remember: AX contains the mean
_mean    ENDP
         END
```

Fig. 6.14. *Compilation, assembly, and execution of the* `c_avg0.c` *program.*

```
C>tcc c_avg0
Turbo C  Version 2.0  Copyright (c) 1987, 1988 Borland International
c_avg0.c:
Turbo Assembler  Version 1.0  Copyright (c) 1988 by Borland International

Assembling file:   C_AVG0.ASM
Error messages:    None
Warning messages:  None
Remaining memory:  165k

Turbo Link  Version 2.0  Copyright (c) 1987, 1988 Borland International

        Available memory 297692

C>c_avg0
The average value of the first test is:  30
The average value of the second test is:  5

C>
```

The `c_avg1.c` program in listing 6.18 is a revised version of the `c_avg1.c` program from listing 6.16. `c_avg1.c` is designed to reference `mean()` as an external function; however, no other changes have been made.

Listing 6.18

```
/* C_AVG1--calculate an integer average */

extern int mean( int far * ValuePtr, int NumberOfValues );

#define  TEST_1  4
int TestValues_1[ TEST_1 ] = { 15, 25, 35, 45 };
#define  TEST_2  20
int TestValues_2[ TEST_2 ] = { 1, 9, 2, 8, 3, 7, 4, 6,  5, 5,
                               6, 4, 7, 3, 8, 2, 9, 1, 10, 0 };

main()
{
   printf( "The average value of the first test is:  %2d\n",
           mean( TestValues_1, TEST_1 ) );

   printf( "The average value of the second test is: %2d\n",
           mean( TestValues_2, TEST_2 ) );
}
```

Figure 6.15 shows the displays during compilation, assembly, link, and execution of the c_avg1.c and A_AVG1.ASM programs.

Fig. 6.15. *The compilation, assembly, and execution of the* c_avg1.c *and* A_AVG1.ASM *programs.*

```
C>tcc c_avg1 a_avg1.asm
Turbo C  Version 2.0  Copyright (c) 1987, 1988 Borland International
c_avg1.c:
a_avg1.asm:
Turbo Assembler  Version 1.0  Copyright (c) 1988 by Borland International

Assembling file:   A_AVG1.ASM
Error messages:    None
Warning messages:  None
Remaining memory:  170k

Turbo Link  Version 2.0  Copyright (c) 1987, 1988 Borland International

        Available memory 299604

C>c_avg1
The average value of the first test is:  30
The average value of the second test is:  5

C>
```

Calling C Routines from Assembly Language

Listing 6.19 contains yet another way to calculate an average. The c_avg2.c program is designed to call the external function mean2() that, in turn, will call the C function discussion().

Listing 6.19

```
/* C_AVG2--calculate an integer average */

extern void mean2( int SeqNum, int far * ValuePtr, int NumberOfValues );

#define  TEST_1  4
int TestValues_1[ TEST_1 ] = { 15, 25, 35, 45 };

#define  TEST_2  20
int TestValues_2[ TEST_2 ] = { 1, 9, 2, 8, 3, 7, 4, 6,  5, 5,
                               6, 4, 7, 3, 8, 2, 9, 1, 10, 0 };

void discussion( int TestNumber, int Average, int Total, int Counter )
{
   printf( "Results of test%2d:\n",         TestNumber );
   printf( "   Number of values: %4d\n",    Counter    );
   printf( "   Total of values: %4d\n",     Total      );
   printf( "   Arithmetic mean: %4d\n\n",   Average    );
}

main()
{
   mean2( 1, TestValues_1, TEST_1 );
   mean2( 2, TestValues_2, TEST_2 );
}
```

The A_AVG2.ASM program in listing 6.20 calculates an integer average, then passes its result to the `discussion()` function.

Listing 6.20

```
        DOSSEG
        .MODEL  SMALL
        EXTRN   _discussion:PROC
        .CODE
        PUBLIC  _mean2
_mean2  PROC
        push    bp              ; save BP
        mov     bp,sp           ; set BP to SP
        les     bx,[bp+6]       ; point ES:BX to input values
        mov     cx,[bp+10]      ; load number of values into CX
        mov     ax,0            ; initialize AX to 0

MLoop:  add     ax,es:[bx]      ; add next value to AX
        add     bx,2            ; move to next value in array
        loop    MLoop           ; loop CX times

        push    WORD PTR [bp+10] ; push the number of values
        push    ax              ; push the total
        mov     dx,0            ; clear the DX register
        mov     bx,[bp+10]      ; set BX to number of values
```

Listing 6.20 continues

Listing 6.20 continued

```
          div     bx                          ; divide AX (total) by
                                              ;    BX (number of values)
                                              ;    Quotient (mean) is in AX
          push    ax                          ; push the quotient (mean)
          push    WORD PTR [bp+4]             ; push the number of values
          call    _discussion                 ; call discussion()
          add     sp,8                        ; remove parameters from stack
          pop     bp                          ; restore original BP
          ret
_mean2    ENDP
          END
```

The displays during compilation and execution of the c_avg2.c and A_AVG2.ASM programs are shown in figure 6.16.

Fig. 6.16. *The compilation, assembly, and execution of the* c_avg2.c *and* A_AVG2.ASM *programs.*

```
C>c_avg2
Results of test 1:
     Number of values:      4
     Total of values:     120
     Arithmetic mean:      30

Results of test 2:
     Number of values:     20
     Total of values:    100
     Arithmetic mean:      5


C>
```

Summary

In this chapter, you have learned two ways of developing an executable program from source text written in both assembly language and C.

The first method, called *inline assembly*, uses Turbo C's asm instruction to insert assembly language source statements directly into a C program. In order to compile a program that contains inline assembly code, the tcc.exe command-line compiler generates assembly language source text for the entire module. Any inline assembly statements contained in the program are simply passed along to this file. Next, this assembly language source text is used as input to the TASM.EXE Turbo Assembler. Finally, the output from the assembler is linked to produce an executable program.

The second method involves linking separate object modules produced by the Turbo Assembler with those produced by the Turbo C compiler. Turbo C places program code and data into segments whose names depend on the particular memory model in force. If an assembly language module uses these same segment names, the compiled modules can be linked together to form a single program. All public names must comply with the Turbo C naming convention.

Part II

Compiling and Linking

Alan
Plantz

CHAPTER

7

Compiling, Checking, and Linking the Program

This chapter covers the final steps of program development related to compiling and linking the final executable. Some utilities that can be used when problems arise—map files, symbol tables, removing debugging information from binary files, and so on—are discussed here, as are TLINK and MAKE. This chapter includes also an overview of testing and debugging techniques, which are discussed more fully in Part III.

Studies have shown that the number of compilations is directly correlated to the number of errors in the final program. This is open to debate, especially when you use an interactive environment such as that provided by Turbo C Professional. The reasoning here is that debugging cannot be used until a unit of code successfully compiles, and the debugger greatly enhances unit and program testing.

Compiling the Program

Compiling is the process of checking source code syntax, and, when the syntax is correct, turning the source into assembly language and or .OBJ files to be handed over to the linker at some point.

In the simplest C programs, a single source file can be compiled and linked without a make or project (.PRJ) file, unless a special library must be included. Note that in Turbo C you have an option to tell the compiler where to find the graphics library. If this information is not given, you use a project file or make file to pass along this data. Be aware that make files are used with TCC, the command-line compiler version, and that project files are used only with the IDE version of Turbo C.

In larger programs with more than one module, you can create a project file to give the name of each module in order, as well as any special libraries and header files required. You can provide the same information, in more detail, in a make file if the stand-alone compiler (TCC) is used.

The first time you press Alt-C (or Alt-R) after writing code, compiling may not go well. If you have forgotten to change the .PRJ file to the correct one, you may end up with something entirely different than you expected. Or you may end up with a long list of error messages.

Use Maximum Error Checking for the First Compile

Using the maximum amount of error checking available in Turbo C will help you catch most errors during your first round of compiling. The more errors you turn off, the easier your compilations will be, but the more inexplicable errors you will find in your programs (if they even run). Because Borland's defaults turn off some levels of error checking, change the defaults. If the code you are writing will be ported, make certain that ANSI settings are on, as well as other portability features affecting pointers, boundary alignment, and so on, so that nonstandard features will be flagged.

Using TC's Built-in Syntax Checking

The built-in LINT-like features of Turbo C are extremely helpful. The LINT utility provides a more rigorous form of syntax checking than does the compiler. The warnings and errors are usually quite specific. While you look at the error list, you can get more explanation of the error by placing the cursor on the line in question and pressing F1. This brings up a help window similar to the window that appears when you press Ctrl-F1. For an error message, the window contains the message along with a brief description of the message, which may lead to how the error condition can be corrected.

Turbo C's error-checking facilities are more extensive than those in some other compilers. You get a message for each error and can immediately find the location in the source code from which the condition occurred within the IDE. This is much more desirable than just getting an error code or an approximate location of the condition. Note, however, that due to the multiple-statement lines allowed by the C language, the actual error may be located a line or two before the location stated by the error message. Messages on precision problems, pointers, and other features can be especially helpful.

One of the greatest boons to the C language has been the implementation of prototyping. This enables the number of arguments and the type of each argument—except in variable argument lists denoted by an ellipsis—to be checked by the compiler. This feature alone can weed out a significant number of errors. For example, prototyping is helpful when you use a library of routines you have not developed yourself. As you type unfamiliar code, omitting a parameter (or switching the position of two) is easy. Function prototyping, properly used, would catch these conditions. At compile time, omitting a parameter could be caught as a condition of incorrect number of arguments; switching two parameters might be caught if each were a different type. Note, however, that prototyping would *not* catch it if the arguments switched were of the same type. If the prototyping were turned off, crashes or erratic program behavior could occur.

For function prototyping to operate properly, one of the Error menu's Less Common Errors options, `Call to function with no prototype`, also must be on. (For a more detailed discussion, see Chapter 8, "Using TCC, the Command-line Compiler.")

Is the Compiler Telling the Truth?

Remember that due to the limited look-ahead capabilities of the parser, the compiler may generate more error messages than are actually there.

Normally, the compiler displays both warnings and real error conditions. The `Display warnings` option can be turned on or off. With this option off, you can get to just the errors to correct them first, then turn on the warnings later during compilation. Even warnings should be dealt with and corrected; they can lead to errors down the road.

The result of the error detection will be accurate for the first warning or error, but perhaps not for successive messages unless they are separated from the first report by several lines. Errors often are accurate, but warnings should be held under suspicion, especially if more than one warning is reported for a single line. This cascade of messages is typical in compilers and LINTs, almost seeming to be the nature of the beast. A possible cause of the overflow of errors is omission of the semicolon from the end of a statement, which then does not signal the end of that statement to the compiler. The parser would be off course from the point of the missing semicolon on. Many parsers, however, are smart enough to detect the missing semicolon and still sense the end-of-line, thus inferring the end of statement.

Using Compiler Options

Compiler options can sometimes greatly affect the efficiency and speed of the executable code produced. Code size differences of 10 to 20 percent are not uncommon; the same percentages apply to speed enhancements of the final program. The three areas of optimization, debugging information, and memory models can dramatically affect the final code produced. If you are really trying to develop a fine product, do not overlook the options for increasing performance and putting the polish on your application.

Optimization

Optimization is the fine-tuning of code to squeeze as much as possible out of it. It may be possible to get performance increases of 5 to 20 percent, or maybe more, just by answering "on" or "off" to simple questions about compiler performance.

The time to apply optimizations is when your program runs correctly, or almost correctly. You should also test your program with the optimizations you will use, because they may at times have some side effects not foreseen during coding.

The Optimization menu has several options for allowing either speed or code size improvements.

Optimize can be set for speed or code-size optimization. Your choice will depend upon the application. For example, ROM-able code or code for floppy-based systems may need size optimization, and other systems for real-time programming, database operations, graphics, and so on, may need speed optimizations. Arrays are a special area for which an "either-or" situation exists and you must choose between size or speed.

Use Register Variables turns off or on the use of variables with the register storage modifier. In other words, even if the keyword register were used, it would be ignored by the compiler if this option had the value of off. The on option uses register variables; they will be placed in machine registers for faster execution. This is helpful for loop counters and other such program elements. Note that only the SI and DI registers are available for optimization.

Register Optimization is not the same as the Use Register Variables option. The Register Optimization option enables the compiler to remember the contents of registers it will use later. However, this practice can lead to problems when the value in the register is referenced by a pointer. Because of this problem, optimization is not a wise choice for registers unless you are extremely careful. In one example of trying to duplicate the strcmp() function from the run-time library, as little source code as possible was written. In fact, the routine was condensed from several lines to just one line of code. Even then it did not quite achieve the same timings as the run-time library version of the routine. Only after applying register optimizations did it match the run-time library.

Jump Optimization has an effect of decreasing code size by removing excess (duplicated) jumps and manipulating switch and loop statements. Due to the reorganization of these statements, source debugging may be confusing when you try to follow the instructions. It is best to turn this optimization technique off when you are debugging—it can always be turned on afterward—and especially retest those features using the optimization to ensure that no bugs have crept into the program.

Debugging Information

Debugging information deals with symbol information and other address information used by the debugger for its operation. Debugging information is a necessary evil while the program is being developed, tested, and then tested at the first few customer sites. It should not be removed until the product has been thoroughly examined and tested, and runs correctly.

The Turbo C `TDSTRIP` utility can be used to remove debugging information from an executable. If you use `TDSTRIP`, you will not have to recompile the entire program with the option `OBJ debug information` turned off. A handy option of `TDSTRIP` allows you to write the extracted debugger data to a disk file, which can then be used in lieu of rerunning `TDSTRIP` on the program.

Deleting debugging information from the final .EXE file can reduce the file size considerably—in the range of 10 to 40 percent—and execution time savings can also result.

Just remember that without this special information, you will not be able to use your program properly with either of the debuggers.

Memory Models

As mentioned earlier, memory models also can affect the size and speed performance of a program.

The rule of thumb is to use the smallest memory model possible for your program's code and data. Larger models tend to be slower, due to increased math needed for calculating addresses of information. The smaller models, even though they execute faster, may not have the storage capabilities needed for either data or code.

The medium and compact models are perhaps the trickiest, because they are just the opposite in terms of code and data usage, but you rarely will be in such a tight situation that you have to decide between the two. Usually it is a matter of deciding between the small and the large models.

Using the CPP Preprocessor Separately

You might need to use the preprocessor separately. Doing so enables you to view macro expansion, which may be critical when you work with macros as "functions," but can be useful also in other instances. This means working with CPP from the DOS command line and not within the Integrated Development Environment, where compilation would follow directly without any way of breaking the operation.

If you use conditional compilation to some degree, viewing the output from the preprocessor before compiling can provide a clearer picture of just which paths are being taken and whether the compilation will be successful. Make sure that adequate disk space is available. Because of the substitutions, the file produced could be considerably larger than you think. Sometimes just using an incorrect exclamation point can cause different conditions to occur. Working with the preprocessor and changing the value of #define lines can be useful for tracking down problems.

Substitutions also can allow tiny bugs to creep in, but they may have a big bite! Just putting a semicolon at the end of a #define line can cause it to be placed in the code and could signal a preliminary end-of-line to the compiler. Not using enough parentheses with "parameter lists" for function macros can produce strange results and even compilation errors.

Linking the Program

This section outlines the final steps in creating a program (other than testing, which is covered in depth in Chapter 9, "Testing and Debugging Strategies"). The pieces you have created must be put together to form a whole entity. Some link-time problems may occur also, of which you must be aware. There are methods of making the process easier and automating it, such as make files. Configuration management can make the entire process less error-prone and quicker after careful planning.

Linking is the final step in joining pieces to form an executable program. The linker provides this glue for the pieces. You still have testing to do after an executable file is produced, but linking is what makes the "finished product." Just like putting the pieces (links) of a chain together, linking in computer terminology puts pieces of a program together. The object modules and libraries are combined to form the executable program, which usually is an .EXE file (but a .COM file for use with the tiny memory model). The relocatable object modules, which were compiled using fake addresses for the externals, public variables, and function names, are given real addresses starting from the offset of the beginning of the program. These names and addresses are kept in the symbol table, which you can obtain by using .MAP files.

This chapter concentrates on using TLINK. Part of the Turbo C package, TLINK is fast and efficient. You might want to switch to a different linker if you must use overlays, which TLINK does not support, or if you must use modules compiled with either Microsoft's C or FORTRAN compilers. Their object-file formats are not compatible with Turbo C's object-file formats.

Symbol Tables

The compiler and linker must have a method of tracking the various identifiers (symbols) for variables and functions inside the source code and within the executable program. A symbol table is the tracking method used in Turbo C and most other compilers.

The symbol table contains names that are both global or static in scope and, at times, identifiers that also are local in scope. The symbol table is similar to a stack in that names are added and removed from one end; however, it is different from a stack in that the symbol table can be scanned from the end to the beginning to find the occurrence of an identifier without destroying the table's contents. This makes it more like a linked list in structure. The symbols are not just added and then left in the table. When the compiler finishes using a symbol, especially a local identifier, the symbol is removed from the table to provide room for other identifiers.

The symbol table contains not only the location of the identifier, but also such other information as the type of the identifier and its storage class—whether it is global or static, external or automatic, and so on. If the identifier is a function, the type is the return type of the function.

The location of the identifier can be either a fixed memory address for statics and globals (because they are at absolute memory locations within the data segment) or the location could be an offset from the beginning of the frame pointer. The frame pointer is an offset value contained in the BP register and is relative to the data segment within the SS register. Remember that the frame pointer is part of the stack, and is where local variables (auto storage class) are kept.

For a function, the symbol table takes the value of the first executable line of the function. The symbol table is handy also for keeping track of the parameters of a function that have been placed on the stack, because C does not know which parameters have or have not been loaded. This is the same "free-wheeling" method that allows C to permit a function with a variable number of arguments, whereas Pascal and other languages cannot handle this type of function. It is also the same method that was used before function prototyping to enable C programmers to hang their code by omitting an argument or using one of the wrong type.

The function prototype, a type of advanced declaration, lets the compiler know ahead of time what the function's argument information and return type will be. It is feasible to place this information—the prototype and address—into the symbol table before the compiler and linker actually get to a function call. This way, they have a method of comparing the function call with the declaration to see whether a mismatch has occurred either in the number of arguments present or in the argument type. A warning or error message can then be displayed to the programmer.

The compiler's and linker's ability to search through the symbol table from the end to the beginning helps to allow the concept of scope. Languages such as older BASIC dialects, which allow only global variables, have no scope capability because the symbol table is searched from beginning to end, until a match is found anywhere in the table.. Finding an occurrence of count (a local C variable used to count the iterations of a for loop) in one function can be kept totally separate from the count found in a second function, or even separate from a global named count.

You also can use the View/Variables option in the stand-alone Turbo Debugger to see information similar to what you see in the symbol table.

Linking and .MAP Files

Although you cannot get a copy of the symbol table directly, a similar type of output can be produced. The linker can output a .MAP file, which contains the names of public and global symbols and their addresses. This may be useful in debugging.

The Turbo Linker (TLINK) includes the following options for producing four kinds of map files:

/l   A section of the map file uses source code line numbers.
/m   The map file will include publics.
/s   The map file will be a detailed map of the segments.
/x   No map file will be produced.

To get a detailed map-file listing, use the Detailed option under Map file under Linker on the Turbo C Integrated Environment Options menu, or use the /s option in the command-line version, TCC.

The first part of the file gives addresses of the start and stop locations of major portions of the program, such as the code and data segments, and the stack. Table 7.1 shows an example of this portion of a map file.

Table 7.1. *Major Program Portions from a Map File*

Start	Stop	Length	Name	Class
00000H	015ADH	015AEH	_TEXT	CODE
015B0H	01A09H	0045AH	_DATA	DATA
01A0AH	01A0DH	00004H	_EMUSEG	DATA
01A0EH	01A0FH	00002H	_CRTSEG	DATA
01A10H	01A11H	00002H	_CVTSEG	DATA
01A12H	01A17H	00006H	_SCNSEG	DATA
01A18H	01A63H	0004CH	_BSS	BSS
01A64H	01A64H	00000H	_BSSEND	STACK
01A70H	01AEFH	00080H	_STACK	STACK

Note that the addresses are relative to the start of the program, and not to the computer's RAM.

The next portion of the detail map file is a listing of segment information with addresses, length in bytes, class (such as CODE, DATA, and BSS), the name of the segment in which the information is found, the group, module name, and the alignment/combining information. The alignment information includes whether alignment occurs on byte or word boundaries. Table 7.2 shows a portion of this section of the map file.

Alignment may start at different memory locations: with *byte* alignment, a segment may start at any address; with *word* alignment, only at an even address; *paragraph* alignment starts a multiple of 16 bytes; and *page* alignment starts on page boundaries or in multiples of 256 bytes.

Table 7.2. *Detailed Segment Map from a Map File Segment*

Address	Length	Class	Type	Group	Module	Alignment Combining
0000:0000	01FA	C=CODE	S=_TEXT	G=(none)	M=C0.ASM	ACBP=28
0000:01FA	0071	C=CODE	S=_TEXT	G=(none)	M=QSORT.C	ACBP=28
0000:026B	003B	C=CODE	S=_TEXT	G=(none)	M=IOERROR	ACBP=28
0000:02A6	0030	C=CODE	S=_TEXT	G=(none)	M=EXIT	ACBP=28
0000:02D6	00F1	C=CODE	S=_TEXT	G=(none)	M=SETARGV	ACBP=28
0000:03C7	004A	C=CODE	S=_TEXT	G=(none)	M=SETENVP	ACBP=28
.						
.						
.						
01A1:0050	0004	C=BSS	S=_BSS	G=DGROUP	M=QSORT	ACBP=48
01A6:0004	0000	C=STACK	S=_BSSEND	G=DGROUP	M=C0.ASM	ACBP=28
01A7:0000	0080	C=STACK	S=_STACK	G=(none)	M=C0.ASM	ACBP=74

The ACBP information in the table's rightmost column consists of hexadecimal values and is encoded. Turbo C uses only three codes of alignment (A), combining (C), and big (B). The alignment value tells the type of boundary alignment for the segment map module. The combining value tells the type of segment combining performed by the linker, where public segments are appended one to another to form a larger segment, and where common segments overlay each other. The B field tells whether the size of the segment is exactly 64K or smaller.

The last part of a detailed map, mfile, is the list of publics and their addresses within the program, along with any error messages that might be produced. Table 7.3 shows an example of the public section.

Table 7.3. *Publics Section of a Map File (Publics by Name)*

Address	Public Name
015B:01A8	arrElem
0000:0411	atexit
0000:05DC	brk
0000:01FA	compareStrings
0000:01F8	DGROUP@
015B:0188	emws_adjust
015B:018C	emws_BPsafe
015B:0184	emws_control
015B:018A	emws_fixSeg
.	
.	
.	
015B:009E	___brklvl
015B:009C	___heapbase
015B:00A0	___heaptop

The publics are arranged in two ways: alphabetically by name within a module, and strictly by address value. The names of the modules/routines are all uppercase, preceded by two underscores in the publics map file.

The final section is reserved for any error messages that may be produced. These messages would appear at the end of the map file like this:

```
Undefined symbol '__stklen' in module CO.ASM
Undefined symbol '__heaplen' in module CO.ASM
Undefined symbol '_main' in module CO.ASM
Undefined symbol '_exit' in module CO.ASM
Undefined symbol 'errno' in module IOERROR
Undefined symbol '_malloc' in module SETENVP
Program entry point at 0000:0000
```

Note that the linker does not produce friendly messages as it creates the map file. Information is not really produced in a columnar format, and headings for information often are nonexistent. The headings for tables 7.1 through 7.3 have been added here to help you identify quickly what is in the map file.

If the .MAP file is of little or no help in finding duplicate identifiers, unknown identifiers, or other conditions, the utility program, OBJXREF, may be of help. This utility prints the contents of object and library files by listing the public symbols and any references to these symbols. A second type of report from OBJXREF prints the contents of the object modules in terms of segments and segment size. OBJXREF reports can be broken down to give less information than what is presented in the map file by using the appropriate command-line option, such as /rp, to produce only public symbol definitions. OBJXREF may be most useful because you do not have to wade through so much information to find the answer.

The following is an example of output from OBJXREF:

```
WARNING: Unresolved symbol OVERFLOW@ in module LST54
WARNING: Unresolved symbol _printf in module LST54
WARNING: Unresolved symbol ___brklvl in module LST54
WARNING: Unresolved symbol _coreleft in module LST54
WARNING: Unresolved symbol _farcoreleft in module LST54

PUBLIC SYMBOL DEFINITIONS BY SYMBOL NAME

SYMBOL                              DEFINED IN

OVERFLOW@                           -undefined-
_coreleft                           -undefined-
_farcoreleft                        -undefined-
_main                               LST54
_printf                             -undefined-
_printMemoryModel                   LST54
___brklvl                           -undefined-

Symbols  = 7
Modules  = 2
```

Addressing Problems in Linking

Linking is not without its error and warning messages, but they usually are not as frequent as compilation messages. A common message involves "unresolved externals," or identifiers that cannot be found in the files and modules to be linked. Other sources of error include conflicts within modules compiled under different memory models or when trying to link .ASM modules. Other errors are much more infrequent, such as exceeding a stack size of 64K or total program size when you are trying to produce a .COM file with the /t (tiny) option.

TLINK will use the address of the first occurrence of a function name. This address is part of the information you can find in a map file. If a programmer knows the address of a standard library routine, he or she can use the address and replace the function with a routine developed by the programmer. The programmer must ensure that the linker sees the user-written version before it sees the standard library version.

The linker has warnings as well as fatal and nonfatal errors. Some of the fatal errors—which stop linkage from taking place—deal with undefined symbols; the inability to read a file; running out of memory; lack of disk space; and invalid offset calculations from the beginning of a code, data, stack, or other segment. Most fatal errors are obvious; you know what to look for to remedy the problem. In the case of undefined symbols, the definition may have been omitted from the file, or the file may have been left out of the file list. The symbol or the module name could have been misspelled, leaving the linker unable to find the correct module.

There are few nonfatal errors, and their range usually is related to an unresolved external or file overflow. An unresolved external message occurs when the symbol was used but not defined in any of the modules given to the linker. Sometimes giving the linker another file name in which the definition of the symbol is located solves the problem. Using different memory models can cause file overflow messages.

TLINK has just a few warnings. The most common are duplicate symbol definitions that will occur in two different modules. You simply may need to delete a definition or use conditional compilation to define the symbol only once.

Some messages concern the production of .COM files using the tiny memory model option (/t). A likely cause is that your code compiles and links to a size greater than 64K, which is the maximum size allowed for a tiny model's .COM file. Condense some code and try to use library routines that take up less room. In another case, you may just have to switch to a larger model.

Table 7.4 shows briefly the possible error messages of TLINK and their meaning.

Table 7.4. TLINK Warning and Error Messages

Fatal Errors

Message: `<lsegname>:segment/group exceeds 64K`
Correction: Too much data for segment; reduce the amount of data stored.

Message: `32-bit record encountered in module XXXX: use "/3" option`
Correction: Need to generate 80386 code

Message: `Bad character in parameters`
Correction: A punctuation character was found; remove it.

Message: `Base fixup offset overflow`
Correction: 32-bit record with offset > 64K; try larger memory model.

Message: `Cannot gen. COM file: segment-relocatable items present`
Correction: A .COM file must have fixed addresses.

Message: `Cannot gen. COM file: invalid initial entry point address`
Correction: .COM file with 100H as address needed

Message: `Cannot gen. COM file: program exceeds 64K`
Correction: .COM file must be under 64K.

Fatal Errors

Message: `Cannot gen. COM file: stack segment present`
Correction: No stack segments are allowed in a .COM file.

Message: `Invalid group definition`
Correction: Replace the bad .OBJ file.

Message: `Invalid initial stack offset`
Correction: Stack pointer exceeds 64K; reduce its size.

Message: `Invalid entry point offset`
Correction: 32-bit record is larger than 64K; reduce the record size.

Message: `MSDOS error, ax = xxxxh`
Correction: Unexpected error due to DOS call; check file or disk drive.

Message: `Not enough memory`
Correction: More RAM is needed.

Message: `Relocation table full`
Correction: Fixups exceed capacity of table; try to reduce calls to `far` digital
   functions.

Message: `Undefined symbol name`
Correction: Omission or misspelling of symbol name; reenter it.

Message: `Unknown option`
Correction: Slash without option; enter an option.

Message: `Write failed, disk full?`
Correction: Check disk space; erase files no longer needed to free additional
space.

Message: `XXXXXXXX.XXX: bad object file`
Correction: Object file is not completely built; recompile the code.

Message: `XXXXXXXX.XXX: unable to open file`
Correction: File name does not exist or was misspelled; reenter the name.

Nonfatal Errors

Message: `Fixup overflow in module XXXX, at <lsegname>:xxxxh,`
   `target=<sname>`
Correction: Incorrect code or data reference.

Message: `XXX is unresolved in module YYY`
Correction: No definition was found; revise code to include one.

Table 7.4 continues

***Table* 7.4** *continued*

Warnings

Message: `Warning: XXX is duplicated in module YYY`
Correction: Symbol is defined twice; eliminate one definition.

Message: `Warning: XXX defined in module YYY is duplicated in`
`    module ZZZ`
Correction: Symbol is defined in each module; eliminate all duplicates.

Message: `Warning: no stack`
Correction: Define a stack segment.

Making the Program

You can automate the program-creation process easily during the linkage and compilation steps. The old standby is the *make file*, in which the programmer specifies each rule and dependency needed to put everything together. Turbo C, especially in the Integrated Development Environment, has made automation even simpler, turning it into child's play. This type of `make` file is the project file.

Creating a Project File

Creating a project file is extremely easy. It can be created with any ASCII editor, including the Turbo Editor. It consists mainly of the names of source code modules and library names that will be compiled and linked together to form the final executable. You may include also the names of special libraries needed, especially those not found in the default directories. The names of the source code modules can be listed in any order in the project file—they do not have to be placed in the order of compilation.

In earlier versions of Turbo C (before 2.0), the name of a source file had to be followed by any user-defined header files required for compilation, as in

```
windows (win.h)
crtwind (crt.h)
```

Now, only `windows` and `crtwind` are needed in the project file; a built-in dependency search can look automatically for dependencies. Also, before TC 2.0 you had to have the `graphics.lib` file as part of the project file if you wanted to use any of the graphics routines; Turbo C Professional has an option to control this placement—`graphics.lib` no longer must be placed in the project file. You do not have to specify the floating-point routine libraries in the project file, because Turbo C finds them automatically.

A project file is not necessary if your program consists of a single source code module and the run-time library routines. These can all be found by the compiler and processed without any further information. But if you use more than one source code module, such as one module containing the `main()` function and another module with other functions you have written, or an outside library of routines, a project file is a must with the integrated environment. Because TCC allows you to name library modules on the command line, a `make` file would not be needed for the single source code module or even for the module if it required a user-written library.

To ensure that an object file is dependent upon a header file it contains, or is dependent upon multiple header files, give the file names in parentheses after the name of the source module. This verifies that the source module will be compiled/linked if the header file has changed.

File Dependencies and the Autodependency Feature

In the simple technique of autodependency checking, the compiler opens the .OBJ file listed in the project file and reads information placed there by the compiler and linker.

The theory behind the file checking is that if the .OBJ module has a date and time earlier than the date and time of the source module from which it was created, the source module from which the .OBJ was created is recompiled. When the .EXE file has a date and time earlier than any of the component object modules, the .EXE file will be relinked and any out of date object files will be made current by recompiling them. Another part of the dependency factor is the project file itself. If it has a date later than the files it contains, those files are compiled and or linked.

Accessing .OBJ files, Vendor Routines, and Graphics

Your project file need not consist of just C source code files. You can even enter object files, libraries of routines, and modules from vendors other than Borland. Placing these files in a .PRJ file is as simple as inserting your own source modules there.

Just give object files the .OBJ extension—the compiler/linker will know how to process them. Use the .LIB extension for a library file. This method is especially useful if you have purchased routines from outside vendors and want to use them with your own program. Just create a project file and give the names of your modules along with those from the vendor, with the appropriate extension, and you should be on your way to creating an executable.

Remember that in Turbo C 2.0 you do not have to specify the graphics library file in the project file. If you turn off the option for using the graphics library, you must name the file explicitly; otherwise, the compiler uses the graphics library file by default.

Problems may occur, however, if outside modules were not compiled specifically with Turbo C in mind. Clashes between modules arise because of leading underscores on external modifiers in the Turbo C libraries. The leading underscores can be eliminated if you purchase and recompile the Turbo C run-time library source code using the −u− option; then non-C routines could be linked into your program. The source code is a separate package available only from Borland International.

There are several disadvantages to working with the Turbo C run-time library source code. First, it takes up a lot of room. The source code by itself, as installed by the diskettes onto a hard disk, consumes more than 1.5M of space. Several batch files can be used to recompile the files and create new libraries or replace the modules in existing libraries. Unless you modify these batch files, they do not clean up after themselves, and you will be left with the .OBJ file from each memory model for which you compile. If you use the ALL option to do the entire process, you should have about 5.5 to 6M of free space on the disk for all to go smoothly. Second, recompiling all of the files takes a lot of time. On a 10MHz AT-compatible the process of recompiling and creating libraries for the run-time libraries and the math routines took about four hours. Luckily, you can let this process run while you are away, so that you are spared the boredom. Do oversee the process for about the first 15 to 20 minutes, however. If an error occurs, such as one due to improper setup or the wrong command-line parameters, it will happen early on, and you can correct the problem and allow the compilation to continue.

If the outside routines were compiled or placed into libraries to be used with Microsoft C, they cannot be used by Turbo C because of incompatible .OBJ file formats. You are still stuck in this case.

Blending in Modules from Other Languages

Turbo C can integrate modules from any of the Borland family of languages, except for Turbo Pascal (which doesn't produce .OBJ modules) and Turbo BASIC. This means that you can write modules in assembly language using TASM, or you can write in Turbo Prolog and then import the routines into Turbo C. For assembly language code, the inline assembly possible with Turbo C can perform across memory models or language calling conventions. Prolog may have logic or development advantages over C, such as using a natural language front end. Prolog's handling of logic by means of "backtracking," "cuts," and other methods is very different from what goes on in a normal C program.

The topic of linking in assembly language modules is covered in Chapter 6, "Working with Turbo Assembler." There is yet another way to place assembly code inside C functions. This method, which uses __emit__()—a new function in Turbo C Version 2.0—is similar to the Turbo Pascal method of using inline hexadecimal codes in place of assembly language. This enables you to use the Turbo C Integrated Development Environment to perform compilation instead of having to use the command-line version. You are on your own here, however, because no checking at all is made on the arguments of the __emit__() function, which are the hex codes. The __emit__() function is similar to the inline code option that can be used with Turbo Pascal; hex codes are used in both. Having examples from Turbo Pascal would be more helpful than trying to convert the assembly language statements into hex codes yourself. The *Turbo C Reference Guide* has more information on the use of this function.

This does not mean that you cannot call Turbo C routines from Turbo Assembler. You can reference functions, for instance, if they are declared as external in the assembly code module using the EXTRN statement; the same method can be applied to get data from variables.

For Turbo Prolog, several rules apply to Turbo C:

❑ Functions that write to the screen—such as printf(), cprintf(), putc(), and cputc()—do not work correctly when Turbo Prolog and Turbo C are linked. There are corresponding functions in Turbo Prolog, however (such as wrch and zwf), which you can use in place of the C functions. This means your C source code will not convert directly.

❑ Memory allocation in Turbo Prolog is accomplished with routines other than those named in Turbo C. In Turbo C, calloc(), malloc(), and free() are used for memory management, but in Turbo Prolog, alloc_gstack, _malloc, and _free are used. There is no real correspondence between Turbo C's calloc() and calloc() in Turbo Prolog, and alloc_gstack works with the global stack and has no equivalent in Turbo C.

❑ Use void functions when they will be linked with Turbo Prolog. Predicates in Prolog, the "verbs" of that language, just as functions are the "verbs" of C, do not return values directly.

❑ Standard Turbo C library functions must be preceded with an underscore in the code. You must add this underscore rather than thinking that the –u option of the compiler does this adequately—it does not. In fact, the underscore option should be turned off (– u–) when you compile your Turbo C modules, and you should use the large-memory model.

❑ The memory usage of Turbo Prolog requires it to use the large-memory model in place of the smaller models. End user-defined functions with _▯ instead of having a leading underscore.

❏ The C functions must be declared as global predicates in Turbo Prolog so they will be properly recognized in the program; append `language c` to the declarations to further signal the Prolog compiler it is working with a routine from a "foreign" language.

These main rules should ensure success of code conversion for compatibility with Turbo Prolog.

One of the largest issues to consider in compiling a mixed-language program of Turbo C and Turbo Prolog is that the main program module of Turbo Prolog takes the place of the C `main()` function. Your program, therefore, essentially becomes a Prolog program. This Prolog module contains a goal in its logic of declarations and predicates.

These steps are not particularly difficult, but it is easy to forget an underscore at the beginning of a library routine, to leave in a `printf()`, or to neglect some other fine point. Any of these will, of course, cause problems in the final compilation and linking of the mixed-language modules. When you use mixed-language modules you can prevent a lot of code rewrites from one language to another. Some conversions could be extremely difficult or even impossible. The bridge to gap is much narrower between Pascal and C than between a declarative language like Prolog and a procedural language like C.

Using a Make File with the Turbo C Compiler

`MAKE` is a utility that helps keep your files up-to-date, compiling those you have not yet compiled, recompiling those with dates earlier than their source modules or header files, and linking and creating a final .EXE file. The `MAKE` utility is extremely handy. It is not the same as the Project-Make used in the Turbo C integrated environment, because it is an independent program, but `MAKE` handles the same types of file dependencies as Project-Make. `MAKE` can be used with the command-line version of Turbo C and with TLINK.

The larger your project, the more valuable `MAKE` becomes. Used for anything longer than a couple of modules, `MAKE` is well worth any effort needed to master it and put it into action. `MAKE` can save enormous amounts of time by avoiding recompilations and faulty linkages caused by omitting a file name from the command line or forgetting to include a library. The same is true for Project-Make, which you must use with multimodule programs in the integrated environment. It is a simple tool often overlooked in the role of version control.

`MAKE` is particularly useful when you need to recompile or relink a program you worked on long ago (and now you can't remember exactly what you did to create the program). Another nice feature of `MAKE` is that it generates not only object files but also executable files and even libraries.

Invoking MAKE

`MAKE` looks first for a file called `makefile.mak`. The convention for giving it a different file name with instructions is

```
make -ffindf.mak
```

where `-f` means that the following parameter is a file name and should be used in place of `makefile.mak`. `MAKE` also looks automatically for a file called `builtins.mak`, which contains frequently used macros and rules. The `builtins.mak` program is discussed later in this section on `MAKE`.

`MAKE` can also be called with command-line options, which are case sensitive. These options cover include-file names, defines, and help. Another option is whether `MAKE` is "verbal" in displaying each command executed. Table 7.5 summarizes the options.

Table 7.5. *MAKE command-line options.*

Option	Action
-a	Turn on autodependency
-Diden	Make identifier true
-Diden=str	Make identifier assume value of `str` (string)
-Idir	Find include files in directory `dir`
-Uiden	Undefine identifier
-?, -h	Display help for Make
-ffilnam	Use `filnam` as makefile
-n	Display but do not execute commands ("Noisy")
-s	Do not display commands ("Silence")

Creating a Make File

A `make` file is created with any ASCII editor, such as the Turbo C editor. When you create a `make` file, you customarily start with the executable files as product, use it as the "root," and then work your way up the trunk and branches of a "tree" until you come to the "leaves" (or at least to the branches). The root, or executable, is followed by a list of the modules of which the program is made. Basically, each module is listed in turn, again followed by any modules upon which it is dependent, including C source modules, assembly code, libraries, and header files. Normally, after the line or lines listing the modules, an instruction or instructions are given telling the compiler or linker what to do to put together the modules on the preceding line or lines. The first line of the `make` file, if it is to produce an executable, usually has a `tlink` instruction under it, and `tcc` commands would be below the other lines to create .OBJ modules. Library modules would use `tlib` with parameters under the dependency list.

Listing 7.1 shows a sample make file. Some say that languages like Prolog enable programmers to tell the computer "how" to do something, and then the computer solves the problem. MAKE is not that intelligent; you must tell it not only "how" to do the problem, but also "what" should go together.

Listing 7.1

```
findf.exe : readfil.obj scanlin.obj maklst.obj prtres.obj
    tlink lib\c0s readfil scanlin, maklst, prtres \
        lib\cs
readfil.obj : openfil.c readfil.c closfil.c readfil.h
    tcc -c -ms -f readfil.c

scanlin.obj : scanlin.c lexan.c lex.h
    tcc -c -ms -f scanlin.c

maklst.obj : maklst.c maklst.h
    tcc -c -ms -f maklst.c

prtres.obj : sprt.c prtrpt.c prtres.c prtres.h
    tcc -c -ms -f prtres.c
```

Note that the backslash at the end of the second line in listing 7.1 acts as a *continuation character*, telling MAKE to look on the next line for part of the command. Note also certain paths, such as lib\, before some file names. These paths signify that lib\ is a subdirectory within the current directory. If your system is not arranged in this way, you must specify a different path.

Here the program findf.exe is intended to find the functions in a source file and create a list of those functions as declarations. The executable is composed of the modules readfil.obj, scanlin.obj, maklst.obj, and ptrres.obj. If MAKE sees that any of these object files is newer than findf.exe, it relinks the executable using TLINK.

In the next line, the object file readfil.obj is made of openfil.c, readfil.c, and closfil.c, and uses readfil.h. Notice the use of tcc to compile the module rather than TLINK to link pieces together. If you leave out the -c option, TLINK would be called to link the modules after compilation. If any of the C source files or the header file here is newer than readfil.obj, the source files are recompiled. The same goes for the remaining object modules such as scanlin.obj, maklst.obj, and ptrres.obj. Building this hierarchy within a make file allows MAKE to examine any C source file, header file, library, and so on that composes the executable. MAKE does a date comparison between the files. Anything older than the newest module is recompiled or linked, ensuring that your object file is current with the latest changes.

Again, MAKE works by comparing file dates. If an object module or executable—or perhaps even a library—is older than a source module or header file upon which it depends, the module will be rebuilt. Suppose that you created a C source file and a header file it uses (cscan.c and cscan.h) on 2/11/89. You also compiled cscan.c on 2/11/89 and have an .OBJ file of cscan.obj with the same date (date includes the time). Later, on 2/25/89, if you open the header file and add a field to the structure, the object file is out-of-date, and the make file will cause cscan.c to be recompiled. Even if the object or executable file exists, each component source module or .OBJ file is checked by date and time. Other utilities that change the time stamp of your files, if used improperly, are likely to cause files to be compiled/linked when they shouldn't be processed.

Another useful feature of make files is that they are constructed similarly between compilers; if you learn how to prepare a make file on one, you basically can use the same technique on another computer system. The punctuation or syntax may be slightly different, but the general principles are the same.

Turbo C Professional's MAKE also works with both explicit and implicit rules. In checking file dependencies, MAKE can take the –a option to signal autodependency checks, thus enabling the programmer to keep track of the files more readily. The example in listing 7.1 used all explicit dependencies. An implicit dependency would generalize the situation. For example, each of the .OBJ modules contains at least one module with the same name as the object file (along with other source code files). You could generalize this portion of the instructions and correct them to an implicit dependency:

```
.c.obj:
    tcc -c -ms -f $<
```

This syntax uses a macro, $<, and tells MAKE that all object modules are dependent on a .C file of the same full name. Other implicit rules could considerably shorten the make file and further generalize the files. The full make file with implicit rules appears in listing 7.2.

Listing 7.2

```
#  Implicit Rules--next line uses .C name for .OBJ
.c.obj:
    tcc -c -ms -f $<

findf.exe : readfil.obj scanlin.obj maklst.obj prtres.obj
    tlink lib\c0s readfil scanlin, maklst, prtres \
        lib\cs

readfil.obj : openfil.c closfil.c readfil.h
```

Listing 7.2 continues

Listing 7.2 *continued*

```
scanlin.obj : lexan.c lex.h

maklst.obj : maklst.h

prtres.obj : sprt.c prtrpt.c prtres.h
```

This version of the `make` file has only implicit rules for compilation. The main differences come in the groups below the first used to actually create the .EXE file. These lines now lack the `tcc` instruction; also, the .C file name that duplicated the .OBJ file has been removed from the file list after each object module. Two lines telling MAKE to use the .C file to create an object file of the same name were added at the beginning. This example follows the old story: "Let the computer do the work for you."

Listing 7.2 also includes a new feature: a comment. The normal C syntax of `/**/` is not used for comments in a `make` file; rather, `make` file comments are marked by a pound sign (#). Each comment line needs only an opening marker because there is no closing marker to tell MAKE where the comment ends.

Using Macros with MAKE

MAKE has other advanced features that make life simpler. *Macros* can be created to replace file lists, memory-model options, or other command-line options. Basically, anything that is repeated can be made into a macro. Macros are just like using a `#define` in a source code file; to change a macro, you simply make the change once instead of many times.

Macros are simple to create, following the case-sensitive form

```
macroName = text
```

where you can use or omit the white space around the equal sign. To use the macro, a dollar sign and parentheses must be used:

```
$(macroName)
```

MAKE also has several predefined macros, listed in table 7.6.

Table 7.6. *Predefined Macros in MAKE*

Macro	Meaning	Example
$d	Defined test	!if !$d(LARGE)
$*	Base file name	c:\mywrk\readfil
$<	Full file name	c:\mywrk\readfil.c

Macro	Meaning	Example
$.	File name path	`c:\mywrk`
$.	File name and extension	`readfil.c`
$&	File name only	`readfil`

MAKE Directives

Turbo C's MAKE utility even allows conditions to be met through the use of directives. These directives are similar to the conditional compilation directives used by the C preprocessor. The big difference is that MAKE directives start with an exclamation point (!) instead of a pound sign (#).

The directives !include, !if, !else, !elif, !endif, !error, and !undef offer lots of flexibility for developing your make files. The directive !error, which is not a part of the preprocessor language, allows an error message to be displayed. The text for the message is given following the !error directive, and will be output when an error occurs. Table 7.7 lists the directives with examples.

Table 7.7. *Directives in MAKE*

Directive	Example
!include	`!include "make1.mk"`
!if	`!if $d(LARGE)`

!else	`!if $d(LARGE)`
	`        tcc -c -LARGE ...`
	`!else`
	`        tcc -c -SMALL ...`

!elif	`!if $d(LARGE)`
	`        tcc -c -LARGE ...`
	`!elif $d(MEDIUM)`
	`        tcc -c -MEDIUM ...`
	`!elif $d(SMALL)`
	`        tcc -c -SMALL ...`

!endif	`!endif`
!error	`!error Compilation aborted`

Now try living dangerously—use these directives to process modules from the sample `make` file under different memory models, assuming that pointer usage within them was used carefully. Listing 7.3 shows the result of the directives and macros in the file.

Listing 7.3

```
LARGE = l
SMALL = ms
MED = mm

#  Implicit Rules--next line uses .C name for .OBJ
!if !$d(MED)
.c.obj:
        tcc -c -SMALL -f $<
!else
.c.obj:
        tcc -c -MED -f $<
!endif

findf.exe : readfil.obj scanlin.obj maklst.obj prtres.obj
        tlink lib\cOLARGE readfil scanlin, maklst, prtres \
            lib\cLARGE

readfil.obj : openfil.c closfil.c readfil.h

scanlin.obj : lexan.c lex.h

maklst.obj : maklst.h

prtres.obj : sprt.c prtrpt.c prtres.h
```

Remember that the `lib\` subdirectory in this example may be different from what you have on your system. Remember also that the exclamation point in front of the `if` is a signal to MAKE and *not* a sign of negation, as is the exclamation point before the `$d`. The rules require that if the medium memory model has not been defined, the compiler use the small model or the medium model if it has been defined. The rules require linking using the large model, however, and bets are on that this mixing of models does not work!

Even such C operators as `<`, `%`, and `&&` can be used in expressions working with the directives. With operators, the code could convey something like: "If the tiny memory model or the small memory model is defined, then ..." as in

```
!if $d(TINY) || $d(SMALL)
    ...
!endif
```

Turbo C is loaded with extras; it even offers a different way to reuse macros and rules. A special file, called `builtins.mak`, is provided for this purpose as an alternative to both using the include directive and putting these macros and rules in every make file you produce. MAKE looks for this file before any other make file to include the information in its processing of the make file.

As you can see, MAKE is a versatile utility. It beats a batch file hands down (don't use them) in automating compilation and linking files, and it has the power to make decisions, if you want it to. MAKE should be one of your closest friends if you are using the command-line version of Turbo C. Use it often and you should have fewer problems in producing your final program.

Building the Program

You can build a program simply by selecting a Compile menu option of the Turbo C Integrated Development Environment. The Build All option here is distinctly different from the Compile and Link options directly above it. Build All is like performing an entire make on all of the modules and does no date checking on them. Because Build All redoes everything from scratch, prepare to spend some time waiting. You will have to use Build All if you compile a program using the normal make EXE file with one memory model and then need to recompile under a different memory model. You can be assured, however, of having the latest, most complete version when Build All is finished.

This process resembles that of making a change in all of the C source modules and header files and then recompiling and linking. The process also resembles that of the TOUCH utility, which changes the date and time stamps on all the source files to make them newer than the object files and executables so that recompilation and relinking occurs. You may need the TOUCH utility for your code. It lives up to its names and "touches" a file only to the extent of changing the date and time stamp to the current date and time. This makes that file "newer" than the object modules it produced. TOUCH is simpler than using an editor to rewrite the source file as a new version, because the utility does not have to modify the file—and the editor won't even work on binary files.

In another sense, building a program includes all of the steps you have seen so far, and then some. It starts with setting down requirements and supplementing, changing, or deleting them later in the process. A design stage usually follows, especially for more complicated portions of the program or for interfacing pieces of it. Next comes the actual writing of the code, following the algorithms established during the design phase. This is followed by the cycle of compiling, linking, and editing with the hope of creating a product close to what you planned.

By this stage you have spent perhaps two-thirds to three-quarters of the time initially set aside for the project—if you make a fairly accurate guesstimate of the time allotted to the undertaking. If not, you already may have exceeded the original estimate, perhaps by a factor of two or three if problems arose.

If your code deals with multiple hardware configurations, myriad problems can arise. Chips, boards, communications, parity, peripherals, and handshaking can factor into delays. In software, lack of adequate error checking, bad algorithms, misunderstanding requirements, and other considerations can also lead to delays and problems. Group projects can have a different set of factors related to personnel, a lack of communication between members, sick and vacation days, and more. All such elements eventually contribute to "building" a program.

Being successful at a project involves many factors. Although I have covered many of them, there are still quite a few to go. The biggest area is the testing/ debugging cycle to iron out the problems, "spray" out the bugs, and meet the users' requirements to bring them a healthy, usable program.

Testing and Debugging the Program as a Whole

A good portion of this book is devoted to the importance of testing and debugging a program. (Chapter 9, "Testing and Debugging Strategies," covers testing in detail.) These program-development skills seem to be lacking from many programmers' repertoires of tools and utilities. Testing is sometimes not well understood by programmers because they lack training in this area, which is unfortunate. Not only is testing extremely important, but it also can be much more creative and stimulating than you may think. Testing is difficult for a programmer to do on his or her own project or module—it is hard to see someone "attack" your creation and find fault with it. But in most cases you will have to test your own program.

Try to turn that attitude around. Think of it as an opportunity to learn how to avoid generating the same problem twice and to provide greater customer satisfaction. Testing code can increase your efficiency, give you more time to spend on other project aspects, possibly reduce the time needed to complete the project. (If your customers are satisfied, testing may even be instrumental in securing a second project from them.)

Testing is essential. Granted, it can be more beneficial (and less painful) to observe ways to prevent problems before they occur, but testing prevents many problems from getting out the door (your customers won't appreciate doing your testing for you!). This is a difference between quality control and quality assurance: quality control fixes errors, and quality assurance tries to prevent them. Quality assurance groups are becoming more prevalent in the software industry.

Benefits of Testing Code

Getting rid of errors before your code reaches the customers will improve their opinion of the program. Even if the program is meant for your own use, testing will uncover malfunctions that could cause problems later. Getting 100 records into a database only to find that it has mixed up several fields, or worse yet, that you cannot change anything once the data is inside, is better discovered up front.

Testing as a whole helps you view the program as the customer sees it. Try to assume the same frame of reference as your customers and to view the program as if through their eyes. If the program is for your own use, you might not need all of the safeguards and bells and whistles requested by many different users. On the other hand, you may be more tolerant of program aspects that would be unacceptable to customers. Help and error messages are usually good examples of this. "Computerese," readily understood by programmers, is still Greek to most users. For example, users are not likely to understand the message `Error to key for Quicksort Routine`. They should more readily grasp the meaning if the message is reworded (without computer jargon) as `Last name field must be all caps`. By the way, because changing text to all uppercase is another example of something the computer should do automatically for the user, this error message should not be necessary!

Testing is usually a series of steps. You work with pieces of the program or the entire program to find out what the bugs are and list them. Working with an individual function or a module apart from the program is called *unit testing*. It is one of the most fundamental steps and should always be carried out. Bugs not caught here will just pass on to the next steps.

Working with more than one piece of the program, such as two modules that interact, is called *integration testing* and is also very important. For C programs, checking parameters for problems is part of integration testing, which also may involve checking other types of communications and information exchange, side effects, and so on, between modules. Test *drivers*, small programs written to test an individual function, module, or program section, may be used in testing.

In yet another type of testing, called *regression testing*, tests are repeated either to verify that an error has occurred or to retest after fixes or changes have been made, because making changes can cause new glitches to appear. Regression testing is a prime candidate for automation.

Another type of testing is *system testing*, which works with the entire application system. The exercising of the program here is similar to beta testing by customers. Systems testing is sometimes called *alpha testing* when it is done "in-house." This testing then switches to the Greek alphabet character, *beta*, when it is in the potential customers' hands. Sometimes there is even a *gamma*, or *preproduction* release that is probably very close to the final product but still has a few problems. Customer testing is called by a number of names. Acceptance testing, validation testing, system testing, and beta testing can all mean the same thing. *Validation testing* refers to the specific activity of proving that the program does what it is supposed to do. It checks data for correctness and may be compared to older methods, either manual or computerized, done prior to program implementation. Table 7.8 gives an overview of testing types.

Table 7.8. *Types of Program Testing*

Test Name	Purpose
Unit	Test individual functions or modules
Integration	Test two or more modules or program sections
Regression	Test repeated on partial or whole program
System	Test the whole program
Acceptance, Validation	Test (by user) of the whole program

Examples of Testing and Debugging

The process of debugging is part of testing. Once a glitch has been identified, the programmer may do further tests to locate the bug, or perhaps the information is already present from testing. When the bug is located, a fix is attempted, tests are done, and the cycle repeats itself until the bug is actually declared vanquished and removed from the list.

If you still have trouble understanding the difference between testing and debugging, here are some additional ways to distinguish them. Testing usually is done on a higher level than debugging. Code is not normally examined, except perhaps as a secondary process. Testing uses drivers, program portions, sets of data, data dictionaries, and so on, to execute the code and supply information. Debugging is actually locating the line of code in which the problem resides and then providing a fix.

Testing might consist of entering data on a data-entry screen and finding that a number is left-justified instead of right-justified in a field, or using a device driver to operate a printer in a particular font and character pitch. Nothing is fixed during testing: errors are just identified.

Debugging entails locating the data-entry routine, checking to see where the line or lines of C code are to perform justification, and then fixing them. In the example of the device driver, if the font were incorrect, the line sending instructions to the printer for font control would have to be found, a fix applied (such as changing an escape sequence), and then a retest performed.

These are rather opposite examples of both testing and debugging, but sometimes the two do overlap. Whatever the case, both are important steps in producing a program.

Debugging is easier if you have hardware or source code debuggers on hand and specially written debugging routines for performing assertions, displaying error messages, tracking changes in the heap and stack, and so on. Turbo C Professional's integrated and stand-alone debuggers are tremendous assets in this area. Their versatility in looking at the program in different ways can greatly reduce the amount of time needed to write drivers and other routines to find out what is going on inside the code. One of the biggest advantages of the Turbo C stand-alone Debugger is being able to examine source code and either machine code or data, or both, at the same time.

So why are bugs still found in a program? There are a number of reasons. Presumably it is not because testing on the program was done minimally or not at all. The logic of programs—and this logic seems to be proportional to the size of the program—can be very complex. It usually is impossible to test every case and every path. Even for the simplest cases, it might take years to accomplish complete coverage of all cases and paths, if it were possible at all. In the case of path coverage, which is a specialized area of testing, what if the path does not exist in the first place? Not having the path at all might be considered an even larger error than if the path were there but worked incorrectly. The strategy to apply here is to find the most important problems, test and fix them first, and then go after more minor ones. Testing is in part creative, especially when it comes to thinking of test cases. On a one-person project, it is hard for that one person to think of all the ways a user might work with the program. Even a large amount of creativity will not uncover all the cases here.

Types of Bugs and Types of Tests

Bugs can also be classified. *Fatal* and *Nonfatal*, two high-level categories, can be broken down further into categories organized by level of destructiveness. For example, minor bugs normally deal only with appearance or trivial items. Major bugs perhaps cause miscalculations or take a lot of time to fix. The moderate bugs fall in between.

Minimizing the cases left out of the test sequence is part of testing methodology. Techniques were developed to test areas that bugs seem to frequent. Upper and lower boundaries, interfaces, and the like seem to attract glitches. Testing methods are available for these areas. It is amazing how many errors can be caught by checking for numbers less than the proposed lower limit, such as negative numbers below a limit of 0 or fields that accept more than the 10 characters they should. But then there are always the "creepy crawlies"—glitches that appear only intermittently and cannot be reproduced at will—caused by pointer and memory problems. This class of bugs can be especially difficult to track and exterminate.

When you test a program, develop a *test plan*—a strategy you use to go through the code systematically. Testing "by chance" will of course uncover some bugs, but it leaves a far greater likelihood of missing others that will haunt you later. Entire portions of the program may never even be reached if you are haphazard in testing and debugging. Unfortunately, test plans are lackluster and not the most exciting thing to work on. Being creative and thinking of test cases that normally would not occur may not only help to add interest to the subject, but also may actually uncover more problems.

Unfortunately, automation in the area of testing is not well advanced. Some programs work in some cases, but usually not for all kinds of programs. Path analyzers, test-case generators, regression testers, and others are available for certain needs.

Configuration Management and Source Code Control

Earlier in this discussion I mentioned regression testing and its use in retesting programs after changes or fixes are made. A major reason for its use is to check not only that the fix actually worked, but also that no side effects took place, and indeed, that all of the prior changes and the state of the program were preserved in the current program. This process is a matter of version control.

Version control involves a couple of issues. One is that the changes and fixes do indeed go into the current version for testing, updating, and so on. A second issue is that at some time previous versions can be reconstructed and reliably assume the same form they had originally. In some ways, version control is a form of backup or archiving. Version control is also part of a larger picture called *configuration management*, which deals with the entire scope of how pieces are put together, how versions are produced, how bugs are tracked in each version, how changes are authorized and tracked, and other factors.

Version Control Techniques

On a PC, version control is virtually nonexistent without special tools. Turbo C offers only the very primitive form by making backup (.BAK) files of the C source code modules so that you can access the very last version. In many instances this is not even barely adequate. Unlike some other operating systems, DOS has nothing built in for version control, such as file version numbers. A hard disk is essential when you produce previous versions on-line. Disks can be used to archive earlier forms. You can create your own form of version control by using subdirectories for each distinct version and placing the appropriate source code there. Having a thorough project or make file is of utmost importance here for introducing a reliability factor in reconstructing the version. Relying on memory is an extremely poor substitute.

Versions of a certain age can be archived in backup or other formats and put onto disks for storage. Minor versions may not have to be kept at all, but it is advantageous to at least keep versions given to customers. If they report an error, it is essential that you try to recreate the glitch. If it can be re-created, there really is a problem and you can start tracking it down. If it can't be repeated, further investigation is necessary to see whether the user misunderstood the instructions or did something wrong, or whether you have a particularly nasty bug.

In a different matter, version control can help you keep your sanity. You might create a new version of the program, only to test it and find that your fix does not work, although it tested correctly a half hour ago. You investigate and find that an older version of the module was linked in because you gave the link command manually on the command line. You could eliminate the error by using the current version of the module in a make file or project file. There is also no substitute for version control when you are developing version 4.1 of the program and your customer calls with a problem found in 3.5. Without version control, you may have no way to get back to that version, even by attempting to recreate it from old source modules.

Yet another reason for maintaining version control (heaven forbid!) is that a major bug might be found in the version you are now shipping (with the promise of a *free* upgrade). If you can get back to the latest stable version, you can perhaps continue shipping the code until the problem is solved.

Even if you can get back to the earlier version, there are other matters to consider. Perhaps some difference in the operating system has crept in since the last release, or maybe you have set the buffers or files in your CONFIG.SYS file differently from when the version was tested. Getting as much information as possible about the conditions surrounding the problem is vital to solving it.

Version Numbering

When you produce a version, you should have a method of assigning a version number to it. Perhaps this will be just a "major" version number such as 1, 2, or 3. Many times you see numbers like 3.21 or 5.4a. Everybody has some scheme for numbering the versions. These numbers can relate to major fixes, functionality enhancements, or other factors. Sometimes any and all versions are released, and other times releases may occur only on version numbers such as 3.0, 4.0, and so on. It will help you refer to the proper release to have such a number.

Special programs are available for providing source code control and version management on the PC. If you have a fair amount of source code to manage, they could be beneficial to you. Even if they do not fit your needs, you should have some of the programs for configuration management, procedures, and policies to help you control your program environment.

Develop a policy that helps your customers. If you are developing a commercial application, remember that your customers do not want to be notified of an update every three months. Unless major errors occur and must be fixed, it is probably better to release only major versions that provide not only fixes but also significant enhancements to the product in terms of functionality and performance.

The Final .EXE (.COM) File

At this point you have created the finished product. The program has been defined, designed, coded, debugged, tested, stamped for approval, and placed under version control. It is robust, meets user requirements, and you know it can withstand some punishment and recover gracefully. For a commercial product, you may yet have documentation to prepare (user or technical manuals), but the product itself is ready. This is a completely different area, but also an extremely important one. Good documentation can make a big difference in the expectations users have of the product. The process of program development is not a simple one, and every year new models are proposed to make development more efficient or to improve certain steps. There are always repetitive loops along the way, with the size of the cycle changing as you add information, recognize problems, and accomplish solutions. The "Standard Software Development Lifecycle" rarely exists in the real world.

If you have met your customers' wishes and requirements and the program is sound and effective, they should be happy with the product, and you should be proud to have been a part of producing it. You probably learned a great deal along the way, much of which can be applied to future projects to improve them even more.

Summary

This chapter has covered the final steps of program development related to compiling and linking the final executable. Also discussed were some of the utilities that can be used when problems arise—map files, symbol tables, removing debugging information from binary files, and so on. TLINK and MAKE also were examined. Finally, this chapter presented an overview of testing and debugging techniques.

There is still more on testing and debugging, especially related to using the new products of the integrated debugger and the stand-alone debugger. Part III of this book should help you maximize your use of these tools in examining your program for the inevitable quirks and bugs. Study them carefully, gleaning what tips you can for testing and improving your programs.

Alan
Plantz

CHAPTER

8

Using TCC, the
Command-line Compiler

Until now, most of my discussion has centered on the Integrated Development
Environment (IDE) and the use of this version of the Turbo C compiler. Borland also gives you the option of using TCC—a stand-alone, command-line version
of the compiler. Although TCC is more powerful than the integrated version (since
the compiler allows .ASM file generation from C source files and also using inline
assembler), it is not as convenient to use in most cases. It must be used in some
instances, however, such as compiling source within make files. TCC must be used
also when inline assembly code is part of a C module, and it will be helpful when
you work with other languages such as Prolog, and perhaps others in the future.

As with other command-line-driven programs, you will see error messages and
other information scan by on the screen as the program executes. Because these
errors and messages are not caught in a separate window as they are in the integrated compiler, you must be careful or you will lose some of the information. The
output can be redirected to a file if you want to keep track of everything. Because
TCC is not an integrated development environment, you sacrifice other features by
using it. There is no way to get directly from the error message to the line of code
in the editor. There is no way to use a project file; a more detailed make file must
be used instead to demonstrate dependencies and compilation and linking rules.
There is no way to get directly into the editor without having to load it. To produce
an executable file, you must call the compiler and the linker separately.

If you have a favorite editor other than the one supplied with the integrated
environment, using it with the command-line compiler version is not so bad. You
could also use a different linker. If you have worked mainly with command-line
compilers and feel more comfortable with them, you do not have to sacrifice that
comfort with Turbo C.

231

You use the command-line version also when you purchase and use the run-time library source for the C library. This package contains the source for the basic routines but does not include the graphics library or floating-point routines. However, you can learn and accomplish quite a bit by viewing or modifying the source code. Batch files are provided to perform the compilation, linking, and even rebuilding libraries or replacing the modules within the libraries. These batch files can perform their tasks only with TCC and not the integrated version of TC.

If the name of the game is to be more productive, more efficient, and speed up and make more sound the process of producing a program, why use the stand-alone versions of the compiler, linker, and debugger? In most cases, the independent compiler and linker provide no added functionality unless you are working with assembly code; and although the stand-alone debugger offers features not offered by the integrated debugger, probably 80 to 90 percent of normal debugging, unless you use a great deal of assembly code or inline assembly, can be done with the integrated debugger. You might also need to use TCC if you run out of memory while working in the integrated environment. The integrated environment naturally requires more memory than the stand-alone compiler because of on-line help and other extra features. Not only is turnaround time magnitudes shorter with the integrated environment than with the standalones, but the IDE also prevents much trouble and saves many keystrokes. If you have not given it a try, I urge you to strongly consider the Turbo C Integrated Development Environment, because it is easy to use and makes for quicker development time. In this day and age, speed can often mean extra dollars.

Clearly, the command-line parameters and options viable with TCC are important. The following sections discuss these parameters and options and how you can use them effectively for development.

The general form for using TCC is

```
tcc [options] file[s]
```

where [options] could represent any of the options available, and at *least* one file can be given on the command line signifying the .C source file to compile.

The options for the command-line compiler can be broken into several major groups:

Environment options   Source code   Linker options

    Compiler options
    Code generation
    Error messages
    Macros
    Memory models
    Optimization
    Naming segments

Actually, the options and parameter specification can be obtained by just entering **tcc** at the DOS prompt. A data screen shows which options are available.

Environment Options

The environment options (`-I`, `-L`, `-n`) manage where the compiler looks for files and where it places the files it produces. Note that TCC's options are case sensitive. For example, `-I` tells the compiler the names of include files, whereas `-i` is used to set the length of identifier names.

`-Idirectory` — This option searches the directory specified for include files, in addition to the current directory. More than one `-I` option may be cited, and valid drives and directory paths may also be part of the directory name. More than one directory could be given by placing a semicolon between directory names, as in

    -Ic:\tc\incl;c:\mywork\myincl

`-Ldirectory` — This option, `-L`, is for the linker. It causes the linker to get the Turbo C start-up files from the standard library, because the linker usually looks for them in the current directory. These start-up files include c0X.cbj, cX.lib, mathX.lib, emu.lib, and fp87.lib. The X stands for a single-letter abbreviation for a memory model: T = tiny, S = small, C = compact, M = medium, L = large, and H = huge. Again, the semicolon could be used to separate more than one directory with this option, as used in the `-I` option.

The compiler can accept multiple `-I` or `-L` options per line, or you can specify all directories to search using a single option indicator and multiple directories, as in:

    -Lc:\tc\incl -Lc:\tc\obj

or

    -Lc:\tc\incl;c:\tc\obj

`-nxxx` — This option (`-n`) forces the output to be placed on the drive, directory, or path as specified by xxx, or the output files are placed in the current directory.

Compiler Options

The compiler options can be separated further into the following categories: code generation, error messages, macros, memory models, optimization, naming segments, and source code options. These are items the compiler can affect in its operation.

Code-Generation Options

Code-generation command-line options may be used often, because they directly affect the .OBJ file produced. The options can also affect debugging, floating-point operations, and other tasks.

-1	(One, not lowercase *L*) tells the compiler to produce 80186 instructions and 80286 real-mode instructions. Be careful. Code compiled with this option will not execute on 808x-based machines like older PCs.
-a	Alignment is affected here and is either on a byte or word boundary. Alignment can be a problem when you use a C struct to overlay a data structure already in memory, especially one created by another process.
-d	Literal strings are merged when the strings match. This consumes less space.
-f*xx*	This option affects floating-point math in several ways:

f87 Causes 8087 instructions, rather than emulation, to be used. Use this option with caution; remember that this code does not run on a machine that does not have a math coprocessor.

f Because the 8087 instructions are emulated instead of being produced inline, this code runs on any machine.

-f Turns off both emulation and inline production of floating-point math code. Beware of erratic behavior or error messages if your program contains floating-point math and you have turned off this parameter.

-K	Forces unsigned char types. This may be a portability consideration, depending on which type of processor the code is targeted for. The problem appears when you try to promote a char into larger types such as short, int, or long.

-k	A standard stack frame is generated. The compiler or debugger can trace through the stack frame in case of an error (caused perhaps by misuse of routines with a variable number of arguments or runaway recursion). Because a frame is created for each function and can overlay stack frames from other functions, information for a function other than the one currently executing may be corrupted.
-N	This option provides stack-overflow error-message generation. The code for producing the error is placed at the beginning of every function. Program execution speed and size is increased but, because a stack overflow can be almost impossible to detect, is well worth the trouble. Processes such as recursion can cause stack overflow.
-p	The Pascal type of parameter passing and stack cleanup are employed instead of the normal C sequence (right to left). A function with a variable number of arguments cannot be written unless specified as cdecl. Execution is quicker than usual.
-u	Identifiers in the C language are preceded by an underscore. If this option is turned off, your source will not be compatible with the run-time library routines unless you have recompiled the run-time library with this same option turned off. Pascal-type identifiers are not preceded by an underscore.
-v	Debugging information is placed in the object file and is also passed along to the executable. Again, because this can add bulk to the files, it could be turned off at the last compilation to produce smaller, quicker programs.
-y	Line numbers are placed in the .OBJ file to be used by a debugger (other than Borland's debuggers, which know the line-number information). This option could be turned off during the "last" compilation to produce a smaller object file after all debugging has taken place.

Error Message Options

Error messages enable the programmer to turn warnings and error messages on or off and to specify the maximum number of messages to be generated before the compiler stops. The messages are further grouped as in the Integrated Development Environment. ANSI Violations, Common Errors, Less Common Errors, and Portability Warnings are included, with default ON/OFF information shown.

-g#	Specifies the number of error messages *and* warnings that can be produced before compilation ceases.
-j#	Specifies the number of error messages only (not warnings) after which compilation ceases.
-wxxx	Turns on error or warning message *xxx*.
-w-xxx	Turns off error or warning message *xxx*.

ANSI Violation Options

-wbig	The associated octal or hexadecimal constant is too large for the compiler to handle properly. Respecify the constant. (ON)
-wdup	The identifier XXXXXXXX has been redefined, but the redefinition does not match the original definition. Look for the original definition and make sure that both declarations or definitions match. (ON)
-wret	The return of the function and the return of a value within the function are used improperly. Examine the syntax of the return. (ON)
-wstr	The identifier XXXXXXXX is not part of the structure specified. Replace with the correct member name. (Or you may have used the wrong structure name.) (ON)
-wstu	The structure signified by identifier XXXXXXXX is undefined. You probably misspelled the structure name or forgot to define it. (ON)
-wsus	The pointer conversion in the statement is suspicious; in other words, it probably needs a cast or is incorrect in some other syntactical way. (ON)
-wvoi	This function is void and should not return a value. Look for a return within the body of the function and remove it or change the return type of the function from void to what is needed. (ON)
-wzst	The structure has no length (zero-length structure). You have forgotten to specify any members for it. (ON)

Common Error Options

-waus	The identifier is assigned a value that is never used. This could be simply because it was declared but you did not need to use it, it was declared but you *forgot* to use it, or perhaps you used it nested in parentheses, such as in an if statement, and the parentheses are not correct. (ON)

-wdef	You may have tried to use the identifier before it was defined. Look for a prototype (or lack thereof), for a function, and whether the declaration of a local variable was missed. (ON)
-weff	This code has no effect; look for too many braces, an incorrect if statement, and so on before this code fragment. The compiler is saying that it cannot execute the statement under any circumstances. (ON)
-wpar	The parameter mentioned is not used. Either you have forgotten to use it correctly, or it may be "extra" and you can delete it from the function's parameter list. (ON)
-wpia	An assignment could be incorrect. You may need to use = = instead of =. (ON)
-wrch	Code that cannot be compiled (unreachable) has been found. Check branches of logic (if statements), placement of return statements (return signals the end of a function), or braces. (ON)
-wrvl	The function has been declared as returning a value (non-void) but does not return a value. The declaration may be wrong or you may have an improperly formed return statement. (OFF)
	Note that this is the only error message in this group that is OFF by default. Because this error is fairly common, you may want to use the -w option to turn on all messages the first time you compile.

Less Common Error Options

-wamb	Operators in the statement are ambiguous and require extra parentheses. Add missing parentheses. (OFF)
-wamp	The ampersand, the "address of" operator in C, has been used with an array name; this is unnecessary, as the name of an array *is* an address. (OFF)
-wnod	No declaration for this function exists. This may be because you have not given the include file for the function or have forgotten to define it. (OFF)
-wpro	A call has been made to a function with no prototype. Add the correct include file or add the prototype. (OFF)

−wstv   The structure was passed by value instead of by address; perhaps the & operator was omitted. This is a warning; the decision is left to the programmer, because a structure can be passed by value in ANSI C. (OFF)

−wuse   This warning means that the identifier was declared but not used; you may have misspelled its name or you may not have wanted to use the variable or constant. (OFF)

Portability Warning Options

−wapt   A nonportable pointer assignment was encountered; a cast should fix the problem. (ON)

−wcln   The constant just found by the compiler is too long and should be shortened to fit the machine used. (OFF)

−wcpt   A nonportable pointer comparison was attempted, perhaps by trying to assign to a pointer, without using a cast, a variable that is not a pointer.

−wrng   The constant is out of range in the comparison just performed. Check the upper and lower limits of the numeric type used for the machine. This most likely deals with chars or ints. (ON)

−wrpt   A conversion of a nonportable return type has occurred. Again, this probably deals with size. (ON)

−wsig   The conversion just performed may lose significant digits. You may need a cast or to change a type here. (OFF)

−wucp   Pointers have been mixed between using signed and unsigned characters; check the cast. The use of these pointers can cause bugs that are extremely difficult to find. (OFF)

Macro Options

Macros affect the #defines within a source file and how they are defined. This is like the Define option of the Integrated Development Environment, except here you give the definitions of macros on the command-line (or in the tcconfig.c configuration file). This saves having to go into the source file to make changes, such as redefining a macro from 1 to 0 or vice versa.

Memory-Model Options

Memory models can be selected by using the −mx option, where the x stands for a memory model by the letters c, h, l, m, s, or t for compact, huge, large, medium, small, or tiny, respectively.

Optimization Options

Optimization options allow you to choose the optimizations available in the IDE:

-G   Allows the compiler to use speed (rather than size) optimizations.

-O   Works on jumps and loops to make statements such as `for` and `switch` more efficient.

-r   Affects register variables by turning them on or off. This can cause complications when you use assembly language because of preserving register status; be extra careful if you turn it off.

-Z   Signals to the compiler to use the contents of registers as often as possible instead of reloading them all the time. This option, which is extremely prone to errors, is best left alone.

Naming Segment Options

Naming segments is a little-needed function unless you are an expert with the architecture of the processors under which Turbo C works. All of the options begin with −z and can work on initialized or uninitialized segments. These options normally do not have to be changed.

Source Code Options

Source code options include three options affecting your uncompiled programs.

-A   Causes ANSI C-only identifiers (keywords) to be used, so that keywords in Turbo C (such as `near`, `far`, and `huge`) become nullified. This option makes code more portable. You can cause problems by turning off this option in code that uses pointers requiring these modifiers (for example, graphics and code with arrays larger than 64K).

-C   Allows comments to be nested one inside the other. This is *not* allowed in ANSI C and reduces portability but may be needed on some source code obtained from other systems.

       You can maximize portability by using conditional compilation statements (`#ifdef` and `#endif`, etc.) to block out code sections containing comments (instead of nesting comments). If you use different values after `#ifdef`, you can regulate different sections of code by turning off some sections and leaving others on. Even source code that already contains conditional compilation statements can use this method of separating out code sections; nesting conditional compilation statements inside one another is both valid *and* portable.

−i#   Specifies a number of characters to be recognized in an identifier. The default is 32 (the same as for ANSI C). You may specify up to 255 characters. Systems other than Turbo C may or may not allow that many characters, as older versions of C often recognized only 8 or fewer characters in a name.

Linker Options

Linker options compose the last group of options.

−efilnam   Allows a file name to be specified immediately after the −e option (no spaces can be used) as the name for the .EXE file produced. Otherwise, Turbo C will take the name of the first file in the file list as the name of the executable image.

−M   Produces a link map.

−lx   Passes a linker option to the linker using this switch.

If you are in the habit of using several options with the command-line compiler, it will be much simpler to work with the `turboc.cfg` (configuration) file specifying the options you use.

The following example shows a configuration file consisting of a single line. TCC first looks for the configuration file in the current directory, or in the directory in which TCC is located. Inside the `turboc.cfg` file, the path is given for include files as − `Ic:\tc\incl`. The medium memory model is specified as the second parameter. −`L\tc\lib;mywrk\lib` gives two places to look for library files. The next parameter, `\mywrk\src\tstats`, tells the compiler to look in the `\mywrk\src` directory for the file named `tstats`. The second specification tells it to also compile `\usr\myfloat.c`.

For example, the .CFG file could consist of

```
-Ic:\tc\incl -mm -L\tc\lib;\mywrk\lib \mywrk\src\tstats \usr\myfloat
```

When using it, you would just have to call `tcc`, which automatically looks for the `turboc.cfg` file and uses the information inside it to compile. This works as if you had used the following on the command line:

```
tcc -Ic:\tc\incl -mm -L\tc\lib;\mywrk\lib \mywrk\src\tstats \usr\myfloat
```

meaning that you had to specify only the `tstats.c` file name and the name of the source module to compile with it (`\usr\myfloat`). The actual use of `tcc` with the configuration file already set up would be

```
tcc \mywrk\src\tstats \usr\myfloat
```

Using the configuration file is similar to using a .BAT (batch) file by specifying data normally given to the program via the command line, but in this way it can be done through a file. This can save you a lot of typing.

In fact, if you need to switch from the command-line version to the integrated version of Turbo C or vice versa, there is a utility (`TCCONFIG.EXE`) to convert the `turboc.cfg` file quickly to a `tcconfig.tc` file. The `tcconfig.tc` file is the file used by the integrated Turbo C compiler. This makes any switching between compilers one degree less painful.

You should make sure, if you are using the graphics routines, that the file `graphics.lib` is part of the files on the command line or is in the `make` file when you use TCC. TCC is not like the integrated environment version where `graphics.lib` will be compiled automatically with the other files; the library file must be specifically present to work correctly.

Summary

In general, TCC, the command-line version of Turbo C, is more powerful than the integrated version. In fact, you *must* use it when you work with assembly language modules or inline assembly. However, TCC is not as fast to work with the software development cycle as is the integrated environment. Luckily, a configuration file is available for either compiler, and Borland has provided ways to convert the configuration file into the correct format needed by the specific version of the compiler.

This chapter covered the use of command-line options, what to do with error messages and how to switch them on or off, and how to use configuration files. Also discussed here were the pitfalls and advantages of other command-line options such as those for optimization and miscellaneous features. You should now have enough background information to know which compiler to choose and how to avoid some problems working with it.

Part III

Testing and Debugging

Lee
Atkinson

CHAPTER 9

Testing and Debugging
Strategies

This and the next two chapters explain in some detail how you can test and debug your Turbo C programs. This is the part of the programming process that separates the serious from the casual programmer.

Why are testing and debugging so important to the program development process? Because programmers are *human*, and sometimes make mistakes. Essentially, the problem is that normal people rarely think of *everything*, and that is what a computer requires if it is to function entirely correctly. Some of the likely sources of error are

❑ *Requirements research:* Despite the best intentions in the world, the person who gives you the program specifications will *leave something out*. Humans often function from *habit* and *assumption*, rather than considering the most minute details analytically. Something important will very likely be left unsaid and therefore left out of your program or implemented in the "wrong" way.

❑ *Procedure translation:* Foreign language students often observe that there is no such thing as a perfect translation from one language to another. Some of the subtleties are lost in the process. The same concept applies to translations from human-oriented procedures to sets of instructions a computer can follow.

❑ *Typographical errors:* Just when you know *exactly* what you want to code, you hurry up, and a "finger check" slips into the code (perhaps Murphy thought of this one). The error is sometimes one that can get by the compiler, finally to reveal itself just when you are proudly demonstrating your snappy new program to the boss or client. Sadly, typos can be the hardest to find of all program bugs. If you don't believe this, try typing in a program from a magazine.

❏ *Human factors:* How you *feel* while writing your program can greatly influence its quality. Three factors above all others can throw you off track: *distraction*, *pressure*, and *fatigue*. Then it becomes easy to get ahead of yourself, to fail to organize, or to fall prey to temporary dyslexia and get turned around and confused.

The quest for perfect programs is at best illusory. Athough always the goal, a truly error-free program, written perfectly on the first effort, is an oddity even for the seasoned professional programmer. The professional, however, knows what to do when errors are made and has enough pride in his or her work to correct mistakes effectively.

The Difference between Testing and Debugging

The first step in correcting errors is, naturally enough, finding them. *Testing* is the process of finding errors, and *debugging* is the process of fixing them.

This is a simple and intuitive distinction. What remains is to refine the idea and learn how to apply the tools Borland has provided in Turbo C Version 2.0 and Turbo C Professional.

When Do You Have a Bug?

Some program bugs are very obvious; others are pervasive and subtle. A system crash is an obvious bug, but there is little need to coach you on how to recognize that, and usually the obvious bugs are fairly easy to fix. So other than this, how do you know when you have a bug?

Recognizing that a Bug Exists

A bug advertises its existence in one way: improper program behavior. Proper behavior, of course, is for a program to fulfill its set of functional requirements. Make a checklist of the requirements and keep it handy when you begin testing the program. Better yet—first develop a test procedure from the requirements.

In addition to verifying whether the program does the tasks it was designed to do, observe and note *how it does them*. Some problems you can look for are

❏ incorrect or unexpected output.

❏ poor user-interface behavior.

❏ inconsistent behavior.

❏ module-interface problems.

❏ loss of database/file integrity.

Incorrect output takes many forms; slight inaccuracies on a hardcopy report, wrong formats in output records, difficult-to-read displays, and wild and impossibly wrong computational results are examples. The key here is to examine the output with a fine-toothed comb, never assuming that the program works correctly. Look for improperly written expressions or other noncritical (to the compiler) syntax problems, incorrectly used or poorly understood Turbo C built-in functions, or algorithms that do not handle boundary value extremes well (see Chapters 7 and 10).

An example of *unexpected output* is a line (that should not be there) on a printed report. The problem probably is caused by lack of work-flow control in the program, but can also arise from corrupted *input*.

Poor *user-interface behavior* may or may not be an error, depending on how you look at it. Users almost certainly will consider it to be one. A confusing, incomplete, or misleading screen display causes unnecessary mistakes and aggravation to the user. Resist the temptation to skimp on this part of your program.

Does the program perform a task in exactly the same way every time? *Inconsistent behavior* of the program is a signal that one or more algorithms, functions, or other parts of the program need more research and rewriting. Inconsistent behavior always produces undependable results. When a program behaves this way, it means that some factor escaped your attention during design, that some point seemed clear but was not, or worse—that you could have implemented it incorrectly even though the design was okay.

Module-interface problems occur when you try to pound a square peg into a round hole. C functions are wonderfully flexible, but they require certain parameters and no others. The best way to control this problem is to use the modern style of writing formal function prototypes, so that the Turbo C compiler can at least enforce variable types at compile time, if not variable values at runtime. Data values must be checked at run time by validation routines you write.

Finally, do not forget the "invisible" output—the files and databases you build. There are two good ways to test the *integrity of file output*. Write short reporting programs to examine the file(s) and report on field contents, record types, and so on. The confidence you gain about the data makes doing this worth the effort. Second, you can use the Turbo Debugger to spot check suspected problem points (see the discussion of the File window in Chapter 10).

Discovering the Type of Bug

Chapters 10 and 11 discusses in detail the concept that logic is data driven and what that means in terms of using the Turbo Debugger. The important point here is that there are two (and only two) kinds of bugs: *faulty program logic* and *corrupted data*. This means either that program statements do not match the logical requirements of the task (assuming that these are correct), or that the data the program uses is bad in the first place. These two root causes often overlap.

How can you tell what type of bug is causing the problem? Primarily, you apply a detailed knowledge of what the program is *supposed* to do compared to what it *does* do, using the rules of thumb mentioned earlier. Table 9.1 summarizes these rules of thumb, citing the most likely causes.

Table 9.1. *Probable Causes of Program Bugs*

Symptom	Probable Cause
Incorrect output	Logic, data
Unexpected output	Data, logic
Poor user-interface behavior	Logic
Inconsistent behavior	Logic, data
Module-interface problems	Logic
Loss of database/file integrity	Data, logic

When both data and logic are suspect, the table lists the more likely of the two first. Notice that in two-thirds of the symptom areas, both data *and* logic are listed. Of those four cases, both types have an even chance (two each) of being the prime candidate. As with all rules of thumb, this list is a suggested starting place and may not apply to each specific case. Simply become familiar with the causes; trust your common sense and be prepared to change your mind.

Locating the Bug

There are three ways to locate a program bug once you realize that one exists. You can sometimes go straight to it; you can guess effectively through a process of elimination; or when really at a loss to pinpoint it, you can use a tool like the Turbo Debugger to help you analyze the program in great detail *as it runs*, verifying every suspected point.

Damon Knight, a noted science-fiction author, says that many times Fred will give him the answer about how to put a story together. Who is *Fred?* Fred is Mr. Knight's comical name for his own subconscious mind. Your variation of Fred can lead you straight to the source of a program bug. As soon as you see the result, you say, "Oh, yes. I know exactly what that is!" The rub is that Fred refuses to perform on demand. Just be grateful when he does.

In lieu of intuition, you can often zero in on a problem just because you wrote the code in the first place and are aware of how tasks are supposed to be done. You know what part of the code any given result comes from. A wrong result naturally leads to its code. A comparison of what you wanted to write with what you did write may quickly yield the answer. This does not always work, either.

The last and most powerful means of locating a bug is the Turbo Debugger. With this tool, you can see everything that is going on in your program, as it happens. The debugger does not have to be a last resort—using the debugger is *fun*, especially if you are fascinated by the way your C program accomplishes its goals. If you don't need the full power of the stand-alone debugger, you might want to try the IDE Debugger first.

Fixing the Bug

The program is finished. You have moved ahead to the testing phase and become aware that there is a bug in its function. You have applied the rules of thumb and have a good idea what the bug's source is. You also know where the bug is. Before you make a quick change to the code, pause and reflect a moment on what will happen when you modify the code. Will the change actually correct the problem? Even more important, will the change throw another part of the program out of kilter?

The program development cycle is in many ways a seamless process, although it does have component parts. Note in figure 9.1 the broad strokes of the process. The process moves in large steps from construction to testing to reconstruction. But in a bit more detail, notice that the return arrow to the first large step does not point to the coding; it returns to the *design*. This does not necessarily mean that the program must be redesigned from scratch. What it does mean is that program fixes *may* alter the program flow and disrupt the originally intended sequence of events. Review the design specifications and determine how well the new code will fit in the existing structure.

Fig. 9.1. *Overview of the program-development cycle.*

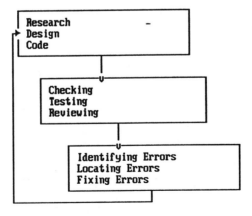

The remainder of this chapter develops a testing and debugging *philosophy* and talks about how to implement that philosophy in a debugging *strategy*.

Types of Testing

The varieties of tests you can use include unit, integration, system, regression, and performance/time testing. I discuss remote and hardware debugging here as they pertain to your testing philosophy.

Unit Testing

Testing ideally begins with the smallest possible amount of code that still makes functional sense. This is called *unit testing*; in the C language, the units involved are functions or very small groups of functions.

Unit testing can (and, in fact, should) begin before the whole program has been completed. Overlapping the design, coding, and testing parts of the process has two great advantages: it speeds the process and provides reliable building blocks as the program grows in size and complexity.

Using a modular approach like this also enables you to respond flexibly to design changes as the program grows. This is a particularly good thing, because almost no program in its finished state completely resembles the original design specifications. Figure 9.2 shows the program design process with overlapping tasks factored in.

Fig. 9.2. Program-development cycle including overlapped unit testing.

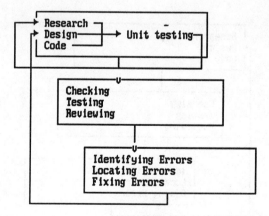

As you might expect, program development with unit testing promotes the completion of separate modules that can be link edited together into a single product. This is an excellent side effect of this approach to program building. You can now change discrete modules with less risk of disturbing the remainder of the program.

If there is a drawback to this approach, it is that you have to write (in the form of *driver* routines) a fair amount of code that never makes it to the final product. A driver routine is really a small whole program that does the following:

❏ sets up the C environment, providing access to command-line arguments, global data areas, and driver logic in the `main()` function.

❏ initializes the environment by defining and priming variables that will be used by the function under test; also sets up or perhaps simulates parameters to be passed to the function.

❏ invokes the function and captures returned values.

❏ analyzes in detail and reports on the results of the test.

The last of these items probably requires the most coding in the driver program, but do not slough over this analysis. The value of the driver lies precisely in its ability to detect and record specific problems. If this portion of the driver program is done correctly, it will almost debug the function for you. Of course, if you are fighting a really tight deadline for completing the program, you can strip down the driver code and run it under the Turbo Debugger. In this case, the inspection and verification of results is completely manual—try not to forget anything. The Turbo Debugger is a super tool for debugging, but debugging is a poor substitute for well-constructed testing.

Integration Testing

Program modules do not function in a vacuum. They operate in the presence of all the other modules that compose the program. Testing the "social" behavior of program modules is called *integration testing*.

Earlier in this chapter I mentioned module-interface problems. Table 9.1 stated that these problems most likely are due to logic problems alone. Like most sweeping generalizations, this is both true and not true.

How? The assertion can be considered not true in that most module-interface problems are caused by improperly passed parameters. On the other hand, a more helpful perspective is that the calling routines have not correctly *generated* the parameters to pass. Assuming that unit testing has been carried out successfully, the problem rests with the calling, not the called, functions.

In figure 9.3 you can see the program-development cycle revised again to include integration testing. The program as a whole has not yet been run; only parts of it have executed. Now the parts consist of groups of functions rather than individual ones.

Fig. 9.3. Program-development cycle including integrated testing.

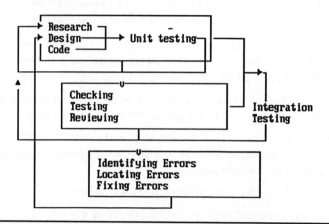

At this level, you may or may not wish to invest the necessary time in what is bound to be more extensive driver logic. Although it is certainly acceptable from the perspective of quality control, a driver program must now provide or simulate a large fraction of the final program environment. Almost all of the global data structures, file-management routines, and user-display interfaces may need to be present.

An alternative approach to testing integrated groups of functions is *prototyping*. A prototype program will later become the production version but begins life as a skeleton framework. You may put all the functions in place, using a "dummy" function (one that returns a fixed response or no response) in undeveloped parts of the code. You may even leave out entire sections until you get to them (the functions that provide the "bells and whistles," for example). A prototyped program grows organically, and the environment for functions under test is real, not simulated.

The advantages of prototyping are that you do not have to write driver code, testing is realistic, the resulting program is highly modular and easy to control, and the entire process is comparatively fast. And a prototyped program usually tends to more closely resemble what the ultimate user wants.

System Testing

For the purposes of this chapter, a *system* is one or more complete and related Turbo C programs. *System testing* is the process of determining the accuracy, reliability, availability, and serviceability of the whole and its component parts.

A software system is *accurate* if it produces correct results for correct inputs, within the limits of precision specified by the system requirements. Further, a system can be considered accurate only if it can detect and handle corrupted input without damaging existing valid data (associated files, and so on). Even more important, a system is only as accurate as its least accurate part or module. Factors that affect accuracy are

❏ internal accuracy of number-representation methods. For example, integers are 100 percent accurate, whereas no floating-point number is ever completely accurate. The question is whether the specific method is accurate *enough*. It may be necessary, for example, to choose `double float` rather than just `float` to maintain sufficient precision. Mathematically, accuracy and precision are different, but for coding purposes the difference is academic.

❏ completeness and efficiency of input-data editing routines. Lack of input editing is a guarantee of eventual failure of the system. Each input item should be tested for proper *type* and *range of value*.

❏ completeness and efficiency of error-handling routines. An error-handling routine should make provisions for detecting the error, notifying the user (using a log file, for example), continuing the run for valid work available, correcting the error, and reapplying the corrected work. All of these tasks may not be performed by the same Turbo C function, but they should be present.

Reliability is the quality of performing the required work without failure (without crashing the system or accidentally erasing the database, for example). If unit and integration testing have been carried out, there is every likelihood that the completed system will be reliable, but no system is *totally* reliable. Only one assumption applies to the programming business: Somewhere a condition exists that can, and eventually will, crash your program.

Modern software engineering theory often speaks of software reliability in the same terms as hardware reliability. It is accepted as a fact that a program will fail on a statistically regular basis, although the "failure" may not be a complete crash. The interval between failures is described as *mean time between failures* (MTBF), or sometimes *mean time to failure* (MTTF).

It is important to decide during the design phase just what will be considered a severe failure. A slight formatting error that does not destroy readability in a printed report is technically a "failure," but does not mean that the system is unreliable. A program compilation with warning messages (at least certain ones) may be considered successful, but one producing error messages cannot be. Ideally, a program that fails in any way during the testing phase should not be passed on to a production status.

The *availability* of a program or system is its ability to run (reliably) whenever called upon, in any or all of the ways the system was designed to function, without requiring repair. In a way, availability is a side effect of reliability. A program that must be modified or fixed in order to run under certain conditions most certainly cannot be considered available.

Because it is practically a given that a program will fail sooner or later, *serviceability* is an important quality of the system. How easily can you get to the various parts of your code to make corrections and updates? A modular design is a winner here, because the logic structure of the entire system does not have to be dismantled and reassembled to make a single change.

Now you know what to test *for*. System testing is a flexible process that depends on the importance of the program and the degree of "finish" desired (not all programs are equally significant—a one-shot "fix-up" program need not be polished to total perfection, for example) and on what the system is supposed to do. But you can count on doing the following:

1. Compile a list of all possible tasks the system can be required to perform. If some tasks depend on the successful completion of others, place those other tasks high on the list. If possible, group tasks that can be tested at one time. Testing should be thorough, but it need not be endless. On the other hand, do not try to test too much at one time; repairs may become unmanageable.

2. Design test data carefully for each test run. The point here is to place the system under every possible stress it may encounter during productive use. See Chapter 10 for additional information on designing test data.

3. Make the test run, preserving all output—good and bad. Check successfully completed tasks off the list. If any errors did occur, debug them as described later in the chapter and rerun this phase until the tasks are performed error free.

4. Repeat the process until every part, or every group of parts, of the program or system has been tested successfully.

Regression Testing

What happens when making a change to a working system or program becomes necessary? Change, especially a radical one, can unravel the whole affair. You need to be aware of two kinds of serious change: logic changes required to fix a bug and design changes that affect the way the program or system does its work—or perhaps even what work it is supposed to do.

When you incorporate changes of this kind, you face the possibility that the "social" behavior of other modules will *regress*, or return to operating incorrectly. Modules that were fixed may fail again; modules that always worked correctly may even fail suddenly.

Regression testing is intended to eliminate this kind of behavior. Although straightforward, the process can be the most tedious and difficult of all kinds of testing. There are four steps to regression testing:

1. Repeat unit testing for all changed modules.

2. Repeat unit testing for all modules that: a) must be modified to accommodate the new modules; b) communicate (using parameters) with changed modules; or c) use the output (files, and so on) from changed modules.

3. Repeat integration testing for all changed modules and modules that communicate with them.

4. Repeat system testing from the ground up. Fortunately, this step may be omitted when only minor bug fixes are being implemented.

Regression testing is easy to recommend and rather difficult to do. It is, however, necessary if you wish to restore complete confidence in the reliability of the finished product.

Performance/Time Testing

How valuable, would you say, is a program that works correctly but takes nearly forever to run? Do you enjoy pressing a hot key and then waiting while the seconds tick away? Neither of these performances is desirable. A user considers a program to be "good" if it performs *well* and *performs* well. Program performance is not just a bonus, it is serious business.

The bottom line in program performance is the time it takes to get the job done. There are exactly two ways to make a program run faster: do the tasks more efficiently and do not do anything unnecessary. Leaving out unnecessary steps is a matter of studying the code carefully and pruning selectively. Determining efficiency, however, is a comparative process in which one way of doing things is found to be better than another.

It would be great if you could quantify how fast "fast" is for any given function or module. In other words, benchmark software is needed. Here is an exercise in performance testing that develops some simple yet effective benchmark software.

Following the rules stated earlier, begin by stating program requirements. What do you want the benchmark function to do? It should be easy to use—perhaps just a simple, one-line function call. It would be best if the amount of data gathered could vary as needed, within limits. To be meaningful, benchmark data needs to be realistically precise. Last, having some descriptive data available for each benchmark entry would make entries easy to interpret and evaluate. By refining this descriptive approach just a little, you can state the program specifications like this:

❑ The benchmark service routine will be named `testlog()`. It is a type `void` routine.

❑ `testlog()` must support the following passed parameters:

`int type`   The type of call being made. Valid types are `START` (initialize the benchmark data array), `LOG` (place a time-stamped entry and comment in the array), and `REPORT` (display the benchmark data for the user to examine). The corresponding integer values for `type` are

                               `START`   0

                               `LOG`   1

                               `REPORT` 2

`int entries`   The maximum number of entries that will be placed in the benchmark array. The `entries` must be less than or equal to the number defined in the global definition of the array. This parameter is nonzero only when the type of call is `START`. Otherwise, it must be zero. The number of entries specified must be evenly divisible by two.

`char *comment` A C string, up to 40 characters long, containing any descriptive comment the user wants to add. Entries should occur in pairs, marking the start and end of a process. A null comment string in the second entry allows for easy visual inspection when `REPORT` is invoked.

❑ Memory allocation is performed by `calloc()` to allow dynamic sizing of the benchmark array. Each entry must contain a time stamp from the Turbo C function `time()` that is accurate to 10^{-2} seconds, as well as the 40-character `*comment`.

❑ The expected calling sequence is as follows:

`testlog(START,n,"")`

                 Call with START causes array setup.

```
testlog(LOG,0,"Comment for this pair");
/* invoke module under test here */
testlog(LOG,0,"");
```

                 Benchmark various functions with calls of type LOG to record start and stop pairs of time stamps.

```
testlog(LOG,0,"Comment for this pair");
/* invoke another module here */
testlog(LOG,0,"");
```

```
testlog(REPORT,0,"");
```

One final call with type REPORT generates a benchmark report on stdout.

A driver program is needed to unit test the function. For this purpose, we will test a home-grown algorithm to evaluate e^x compared to Turbo C's exp(x) built-in function. Because this test was run on a PC without an 80x87 coprocessor, both routines were simulating floating-point arithmetic. Which one does it more efficiently (that is, faster)? The driver routine is implemented in benchmrk.c in listing 9.1.

Listing 9.1

```
/*
      BENCHMRK.C.
      sample driver for the TIMELOG performance
      benchmarking function. This driver allows for 64
      time-stamped benchmark entries. The benchmark
      array is acquired from the near heap
*/

#include <stdlib.h>
#include <stdio.h>
#include <dos.h>
#include <math.h>

#define START   0   /* define TIMELOG request types */
#define LOG     1
#define REPORT  2
#define MAXENT 64

struct logentry {
            struct time ltime;
            char lcomment[41];
          };

            /* single pointer to an array */
struct logentry (*elog)[MAXENT];

            /* LOG benchmark entries */

void timelog( int type, int entries, char *comment )
{
   static int num_entries = 0;
   static int last_entry  = 0;
   int i;

   switch ( type ) {
      case START:  if ( entries % 2 != 0 ) {
                   printf( "TIMELOG requires pairs of\
```

Listing 9.1 continues

Listing 9.1 continued

```
                                entries\n." );
                                abort(); }
                        num_entries = entries;
                        if ( NULL ==
                          (elog =
                            calloc(entries,
                             sizeof(struct logentry))) ) {
                          printf( "TIMELOG could not allocate\
                            benchmark array.\n");
                        abort(); }
                        break;
            case LOG:    if (last_entry >= num_entries) return;
                        gettime(&elog[last_entry]->ltime);
                        strcpy(elog[last_entry]->lcomment,
                            comment);
                        last_entry++;
                        break;
            case REPORT: for ( i=0; i < last_entry; i++ )
                        printf( "Time: %02d.%02d.%02d.%02d %s\n",
                        (int)elog[i]->ltime.ti_hour,
                        (int)elog[i]->ltime.ti_min,
                        (int)elog[i]->ltime.ti_sec,
                        (int)elog[i]->ltime.ti_hund,
                        elog[i]->lcomment );
                        break;
            default:     printf( "\nTIMELOG illegal request\
                            type.\n" );
                        abort();
    }
}


                /* MACLAURIN series for      e^x */
double raise( double power )
{
  double answer,cntr,factor,newx;

  answer = cntr = factor = 1;
  newx = power;
  for( ; cntr <= 20.0 ; cntr++, factor *= cntr,
    newx *=      power ) answer += newx / factor;
  return(answer);
}

main()
{
    /* benchmark my exp() algorithm against Turbo C */

    double my_answer,tc_answer;
```

```
                    /* initialize the benchmark array */

    timelog(START,4,");

                    /* benchmark the two functions */

    timelog(LOG,0,"My exponent routine.");
    my_answer = raise(3.0);
    timelog(LOG,0,");

    timelog(LOG,0,"Turbo C's exponent routine.");
    tc_answer = exp(3.0);
    timelog(LOG,0,");

                    /* report the results */
    printf("My answer for E cubed is %f\n", my_answer);
    printf("Turbo C's answer for E cubed is %f\n",
        tc_answer);
    timelog(REPORT,0,");
}
```

The specific benchmark task chosen was to calculate exponential 3; that is, to raise the base *e* to the third power. The benchmark report, shown next, reveals that *within the limits of precision* of the *time()* function, both routines perform equally well (100+ exponentials per second) and achieve the same answer. Note also that this test was run on a compatible PC running at 7.16 MHz. The results may vary somewhat on your machine, if the system clock is faster or slower.

```
My answer for E cubed is 20.085537
Turbo C's answer for E cubed is 20.085537
Time: 00.06.45.00 My exponent routine.
Time: 00.06.45.00
Time: 00.06.45.00 Turbo C's exponent routine.
Time: 00.06.45.00
```

In fact, you can see that *both* routines together completed in less than one one-hundredth of a second. This is quite practical for real-world applications, such as time value of money calculations (for banking, real estate, insurance), engineering and scientific problems (harmonic functions, decay rates, statistics), or complex geometry (computer graphics!).

If you should need really high-precision timing, the `timelog()` function (and data structures) could be modified to use the Turbo C `ftime()` function. This function can time events with a resolution of one millisecond (10^{-3} seconds).

A number of interesting techniques in this program help to make it short, efficient, and powerful. Look first at the way benchmark array entries and the array itself are defined.

```
struct logentry {
        struct time ltime;
        char lcomment[41];
        };
```

```
struct logentry (*elog)[MAXENT];
```

The declaration `struct logentry { ... }` does not cause the compiler to insert anything in the data segment. It merely describes the layout for a compound variable whose type is `struct logentry`. It does not define the variable itself. The most interesting aspect of this declaration is that the structure is composed entirely of more compound variables. Note that `ltime` is a variable with type `struct time`, and `lcomment` is a C string composed of up to 41 characters (signed characters, by default).

A benchmark composed of only one data point (one entry of type `struct logentry` in this case) would be useless. What users want is an array of these structures. And because program requirements state that the array must be dynamically sizable, you have to allocate the memory from the heap and use a pointer to get to it. Drive the nail all the way home and realize that you especially want *one* pointer to the array. Access to individual entries is to be by indexing, not pointer arithmetic. To understand how this can be done, compare the following two similar statements:

```
struct logentry *elog[MAXENT];
struct logentry (*elog)[MAXENT];
```

Obviously, the intention is to define an array containing `MAXENT` elements/structures. Whether the result turns out to be an *array of pointers* to structures or a *pointer to an array* of structures depends entirely on operator precedence. The way the compiler will handle these two statements is determined completely by the fact that `[ ]` (index brackets) have higher precedence than `*` (the indirection, or pointer, operator).

The compiler will determine the first statement to mean an array of pointers to structures. Why? Because the scanner sees `*elog[MAXENT]` as a single expression and begins by noting that `[ ]` has the higher precedence. Thus it is an array that is being referenced. An array of what? Of `*elog`, which in a declaration means a *pointer to a variable*. Therefore, you have an array—of pointers.

The second statement is handled differently because of the parentheses. Because they have higher precedence than anything else in the statement, the scanner begins by noting that this is a pointer (`*elog`). Only then does the scanner see that this pointer refers to an array with `[MAXENT]` entries. This is the syntax you want for `timelog()`. Figure 9.4 depicts the overall structure for benchmark data that this generates.

Fig. 9.4. *Array of structures for benchmark data.*

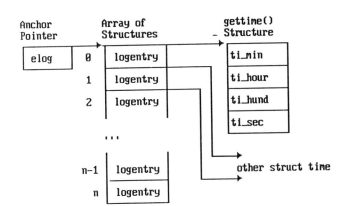

Within the body of timelog() you find the first two local variables, num_entries and last_entry, defined as static variables. The static modifier is used for two reasons. First, these variables must remain intact throughout a whole series of calls, or the current location in the array will be lost. Without the modifier, the variables would default to a storage class of automatic, and would disappear after each call. Second, using static storage class provides an easy way to initialize the variables in the definition statements. This is not possible with automatic variables, because they are undefined between calls to the function.

The manner of allocating storage for the array is instructive in a couple of ways. Take a closer look at the if statement that performs this task:

```
if ( NULL == (elog =
        calloc(entries,sizeof(struct logentry))) )
```

C syntax rules enable you to use both the assignment operator = and the logical equality operator == within the body of an if statement. This makes possible the compact notation used here. The memory is allocated, its location returned and placed in a pointer, and the pointer tested for an error condition (==NULL), all in one statement. You can use this same sort of construction for a fair number of Turbo C functions, particularly file openings and closings.

By using calloc(), the correct amount of memory can be allocated without translating the passed parameter entries. The number of entries is stated directly as the first parameter, and the size of each entry is given as the second using sizeof(). Here, sizeof() is not a function call—it is an *operator*. For this reason, the object specified within the parentheses can be a variable, a basic type (int, double, and so on), or a derived type (struct or user typedef).

As you move down to the code for case `LOG` and case `REPORT`, check how the array entries are *dereferenced*. Strictly speaking, *pointers* are dereferenced, but that distinction is perfectly in line with this discussion, because the entire array is accessed through the pointer `elog`. Two statements in case `LOG` provide an informative contrast:

```
gettime(&elog[last_entry]->ltime);
```

and

```
strcpy(elog[last_entry]->lcomment,comment);
```

both refer to the *address of* an element within a single array entry. To show how it works, the completely referenced element syntax is built up a part at a time:

`elog`	Pointer to the whole array of structures
`elog[last_entry]`	Pointer to a particular array entry
`elog[last_entry]->`	`elog` dereferenced to a particular array entry
`elog[last_entry]->ltime`	The (value) variable `ltime`
`&elog[last_entry]->ltime`	Address of structure `ltime`
`elog[last_entry]->lcomment`	Address of string `lcomment`

The last complete statement here is an address (pointer) because the dereferenced item is a string, not a basic type or structure. To reference the first character in `lcomment`, you could code either

```
elog[last_entry]->lcomment[0]
```

or

```
*(elog[last_entry]->lcomment)
```

The last possibly obscure point in this routine is the *type cast* operator in the `REPORT` case statement. Because entries in `struct time` are defined to be unsigned characters, they must be cast as integers before you display them as decimal values. Note that the cast operator `(int)` simply precedes the completely dereferenced variable; enclosing the complex variable name in parentheses is not necessary.

Remote Debugging

In the past, *remote debugging* meant sitting at a remote terminal and running both the debugger and target program on the same system. What if the program being tested is so large that it will not fit on the same system with the debugger? Or what if your program runs fine on your machine, but not on another (a different compatible, for example)? If you have two PCs (or a cooperative friend with a PC),

Turbo Debugger solves this problem by supplying an extra utility program, TDREMOTE. You just run Turbo Debugger on one system and TDREMOTE with the program under test on the other one.

Actually, the process is a bit more complicated than that. First, the two PCs probably will have to be physically adjacent to one another, because the slowest communications speed that TDREMOTE uses is 9600 baud. Because a modem supporting this kind of speed is rather expensive, individual computer owners may prefer to cable the two machines together with a null modem cable.

As implied by mention of modems and communications speeds, both computers must be equipped with one or more asynchronous communications adapters ("serial ports"). Your machine very likely has a serial port, now considered standard equipment by most computer manufacturers; if it does not, you cannot run Turbo Debugger using a remote link.

Last, you must somehow get a copy of TDREMOTE from your machine to the other one. There are two ways you can do that.

If the two computers use compatible diskettes, just use the DOS COPY command to transfer the TDREMOTE.EXE file to another diskette.

In these days of compatible (and flexibly configured) hardware, you may need to transfer from a 5 1/4-inch diskette to a 3 1/2-inch diskette, but not have both types on one machine. If communications software is available on both machines, you can use an error-checking transfer protocol (such as XMODEM) to send the file to the other machine.

If neither of these options is available to you, you may not be able to do remote debugging. You might think from the *Turbo Debugger User's Guide* that you can use the TDRF file-transfer program to move the file over. However, TDRF works only in conjunction with TDREMOTE on the companion system. If the second machine has neither program available already, you are without recourse. The best bet probably will be to find another friend who has a PC that supports both types of diskettes and COPY the file.

Remote debugging is not difficult, but it may be a little intimidating if you are not accustomed to PC communications procedures. To help you get the feel of debugging with two computers, a sample remote debugging session is documented in figure 9.5. In this figure, the machine labeled **CPU1** is the development system running Turbo Debugger; **CPU2** is the companion PC that runs TDREMOTE and the test program. The `benchmrk.c` program was used for this session. At the beginning of the scenario, the two machines already have been coupled with a null modem cable and powered on.

Fig. 9.5. Remote debugging session using TDREMOTE.

CPU2:

    Command at A›   `tdremote -rpl -rsl [Enter]`

    Messages: `TD Remote Program Loader Version`
    `1.0 Copyright (c) Borland`
    `International`

    `Waiting for handshake (press Ctrl-`
    `Break to quit)`

CPU1:

    Command at A›   `td -rpl -rsl b:benchmark [Enter]`

CPU2:

    Message: `Link established`

CPU1:

    Promt: `Program out of date on remote; send`
    `over link? (Y/N)`
    [Note: BENCHMRK.EXE did not exist on CPU2.]

    User Response: `Y`

CPU2:

    Messages: `Reading file "BENCHMRK.EXE" from`
    `Turbo Debugger`

    `27206 bytes downloaded`
    [Note: This number is updated
    every 2K bytes until file
    transfer is complete.]

    `Download complete`

    `Loading program "BENCHMRK.EXE" from`
    `disk`

    `Program load successful`

CPU1:

    ...   [Debugging commands performed exactly as
    normal. The CPU window shows the CPU
    type of the remote system, with the word
    REMOTE in front of it.]

    User Command: `Alt-x`

CPU2:

    Message: `Link-broken`

Hardware Debugging

Hardware debugging refers to the use of additional option cards in your PC, the purpose of which is to give a debugging program access to the hardware right down to the card, bus, and chip level. Hardware debugging is a *very* sophisticated practice.

Although the details of the hardware debugger interface are beyond the scope of this book, you should know that it exists, what Borland's main purpose for it is, and the basic methods used for hardware debugging.

Borland's main purpose for the hardware debugging interface is to provide a means of debugging that allows a program under test to run at full machine-cycle speed, with no interference from debugging *software*, until a hardware breakpoint occurs. You can imagine how much such a process speeds up debugging.

A hardware breakpoint can be defined to occur for access to a particular RAM address (or range of addresses), or a particular I/O port address. Some debugging boards have extra memory available for instruction trace-back and symbol table storage, but TD does not support these features in Version 1.0.

When a hardware breakpoint does occur, TD uses 80386-specific hardware features to speed up breakpoint processing. This means that hardware debugging is restricted to those who have PCs with an 80386 CPU in addition to the debugging option card.

Hardware debugging services are implemented through a DOS *device driver*. The name of the device driver program file is TDH386.SYS. It is a character (as opposed to block) generic I/O-handling routine that enables you to have hardware-independent access to the debugging hardware produced by several vendors. Borland has not attempted to provide compatibility with every feature from every manufacturer—only a representative subset of them.

General Testing Strategies

The first section of this chapter discussed in some detail the *need* for testing, as well as the basic *steps* and *tools* used in testing. To complete the picture, an overall strategy is needed to define specific testing *procedures*. Specifically, you need to learn how to

- ❏ match testing strategy to design and coding techniques.
- ❏ automate testing procedures and documentation.
- ❏ select the most useful debugging environment (integrated or stand-alone).
- ❏ simplify the debugging process.
- ❏ use the basic debugging tools.
- ❏ automate an audit trail of events during testing.

Debugging topics are covered both here and in the following chapters, because debugging can be viewed as an integral part of the testing process. Test, debug, and test again—all programmers are familiar with the cycle. When it is not done correctly, this cycle can eat up your time and get you nowhere. This section explains how to avoid that dead end.

Top-Down, Bottom-Up, or Topsy-Turvy

Just as code design and development can be structured, program testing also can be organized to maximize its effectiveness and hasten its completion. In fact, testing that is not organized cannot be called testing in the proper sense.

Some testing strategies work better than others with a given development method. Choosing which methods to use depends on the kind of timing involved and the degree of completeness of the code at that point. Matching the methods incorrectly can, as the title of this section suggests, result in a topsy-turvy situation (and unreliable code).

Top-down testing procedures begin with the highest-level modules, just as top-down coding does. For a Turbo C program this is the `main()` function. Top-down procedures lend themselves very well to prototyped program development.

Prototyping code is much like pencil sketching—the broad outlines are quickly blocked in and checked for reasonable proportions, scale, and overall position in the layout. Details are either absent or in dummy blocks. Testing that begins at this point has the value of checking and verifying the overall program flow before the accumulating details force you to commit to a fixed flow. As more and more of the low-level routines are added, like details to a sketch, testing descends into more detailed levels of code, fleshing out the picture and continuing to verify program flow in manageable pieces.

Bottom-up testing moves from the most detailed level (low-level "service" functions) toward the highest level. Bottom-up testing therefore has no place in a prototyping environment. Although this method is much more detailed, software developed and tested from the bottom up is more likely to be well engineered. Interestingly, bottom-up development and testing follow *top-down design*. In fact, if you think about it, the concept and design of a program can *only* proceed from the top downwards. The "what" must always precede the "how."

Each of the factors of coding and testing, in summary, can be either top-down or bottom-up—a total of four combinations. On top of that, recall that four test *types* exist (unit, integration, system, and performance). That brings the total combination of methodologies to 16. What combinations are profitable (or even possible)? Table 9.2 matches appropriate implementation strategies against the test types covered earlier in the chapter.

Table 9.2. *Implementation Strategies versus Test Types*

Test Type	Testing Strategy
Unit	BU[1]
Integration	BU, TD[2]
System	TD, BU
Performance	TD, BU

[1]BU = Bottom-up
[2]TD = Top-down

Unit testing can be carried out in a top-down strategy only with some awkwardness. By definition, unit testing begins with low-level functions at the bottom (most detailed part) of the program structure hierarchy, making it much more suitable for a bottom-up approach.

Whether you apply a top-down or bottom-up strategy during integration testing depends on how you choose to view the modules grouped together for the test. Clearly, it is feasible to view the group as a subunit of the whole program, in which case a bottom-up approach is called for. And it is certainly possible to view the group of modules as a higher-level entity, allowing a top-down approach. The key here is consistency. Whether you begin testing with the main() function and work from top to bottom, or with the lowest-level service routines and work your way up, the need to stay organized dictates that you stick with the chosen method.

Clearly, a global testing strategy at the system level makes sense only if there is more than one program in the system. If so, the same concepts as for unit testing would apply, each unit now being a whole program. The same can be said for performance testing, of course.

Automating Testing Procedures and Documentation

When you deal with large numbers of modules or programs, simply staying organized during the testing and debugging process can become a chore. Documentation is imperative. You need to know at least two basic facts about a test run: what was run and the results.

How convenient it would be if there were a program that automated these functions. In fact, writing a basic skeleton for such a program is not at all difficult. There are just a few tasks it should do.

1. It should accept commands from either the console or an ASCII text file that scripts the sequence of programs to run for testing.

To allow this flexible arrangement, it is only necessary to use Turbo C stream I/O functions, directing input and output to stdin and stdout, respectively. Functions that can be used then are

```
fgets();
fprintf();
printf();
```

The fgets() and fprintf() functions specifically state the name of the stream to be used. The printf() function operates the same as fprintf() using stdout.

2. It should keep in RAM a log of which programs were run and how they terminated. The log is basically a text file that can be implemented as an array of strings.

Every program executed by DOS V2.0 and greater also produces an *exit code*, whether it intends to or not. The Turbo C spawn... family of functions can execute a program as a "child process" and return to you the process's exit code (type int).

3. It should output the run log when testing is finished. The program should be able to route the log output to the console, a disk file, or the system printer. Again, DOS I/O redirection of stdout is the answer for this requirement.

These requirements are put together in the program runlog.c in listing 9.2. This skeletal version of the program only indicates what might be done to automate your testing process.

Listing 9.2

```
/*
    RUNLOG.C--Automated Testing system log
    (1) Replace the A> etc. prompt with Log> prompt
    (2) Accept and scan user commands
    (3) Initiate child processes:
        EXTERNAL COMMANDS: pgm[.ext] [parameters]
    (4) Log programs run and exit codes
    (5) Accept EXIT command and print log

    NOTE: stdin, stdout used for I/O so that
          DOS redirection available
*/

#include <stdlib.h>
#include <stdio.h>
#include <string.h>
#include <process.h>
```

```
char cmdline[129];

char *token;
char *uargs[16];
char *log[64];
char path[41] = "";
int  exitcode;
int  n = 0;

void init_args(void)
{
  int i;

  for ( i=0; i<16; uargs[i++]=NULL );
}

void init_log(void)
{
  int i;

  for ( i=0; i<64; log[i++]=NULL );
}

void get_args(void)
{
  int i;

  i = 0;
  token = strtok( cmdline, " " );
  realloc( uargs[i], strlen(token)+1 );
  strcpy( uargs[i++], token );
  strcpy( path, token );
  do
    {
    token = strtok( NULL, " ");
    realloc( uargs[i], strlen(token)+1 );
    strcpy( uargs[i++], token );
    } while ( token != NULL );
}

void log_cmd(void)
{
  if ( NULL != ( log[n] = malloc( strlen(cmdline)+1 )))
    strcpy( log[n++], cmdline );
}

main()
{
  int i;
  char *ptr;
```

Listing 9.2 continues

Listing 9.2 *continued*

```
printf( "RUNLOG Test Automation Program Version\1.0\n" );
init_args();
init_log();
strcpy( cmdline, "" );
for ( ;; )
    {
    printf( "Log> " );
    fgets(cmdline,129,stdin);
    ptr = cmdline;
    while ( *ptr )
      if( *ptr++ == '\n' ) *(ptr-1) = '\0';
    if( 0 == strncmpi( cmdline, "exit", 4) ) break;
    log_cmd();
    get_args();
    exitcode = spawnv( P_WAIT, path, uargs );
    *cmdline = '\0';
    sprintf( cmdline,"  Exit Code = %03d", exitcode );
    log_cmd();
    }
  for ( i=0; i<n; i++ ) fprintf(stdout,"%s\n",log[i]);
}
```

The heart of the program is the `spawnv()` function. This function (discussed also in an earlier chapter) is one of a family of functions that require three parameters: a mode, a disk path to the child process, and an argument list for the child process.

The function *mode* determines whether the child process is to be created in a true multitasking mode—executed while the parent process is also still running. This is a holdover from multitasking operating systems; MS-DOS and PC DOS are not multitasking systems. The possible values for *mode* are

`P_WAIT`   The parent process remains in a wait state while the child process executes. This is the mode you normally choose while running Turbo C under DOS.

`P_NOWAIT`   The parent process continues to run in multitasking mode while the child process executes. It is not available in the DOS version of Turbo C.

`P_OVERLAY`   The child process replaces the parent in RAM. When the child completes execution, control is returned to DOS (COMMAND.COM) or a higher level parent, but not to the parent creating this process.

The disk path to the child process is a pointer to a string that contains the keystrokes you would type in DOS commands to execute a program. Path can therefore specify a full drive/path designation before the name of the program, but you do *not* have to give the program extension. The program is searched for, using the standard DOS search algorithm:

No extension and no period:	First look for the exact file name. If none is found, look for one with a .EXE extension.
Extension is present:	Search only for the exact file name. Both name and extension must match.
Period only is present:	The file name must match, but an extension is not allowed.
No path specified:	Look in the current drive and directory first. If it is not found there, look in the directory specified in the DOS SET PATH=... command.

The argument list for the child process can be a list of pointers to arguments or an array of pointers to arguments.

The `runlog.c` program requests `P_WAIT`, the path is dynamically determined by `get_args`, and the address of an array of pointers specifies the argument list in the `spawnv()` function call.

In its coverage of the `spawn...` functions, the *Turbo C Reference Guide* Version 2.0 gives an example of its use in the `spawnfam.c` program. In that example, you will notice that the hard-coded argument list is terminated with a `NULL` pointer. Argument lists for the entire family of `spawn...` functions must be terminated with a `NULL` regardless of how the argument list is structured. The algorithm used by `runlog.c` must take this into account and generate a `NULL` pointer after locating all the arguments in the input command line. This is accomplished using a `do-while` loop structure; the `do-while` guarantees that there will always be at least one pass through the loop. Even if there are no parameters following the command name itself, the loop generates a last `NULL` pointer for the list.

A useful and instructive feature of the `get_args()` function is the way `realloc()` is used to obtain heap space for the argument strings. The point is that *only* `realloc()` is used for this purpose. Program initialization logic sets all the `uarg[]` pointer array entries to `NULL`. When `realloc()` is invoked with a `NULL` pointer to the object to be resized, this function behaves just like `malloc()`; new heap space is obtained, and the pointer is set to reference it. Successive calls to `realloc()` that reference the same pointer variable then resize (and possibly relocate) the object in the heap. C garbage collection for the heap is automatic during this process, and you never have to worry about different code for *first* and *successive* string (re)allocations.

One other technique that needs a little explaining is the method used to input the user commands. This is done in `main()` with the following statements:

```
fgets(cmdline,129,stdin);
ptr = cmdline;
while ( *ptr )
  if( *ptr++ == '\n' ) *(ptr-1) = '\0';
```

The reference to `fgets()` is pretty clear: up to 128 characters (129–1) are input from the command source (console or text file, depending on DOS redirection) and placed in the string variable `cmdline`. But what is all that pointer work in the while statement for?

Unfortunately, the `while` is necessary because the *Reference Guide* is in error in documenting `fgets()`. It states that the string is read from the named stream, up to $n - 1$ characters, and placed in the pointed-to location, but the newline character is *not* included in the input. A little work with Turbo Debugger shows that this turns out not to be the case; the newline (`'\n'`) *is* placed in the input string. The purpose of the `while` is to find it and replace it with the null (`'\0'`) string terminator character. The compact notation makes this a fast loop. It is worth taking a moment or two to study the way in which it is done.

The ability to redirect I/O with Turbo C stream functions using `stdin` and `stdout` makes execution of RUNLOG very flexible. Table 9.3 lists the command options you can choose from.

Table 9.3. *RUNLOG.C Execution Options*

Command/Parameters	I/O Sources
`runlog`	Console input, screen output
`runlog <infile`	Text file input, screen output
`runlog >outfile`	Screen, text file, or printer output; console input
`runlog <infile >outfile`	Text file input, screen, text file, or printer output

To demonstrate the program, a text input file `masstest` was created with a text editor. Its contents were

```
b:benchmrk
b:mcalc
exit
```

My benchmark program and Borland's MicroCalc program were executed in turn, with the results logged as they executed. The last command is trapped by `RUNLOG` and causes termination of the testing process. This command is not peculiar to text-file input; you must enter it during console operation as well. Next, the program was run with the following command:

```
runlog <b:masstest >b:syslog.txt
```

Execution results were recorded in `syslog.txt`. Here are the results of the test run.

```
RUNLOG Test Automation Program Version 1.0
Log> My answer for E cubed is 20.085537
Turbo C's answer for E cubed is 20.085537
Time: 20.36.57.00 My exponent routine.
Time: 20.36.57.00
Time: 20.36.57.00 Turbo C's exponent routine.
Time: 20.36.57.00
Log> Log> b:benchmrk
    Exit Code = 019
b:mcalc
    Exit Code = 007
```

Notice that I/O redirection for the parent process was still in effect for the child process benchmark.c. The reason for this is that the child process inherits the I/O environment from the parent. C programs that use stream I/O to stdin and stdout have their I/O redirected. I/O that does not use DOS standard input and output devices (handles 0–4), or that does use ROM BIOS calls for console I/O, are not subject to redirection. You can see also that the Log› prompts did not appear on the screen but are part of the redirected log file. This is no great problem, as long as you know what they are.

Last, notice the exit codes from benchmark and mcalc. They are not zero as they should be for clean execution. The reason for this is that neither program explicitly set the exit codes when it terminated. Whatever happened to be in the AL 8086 register was left there, and DOS interpreted that as the exit code. In this case, there was no real error, but you should use the exit(0) function call to end the program, if you do not want to guess whether a code really indicates an error.

Tips for Simplifying the Debugging Process

Everyone is familiar with the Boy Scout motto, "Be Prepared!" Being prepared when you start a new programming project is the key to making both the development and debugging processes easier. There are many steps you can take beforehand to take the sting out of debugging.

Write for the Most General User Audience

The characteristics of those who will use your program determine to a great extent the characteristics of the program itself. Writing a program is in a sense like writing a letter: both are written *to* someone.

This is where human factors again enter the picture. The eventual users of the program (and you may be one of them), will always do one thing as they become accustomed to and comfortable with the program. They invariably will push it to and beyond its design limits. This happens because users are not aware of (and you may forget, too) design constraints that you unconsciously have come to accept.

Write the program to the broadest possible group of users. Some have considerable computer experience, some have none, and many fall in between. Those at either extreme place the absolute maximum of stress on the program, although they do so in different ways. What this bit of advice boils down to is that you should not only bulletproof your program, you should bulletproof *everything*.

If you hope to write code that can be commercialized, you may be faced with another audience-targeting problem. Will the program run on more than one kind of computer and/or operating system? If this is a possibility, you may have to reconsider seriously how to implement certain functions.

Compiler vendors do not often tell you that *their* "standard" version of a widely used compiler is not truly standard. There is no such thing as a standard and universal C compiler, except in the abstract sense. Turbo C is no exception to this rule, for it has many extensions to the original language specifications.

You can insulate yourself from most (but certainly not all) portability problems by limiting the C code to the basic Kernighan and Ritchie specifications for syntax, plus the American National Standards Institute (ANSI) extensions. The ANSI extensions *do* include the modern style of full-function prototyping but *do not* include the following Turbo C extended keywords:

```
_cs
_ds
_es
_ss
asm
cdecl
far
huge
interrupt
near
pascal
```

You probably will have problems also with identifiers when you port programs to other systems. Turbo C allows 32 significant characters in an identifier, but many other compilers recognize only 8. Turbo C includes a setup option to limit identifier significance to 8 characters for this very purpose.

Use a Top-Down Design and Bottom-up Coding Strategy

Clearly, large-scale projects require the most effort and are the most likely to have numerous bugs. The best prevention for future problems is a solid functional foundation on which to raise the superstructure.

Such a foundation implies *very* thorough preparation. Time spent on the design phase of a large-scale project will turn out to be time saved. Plan, replan, and plan again.

Detailed planning enables you to begin the coding, unit testing, and debugging phases at the bottom—at the most detailed level of service routines. Because you know in advance what the low-level routines are supposed to do, write them first. You will have to write a lot of driver code for these routines, but testing is confined at any given time to one single function. That function can be honed to perfection, or near it, and when high-level coding begins, you already have a library of super-bulletproof support routines. An additional benefit of prewriting the support routines is that they can often be used over and over again, simply by linking them into the programs where necessary. Slow start, fast finish.

Prototype Code To Make Testing Incremental

Prototyping the code for smaller projects can help you get off to a fast start *and* a fast finish. It is easy to recompile small programs many times as more and more functionality is added to them. The benefit here, as stated before, is particularly that overall flow control and program "handling" characteristics are under control from the beginning.

Use Only One Development Language

Many advanced and richly functional programs must be composed of modules written in more than one language. Some modules require complex calculation algorithms that are best written in a high-level language. Other modules perform functions very close to the hardware or must perform them extremely rapidly. These should be written in assembly language.

Two problems are common in mixed-language programming. First, it can be difficult to immerse yourself deeply in one language and then have to pull up short and switch your mental gears to requirements of the other language. This is fertile ground for logistical errors, even when you have no difficulty in getting the code to compile (assemble). Switching language mindsets frequently during debugging can lead you to overlook errors and can create a kind of mental block.

Second, modules that need to be written in another language are often by definition complex or involved. For example, screen handling in Turbo C is quite simple, but there are tasks you cannot do with it. Detecting the vertical retrace to eliminate "snow" on CGA adapters (depending on your particular CPU's clock speed) is one of them. The assembly language routine that this requires is somewhat more complex than a simple `cprintf()` call. As the development cycle progresses, and the inevitable "on the fly" changes appear, these modules may have to be rewritten. Here is more opportunity for errors to creep in.

The solution to these problems is to accept the performance penalties (or increased code size) *during the development phase* and write the special modules in the principal language—Turbo C in this case. When testing and debugging are complete, you can then go back and convert the problem modules to assembly language, Turbo Prolog, or another language. Besides eliminating the problems just cited, this procedure also makes it simpler to write the special modules, because you already have boilerplate code for it.

Formalize the Data Validation and Analysis Process

Even the best program can do little with garbage data. The programmer's old saying, "Garbage in, garbage out," is perfectly accurate. Chapter 10 covers this topic in detail.

Learn the Full Range of Function in the Debugger

Using the Turbo Debugger (TD) is similar to flying an airplane. There is a great deal of theory behind both activities, and you need to know that theory to do either effectively. But the other half of being proficient with TD or with an airplane is hands-on experience. Without it, you will spend more time trying to control the debugger than debugging your program.

By all means, read the material in this and the next two chapters for some pointers on how to use TD, and look up the rest of the details in the *Turbo Debugger Reference Guide* to become more proficient. Then start up TD when you have some spare time and are not under fire to bring in a project. Tinker with it, explore the possibilities, make a friend of it. Time spent now doing this is an investment that will pay off later—when it really counts.

Use the Black Box Approach

The term *black box* comes from electronics engineering, which is often called upon to analyze the behavior of a circuit of unknown construction, or one with an undetermined problem. The circuit under scrutiny is called a black box because the process using the unknown circuit does not initially care what the circuit's internal makeup is. Only the behavior of the circuit is significant. Input signals are thoroughly measured and analyzed, and the same is done for the output signals. Then the circuit elements necessary to transform the signal in exactly that way are deduced, yielding an equivalent circuit. In other words, a process of elimination is used to determine what the circuit is actually doing and therefore how it does it.

The same sort of approach can be used in debugging functions or whole programs. You know (or can determine) what the inputs to the functions are and can observe what the outputs are. With that information in hand, you can deduce at least approximately where and what the error is. A good way of looking at it is like Sherlock Holmes' method of solving a crime: carefully eliminate everything that it cannot be; whatever remains, however unlikely, is what it *must* be.

Debugging Program Internals

At times you may be left without the foggiest notion of the cause of a problem. The black-box approach and intuition together leave you with nothing but more questions. In such circumstances, you must descend with a vengeance into the program details.

The secret to successful internals debugging is skepticism. *Assume* only one thing—that you did it wrong. Accept nothing at face value. Trace every single line of code; inspect every single variable being used.

A paper log of program execution may be necessary for internals debugging. Make a note of everything that happens and, if possible, make a table of every variable being used, log its value and when it changes. When variables change in an unexpected way, you are beginning to get close to the cause of the problem.

When you debug internals, be persistent. Never accept a fix that simply works. Know why it works, which is the same thing as saying you know why the bug did what it did. If you do not, the bug may recur at the least convenient time.

Beta Testing Your New Code

Reputable software manufacturers never let a piece of code reach the marketplace if it has not been beta tested over a period of time.

Beta testing differs from the previously described testing methods in that someone else does it (maximizing the chance that weak spots will show up), and they test it in the real world in a production environment. This is the best way to ensure that the program actually does what it was designed to do.

You do not have to give your source code away, but let groups of users who were not involved in writing the program use it, provided that they report back to you anything out of the ordinary about it. Without this feedback, the whole process is useless.

It is not always possible to truly beta test code. Writing custom software on contract, for example, is one instance in which letting an outside party have access to the program is strictly out of bounds. But try to get as close to it as you can.

Selecting the Most Useful Debugging Environment

Both the stand-alone Turbo Debugger and the Turbo C Integrated Development Environment offer considerable power for debugging your programs. Which one is the most useful for a given program? Each has advantages.

Debugging in the integrated environment can be very quick. You can toggle the active window among the Edit, Watch, and Message windows. You can view the source file as debugging proceeds, just as you can with the stand-alone debugger. Perhaps best of all, you can stop debugging and modify the program without having to leave the environment.

A surprisingly wide range of debugging functions is available in the integrated environment. Table 9.4 summarizes options available by menu.

Table 9.4. *Turbo C Integrated Environment Debugging Options*

Run Menu	Debug Menu	Break/Watch Menu
Go to Cursor	Evaluate	Add Watch
Trace Into	Find Function	Delete Watch
Step Over	Call Stack	Edit Watch
Run	Source Debugging	Remove All Watches
		Toggle Breakpoint
		Clear Breakpoints
		View Next Breakpoint

What does the stand-alone debugger have that the integrated environment does not? Quite a bit, actually. The stand-alone debugger gives you

- CPU status displays.
- assembly language-level debugging.
- file display and modification.
- a dedicated variables window.
- a dedicated memory dump window.
- extensive scope override for inspecting and modifying data.
- a greatly expanded breakpoint facility.
- an automated debugging log.
- macros to automate the debugging process.
- remote debugging.

The integrated debugger can be most useful when you are unit testing a new function, performing first-time testing, or debugging code that is not too complex. Because of its much greater power, the stand-alone debugger is invaluable for extensive debugging, locating subtle problems in very complex code, or performing detailed analysis or debugging of program internals.

Using the Basic Debugging Tools in the Turbo Debugger

The rest of this chapter is devoted to giving you a headstart in using the Turbo Debugger. It is not intended to be an exhaustive reference—that is what the manual is for—but to show you quickly how to move around in the debugger and get some basic results without too much of a struggle.

The Turbo Debugger is a large and complex piece of software. It can be intimidating and confusing, but it need not be. The routes to similar functions are consistent throughout. TD has a consistent user interface. You should get a basic understanding of that interface from this discussion.

Getting Started with the Turbo Debugger

TD runs most quickly when you install it on a hard disk, but Borland still thinks about the "small" PC user out there and allows floppy disk operation. The debugging session from which the following examples were taken was run on a laptop computer with two floppy (720K) drives. Although 3 1/2-inch floppies typically are slower than other drives, response time is good enough not to be too frustrating.

RAM size is another matter. The day of the 128K PC is pretty much gone. The *Turbo Debugger User's Guide* states that TD will run on a machine with 384K, but be advised that you will not fit a very large program into that memory together with TD itself. For all practical purposes, a 640K machine should be considered the minimum. With less than that, you soon may have to resort to the remote debugging procedure described earlier. It is cheaper to "max out" the RAM.

Running TD is straightforward.

1. Switch to the drive and directory in which TD resides.

2. Execute TD at the system prompt, like this:

    A>td

3. Press Enter to execute the command.

On a floppy drive system, it takes 30 seconds or so for TD to load correctly. When loading is complete, you will see the start-up screen display, as shown in figure 9.6.

Loading the program you want to debug is also part of the start-up process. The only guideline to keep in mind here is that you load the .EXE file, *not* the source file. Loading the .EXE file brings the source file with it, however.

To perform the load, press Alt-F (this is not a function key—it is the letter *F*) to pull down the File global menu. Then either press **L** or use the arrow keys to move the highlighted cell to the load option; then press Enter. Figure 9.7 shows the screen while TD is loading the .EXE file. The prompt box overlays the File global menu.

Fig. 9.6. Turbo Debugger start-up screen display.

```
  File    View    Run   Breakpoints   Data   Window   Options            PROMPT
┌CPU 8086━━━━━━━━━━━━━━━━ds:0000 = 20CD━━━━━━━━━━━━┐1┐
│ cs:0100▶2900           sub   [bx+si],ax    │ax 0000 │c=0│
│ cs:0102 FD             std                 │bx 0000 │z=0│
│ cs:0103 5B             pop   bx            │cx 0000 │s=0│
│ cs:0104 005000         add   [bx+si],dl    │dx 0000 │o=0│
│ cs:0107 0000           add   [bx+si],al    │si 0000 │p=0│
│ cs:0109 5B             pop   bx            │di 0000 │a=0│
│ cs:010A 0002                               ├────────┤i=1│
│ cs:010C 5C             ┌─────────────────────────┐  │d=0│
│ cs:010D 005100         │                         │  │   │
│ cs:0110 0000           │      Turbo Debugger      │  │   │
│ cs:0112 5F             │                         │  │   │
│ cs:0113 0002           │      Version 1.0         │  │   │
│ cs:0115 5C             │   Copyright (c) 1988     │  │   │
│                        │   Borland International  │  │   │
├────────────────────────│                         │──┤4
│ ds:0000 CD 20 00       └─────────────────────────┘
│ ds:0008 0D F0 B0 01 B2 05 0C 00 .=▌.▐..     │ ss:0084 2E2A
│ ds:0010 64 38 2F 02 6D 34 80 1A d8/.m4§.   │ ss:0082 3A62
│ ds:0018 01 01 01 00 02 03 04 FF ... ...    │ ss:0080▶0D00
└────────────────────────────────────────────┘

F2-Bkpt F3-Close F4-Here F5-Zoom F6-Next F7-Trace F8-Step F9-Run F10-Menu
```

Fig. 9.7. Loading an .EXE file into Turbo Debugger.

```
  File    View    Run   Breakpoints   Data   Window   Options            PROMPT
┌C━━━━━━━━━━━━━━━━━━━━━━━━ds:0000 = 20CD━━━━━━━━━━━━┐1┐
│ ┌Load...                sub   [bx+si],ax    │ax 0000 │c=0│
│ │Enter program name to load─┐              │bx 0000 │z=0│
│ │b:benchmrk.exe            │               │cx 0000 │s=0│
│ ├──────────────────────────┤+si],dl        │dx 0000 │o=0│
│ │Quit      Alt-X           │ add   [bx+si],al │si 0000 │p=0│
│ └──────────────────────────┘ pop   bx      │di 0000 │a=0│
│ cs:010A 0002           add   [bp+si],al    │bp 0000 │i=1│
│ cs:010C 5C             pop   sp            │sp 0080 │d=0│
│ cs:010D 005100         add   [bx+di],dl    │ds 54C1 │   │
│ cs:0110 0000           add   [bx+si],al    │es 54C1 │   │
│ cs:0112 5F             pop   di            │ss 54C1 │   │
│ cs:0113 0002           add   [bp+si],al    │cs 54C1 │   │
│ cs:0115 5C             pop   sp            │ip 0100 │   │
├────────────────────────────────────────────┤
│ ds:0000 CD 20 00 A0 00 9A F0 FF = á ü≡     │ ss:0086 7874
│ ds:0008 0D F0 B0 01 B2 05 0C 00 .=▌.▐..     │ ss:0084 2E2A
│ ds:0010 64 38 2F 02 6D 34 80 1A d8/.m4§.   │ ss:0082 3A62
│ ds:0018 01 01 01 00 02 03 04 FF ... ...    │ ss:0080▶0D00
└────────────────────────────────────────────┘

F1-Help ↵-Select Esc-Abort
```

Turbo Debugger normally assumes that you will load the .EXE file from the default drive and directory, which in this case is the same as the ones from which TD itself was loaded. As you can see, you can load the .EXE from another drive (B: here). If you specify and override drive and/or path name, TD will attempt to load the corresponding source file from the same location. Note that you can also use TDINST to specify additional directories to search.

TD Menus

The primary means of controlling a debugging session is the menu system. Looking back at either figure 9.6 or 9.7, you can see, across the top of the screen, a strip of options called the *global menu*.

You saw an example of using a global menu when you loaded the .EXE file by pressing Alt-F. You can access the global menu in two ways:

- ❑ Press F10. A highlight will appear in the strip of options across the top of the screen. Use the left- and right-arrow keys to move the highlight to the menu option you want; press Enter to select it.

- ❑ Hold down the Alt key while you press a letter key that corresponds to the first letter of the option you want.

In either case, the associated global menu is "pulled down" in the window appearing just under the option. Now a highlight appears in the menu box. You can press the letter key for the option (without Alt), or you can again use the arrow keys to move the highlight to your choice, and then press Enter.

Generally, screen windows are created through a global menu option. The `Window` global menu option produces a pull-down menu with options for moving the active window around on the screen or resizing it.

Lower levels of menus also are associated with each window you create. These are called local, or "pop-up" menus. To see the pop-up menu for the active window, press Alt-F10. Figure 9.8 shows an example of a local menu (for the Watches window).

TD Windowing

Clearly, TD supports the presence of many windows concurrently. Figure 9.9 shows a debugging session with multiple concurrent windows defined. The *active* window is the one that appears on top of all the others, with no part of its display covered. If there are several windows on-screen that fit without interfering with each other, you can find the active window by noticing which one has a line or option highlighted. There may be some color or shading differences on other lines and in other windows, but the highlighted line stands out clearly.

Fig. 9.8. *Local (pop-up) menu for a window.*

```
     File   View   Run   Breakpoints   Data   Window   Options              MENU
 ┌CPU 8086──┌Module: BENCHMRK  File: B:\BENCHMRK.C 62─────────────────────────┐3─
 │_main: main│         answer += newx / factor;                              │
 │  cs:01FB▶5│         return(answer);                                       │
 │  cs:01FC 8│  }      ┌Watches─────────────────────────────────────────┐4─
 │  cs:01FE 8│         │nt_anser                        ????              │
 │  cs:0201 1│▶ main() │                                                  │
 │  cs:0202 B│  {      │   ┌──────────────┐                              │
 │  cs:0205 8│    /* Benchmark│ Watch     │                              │
 │BENCHMRK#68│         │   │ Edit...      │                              │
 │  cs:0207 1│    double my_an│ Remove     │                              │
 │  cs:0208 B│         │   │ Delete all   │                              │
 │  cs:020B 5│    timelog(START│─────────── itialize the benchmark array */
 │  cs:020C B│         │   │ Inspect      │                              │
 │┌Variables─│    timelog(LOG,0│ Change     │routine.");                   │
 │DGROUP@    │    my_answer = raise(3.0);                                  │
 │FIARQQ     │    timelog(LOG,0,"");                                       │
 │FICRQQ     │                                                            │
 │FIDRQQ     │    timelog(LOG,0,"Turbo C's exponent routine.");           │
 │FIERQQ     │    tc_answer = exp(3.0);                                    │
 │FISRQQ     │    timelog(LOG,0,"");                                       │
 │FIWRQQ     │                                                            │
 │FJARQQ     │    printf("My answer for E cubed is %f\n", my_answer);      │
 F1-Help Esc-Abort
```

Fig. 9.9. *Multiple windows defined to TD.*

```
     File   View   Run   Breakpoints   Data   Window   Options             READY
 ┌CPU 8086──┌Module: BENCHMRK  File: B:\BENCHMRK.C 62─────────────────────────┐3─
 │_main: main│         answer += newx / factor;                              │
 │  cs:01FB▶5│         return(answer);                                       │
 │  cs:01FC 8│  }                                                            │
 │  cs:01FE 8│         ┌Watches──────────────────────────────────────────┐4─
 │  cs:0201 1│▶ main() │my_answer                   double 1.96405e-292    │
 │  cs:0202 B│  {      │                                                   │
 │  cs:0205 8│    /* Benchmark                                             │
 │BENCHMRK#┌Registers─────5┐                                               │
 │  cs:0207 │ax 0000  c=0│n                                                │
 │  cs:0208 │bx 0010  z=1│                                                 │
 │  cs:020B │cx 000E  s=0│RT,4,"");  /* Initialize the benchmark array */  │
 │  cs:020C │dx E23F  o=0│                                                 │
 │┌Variables│si 100D  p=1│,0,"My exponent routine.");                      │
 │DGROUP@   │di 001D  a=0│ raise(3.0);                                     │
 │FIARQQ    │bp 1008  i=1│,0,"");                                          │
 │FICRQQ    │sp 0FF6  d=0│                                                 │
 │FIDRQQ    │ds 5C02     │,0,"Turbo C's exponent routine.");               │
 │FIERQQ    │es 5641     │ exp(3.0);                                       │
 │FISRQQ    │ss 5C8A     │,0,"");                                          │
 │FIWRQQ    │cs 56D1     │                                                 │
 │FJARQQ    │ip 01FB     │answer for E cubed is %f\n", my_answer);         │
 F2-Bkpt F3-Close F4-Here F5-Zoom F6-Next F7-Trace F8-Step F9-Run F10-Menu
```

Identifying Windows

Each window has an identifying number in the upper right corner of the border box. Note the window number as you create new windows, so that you can navigate directly from one window to another. To make another window active, hold down the Alt key while you press the number key for the selected window (it must have already been defined). Pressing Alt-0 presents a Window pick list from which you can select the one you want to navigate to. This is useful if you have many windows open; remembering which one is doing what is difficult.

The Module Window

Perhaps the most important, and certainly the most frequently used, window is the *Module window*. This is the window that displays the source code for the program being debugged.

TD indicates the *current position* in the program by placing a bullet character (▸) to the left of the line. The current position is the line of code that will be executed *next*, when some tracing action is taken, or when you tell TD to run the program at full speed. Figure 9.10 shows the benchmrk.c program in the Module window, ready to begin debugging.

Fig. 9.10. The TD module window.

```
    File   View   Run   Breakpoints   Data   Window   Options          READY
┌CPU 8086──┬Module: BENCHMRK  File: B:\BENCHMRK.C 62═══════════════════════3┐
│_main: main│        answer += newx / factor;
│  cs:01FB▸5│        return(answer);
│  cs:01FC 8│     }
│  cs:01FE 8│
│  cs:0201 1│▸ main()
│  cs:0202 B│    {
│  cs:0205 8│        /* Benchmark my exp() algorithm against Turbo C */
│BENCHMRK#┌R│
│  cs:0207 │        double my_answer,tc_answer;
│  cs:0208 │
│  cs:020B │        timelog(START,4,"");   /* Initialize the benchmark array */
│  cs:020C │
│Variables │        timelog(LOG,0,"My exponent routine.");
│DGROUP@   │        my_answer = raise(3.0);
│FIARQQ    │        timelog(LOG,0,"");
│FICRQQ    │
│FIDRQQ    │        timelog(LOG,0,"Turbo C's exponent routine.");
│FIERQQ    │        tc_answer = exp(3.0);
│FISRQQ    │        timelog(LOG,0,"");
│FIWRQQ    │
│FJARQQ    │        printf("My answer for E cubed is %f\n", my_answer);
```

F2-Bkpt F3-Close F4-Here F5-Zoom F6-Next F7-Trace F8-Step F9-Run F10-Menu

TD Hot Keys

Besides requesting options from menus, you can select options quickly by using TD's hot keys. A hot key is a software-specific key that performs some immediate action when pressed, no matter where you are in the program. The Alt-F key that accesses the File global menu is an example of a hot key.

The *Turbo Debugger User's Guide*, Version 1.0 contains a table of all available TD hot keys. Take a few minutes and familiarize yourself with them. Doing so is worth the time because it will save you much grief, as well as time.

Writing TD Macros for Automation and Retesting

Turbo Debugger has a useful feature that can save you thousands of keystrokes and a lot of time: keystroke macros.

A *keystroke macro* is a sequence of keystrokes (commands, data input, hot keys—the whole works) that can be accessed through *one* special keystroke or key combination (such as Alt-O). An example will demonstrate how the macro works.

Suppose, for example, that you are debugging the benchmrk.c program, and you find it necessary to inspect the variable tc_answer frequently—yet you do not wish to slow down execution by defining a new Watch variable. You can save a great deal of work by defining a macro that contains the keystroke sequence for the Inspect command, assigning that sequence to the ? key.

First, you have to tell TD that you want to define a macro. Press Alt-O to invoke the Options global menu. Then select Macros (press **M**) and finally select the Create option by pressing **C**. Figure 9.11 shows the menu structure just before selection of the Create option.

When you select the Create option, you are prompted to type the character that will invoke the macro (the macro name). This must be a single keystroke, but can be a complex one, such as Shift-F1. For this example, the question mark (Shift-/) was chosen.

After responding to this prompt, all you have to do is type the various keystrokes and commands you want the macro to execute automatically. This is where the keystroke sequence for Inspect/tc_answer was entered. When all keystrokes have been typed (and thus recorded), press Alt-- (Alt-Minus) to complete the macro.

Now, whenever you type **?** the Inspect command will be executed; the result will be similar to that shown in figure 9.12. When you have seen all you want to see, press Esc to remove the Inspecting display from the screen.

Fig. 9.11. The Options/Macros/Create global menu.

```
    File   View   Run   Breakpoints   Data   Window   Options              MENU
┌CPU 8086──┌─Module: BENCHMRK  File: B:\BENCHMRK.C 6┌──────────────────────═3┐
│_main: main│        answer += newx / factor;       │ Language          C    │
│  cs:01FB▶5│        return(answer);                 │ Macros                 │
│  cs:01FC 8│     }                                  │                        │
│  cs:01FE 8│                                        ├────────────────────────┤
│  cs:0201 1│▶ main()                                │ Create         Alt =   │
│  cs:0202 B│  {                                     │ Stop recording Alt -   │
│  cs:0205 8│     /* Benchmark my exp() algorithm aga│ Remove                 │
│BENCHMRK#68│                                        │ Delete all             │
│  cs:0207 1│     double my_answer,tc_answer;        └────────────────────────┘
│  cs:0208 B│
│  cs:020B 5│     timelog(START,4,"");  /* Initialize the benchmark array */
│  cs:020C B│
├Variables─┤     timelog(LOG,0,"My exponent routine.");
│DGROUP@    │     my_answer = raise(3.0);
│FIARQQ     │     timelog(LOG,0,"");
│FICRQQ     │
│FIDRQQ     │     timelog(LOG,0,"Turbo C's exponent routine.");
│FIERQQ     │     tc_answer = exp(3.0);
│FISRQQ     │     timelog(LOG,0,"");
│FIWRQQ     │
│FJARQQ     │     printf("My answer for E cubed is %f\n", my_answer);
```

F1-Help Esc-Abort

Fig. 9.12. Single keystroke Inspect-macro result.

```
    File   View   Run   Breakpoints   Data   Window   Options              READY
┌CPU 8086────┌─Module: BENCHMRK  File: B:\BENCHMRK.C 62──────────────────────═3┐
│_main: main │        answer += newx / factor;     ┌Inspecting tc_answer═══6┐
│  cs:01FB▶5 │        return(answer);               │@5C8A:0FEC              │
│  cs:01FC 8 │     }                                │double        1.59774e+110│
│  cs:01FE 8 │                                      └────────────────────────┘
│  cs:0201 1 │▶ main()
│  cs:0202 B │  {
│  cs:0205 8 │     /* Benchmark my exp() algorithm against Turbo C */
│BENCHMRK# ┌R│
│  cs:0207   │     double my_answer,tc_answer;
│  cs:0208   │
│  cs:020B   │     timelog(START,4,"");  /* Initialize the benchmark array */
│  cs:020C   │
├Variables ┤     timelog(LOG,0,"My exponent routine.");
│DGROUP@    │     my_answer = raise(3.0);
│FIARQQ     │     timelog(LOG,0,"");
│FICRQQ     │
│FIDRQQ     │     timelog(LOG,0,"Turbo C's exponent routine.");
│FIERQQ     │     tc_answer = exp(3.0);
│FISRQQ     │     timelog(LOG,0,"");
│FIWRQQ     │
│FJARQQ     │     printf("My answer for E cubed is %f\n", my_answer);
```

F2-Bkpt F3-Close F4-Here F5-Zoom F6-Next F7-Trace F8-Step F9-Run F10-Menu

There is also a hot key for defining macros: the Alt-= (Alt-Equal sign). The rest of the macro definition is the same.

Automating an Audit Trail of Events during Testing

The need for documenting the testing and debugging process has already been mentioned, and I even went so far as to write a couple of programs to help meet that need in testing. If those two programs are Volkswagens, the TD Log is the Cadillac of the debugging fleet. The Log records

❑ locations of breakpoints reached.

❑ any comments you want to add.

❑ expression values, when requested by a breakpoint action.

❑ the contents of a window pane (such as the system registers) when you invoke Window/Dump Pane to Log.

The Log window is created by the View/Log menu option. By default, the Log records the last 50 events in RAM. If that is not sufficient, you can press Alt-F10 to pop up the Log local menu and request Open Log File. This will cause the Log to be stored continuously to disk, where it can be as large as you need it to be.

Summary

At the beginning of this chapter I commented that testing and debugging are what separate the serious from the casual programmer. You have seen why this is so, and you have been introduced to the major concepts, methods, and tools you can use to carry out successful testing and debugging. Now tie it all together with this question: What is the *ultimate purpose* of testing and debugging? The answer is as simple as it is profound. The ultimate purpose of testing and debugging is to produce *quality software*. How does what you have just learned promote this goal?

If you ask the typical end-user of software what he or she considers to be quality software, the answer is likely to be, "Well, that's software that *works*." Experience shows that he or she means several things that are not said directly. Generally, users will admit, under further questioning, that they mean that quality software works:

❑ Correctly

❑ Consistently (without failure)

❑ Quickly, with no obviously unnecessary waiting time

❑ In a pleasing way, with no irritating quirks or unnatural behavior

It is the addition of the preceding qualities to software products that make testing and debugging so critical. Without an organized method of testing, you cannot know whether your program has these qualities.

When testing reveals a deficiency, debugging begins. You must know how to recognize that a bug exists, determine what kind of bug it is, locate it, and fix it. Adequate recognition of problems is probably the most difficult part, but you can use several rules of thumb to look for bugs:

- ❑ Incorrect or unexpected output
- ❑ Poor user-interface behavior
- ❑ Inconsistent program behavior
- ❑ Module interface problems
- ❑ Loss of database or file integrity

Not every testing methodology is suited to every need and environment. *Unit testing* is applied to the atomic parts of the program (usually discrete functions), whereas *integration testing* verifies how those parts all work together. *System testing* is aimed at the overall or macroscopic behavior of the entire product, and *regression testing* verifies continued functional integrity after changes have been made. Performance and time testing ensure that the job can be done in a realistic time frame.

Although the nomenclature is a little odd, you can consider *remote debugging* and *hardware debugging* also to be highly specialized forms of testing. In addition to permitting the debugging of very large programs, remote debugging is a good vehicle for verifying the correct performance of a program on other, slightly different machines. Hardware debugging, of course, can be used to verify program behavior at the machine level.

Where testing methods are the *tactics* of test implementation, testing *strategies* give you a plan of attack. You can test top-down or bottom-up—just keep in mind that not all methods are suited to every strategy. You can prototype code if you want to, and that often works well, but for the highest quality code, use a top-down design and a bottom-up coding strategy. Know your tools thoroughly (debugger, multiple languages, test automation software, development environment), and use them in the correct mix and in the right order.

Of all the tools available, perhaps the most difficult to learn and the most profitable to use is the *source-level debugger*. The debugger is much like a complex musical instrument, in that you must understand it intimately to get the best results from it. You now have the fundamental knowledge to use the Turbo Debugger. Just remember the three cardinal rules for its *effective* use: Practice! Practice! Practice!

Lee
Atkinson

CHAPTER 10

Logic, Branch, and Path Testing

Daily, professional programmers face a problem that less experienced programmers may not be consciously aware of: a real-world program (one that actually
does something useful) handles conditions and contains logic so complex that it
easily can be forgotten. The plain truth is that you can get lost trying to follow your
own code.

Can you bulletproof a program this complex? Yes, you can, but you will need
discipline, attention to detail, and (there is no way around it) some experience. To
make a program bulletproof, you must do three things successfully. First, you must
create a firm, clear program design. If you are uncertain about what you want the
program to do, it will behave in an uncertain fashion.

Second, logic structure must follow task requirements. Structured programming
is a useful tool but not a magic wand that solves all logic design problems. You must
be aware that some structuring techniques fit some design requirements, whereas
others are inappropriate even if they can be forced to work. If you force the wrong
technique, you almost certainly will find that the logic will not handle boundary
value extremes. (Chapter 11, "Data Validation and Analysis," examines this condition in detail.)

Third, a bulletproof program must be carefully tested and *correctly debugged.*
This chapter looks at some of the ways the Turbo Debugger (TD) can help you with
the third requirement.

Preliminary Definitions

Before you begin debugging logic structures, you should have in hand the terminology for describing logic conditions and errors.

289

Logic is just the required sequence of steps necessary for accomplishing a specific task. Actions must happen in a certain way, or the results will be undependable. This is why design begins with a clear understanding of the task requirements as listed in the requirements analysis (discussed in Chapter 11). Constructing program logic is the detailed process of writing source statements (C language statements, in this case) that accurately follow the work flow. This is not necessarily as easy as it sounds, which is why debugging methods are discussed in this book.

In Turbo C there are only two ways to cause an explicit unconditional branch (sometimes called a *jump* by assembly language programmers). A function call causes physically out-of-line code to be executed, and redefines the local scope (that is, another routine assumes control and is *live*). The only *local* variables that can be referenced are those defined in the called function. Global variables defined outside any function but within the same source file can always be referenced. Global variables in another source file can be referenced if they have been declared as `extern` in the current source file. The other means of causing an unconditional branch is the `goto label;` statement. The `goto` works only in the local scope, meaning that you can jump only to a label in the same function.

In Turbo C there are, however, several ways to cause an implicit branching operation. This kind of branch is "hidden" beneath the C source code. Table 10.1 shows which statements can cause implicit branching and the type of branching action they use.

Table 10.1. *Turbo C Verbs Causing Implicit Branching*

Verb/Statement	Branch Action
`if-then-else`	sequential
`switch, case`	sequential
`continue`	loop
`break`	loop
`for`	loop
`while`	loop
`do-while`	loop
`return`	sequential
`exit`	sequential

As you can see, there are basically two kinds of branching action: *loop continuation* and *sequential branching*. Loop continuation is simply the branch taken to go back to the top of a loop structure in order to perform repetitive work. When no more repetitions are needed, execution "falls through" the bottom of the loop structure and continues sequentially. Sequential branching occurs when the next executed instruction is physically out of line with the previous one, but execution continues sequentially after the branch.

Closely related to the concept of branching is *instruction-path analysis*. If no branch is ever taken, the instruction path is simply all the machine instructions (or Turbo C statements) in the program, from beginning to end, in the order of appearance. Naturally, real programs do not look anything like that.

A program's instruction path, taken as a whole, is the set of instructions actually used, taken in the order of execution. Typically, a program can be considered as a group of related subtasks; the instruction paths for the individual subtasks are considered separately. In the past, instruction-path analysis was a tedious process performed manually on paper. Now you can use Turbo Debugger's Trace Into to examine every instruction in a path, without first having to predict what it will be.

Instruction-path analysis serves two purposes. It reveals instruction paths that are too long as well as those that, at least potentially, are never used. Paths that are too long are inefficient and slow. They may need to be pruned to shorter lengths for better program performance. It is not very surprising that properly tuned instruction paths also tend to be inherently more reliable. Paths that are never used do nothing but consume memory in the program. The RAM they occupy could be better used elsewhere. They also are warning flags indicating that a program may be poorly designed. The logic in seldom-used paths should probably be reviewed to see whether it can be better handled by integrating the instructions with other functions and paths.

Now you are ready to put all this general theory to work—to see what the theory yields in terms of testing, debugging, and tuning Turbo C programs. This discussion uses the standalone Turbo C source-level debugger (the Turbo Debugger, or TD) to check out a financial analysis program named `finance.c`.

Tracing

Because `finance.c` contains different financial analyses, much of the code is concerned with user interfaces. In the sample discussion that follows, it is assumed that the financial algorithms themselves have been thoroughly tested and found reliable.

The problem you face is why the menu selection function, `bullet()`, is not working properly. Figure 10.1 shows (in the form of a hierarchical tree) the instruction path to `bullet()`.

The `main()` function sets up the program to run by initializing a few variables and then invoking `menu_0()` exactly one time. When `menu_0()` returns to `main()`, the program terminates.

The `menu_0()` function repeatedly calls `bullet()` to determine what financial calculation to carry out next, each time invoking a lower-level menu function, which also calls `bullet()`. To give some meaning to this tracing exercise, pause a

Fig. 10.1. `finance.c` *instruction path by function name.*

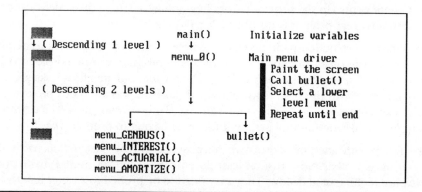

moment and ponder what these routines are doing. You may find this technique useful also for writing some of your own programs.

The "bullet" menu selection process presents the user with a menu selection list that generally looks like this:

▶ This is Item 1.

  This is Item 2.

  ...

  This is Item *n*.

The arrowhead to the left of the item is the "bullet;" it indicates the item that will be selected if the user presses Enter. This character shows up on the display as a solid right-pointing arrowhead. The bullet (and hence the current item) can be moved by using the up- and down-arrow keys in an intuitive manner.

It is up to the menu "driver" function to paint the menu screen, placing the selection items on specific screen lines and at a specific offset from the left edge of the screen. Then the driver function invokes `bullet()`, passing those locations as parameters. The following code shows the way that `menu_0()` paints the menu-selection screen:

```
void menu_0() /* master menu (0) */
{
while ( !endjob ) {
   clrscr();
   printf("%48s","Finance/PC Master Menu");
   gotoxy(1,6);
   printf("%s%s%s%s%s%s%s%s%s%s%s%s%s%s%s%s",
   "_____",
   "_____\n\n",
```

```
   "                          General Business\n",
   "                          Interest Rate Conversions\n",
   "                          Cash Flow Calculations\n",
   "                          Forecasting\n",
   "                          Sum and Statistics\n",
   "                          Time Value of Money\n",

   "                          Amortization\n",
   "                          Create, Edit Tables\n",
   "                          Handle Case Files\n",
   "                          Control Display Windows\n",
   "                          QUIT BUSINESS/PC\n",
   "_____",
   "_____"
      );
   printf("\n");
   printf(
   "      Use the Up- and Down-Arrow keys to move the bullet\
beside the item",
   "       to select. Then Press RETURN (ENTER).''
      );
   bullet(&rc,26,8,18);
       switch ( rc ) {
           case 1: menu_GENBUS(); break;
           case 2: menu_INTEREST(); break;
           case 6: menu_ACTUARIAL(); break;
           case 7: menu_AMORTIZE(); break;
           case 11: return;
       }
   }
}
```

When the menu screen has been painted, together with some comments that make the screen intelligible to the user, it is time to invoke bullet() and process the returned selection item number. The code for this function follows:

```
void bullet (int *rc, int xvol, int line 1, int line 2)
{
   char ch;
   int  fine;

   fine=FALSE;
   gotoxy(xcol,line1); printf( "%c",0x10 );
   while ( !fine ) {
      ch = getch(); if ( ch == 0 ) ch = getch();
      switch (ch) {
          case 13:  fine=TRUE; break;
          case 72:  gotoxy(xcol,wherey()); printf( " " );
                    if ( wherey()==line1 ) gotoxy(xcol,line2);
                    else gotoxy(xcol,wherey()-1);
                    printf( "%c",0x10 ); break;
          case 80:  gotoxy(xcol,wherey()); printf( " " );
                    if ( wherey()==line2 ) gotoxy(xcol,line1);
                       else gotoxy(xcol,wherey()+1);
                    printf( "%c",0x10 ); break;
      }
   }
   *rc = wherey()-line1+1;
}
```

To understand how this function performs its task, you need to know that:

❑ 0x10 = ASCII 16 = the bullet character

❑ The C code sequence:

```
ch = getch(); if ( ch == 0 ) ch = getch();
```

is used to read keystrokes that may include function keys, arrow keys, or any other keys that generate codes in the *extended ASCII* character range (128 through 255). When such a key is pressed, Turbo C first returns 0x00, and then, on the second call to getch(), the extended ASCII scan code.

❑ The following key codes are used in this function:

13 The normal (low range) character code for the Enter (Return) key.

72 The extended ASCII scan code for the up-arrow key.

80 The extended ASCII scan code for the down-arrow key.

❑ C normally treats char type variables as integers. The switch(ch) statement body contains case statements referencing simple integer values corresponding to the ASCII values of the characters or scan codes.

The bullet() function does nothing but move the bullet character up and down the selection list and return the selection item number, relative to 1, when the user presses Enter. The expression

```
wherey() - line1 + 1
```

converts the screen cursor position to this relative line number.

menu_0() invokes bullet() with the following calling sequence:

```
bullet(&rc,26,8,18);
```

The first parameter, rc, is given together with the "address of" operator, so that bullet() can reference and modify this variable. This peculiar way of returning a result from a C function exists here primarily because this is a converted Turbo Pascal procedure (rc was originally a variable parameter). You could rewrite the function in classical C style, as follows:

```
int bullet(xcol,line1,line2)
   int xcol,line1,line2;
{

   . . .
   return(wherey()-line1+1);
}
```

The other parameters indicate that the bullet is to appear in column 26, the first selection item is on line 8, and the last selection item is on line 18.

In tracking a problem down into the `bullet()` function, you need to ask the debugger to "descend" into functions as they are called. To do this (after starting TD and loading `finance.exe`), use the F7 (Trace Into) key. (F7 is called the Trace Into key because it traces an error down into a called function, switching the local scope to that function.) Figure 10.2 shows the debugger screen after you have pressed F7 several times and are poised to trace into `menu_0()`.

Fig. 10.2. *Ready to trace into* `menu_0()`.

```
   File   View   Run   Breakpoints   Data   Window   Options        READY
┌CPU 8086──┌Module: FINANCE  File: B:\FINANCE.C 646══════════════════════3┐
│FINANCE#645│     }
│  cs:1E4F B│    }
│  cs:1E52 5│   }
│  cs:1E53 9│
│  cs:1E58 5│ main()
│  cs:1E59 B│ {
│  cs:1E5C 5│   amtmort=0; levelpay=0; payno=1; prinpay=0;
│  cs:1E5D 9│   intpay=0; apr=0; freq=0; numpay=0;
│  cs:1E62 5│   textbackground(BLUE); textcolor(LIGHTGRAY);
│FINANCE#646│▶  clrscr(); endjob=FALSE; menu_0(); clrscr();
│  cs:1E63▶9│ }
│  cs:1E68 C│
┌Variables─┤
│DGROUP@    │
│FIARQQ     │
│FICRQQ     │
│FIDRQQ     │          @0000:5C32
│FIERQQ     │             ????
│FISRQQ     │             ????
│FIWRQQ     │          @0000:A23D
│FJARQQ     │             ????
└───────────
 F2-Bkpt F3-Close F4-Here F5-Zoom F6-Next F7-Trace F8-Step F9-Run F10-Menu
```

At this point, the next time you press F7 the debugger switches local scope and context to the `menu_0()` function and prepares to trace into its individual statements (see fig. 10.3).

Once program tracing has proceeded into `menu_0()`, you can prepare to trace into `bullet()` by continuing to press F7 until the debugger active line pointer is on the function call, or by using the arrow keys to place the cursor on the function call and then pressing F4 (Execute to "Here").

No matter which method you choose, you now are ready to descend into `bullet()`. Figure 10.4 shows the status of the active line pointer at this time.

When you press F7 one or more times, the debugger descends into `bullet()`; you are ready to find the error in that routine. Figure 10.5 shows this process.

Fig. 10.3. *Local scope switched to* `menu_0()`.

```
    File   View   Run   Breakpoints   Data   Window   Options            READY
┌CPU 8086──┌Module: FINANCE  File: B:\FINANCE.C 602════════════════════════3┐
_menu_0: vo│  }                                                            │
  cs:1C77►5│                                                               │
  cs:1C78 8│► void menu_0() /* MASTER MENU (0) */                          │
  cs:1C7A 1│  {                                                            │
  cs:1C7B B│  while ( !endjob ) {                                          │
  cs:1C7E 8│    clrscr();                                                  │
  cs:1C80 E│    printf("%48s","Finance/PC Master Menu");                   │
FINANCE#605│    gotoxy(1,6);                                               │
  cs:1C83 9│    printf("%s%s%s%s%s%s%s%s%s%s%s%s%s%s",                     │
FINANCE#606│      "─────────────────────────────────────────",            │
  cs:1C88 1│      "─────────────────────────────────────\n",              │
  cs:1C89 B│      "                          General Business\n",          │
┌Variables─│      "                          Interest Rate Conversions\n", │
DGROUP@    │      "                          Cash Flow Calculations\n",    │
FIARQQ     │      "                          Forecasting\n",               │
FICRQQ     └───────────────────────────────────────────────────────────────┘
FIDRQQ            @0000:5C32
FIERQQ                 ????
FISRQQ                 ????
FIWRQQ            @0000:A23D
FJARQQ                 ????
 F2-Bkpt F3-Close F4-Here F5-Zoom F6-Next F7-Trace F8-Step F9-Run F10-Menu
```

Fig. 10.4. *Ready to trace into* `bullet()`.

```
    File   View   Run   Breakpoints   Data   Window   Options            READY
┌CPU 8086──┌Module: FINANCE  File: B:\FINANCE.C 630════════════════════════3┐
FINANCE#630│      "     to select, Then Strike RETURN (ENTER),"           │
  cs:1D1F►B│      );                                                      │
  cs:1D22 5│►   bullet(&rc,26,8,18);                                      │
  cs:1D23 B│    switch ( rc ) {                                           │
  cs:1D26 5│      case 1: menu_GENBUS(); break;                           │
  cs:1D27 B│      case 2: menu_INTEREST(); break;                         │
  cs:1D2A 5│      case 6: menu_ACTUARIAL(); break;                        │
  cs:1D2B 1│      case 7: menu_AMORTIZE(); break;                         │
  cs:1D2C B│      case 11: return;                                        │
  cs:1D2F 5│    }                                                         │
  cs:1D30 0│  }                                                           │
  cs:1D31 E│  }                                                           │
┌Variables─│                                                              │
DGROUP@    │  main()                                                      │
FIARQQ     │  {                                                           │
FICRQQ     └───────────────────────────────────────────────────────────────┘
FIDRQQ            @0000:5C32
FIERQQ                 ????
FISRQQ                 ????
FIWRQQ            @0000:A23D
FJARQQ                 ????
 F2-Bkpt F3-Close F4-Here F5-Zoom F6-Next F7-Trace F8-Step F9-Run F10-Menu
```

Fig. 10.5. Descending into bullet() *and debugging.*

```
     File   View   Run   Breakpoints   Data   Window   Options              READY
  ┌CPU 8086──┌Module: FINANCE  File: B:\FINANCE.C 76════════════════════════3┐
  _bullet: vo│                            LINE2  :Bottom y-position.
   cs:0145►5 │         ═══════════════════════════════════════════════════
   cs:0146 8 │► void bullet(rc,xcol,line1,line2)
   cs:0148 8 │    int *rc,xcol,line1,line2;
   cs:014B 5 │    {
   cs:014C 5 │    char ch;
   cs:014D 1 │    int  fine;
   cs:014E B │
   cs:0151 8 │    fine=FALSE;
   cs:0153 8 │    gotoxy(xcol,line1); printf( "%c",0x10 );
   cs:0156 8 │    while ( !fine ) {
  FINANCE#82:│      ch = getch(); if ( ch == 0 ) ch = getch();
  ┌Variables─│      switch (ch) {
  DGROUP@     │        case 13:  fine=TRUE; break;
  FIARQQ      │        case 72:  gotoxy(xcol,wherey()); printf( " " );
  FICRQQ      │
  FIDRQQ      │     @0000:5C32│rc               6CF6:0026 [_rc]
  FIERQQ      │           ????│
  FISRQQ      │           ????│
  FIWRQQ      │     @0000:A23D│
  FJARQQ      │           ????│
  F2-Bkpt F3-Close F4-Here F5-Zoom F6-Next F7-Trace F8-Step F9-Run F10-Menu
```

How will you locate the error? As you continue to trace, look for two closely related elements: a particular sequence of events (an instruction path that follows the functional design) and the state of the data being used by the program. These two elements are closely related because *the data is what drives the logic.* This means that branching usually takes place conditionally, based on the value of some variable. Chapter 11 takes a closer look at data debugging. For now, just be aware that this relationship exists.

Tracing Machine Instructions

At times, even the Trace Into facility is not a fine enough comb to sift out an error. This problem may occur when your program works at a level very close to the hardware or if you are uncertain of the exact effect of a particular C statement.

The Turbo Debugger also has a way around this: the Instruction Trace facility traces a single machine instruction at a time whenever you press Alt-F7. To illustrate how this works, this discussion examines the inner workings of a terminate-and-stay-resident (TSR) utility named xehelp.c. (Be careful not to execute xehelp to completion while debugging—unless you want Turbo Debugger resident also!)

It is important to find out two things about the way `xehelp.c` works: how it captures the program segment prefix (PSP) address from Turbo C's `_psp` variable, and how it locates the address of the end of the DOS segment (the area in which DOS stores all its information). Exactly why `xehelp.c` does these tasks has nothing to do with the example here, but you are in the driver's seat, prying into the interior of a TSR utility (before it is made resident).

Capturing the PSP Address

Look first at figure 10.6. The debugger has already started and the `xehelp.exe` module is loaded. In addition, you have already used F7 to trace down to assign `_psp` to a variable named `mypsp`. The triangular bullet indicates the debugger's current line position.

Fig. 10.6. *Ready to instruction trace in* `xehelp.c`.

```
   File   View   Run   Breakpoints   Data   Window   Options          READY
┌CPU 8086──┌Module: XEHELP  File: B:\XEHELP.C 187═══════════════════════3┐
 XEHELP#187:│    oldptr = getvect(5);
   cs:06EF.B│    setvect(5, xehelp);
   cs:06F2 8│  }
   cs:06F4 2│
   cs:06F8 A│  main(argc,argv)
   cs:06FB 8│    int argc;
   cs:06FD A│    char *argv[];
   cs:0700 8│  {
 XEHELP#188:│    if ( argc == 2 ) strcpy(path,argv[1]);
   cs:0704 0│      else strcpy( path,"B:\\" );
   cs:0705 E│    gettextinfo(&s_d);
 XEHELP#189:│    if ( NULL == ( screen_save =
┌Variables─┐│        farmalloc( (s_d.screenheight+s_d.screenwidth)*2 ) )
 DGROUP@   │        ) return;
 PADD@     │    *fname = '\0';
 PCMP@     │    directvideo = 1;
 PSUB@     │    scrseg = 0xB800; scrofs = 0;
 SCOPY@    │    install();
 _8087     │►   mypsp = _psp; myss = _SS; mysp = _SP;
 _IOERROR  │    set_up();
 _Int0Vecto│    reg.x.ax = 0x3100; reg.x.dx = 0x2000; intdos(&reg,&reg);
```

F2-Bkpt F3-Close F4-Here F5-Zoom F6-Next F7-Trace F8-Step F9-Run F10-Menu

There are two ways to begin an instruction trace. The first way is to press Alt-F7 immediately. When you do, notice that the debugger display changes. The module window is moved to the background, and the CPU window is made active in the foreground (see fig. 10.7).

Fig. 10.7. `xehelp.c` *instruction trace started.*

```
   File   View   Run   Breakpoints   Data   Window   Options                    READY
┌CPU 8086══════════════════════════════════════════════1┐                          3┐
│XEHELP#187:   mypsp = _psp; myss = _SS; mysp =   │ ax 6572 │c=0│
│   cs:06EF B87265          mov     ax,6572        │ bx 04A1 │z=0│
│   cs:06F2▸8EC0            mov     es,ax          │ cx 0005 │s=0│
│   cs:06F4 26A17B00        mov     ax,es:[007B]   │ dx 04A1 │o=0│
│   cs:06F8 A37901          mov     [XEHELP#mypsp  │ si 100D │p=0│
│   cs:06FB 8CD0            mov     ax,ss          │ di 001D │a=0│
│   cs:06FD A36F01          mov     [XEHELP#myss]  │ bp 0FF4 │i=1│
│   cs:0700 89266D01        mov     [XEHELP#mysp]  │ sp 0FF2 │d=0│
│XEHELP#188:   set_up();                           │ ds 657F │
│   cs:0704 0E              push    cs             │ es 06CC │
│   cs:0705 E8FEF8          call    _set_up        │ ss 65D0 │
│XEHELP#189:   reg.x.ax = 0x3100; reg.x.dx = 0x    │ cs 6314 │
│   cs:0708 C706EA000031    mov     word ptr [XEH  │ ip 06F2 │)*2 ) )│
│                                                  │
│62B2:0000 CD 20 00 A0 00 9A F0 FF = á Ü≡          │ ss:0FF8 62C2 │
│62B2:0008 0D F0 60 03 2C 3B 2D 03 .=`,,;-,        │ ss:0FF6 00FD │
│62B2:0010 2C 3B 2F 02 5B 40 6E 26 ,;/,[@n&        │ ss:0FF4 1008 │
│62B2:0018 01 01 01 00 02 FF FF FF ... .           │ ss:0FF2,6572 │
│                                                  │
│__IOERROR          set_up();                      │
│__Int0Vecto        reg.x.ax = 0x3100; reg.x.dx = 0x2000; intdos(&reg,&reg);│
└───────────────────────────────────────────────────────┘
 F2-Bkpt F3-Close F4-Here F5-Zoom F6-Next F7-Trace F8-Step F9-Run F10-Menu
```

The first feature to notice about the new screen is that it contains several machine instructions associated with this Turbo C statement (not very surprising). Note also that Alt-F7 executed the first instruction before swapping to the CPU window. The first three lines of that window are reproduced here (for clarity, asterisks mark the new current position:

```
      XEHELP#187:   mypsp = _psp; myss = _SS; mysp = ...
         cs:06EF B87265          mov      ax,6572
   **    cs:06F2>8EC0            mov      es,ax
```

You will see how to avoid executing the first machine instruction in a moment.

To understand what is going on here, you have to know something about how Turbo C handles the environment in which Turbo C executable programs run.

When you type in the name of a Turbo C program at the DOS prompt and begin to run the program, Turbo C first executes some setup code that is both invisible to the programmer and not under the programmer's control (except in the sense of choosing the memory model at compile time)—unless you recode c0.asm yourself. One of the first tasks accomplished is that of extracting the PSP address and storing it in the _psp variable. In this example, the ES register is being "borrowed" to hold the segment address (6572) of the area of memory containing _psp, so that AX can be loaded with the segment address of the PSP from _psp.

After the segment address of the PSP has been loaded into AX, it can then be stored into `mypsp`, as illustrated by the current line pointer in figure 10.8.

Fig. 10.8. *Accessing and saving the PSP address.*

```
    File    View    Run    Breakpoints    Data    Window    Options                    READY
 ┌CPU 8086════════════════════ds:0179 = 0000┬──────────┬─1┐                               ─3┐
 │LP#187:  mypsp = _psp; myss = _SS; mysp = _SP │ ax 62B2 │c=0│
 │:06EF B87265       mov     ax,6572            │ bx 04A1 │z=0│
 │:06F2 8EC0         mov     es,ax              │ cx 0005 │s=0│
 │:06F4 26A17B00     mov     ax,es:[007B]       │ dx 04A1 │o=0│
 │:06F8►A37901       mov     [XEHELP#mypsp],ax  │ si 100D │p=0│
 │:06FB 8CD0         mov     ax,ss              │ di 001D │a=0│
 │:06FD A36F01       mov     [XEHELP#myss],ax   │ bp 0FF4 │i=1│
 │:0700 89266D01     mov     [XEHELP#mysp],sp   │ sp 0FF2 │d=0│
 │LP#188:  set_up();                            │ ds 657F │
 │:0704 0E           push    cs                 │ es 6572 │
 │:0705 E8FEF8       call    _set_up            │ ss 65D0 │
 │LP#189:  reg.x.ax = 0x3100; reg.x.dx = 0x2000 │ cs 6314 │
 │:0708 C706EA000031 mov     word ptr [XEHELP#  │ ip 06F8 │)*2 ) )│
 ├──────────────────────────────────────────────┼─────────┤
 │62B2:0000 CD 20 00 A0 00 9A F0 FF = á Ü≡       │ ss:0FF8 62C2 │
 │62B2:0008 0D F0 60 03 2C 3B 2D 03 ,=`.,;-.     │ ss:0FF6 00FD │
 │62B2:0010 2C 3B 2F 02 5B 40 6E 26 ,;/.[@n&     │ ss:0FF4 100B │
 │62B2:0018 01 01 01 00 02 FF FF FF ... .        │ ss:0FF2.6572 │
 ├──────────────┬───────────────────────────────────────────┤
 │ __IOERROR    │ set_up();                                   │
 │ __Int0Vecto  │ reg.x.ax = 0x3100; reg.x.dx = 0x2000; intdos(&reg,&reg); │
 └──────────────┴───────────────────────────────────────────┘
 F2-Bkpt F3-Close F4-Here F5-Zoom F6-Next F7-Trace F8-Step F9-Run F10-Menu
```

You can mix freely your use of F7 (Trace Into) and Alt-F7 (Instruction Trace). In figure 10.8, the instruction trace of the machine instructions associated with `xehelp` (line 187) is only partially complete. If you return to the Module window (F8) and then press F7 here, TD will complete execution of all machine instructions for that source line, and return to the next line (188) of the C code. This result is shown in figure 10.9.

Locating the End of the DOS Segment

The other issue to explore is how `xehelp` managed to locate the address of the end of the DOS segment. Figure 10.10 shows the module window after the program has traced into the `set_up()` function and positioned the current line to 40.

You will recall that the last time you started Instruction Trace, TD switched to the CPU window *after* executing the first machine instruction for the current source line. To get around that, you simply switch to the CPU window (window 1, in the example) by pressing Alt-1 before you press Alt-F7. The CPU window now displays the machine code used to calculate and store this address (see fig. 10.11).

Fig. 10.9. *Resuming trace into in* `xehelp` *after you use Instruction Trace.*

```
    File   View   Run  Breakpoints  Data   Window   Options              READY
┌CPU 8086──┌Module: XEHELP  File: B:\XEHELP.C 188══════════════════════════3┐
│XEHELP#187:│    oldptr = getvect(5);
│  cs:06EF B│    setvect(5, xehelp);
│  cs:06F2 8│  }
│  cs:06F4 2│
│  cs:06F8 A│  main(argc,argv)
│  cs:06FB 8│    int argc;
│  cs:06FD A│    char *argv[];
│  cs:0700 8│    {
│XEHELP#188:│    if ( argc == 2 ) strcpy(path,argv[1]);
│  cs:0704.0│      else strcpy( path,"B:\\" );
│  cs:0705 E│    gettextinfo(&s_d);
│XEHELP#189:│    if ( NULL == ( screen_save =
│  cs:0708 C│       farmalloc( (s_d.screenheight+s_d.screenwidth)*2 ) )
│           │         ) return;
│62B2:0000 C│    *fname = '\0';
│62B2:0008 0│    directvideo = 1;
│62B2:0010 2│    scrseg = 0xB800; scrofs = 0;
│62B2:0018 0│    install();
│           │    mypsp = _psp; myss = _SS; mysp = _SP;
│_IOERROR   │►   set_up();
│_Int0Vecto │    reg.x.ax = 0x3100; reg.x.dx = 0x2000; intdos(&reg,&reg);
└───────────┴──────────────────────────────────────────────────────────────┘
 F2-Bkpt F3-Close F4-Here F5-Zoom F6-Next F7-Trace F8-Step F9-Run F10-Menu
```

Fig. 10.10. *Tracing into* `xehelp set_up()`.

```
    File   View   Run  Breakpoints  Data   Window   Options              READY
┌CPU 8086──┌Module: XEHELP  File: B:\XEHELP.C 40═══════════════════════════3┐
│XEHELP#40: │    "2. Capture Screen to Disk",
│  cs:004A.8│    "3. Commands"
│  cs:004E 8│      };
│  cs:0050 8│
│  cs:0054 8│  void set_up()
│  cs:0057 2│  {
│  cs:005A A│    unsigned adr = 0;
│  cs:005D E│
│XEHELP#42: │    reg.h.ah = 0x34; intdos(&reg,&reg); dosseg = _ES;
│  cs:005F 8│    reg.h.ah = 0x52; intdos(&reg,&reg); enddos = _ES;
│  cs:0063 8│►   enddos = peek(enddos,reg.x.bx-2);
│  cs:0065 8│    while ( pidctr < 2 && (unsigned)((dosseg<<4+adr)<(enddos<<4))
│  cs:0067 2│      if (peek(dosseg,adr)==mypsp) {
│           │         reg.h.ah=0x50; reg.x.bx=mypsp+1; intdos(&reg,&reg);
│62B2:0000 C│         if (peek(dosseg,adr)==mypsp+1) pids[pidctr++] = adr;
│62B2:0008 0│         reg.h.ah=0x50; reg.x.bx=mypsp; intdos(&reg,&reg);
│62B2:0010 2│      }
│62B2:0018 0│      adr++;
│           │    }
│_IOERROR   │  }
│_Int0Vecto │
└───────────┴──────────────────────────────────────────────────────────────┘
 F2-Bkpt F3-Close F4-Here F5-Zoom F6-Next F7-Trace F8-Step F9-Run F10-Menu
```

Fig. 10.11. *The CPU window positioned at* `xehelp` *line 40.*

```
    File  View   Run   Breakpoints  Data  Window   Options          READY
┌CPU 8086════════════════════ds:0189 = 0116═════════════════1┐════════3┐
│P#40:  enddos = peek(enddos,reg.x,bx-2);    ax 0116 │c=0│           │
│004A▶8B1E8901        mov    bx,[XEHELP#enddos]  bx 00F0 │z=0│           │
│004E 8EC3            mov    es,bx               cx 0000 │s=0│           │
│0050 8B1EEC00        mov    bx,[00EC]           dx 0000 │o=0│           │
│0054 83C3FE          add    bx,FFFE             si 0000 │p=1│           │
│0057 268B07          mov    ax,es:[bx]          di 001D │a=0│           │
│005A A38901          mov    [XEHELP#enddos],ax  bp 0FEC │i=1│           │
│005D EB6F            jmp    XEHELP#41 (00CE)    sp 0FE8 │d=0│           │
│P#42:  if (peek(dosseg,adr)==mypsp) {          ds 657F │   │S;         │
│005F 8B1E7501        mov    bx,[XEHELP#dosseg]  es 0116 │   │S;         │
│0063 8EC3            mov    es,bx               ss 65D0 │   │           │
│0065 8BDE            mov    bx,si               cs 6314 │   │)<(enddos<<4))│
│0067 268B07          mov    ax,es:[bx]          ip 004A │   │           │
│                                                         │   │g,&reg);   │
├────────────────────────────────────────────── ss:0FEE 0708 │+] = adr;│
│62B2:0000 CD 20 00 A0 00 9A F0 FF = á ü≡        ss:0FEC 0FF4 │&reg);   │
│62B2:0008 0D F0 60 03 2C 3B 2D 03 .≡`,,;-.      ss:0FEA 100D │         │
│62B2:0010 2C 3B 2F 02 5B 40 6E 26 ,;/.[@n&      ss:0FE8.657F │         │
│62B2:0018 01 01 01 00 02 FF FF FF ... .                      │         │
├──────────────┬──┐                                                      │
│__IOERROR     │ }                                                       │
│__Int0Vecto   │                                                         │
└──────────────┴──┘─────────────────────────────────────────────────────┘
 F2-Bkpt F3-Close F4-Here F5-Zoom F6-Next F7-Trace F8-Step F9-Run F10-Menu
```

The current line is now positioned at source line 40, ready to step through the machine instructions, beginning with the first one associated with this source line.

Stepping Over

When testing or debugging has proceeded beyond the initial stages, you very likely will have already verified the correct operation of many lower-level functions. There is no further need to see every line of code executed in those functions.

The Turbo Debugger provides a tracing facility suited to this need: F8 (Step Over). The operation of Step Over is similar to that of Trace Into, in that one line of source code is executed each time you press F8; it differs, however, in that TD does *not* descend into lower-level functions. Called functions are simply executed without showing them (or treated as a single executable entity, if you will), and the current position is moved to the next line in the calling routine. Consider, for example, the short program in listing 10.1.

Listing 10.1

```
#include <stdio.h>      /* showpix.c */
#include <conio.h>
#include <dos.h>

    int x = 1;
    int y;

void show_line(char *ostring )
{
    char *screen;

    screen = MK_FP( 0xB800, (x-1)*2 + (y-1)*160 );
    while ( *ostring ) {
        *screen = *ostring++; screen += 2;
    }
}

main(argc,argv)
    int argc;
    char *argv[];
{
    FILE *pix;
    char pline[83];
    char ch;

    if ( argc < 2 ) exit(0);
    if ( NULL == (pix = fopen(argv[1[,"rt")) ) exit(0);
    y = 1;
    clrscr(); gotoxy(1,1);
    while ( NULL != (fgets( pline,83,pix )) ) { /* 80+CRLF */
        show_line(pline); y++;
    }
    fclose(pix);
    ch = getch(); if ( ch == 0 ) getch();
    clrscr();
}
```

The purpose of the showpix program is to read a short ASCII text file and quickly display it on the screen. The program assumes that the file is composed of text strings terminated by a carriage return/line feed pair of characters, that the file contains no more than 25 lines, and that a CGA video adapter is being used.

The real meat of the program is in the main() function's solitary while statement. This statement repetitively performs the read from a stream and calls the show_line() function to place each text line on the screen. The purpose of the exercise is to verify that the variable y is being incremented properly in the while loop. Figure 10.12 shows the current position located at the while.

Fig. 10.12. *Ready to step over* show_line().

```
    File   View   Run   Breakpoints   Data   Window   Options              READY
 ┌CPU 8086──┌Module: SHOWPIX  File: B:\SHOWPIX.C 33══════════════════════════3┐
 │SHOWPIX#33:││    }
 │  cs:00DB▶F││  }
 │  cs:00DE F││
 │  cs:00E1 B││
 │  cs:00E4 5││  main(argc,argv)
 │  cs:00E5 1││    int argc;
 │  cs:00E6 8││    char *argv[];
 │  cs:00E9 5││  {
 │  cs:00EA 9││    FILE *pix;
 │  cs:00EF 8││    char pline[83];
 │  cs:00F2 0││    char ch;
 │  cs:00F4 7││
 ├Variables─┤│    directvideo = 1;
 │DGROUP@    ││    if ( argc < 2 ) exit(0);
 │PADD@      ││    if ( NULL == (pix = fopen(argv[1],"rt")) ) exit(0);
 │PCMP@      ││    y = 1;
 │PSUB@      ││    clrscr(); gotoxy(1,1);
 │_8087      │▶   while ( NULL != (fgets( pline,83,pix )) ) {  /* 80 + CRLF */
 │_CPUTN     ││      show_line(pline); y++;
 │_IOERROR   ││    }
 │_Int0Vecto ││    fclose(pix);
 └───────────┴──────────────────────────────────────────────────────────────┘
  F2-Bkpt F3-Close F4-Here F5-Zoom F6-Next F7-Trace F8-Step F9-Run F10-Menu
```

If you presume that show_line() has already been tested and debugged, you can use the F8 key to step over the call to that function. As F8 is pressed repeatedly, the current line pointer appears to shuttle back and forth between lines 33 and 34. During this process, it was decided to spot check the value of the Y coordinate to see whether it was indeed on line 3 (in this case), as a count of loop passes would indicate. It was indeed (see fig. 10.13). Note that you can position the cursor under the variable and press Ctrl-I to pop up an inspector window.

When this example was created, the screen being displayed was in fact a captured Turbo Debugger screen, so that there were exactly 25 lines to be displayed. When all the lines have been read and displayed, the current-position pointer should fall through the bottom of the while loop, after incrementing y one last time. Because the value of y at that time should be 26, an inspection of its value was made (see fig. 10.14).

The variable checks out properly and the program is tested and verified.

Fig. 10.13. *Inspecting* Y *during* while *execution.*

```
    File   View   Run   Breakpoints   Data   Window   Options              READY
┌CPU 8086──┬Module: SHOWPIX  File: B:\SHOWPIX.C 34──────────────────────3┐
│SHOWPIX#34:│      }
│  cs:00CC▸1│    }
│  cs:00CD 8│
│  cs:00D0 5│
│  cs:00D1 0│    main(argc,argv)
│  cs:00D2 E│      int argc;              ┌Inspecting y══════════════4┐
│  cs:00D5 5│      char *argv[];          │@6583:000E
│  cs:00D6 5│    {                        │int                3 (0x3)│
│  cs:00D7 F│      FILE *pix;             └────────────────────────────┘
│SHOWPIX#33:│      char pline[83];
│  cs:00DB F│      char ch;
│  cs:00DE F│
├Variables─┤      directvideo = 1;
│DGROUP@   │      if ( argc < 2 ) exit(0);
│PADD@     │      if ( NULL == (pix = fopen(argv[1],"rt")) ) exit(0);
│PCMP@     │      y = 1;
│PSUB@     │      clrscr(); gotoxy(1,1);
│__8087    │      while ( NULL != (fgets( pline,83,pix )) ) {  /* 80 + CRLF */
│__CPUTN   │▸       show_line(pline); y++;
│__IOERROR │      }
│__Int0Vecto│      fclose(pix);
└──────────┴──────────────────────────────────────────────────────────────┘
 F2-Bkpt F3-Close F4-Here F5-Zoom F6-Next F7-Trace F8-Step F9-Run F10-Menu
```

Fig. 10.14. *Final inspection of* Y *in* showpix.

```
    File   View   Run   Breakpoints   Data   Window   Options              READY
┌CPU 8086──┬Module: SHOWPIX  File: B:\SHOWPIX.C 36──────────────────────3┐
│SHOWPIX#36:│      clrscr(); gotoxy(1,1);
│  cs:00F6▸F│      while ( NULL != (fgets( pline,83,pix )) ) {  /* 80 + CRLF */
│  cs:00F9 F│        show_line(pline); y++;
│  cs:00FC 9│      }
│  cs:0101 5│▸     fclose(pix);
│  cs:0102 5│      ch = getch(); if ( ch == 0 ) getch();
│SHOWPIX#37:│      clrscr();
│  cs:0103 9│    }
│  cs:0108 8│
│  cs:010B 8│
│  cs:010F 7│
│  cs:0111 9│
├Variables─┤
│DGROUP@   │
│PADD@     │                             ┌Inspecting y══════════════4┐
│PCMP@     │                             │@6583:000E
│PSUB@     │                             │int               26 (0x1A)│
│__8087    │                             └────────────────────────────┘
│__CPUTN   │
│__IOERROR │
│__Int0Vecto│
└──────────┴──────────────────────────────────────────────────────────────┘
 F2-Bkpt F3-Close F4-Here F5-Zoom F6-Next F7-Trace F8-Step F9-Run F10-Menu
```

Automating Program Analysis with Breakpoints

Testing and debugging large, sophisticated programs is a complex task. Usually, a large number of errors can occur in the execution path, many of them interrelated. This can make debugging by tracing and stepping extremely difficult, if not impossible.

What if you could define to the debugger a condition that might signal a problem, have the debugger execute to the position in the source code where the condition exists, and then tell you about it? With the Turbo Debugger you can do exactly that by *breaking*, or stopping, program execution at a predefined point or time so that you can examine code and data. To break program execution, you set a *breakpoint* by telling TD what line of code, condition defined by an expression, or data value should stop the execution.

Simple Breakpoints and the Log Window

A simple breakpoint can be set at a specific line of code or even at a machine instruction.

Suppose that you want to allow the program to paint an entire screen before pausing, so that you can examine the contents of data fields. Use the down-arrow key to move the cursor (not the current-position pointer) to line 36.

The menu at the bottom of the screen indicates that F2 is the Set-Breakpoint key. If you now press F2, TD should highlight that line. A simple breakpoint can be removed just by moving the cursor to that same line and pressing F2 again; F2 acts as a toggle key for breakpoints. To allow TD to execute the program until the debugger encounters the breakpoint, press F9 (Run).

TD now runs the program, showing that work is being done by occasionally displaying WAIT in the status area at the screen's upper right corner and by moving the current-position pointer as each line is executed. When the breakpoint (an unconditional breakpoint) is encountered at line 36, TD halts execution. Now you can inspect variables, look at other windows, or perform another task.

While all of this is going on, TD is recording all significant events in its Log. To see the Log, press Alt-V to first pull down the View menu. You can either use the down-arrow key to move the highlighting to Log, or simply press L to display the contents of Log. Figure 10.15 shows the Log display in window 4.

Although this is a simple example, it is apparent that the Log display can be an important part of a debugging session. It eliminates the need to step through a program, manually writing down each significant event. More on this in Chapter 11, "Data Validation and Analysis."

Fig. 10.15. Log display showing breakpoint event.

```
    File   View   Run   Breakpoints   Data   Window   Options              READY
┌CPU 8086──┬─Module: SHOWPIX  File: B:\SHOWPIX.C 20──────────────────────────3┐
│SHOWPIX#36:│        }
│  cs:00F6 F│    }
│  cs:00F9 ┌Log══════════════════════════════════════════════4═╗
│  cs:00FC │Stopped at _main                                   ║
│  cs:0101 │Terminated, exit code 0                            ║
│  cs:0102 │Stopped at _main                                   ║
│SHOWPIX#3 │Breakpoint at SHOWPIX#36                            ║
│  cs:0103 │Stopped at _main                                   ║
│  cs:0108 │Stopped at _main                                   ║
│  cs:010B │                                                   ║
│  cs:010F │                                                   ║
│  cs:0111 9│═══════════════════════════════════════════════════╝
┌Variables─┐       directvideo = 1;
│DGROUP@    │       if ( argc < 2 ) exit(0);
│PADD@      │       if ( NULL == (pix = fopen(argv[1],"rt")) ) exit(0);
│PCMP@      │       y = 1;
│PSUB@      │       clrscr(); gotoxy(1,1);
│_8087      │       while ( NULL != (fgets( pline,83,pix )) ) {  /* 80 + CRLF */
│_CPUTN     │          show_line(pline); y++;
│_IOERROR   │       }
│_Int0Vecto │       fclose(pix);
```

F2-Bkpt F3-Close F4-Here F5-Zoom F6-Next F7-Trace F8-Step F9-Run F10-Menu

Setting Conditional Breakpoints

Traditionally, debugging has involved much scratch paper and hair pulling—keeping up manually with changing data values, loop iterations, and so forth can be very difficult. A more sophisticated feature of the Turbo Debugger's breakpoint facility, the *conditional breakpoint*, also can prevent much note-taking.

You can instruct TD to break execution conditionally when a certain number of iterations have occurred (by setting a Pass Count), when a logical condition exists (by setting an Expression Value, or *watch point*), or when a particular variable has been modified (by setting a Changed Data value, or *trace point*). This type of breakpoint is different from a simple breakpoint, in that execution is stopped when the condition has been fulfilled, rather than simply when the indicated line of source code has been reached. A particular line of code may be executed many times before the breakpoint is taken.

To illustrate the use of breakpoints with a pass count, re-execute showpix, and break after the function show_line() has been executed 25 times. Select View/Breakpoints to start setting it up.

Initially, the Breakpoints window will be empty when it pops up because you have not yet defined anything. Notice that a vertical line divides the window into left and right sides, or *panes*. In the left pane, the *breakpoint list* contains an entry for every defined breakpoint; you can move up and down in this list with the arrow (or other navigation) keys. The right side of the window is the *breakpoint detail* pane, which gives detailed information about the breakpoint currently highlighted in the list pane.

How do you control the Breakpoints window? Press Alt-F10 to pop up the local menu (*local* means for one window only). The Breakpoints local menu is shown in figure 10.16.

Fig. 10.16. *Breakpoints local menu.*

```
   File   View   Run   Breakpoints   Data   Window   Options        MENU
┌CPU 8086──┌Module: SHOWPIX  File: B:\SHOWPIX.C 8──────────────────────3┐
│SHOWPIX#3│Breakpoints═══════════════════════════════════5┐
│  cs:00F6│_show_line      │ Breakpoint
│  cs:00F9│┌───────────────┤ Always
│  cs:00FC││ Set action    │ Enabled
│  cs:0101││ Condition
│  cs:0102││ Pass count...
│SHOWPIX#3││ Enable/disable
│  cs:0103│└───────────────┘
│  cs:0108│ Add...          │g;
│  cs:010B│ Global
│  cs:010F│ Remove          │;
│  cs:0111│ Delete all
┌Variables│ Inspect         │FP( 0xB800, (x-1)*2 + (y-1)*160 );
│DGROUP@   └─────────────────┘ring ) {
│PADD@              *screen = *ostring++; screen += 2;
│PCMP@           }
│PSUB@         }
│_8087
│_CPUTN
│_IOERROR  ► main(argc,argv)
│_Int0Vecto   int argc;
```
```
F1-Help ↵-Select Esc-Abort
```

Consistent with TD menu usage, you can move the highlight to another selection by using the arrow keys or by typing the first letter of the selection you want. In this case, you will identify a breakpoint location at the show_line() function header to stop execution just as TD is about to descend into this function.

First, select Add to add a new breakpoint. TD will prompt you for the location in the program at which to set the breakpoint. Because the function header is line 8 in showpix, you can respond by typing **showpix.8**.

This syntax works even in programs made up of multiple source files. In general, you respond by typing the file name of the source file (in other words, the module name) without the .C extension, followed by a period and the line number within the source file. In figure 10.16, this already has been done; the breakpoint identifier is listed as _show_line.

Breakpoint Locations and External Identifiers

> The sample breakpoint (fig. 10.16) was located on a *function header*. In Turbo C (as in all implementations of C) a function name is an external identifier; by default, it is noted in the compiler's symbol table with a leading underscore. Thus, the Breakpoint-list entry name is _show_line. This indicates that C considers its functions to be objects which can be manipulated, in contrast to the Pascal procedure, which is action-oriented only.
>
> If you had added the breakpoint requesting a location within the function body, showpix, line 13, for example (showpix.13), the Breakpoint-list entry would have read SHOWPIX#13.

To complete the breakpoint definition, tell TD how many times to execute past this point before stopping execution. Figure 10.17 shows the Breakpoints window and its local menu after you select Pass count and enter 25 as an argument. TD will stop execution when it "passes by" this location for the 25th time.

Fig. 10.17. Setting the breakpoint pass count.

```
    File   View   Run   Breakpoints   Data   Window   Options              PROMPT
 ┌CPU 8086──┌Module: SHOWPIX  File: B:\SHOWPIX.C 8─────────────────────3┐
 │SHOWPIX#3 ┌Breakpoints══════════════════════════════5┐
 │  cs:00F6 │_show_line        │ Breakpoint
 │  cs:00F9 │                  ┌Always
 │  cs:00FC │ Set action       │ Enabled
 │  cs:0101 │ Condition
 │  cs:0102 │ Pass count...
 │SHOWPIX#3 ┌Enter breakpoint pass count──────────┐
 │  cs:0103 │ 25
 │  cs:0108 │
 │  cs:010B │ Global
 │  cs:010F │ Remove            ;
 │  cs:0111 │ Delete all
 ┌Variables─│ Inspect           FP( 0xB800, (x-1)*2 + (y-1)*160 );
 │DGROUP@   └──────────────────┘ring ) {
 │PADD@            *screen = *ostring++; screen += 2;
 │PCMP@         }
 │PSUB@      }
 │_8087
 │_CPUTN
 │_IOERROR  ▶ main(argc,argv)
 │_Int0Vecto     int argc;
 F1-Help ,⌐-Select Esc-Abort
```

As soon as this request has been made, TD updates the breakpoint information and displays it in the Breakpoints detail pane (see fig. 10.18).

Fig. 10.18. *The completed breakpoint definition with pass count.*

```
    File   View   Run   Breakpoints   Data   Window   Options          MENU
┌CPU 8086──┌Module: SHOWPIX  File: B:\SHOWPIX.C 8──────────────────────┐3┐
│SHOWPIX#3 ┌Breakpoints═══════════════════════════════════════════5┐   │
│  cs:00F6 │_show_line          │ Breakpoint                       │   │
│  cs:00F9 │                    ├Always                            │   │
│  cs:00FC │ Set action         │After 25 times                    │   │
│  cs:0101 │ Condition          │Enabled                           │   │
│  cs:0102 │ Pass count...      │                                  │   │
│SHOWPIX#3 │ Enable/disable     │                                  │   │
│  cs:0103 └                    └──────────────────────────────────┘   │
│  cs:0108 │ Add...             │g;                                     │
│  cs:010B │ Global             │                                       │
│  cs:010F │ Remove             │;                                      │
│  cs:0111 │ Delete all         │                                       │
│┌Variables│ Inspect            │FP( 0xB800, (x-1)*2 + (y-1)*160 );     │
││DGROUP@   └────────────────────ring ) {                               │
││PADD@           *screen = *ostring++; screen += 2;                    │
││PCMP@         }                                                       │
││PSUB@       }                                                         │
││__8087                                                                │
││__CPUTN                                                               │
││__IOERROR  ▶ main(argc,argv)                                          │
││__Int0Vecto    int argc;                                              │
└─────────────────────────────────────────────────────────────────────┘

F1-Help Esc-Abort
```

As you can see, the detail pane indicates that this is a breakpoint, that it is to occur always when this location is being passed for the 25th time, and that it is enabled. If a breakpoint definition is disabled, no breakpoint will be taken, even though the breakpoint definition exists.

When you have defined how you want program execution to break, simply press F9 (Run) to begin execution. TD quickly executes the program one line at a time. You do not have to press F7 or F8 for each line. Figure 10.19 shows showpix after the pass-count breakpoint has been reached. The Breakpoints window has been moved out of the way so that you can see the current-position pointer. You can move a window quickly by pressing Scroll Lock, using the arrow keys to position, and then pressing Enter to complete the move.

Setting a breakpoint to halt execution when a specified condition is met is a more sophisticated way of tracking events during program execution. The showpix program again provides a good example of this type of breakpoint. As written here, showpix displays the ASCII graphic character for a line feed at the end of the line, when the display is less than 80 characters long. To determine what is going on, set a breakpoint that will detect a display line shorter than 80 characters.

To do this, select showpix, line 36, as the breakpoint location. This is the source line in main() that invokes show_line(pline), where pline is the display line string (see fig. 10.20).

Fig. 10.19. Current position after pass count break.

```
      File   View   Run   Breakpoints   Data   Window   Options          READY
┌CPU 8086──┬Module: SHOWPIX  File: B:\SHOWPIX.C 8─────────────────────────3┐
│_show_line:│    #include <stdio.h>
│  cs:000A▶5│    #include <conio.h>
│  cs:000B┌L│    #include <dos.h>
│  cs:000D│S│
│  cs:0010│T│       int x = 1;
│  cs:0011│S│       int y;
│  cs:0014│B│
│SHOWPIX#1│S│▶  void show_line( ostring )
│  cs:0016│S│       char *ostring;
│  cs:0019│T│    {
│  cs:001A└─│       char *screen;
│  cs:001C 5│
├Variables─┤       screen = M┌Breakpoints═══════════════════════════════5┐
│DGROUP@   │       while ( *o│_show_line      │ Breakpoint
│PADD@     │         *screen │                │ Always
│PCMP@     │       }         │                │ Enabled
│PSUB@     │    }            │
│__8087    │                 │
│__CPUTN   │                 │
│__IOERROR │    main(argc,ar └
│__Int0Vecto│      int argc;
└──────────┴──────────────────────────────────────────────────────────────┘
 F2-Bkpt F3-Close F4-Here F5-Zoom F6-Next F7-Trace F8-Step F9-Run F10-Menu
```

Fig. 10.20. Adding a breakpoint at `showpix.36`.

```
      File   View   Run   Breakpoints   Data   Window   Options          PROMPT
┌CPU 8086──┬Module: SHOWPIX  File: B:\SHOWPIX.C 36────────────────────────3┐
│_main: ma┌Breakpoints═══════════════════════════════════4┐
│  cs:006B│                  │
│  cs:006C│
│  cs:006E│ Set action
│  cs:0071│ Condition
│  cs:0072│ Pass count...
│  cs:0075│ Enable/disable
│SHOWPIX#3│
│  cs:0077│ Add...
│  cs:007A┌Enter code address for breakpoint┐
│  cs:007C│ showpix.36
│SHOWPIX#31│
├Variables─┤ Inspect          │= 1;
│DGROUP@   │         └────────┘2 ) exit(0);
│PADD@     │      if ( NULL == (pix = fopen(argv[1],"rt")) ) exit(0);
│PCMP@     │      y = 1;
│PSUB@     │      clrscr(); gotoxy(1,1);
│__8087    │      while ( NULL != (fgets( pline,83,pix )) ) {  /* 80 + CRLF */
│__CPUTN   │        show_line(pline); y++;
│__IOERROR │      }
│__Int0Vecto│      fclose(pix);
└──────────┴──────────────────────────────────────────────────────────────┘
 F1-Help ↵-Select Esc-Abort
```

Defining the condition to check is a simple matter (see fig. 10.21). You select the
`Condition` option from the `Breakpoints` local menu, then select `Expression`
`True`, and respond to the prompt.

Fig. 10.21. *Defining an expression true conditional breakpoint.*

```
    File    View    Run    Breakpoints    Data    Window    Options         PROMPT
 ┌CPU 8086──┌Module: SHOWPIX  File: B:\SHOWPIX.C 38───────────────────────────3┐
 │_main: ma┌Breakpoints════════════════════════════════════4┐
 │  cs:006B│SHOWPIX#36      │  Breakpoint
 │  cs:006C│                │ ┌Always
 │  cs:006E│  Set action    │  Enabled
 │  cs:0071│  Condition
 │  cs:0072│
 │  cs:0075│  Always
 │SHOWPIX#3│  Changed memory...├──────────────┘
 │  cs:0077│  Expression true...
 │  cs:007A┌Enter expression for conditional breakpoint┐
 │  cs:007C│ strlen(#main#pline) < 80
 │SHOWPIX#31
 ┌Variables─┐ Inspect        │ = 1;
 │DGROUP@   └────────────────┘2 ) exit(0);
 │PADD@         if ( NULL == (pix = fopen(argv[1],"rt")) ) exit(0);
 │PCMP@         y = 1;
 │PSUB@         clrscr(); gotoxy(1,1);
 │_8087         while ( NULL != (fgets( pline,83,pix )) ) {   /* 80 + CRLF */
 │_CPUTN           show_line(pline); y++;
 │_IOERROR      }
 │_Int0Vecto    fclose(pix);
 └──────────────────────────────────────────────────────────────
 F1-Help ◄┘-Select Esc-Abort
```

Writing Expression True Conditions

When you write expressions, there are two factors to be careful about: symbol
existence and scope.

Function names and data variables (both considered to be symbols) are unreachable if they have not been defined in the program. To define the `Expression True`
condition shown in figure 10.21, for example, a reference was made to the Turbo C
function `strlen()`, which returns the length of the argument string. For this to
work correctly, however, the `showpix` program had to be modified slightly: both
the compiler directive `#include <string.h>` and a dummy call to `strlen()`
were added. This will cause the linkage editor to include the function code in the
.EXE file.

Scope also was an issue in this example. At the time the condition was defined,
the string `pline` was not yet defined; a *scope override* syntax was required to define it. The general syntax for doing this is

```
#file#function#variable
```

where you can include, *in this same relative order*, the necessary identifying references. Because the `showpix` program does not have multiple source files, the file qualifier was not needed.

After defining the `Expression True` condition, it is again necessary only to press F9 to run the program until the condition has been met, or possibly to completion if no such conditions become satisfied. Figure 10.22 shows the debugger display when the breakpoint occurs. TD conveniently makes the breakpoint event almost impossible to miss.

Fig. 10.22. Conditional breakpoint has occurred.

```
    File    View    Run    Breakpoints    Data    Window    Options              STATUS
 ┌CPU 8086──┬Module: SHOWPIX  File: B:\SHOWPIX.C 36═══════════════════════════3┐
 │SHOWPIX#3┌B│      }
 │  cs:00D9│S│    }
 │  cs:00DA│ │
 │  cs:00DD│ │
 │  cs:00DE│ │    main(argc,argv)
 │  cs:00DF│ │      int argc;
 │  cs:00E2│ │      char *argv[];
 │  cs:00E3└─│    {
 │  cs:00E4│ │      FILE *pix;
 │SHOWPIX#3│ │      char pline[83];
 │  cs:00E8└─│      char ch;
 │  cs:00EB F│
 ┌Variables─│      directvideo = 1;
 │DGROUP@   │      if ( argc < 2 ) exit(0);
 │PADD@     │      if ( NULL == (pix = fopen(argv[1],"rt")) ) exit(0);
 │PCMP@     │      y = 1;
 │PSUB@     │      clrscr(); gotoxy(1,1);
 │__8087    │      while ( NULL != (fgets( pline,83,pix )) ) {  /* 80 + CRLF */
 │__CPUTN  ▶│        show_line(pline); y++;
 │__IOER    ├──────────────────────────────────────────────────────────────
 │__Int0    │ Breakpoint at SHOWPIX#36 "strlen(#main#pline) < 80" true.  Press ESC.
 └──────────┘
  F2-Bkpt F3-Close F4-Here F5-Zoom F6-Next F7-Trace F8-Step F9-Run F10-Menu
```

The `Changed Data Condition` breakpoint is especially useful in detecting the corruption of a data field. This error often occurs in a looping structure that is not closely written (a favorite programmer's joke is to blame any unexplained program behavior on a "runaway subscript").

Recall the processing loop from the `bullet()` function in `finance.c`. Figure 10.23 shows that this loop is controlled by a `while (!fine)` statement, in which `fine` means "finished". If `fine` somehow becomes corrupted during loop iterations, the program may never exit `bullet()`.

Figure 10.24 shows how to set this type of breakpoint condition. TD monitors the specified data location (the `while` statement was chosen) as it executes the program, one line at a time. When the contents of that location change in relation to the previous line that was executed, the breakpoint occurs.

Fig. 10.23. *A suspect loop control variable.*

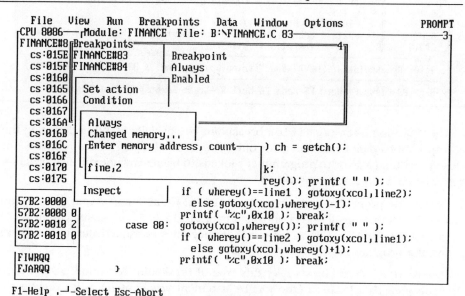

```
   File   View   Run   Breakpoints   Data   Window   Options          READY
┌CPU 8086──┌Module: FINANCE  File: B:\FINANCE.C 96══════════════════════3┐
│_main: main║    void bullet(rc,xcol,line1,line2)                        │
│  cs:1D86►5║      int *rc,xcol,line1,line2;                             │
│  cs:1D87 8║    {                                                       │
│  cs:1D89 1║      char ch;                                              │
│  cs:1D8A B║      int  fine;                                            │
│  cs:1D8D 8║                                                            │
│FINANCE#643║      fine=FALSE;                                           │
│  cs:1D8F C║      gotoxy(xcol,line1); printf( "%c",0x10 );             │
│  cs:1D95 C║      while ( !fine ) {                                     │
│  cs:1D9B C║        ch = getch(); if ( ch == 0 ) ch = getch();         │
│  cs:1DA1 C║        switch (ch) {                                       │
│  cs:1DA7 C║          case 13:  fine=TRUE; break;                       │
│  cs:1DAD C║          case 72:  gotoxy(xcol,wherey()); printf( " " );   │
│          ║             if ( wherey()==line1 ) gotoxy(xcol,line2);     │
│ 57B2:0000 C║                else gotoxy(xcol,wherey()-1);             │
│ 57B2:0008 0║             printf( "%c",0x10 ); break;                   │
│ 57B2:0010 2║          case 80:  gotoxy(xcol,wherey()); printf( " " );  │
│ 57B2:0018 0║             if ( wherey()==line2 ) gotoxy(xcol,line1);   │
│          ║                else gotoxy(xcol,wherey()+1);              │
│FIWRQQ     ║             printf( "%c",0x10 ); break;                    │
│FJARQQ     ║      }                                                     │
└──────────┴────────────────────────────────────────────────────────────┘
F2-Bkpt F3-Close F4-Here F5-Zoom F6-Next F7-Trace F8-Step F9-Run F10-Menu
```

Fig. 10.24. *Defining a changed data condition breakpoint.*

```
   File   View   Run   Breakpoints   Data   Window   Options          PROMPT
┌CPU 8086──┌Module: FINANCE  File: B:\FINANCE.C 83══════════════════════3┐
│FINANCE#8 ┌Breakpoints═══════════════════════════════════════4┐         │
│  cs:015E║FINANCE#83        Breakpoint                         │         │
│  cs:015F║FINANCE#84        Always                             │         │
│  cs:0160║              ┌──Enabled                             │         │
│  cs:0165║┌──────────┐  │                                      │         │
│  cs:0166║│Set action│  └──────────────────────────────────────┘        │
│  cs:0167║│Condition │                                                   │
│  cs:016A╨├──────────┤                                                   │
│  cs:016B║│Always    │                                                   │
│  cs:016C║│Changed memory...│                                            │
│  cs:016F║┌─Enter memory address, count──────┐ ) ch = getch();          │
│  cs:0170║│fine,2                            │                          │
│  cs:0175║└──────────────────────────────────┘ k;                       │
│          ├──────────┤              rey()); printf( " " );              │
│ 57B2:0000│Inspect   │        if ( wherey()==line1 ) gotoxy(xcol,line2);│
│ 57B2:0008 0          │           else gotoxy(xcol,wherey()-1);         │
│ 57B2:0010 2│         case 80:  printf( "%c",0x10 ); break;             │
│ 57B2:0018 0│                   gotoxy(xcol,wherey()); printf( " " );    │
│          │                     if ( wherey()==line2 ) gotoxy(xcol,line1);│
│FIWRQQ    │                        else gotoxy(xcol,wherey()+1);        │
│FJARQQ    │      }              printf( "%c",0x10 ); break;             │
└──────────┴────────────────────────────────────────────────────────────┘
F1-Help ↵-Select Esc-Abort
```

Summary

Some important tools and concepts have been presented in this chapter. I have only scratched the surface of the topics dealt with, but this material, combined with that in Chapter 9, should prepare you for the more extensive discussions in Chapter 11.

The most important underlying concept in this chapter is the notion of *formalized* thinking about program logic, program branching, and instruction paths. By *formal* I mean that you should be deliberately conscious and analytical. It is true that these concepts are basically simple, but their *consequences* can become complex.

Turbo Debugger provides for the analysis of program logic in two fundamental ways: tracing and breakpoint events. The essential difference between the two facilities is that tracing does not presume any knowledge about where a bug may be, or what a program may do next, whereas a breakpoint can be set when you already suspect the location of a bug, or the condition that causes it.

TD's tracing facilities allow you to examine the flow of instructions anywhere in the program (or outside of it, for that matter), and at varying levels of detail.

❑ `Instruction Trace` executes and displays one machine instruction at a time. You can see exactly how each C statement uses the hardware. Nothing is hidden from you, but this type of trace requires the greatest knowledge of both PC and Turbo C internals.

❑ `Trace Into` remains at the C source language level, but traces down into called functions, making every C source statement in the program available for analysis. Most of the time, you will need no more detail than this.

❑ `Stepping Over` works just like `Trace Into`, except that tracing does not descend into called functions. You might think of this as a sumamry trace, to be used when low-level routines are known to be correct.

Using breakpoints can speed up the debugging process considerably, since TD executes instructions (or source lines) continuously until a breakpoint is reached. The tradeoff is that you must plan the debugging session more carefully and develop an idea about where and what the problem is. You can then define breakpoints to help you test your hypothesis.

TD breakpoints encompass three facilities that traditionally have been implemented separately: breakpoints, watchpoints, and tracepoints.

❑ *Simple Breakpoints* have been thought of traditionally as just a location in the program where execution should stop. It might be helpful to think of this kind of TD breakpoint as an "unconditional" breakpoint.

❑ The Condition/Expression True selection on the Breakpoints local menu establishes the criteria for a conditional breakpoint that will occur when a specified expression becomes TRUE (not zero). This type of breakpoint is TD's implementation of a *watchpoint*. A related method is to define a Pass Count breakpoint; execution stops when a location has been passed (or a condition fulfilled) a stated number of times.

❑ TD implements the equivalent of a *tracepoint* in the Condition/Changed Memory selection on the Breakpoints local menu. Each time the specified memory location changes, a breakpoint occurs. You can avoid some of the performance penalty associated with this type of breakpoint by specifying it for a breakpoint at a specific address, if your debugging strategy permits that.

Turbo Debugger's trace and breakpoint facilities allow you to selectively control program execution, and to examine in detail what the program is doing (and how it does it).

Lee
Atkinson

CHAPTER 11

Data Validation
and Analysis

Following the logic of a program per se is not much of a problem. Program verification and debugging become a problem only when you cannot clearly determine just what the sequence of events will be.

The instruction path actually executed will deviate from the predicted route under three circumstances: the program was not properly designed, you did not code the program exactly as you thought you did, or the information entered for the program is not what you think it is.

Earlier chapters have dealt with the first two of these conditions. This chapter deals in some detail with the third. The following topics are discussed:

❏ Manual and automated methods of validating data

❏ Designing test case data

❏ Designing manageable data structures

❏ Common sources of data error

Data Validation

This section explores methods of validating data, including data representations, boundary value analysis, and automated validation techniques.

How Data Drives Logic

Program logic is driven by the data it works with. Exactly what does that mean?

Consider a simple `for` loop structure. The `for` declaration consists of three expressions that initialize variables, check conditions, and perform some sort of control action, respectively. In the following example:

```
for( i=1; i<=10; i++ ) {
   /* do something here */
}
```

the variable i is being used as a loop control variable in a fashion very similar to a FORTRAN loop (although the syntax is much different). The variable is first initialized to 1; it is checked every pass through the loop (at the top) to see whether it is still less than or equal to 10, and it is updated during every pass (at the back end of the loop).

The significant factor for such a simple statement is that *it is controlled entirely by the value of the variable i.*

The same concept applies to the if, switch, while, and do-while statements. In every case, the controlling action is provided by the state (contents or value) of a data variable.

Thus, although it may be true that data validation and analysis are not all there is to testing and debugging a program, they are critical to the process. Having complete control of the data is just as important as having control of the logic flow.

How can you get such control? First, you can *design the program to take control* of its operating environment. Programming is an art much like driving a car. You can easily under control or over control the car, but finding just the right amount of control is quite difficult. Second, you can *design the environment to work effectively and correctly* with the program. This process involves designing an efficient set of variables and structures; it can be compared to building the road on which you drive the car.

In this chapter I explain the tools and techniques you need to achieve program control.

Looking at Live Data

At the risk of beginning at the back end, I start with the easiest method of validating and analyzing data usage within a program. You can simply run the program under the Turbo Debugger (TD) and inspect the data as it is being changed and used.

The Inspect Command

To inspect the state of a variable, the Turbo Debugger must indicate READY. In other words, while TD is running a program, that is all it will do—run. Refer to Chapter 10 in this book, as well as to Borland's *Turbo Debugger User's Guide*, to see how to use breakpoints, Trace Into, and Instruction Trace to position the program properly. When TD has halted execution of program statements and is displaying the READY flag, you can use the Inspect command to examine the contents of variables.

TD gives you two ways to invoke Inspect. You can move the cursor (within the local scope, discussed in the following section) until it is under one of the characters of the variable name you want to inspect. This location does not have to be the definition of the variable. The location can be anywhere the variable name is referenced. Once the cursor is in position, press Ctrl-I. Note that this is a *shortcut key*. If you have used TDINST.EXE to disable shortcut keys, this method will not work. Figure 11.1 shows a displayed TD Inspector window.

Fig. 11.1. *Invoking Inspect by pressing Ctrl-I.*

```
   File   View   Run   Breakpoints   Data   Window   Options          READY
┌CPU 8086──┬Module: FINANCE  File: B:\FINANCE.C 631───────────────────────3┐
│FINANCE#631│      "                       Create, Edit Tables\n",
│  cs:1D37►A│      "                       Handle Case Files\n",
│  cs:1D3A 4│      "                       Control Display Windows\n",
│  cs:1D3B 3│      "                       QUIT BUSINESS/PC\n",
│  cs:1D3E 7│      "_____",
│  cs:1D40 8│      "                                        "
│  cs:1D42 D│          );
│  cs:1D44 2│      printf("\n");
│  cs:1D49 5│      printf(
│  cs:1D4A 1│      "     Use the Up and Down ARROW keys to move the bullet besid
│  cs:1D4D 7│      "     to select. Then Strike RETURN (ENTER)."
│  cs:1D4F 7│          );
├Variables──┤      bullet(&rc,26,8,18);
│DGROUP@    ├──►   switch ( rc ) {
│FIARQQ     │         case 1: ┌Inspecting rc════════════════4┐
│FICRQQ     │         case 2: │@60EA:0026                    │
│FIDRQQ     │         case 6: │int                   7 (0x7) │
│FIERQQ     │         case 7: └──────────────────────────────┘
│FISRQQ     │         case 11: return;
│FIWRQQ     │      }
│FJARQQ     │   }
└───────────┴───────────────────────────────────────────────────────────────
 F2-Bkpt F3-Close F4-Here F5-Zoom F6-Next F7-Trace F8-Step F9-Run F10-Menu
```

When you inspect a variable, keep in mind the difference between the *physical location* of the reference and the *time at which it was executed*. You can place the cursor on any one of multiple occurrences of the variable's name, but the value that Inspect displays is the value as of *the last program statement that TD actually executed*.

The other way to invoke Inspect is from the Data pull-down menu. In figure 11.2 you can see that Data is one of the Global (pull-down) menu selections displayed at the top of the screen. Invoke it directly by pressing Alt-D or indirectly by pressing F10-Menu, using the cursor keys to position the highlight over Data. Then press Enter. When the pull-down menu appears, use the cursor keys to position the highlight over Inspect, and then press Enter.

Fig. 11.2. *Invoking Inspect from the Data menu.*

```
    File   View   Run   Breakpoints   Data   Window   Options              PROMPT
┌CPU 8086──┌Module: FINANCE  File:                                            ─3┐
│FINANCE#631│       "          ┌────────────────────────────────────┬n",
│  cs:1D37▶A│       "          │ Inspect...                          │
│  cs:1D3A 4│       "          │┌Enter variable to inspect──────────┐│
│  cs:1D3B 3│       "          ││rc                                 ││n",
│  cs:1D3E 7│       "_____│└───────────────────────────────────┘│
│  cs:1D40 8│       "_____└──────────────────────────────"
│  cs:1D42 D│              );
│  cs:1D44 2│       printf("\n");
│  cs:1D49 5│       printf(
│  cs:1D4A 1│       "      Use the Up and Down ARROW keys to move the bullet besid
│  cs:1D4D 7│       "      to select. Then Strike RETURN (ENTER)."
│  cs:1D4F 7│              );
┌Variables─┐       bullet(&rc,26,8,18);
│DGROUP@   │  ▶      switch ( rc ) {
│FIARQQ    │           case 1: menu_GENBUS(); break;
│FICRQQ    │           case 2: menu_INTEREST(); break;
│FIDRQQ    │           case 6: menu_ACTUARIAL(); break;
│FIERQQ    │           case 7: menu_AMORTIZE(); break;
│FISRQQ    │           case 11: return;
│FIWRQQ    │         }
│FJARQQ    │       }
```

F1-Help ⌐┘-Select Esc-Abort◙

When you select Inspect, a data-entry box appears on top of the menus, prompting you to Enter variable to inspect. In this example, the variable rc is being inspected. Your choices of variable names depend on the current position in the program, what parts of the program have already been run, and how the variable being referenced was defined initially.

Details on Overriding Scope

Figure 11.3 illustrates what happens if you do not observe *scope* correctly. The user has attempted to inspect the value of a variable that either was not a global variable or was one of the variables defined as belonging to main(): int oldx,oldy,r,s. By displaying Symbol not found. Press ESC, TD quickly tells you that it has no idea what you are talking about—nothing has yet been executed, as indicated by the current-position pointer which is still located at main().

Understanding Scope

The proper entry point into C scope rules is to first understand what a *block* is: a particular sequence of C source statements. Naturally, these statements are assumed to be contiguous and to belong in the same logical grouping. With that in mind, it is easy to name the groups of C statements that can be considered to make up a block:

user-defined functions, a single source file (whether the program contains one or many source files), or the entire program or subfunction level. Some items can be local to a block within the function:

```
void func()
{
    int var1;
    /*do something*/
if (var1 !=1)
{
    int var2;
    /* etc. */
}
```

var2 is local to the if block. As soon as execution moves outside this block, var2 is no longer visible.

Fig. 11.3. *Result of an invalid scope during Inspect.*

```
    File   View   Run   Breakpoints   Data   Window   Options          ERROR
 ┌CPU 8086──┌Module: XE  File: B:\XE ┌──────────────────────────┐         ─3┐
 _main: main │     farfree( holdtcb  │ Inspect...               │
   cs:2EFD▶5 │  }                    │ ┌──────────────────────┐ │
   cs:2EFE 8 │ }                     │ │ Symbol not found.  Press ESC. │
   cs:2F00 8 │                       │ └──────────────────────┘ │
   cs:2F03 5 ▶ main(argc,argv)       └──────────────────────────┘
   cs:2F04 5 │    int  argc;
   cs:2F05 1 │    char *argv[];
   cs:2F06 B │    {
   cs:2F09 8 │      int oldx,oldy,r,s;
 XE#273:  if │
   cs:2F0B 8 │    /*──────────────────────────────────────*/
   cs:2F0F 7 │    /*           Initialize variables        */
 ─Variables─ │    /*──────────────────────────────────────*/
 DGROUP@     │
 PADA@       │    if (argc==2) strcpy(docname,argv[1]);
 PADD@       │      else strcpy(docname,"");
 PCMP@       │    lm=2; rm=78; tm=2; bm=21;
 PSBA@       │    initvid();
 PSBP@       │
 PSUB@       │    if ( vbasead == VCOLOR ) scr_buf = 0xb8000000L;
 _CAPS       │      else scr_buf = 0xb0000000L;

 F1-Help Esc-Abort█
```

A Glance at C Scoping

The whole concept of scope rules—whether in C or another language—arose from the idea of *information hiding*.

Information hiding aims to make certain code and data in a program "visible" or "active" at a certain point. All other data and code are considered "invisible." The reasoning behind this is, of course, that you cannot hurt what you cannot access.

As with all such techniques, scoping has advantages and disadvantages. In the hands of a competent programmer, scoping is a convenient and powerful tool. In the hands of the less competent, neither this nor any other strategy will help to protect data and code.

Now that you know about information hiding, keeping track of scope is easy. A variable defined at the beginning of a block is valid for that entire block, with the single exception of variables whose definitions contain the `extern` scope modifier, which can be made visible anywhere you choose to use the `extern` declaration.

Consider the simple case of a program consisting of one source file, which has variables defined both at the top of the program and within the user-defined functions:

```
#include <stdlib.h>    /* source file A */
#include <stdio.h>

int a,b,c;
void myfunction( void )
{
   double d,e,f;

      ... myfunction logic
}

main()
{
   unsigned long g,h,i;

      ... main program body
   if(i > 5)
   {
      int   j,k,m;
         more logic
   }
}
```

This short (and empty) sample program defines 10 variables in four different places. Table 11.1 summarizes the locations *from which* the variables can be referenced.

Table 11.1. *Availability of Variables*

Variables	Where Defined	Where Available to Reference
a, b, c	Source file	Entire source file Other source files
d, e, f	myfunction()	Only myfunction()
g, h, i	main()	Only main()
j, k, m		Block controlled by if

Note: people seldom use the letter *l* as a variable name because of the similarity with digit *1*.

It is intuitively obvious that the variables d, e, f should be available only in myfunction(), because that is where they are defined. It is not so obvious that variables defined in main() are available only in main(); that, after all, is the main function of the whole program. But main() is in fact only a function with *local scope*, even if it is the only one required.

The variables a, b, c are of more interest, because there are two uses for them in addition to using them in this source file. First, you can reference them in another source file because, being defined outside of any function block, a, b, c have *external scope*. Suppose that you write another source module like this:

```
#include <stdlib.h>    /* source file B */
#include <stdio.h>

extern int a,b,c;

void function_two( void )
{
    if ( a< 2 ) b = c; else b = c/2;
}
```

In source file B, the declaration extern int a,b,c does not set aside any storage, and you cannot initialize the variables in the declaration statement as you can when originally defining them. This code *does* direct the compiler to make a notation in the .OBJ file so that the linker will handle it as it puts together all the modules and resolves the external references. This technique thus enables you to build a very large program one module at a time, saving a great deal of time by preventing much unnecessary recompilation.

The second protective measure for these variables is to prevent access to them from other source files. The static scope modifier can be used at the top of a block (in the "global variable position") to make variables unavailable to other source files. In this example, if you had declared

```
static int a,b,c;
```

in source file A, the variables would be unavailable to B. The compiler would have processed source file B successfully, only to have the linker in its turn inform you that it did not know what these variables are.

Inspecting Variables in Another Scope

Now the foundation is in place for understanding what the Turbo Debugger does when the `Inspect` command is issued and why the `Inspect` in figure 11.3 failed. In that example, a variable local to another function, and therefore *not active in the current scope*, was requested. Further, the variable was an automatic variable, and did not physically exist yet.

In figure 11.4, another variable was requested; this variable was not part of the function being traced at the current position, yet the `Inspect` command was successful. The command was successful because the variable has global scope (that is, the variable was defined at the top of the source file).

Fig. 11.4. *Inspecting a variable with global scope.*

```
    File   View   Run   Breakpoints   Data   Window   Options              READY
┌CPU 8086──┌Module: XE  File: B:\XE.C 310───────────────────────────────────3┐
│XE#310:  sh│   gotoxy(2,22); writechs(196,2,78);   /* bottom bar */
│ cs:31CC▶1 │   gotoxy(80,22); writechs(189,2,1);    /* bottom right corner */
│ cs:31CD B │   for ( x=1,y=2; y<22; y++) {
│ cs:31D0 5 │     gotoxy(x,y); writechs(186,2,1);
│ cs:31D1 9 │   }
│ cs:31D6 5 │   for ( x=80,y=2; y<22; y++) {
│ cs:31D7 5 │     gotoxy(x,y); writechs(186,2,1);
│XE#311:  y=│   }
│ cs:31D8 C │
│ cs:31DE C │   y=23; x=2;
│XE#312:  sp│   sprintf( display,"Document File<>" );
│ cs:31E4 1▶│   show_string(display);
┌Variables──│   y=24; x=2; ┌Inspecting display════════4┐
│DGROUP@    │   sprintf( dis│@6500:0277              │    >" );
│PADA@      │   show_string(│[0]           'D' 68 (0x44)│
│PADD@      │   y=25; x=2;  │[1]           'o' 111 (0x6F)│
│PCMP@      │   show_string(│[2]           'c' 99 (0x63)│
│PSBA@      │              │[3]           'u' 117 (0x75)│
│PSBP@      │   tcb = NULL; │                           │
│PSUB@      │   if ( FALSE =│char [121]            │otoxy(1,1); exit(0)
│_CAPS      │
F2-Bkpt F3-Close F4-Here F5-Zoom F6-Next F7-Trace F8-Step F9-Run F10-Menu
```

These two examples illustrate what TD considers to be the *current scope*. A current scope includes both the global and the local scope for the active function. When TD processes an `Inspect` command, it searches for the named symbol following normal C scope rules.

1. Searching begins with the current source file.

2. The current function is searched for both automatic and static variables, because both are valid in the current scope (the same as the local scope here).

3. Searching continues in the global scope in the same source file (still part of TD's current scope), including references to symbols declared to be `extern`.

4. Finally, other source files are searched for static symbols only.

Why does TD sometimes confine itself to a search for static variables? Depending on the current/local scope, other variables may not be found because they do not yet exist. You may recall that the `static` scope modifier "hides" variables from other blocks of code. Another effect of using the `static` modifier is to make the variable permanently available in the current scope.

The contrast between automatic variables and static variables is an important one for debugging, as well as for some types of advanced program design. An automatic variable is one defined within a *function*; Turbo C allocates the space for it from the *stack* only when the function is actually executed. This means that both before and after the function runs, an automatic variable literally does not exist.

A static variable, on the other hand, is allocated from the *data segment* at compile time, before the program ever runs. Thus, a static variable always exists, and its contents are not disturbed when the current or local scope changes.

Using Scope-Override Syntax

With this in mind, you can inspect variables *outside* the local scope (variables in functions and source files other than those at the current position). Always remind yourself, though, what kind of variable you want to inspect in another scope. Is it an automatic or static variable? If it is not a static variable, it may not be available for inspection. Figure 11.5 shows the Inspector window displaying a variable in another function.

Notice that the current-position indicator is located at the `main()` function header. Clearly, no part of the program has been executed, yet the `Inspect` command was successful. How did it work?

The Inspector window indicates that TD is inspecting `#xprintf#extra`. A scope override was used to display the static variable `extra`, which is located in the function `xprintf()`.

The pound sign (`#`) signals TD to begin looking for scope-override syntax to process this `Inspect` command. Scope-override syntax is flexible and powerful. Write the most powerful scope first, follow it with lower-level block names, and finish with the variable name itself.

You can specify the location of the variable either with the line number in the source file or with the name of the function that contains it. In general, the syntax is

```
[#modulename[#filename]]#linenumber[variablename]
```

Fig. 11.5. *Overriding local scope for a variable.*

```
    File   View   Run  Breakpoints   Data  Window   Options              READY
┌─CPU 8086──┬─Module: XEHELP  File: B:\XEHELP.C 176──────────────────────────3┐
│_main: main│     oldptr = getvect(5);
│  cs:0677►5│     setvect(5, xehelp);┌Inspecting #xprintf#extra═══4┐
│  cs:0678 8│   }                    │@5A8A:001C                    │
│  cs:067A 1│                        │int                  0 (0x0) │
│  cs:067B B│► main(argc,argv)       └──────────────────────────────┘
│  cs:067E 8│     int argc;
│XEHELP#180:│     char *argv[];
│  cs:0680 8│   {
│  cs:0684 7│     if ( argc == 2 ) strcpy(path,argv[1]);
│  cs:0686 C│       else strcpy( path,"B:\\" );
│  cs:0689 2│     gettextinfo(&s_d);
│  cs:068D 2│     if ( NULL == ( screen_save =
├─Variables─┤        farmalloc( (s_d.screenheight+s_d.screenwidth)*2 ) )
│DGROUP@     │        ) return;
│PADD@       │     *fname = '\0';
│PCMP@       │     scrseg = 0xB800; scrofs = 0;
│PSUB@       │     install();
│SCOPY@      │     mypsp = _psp; myss = _SS; mysp = _SP;
│_8087       │     set_up();
│_FPUTN      │     printf( "XEHELP TSR Installation Statistics:\n" );
│_IOERROR    │     printf( "   CS=%04X DS=%04X SS=%04X SP=%04X BP=%04X\n",_CS,_DS
└────────────────────────────────────────────────────────────────────────────
F2-Bkpt F3-Close F4-Here F5-Zoom F6-Next F7-Trace F8-Step F9-Run F10-Menu█
```

---

for requests by line number, or

```
[#modulename[#filename]][#functionname]#variablename
```

for requests by variable name. You can type only enough to make the request un-
ambiguous. For example, if the line number given points to the variable definition
itself, that is all you need to state. If the variable is in a file that is included (via the
#include directive) by the module being debugged, you can specify #filename
to get to it. Figure 11.6 shows how to inspect a variable in a program with multiple
source files.

The main source file in this program is xe.c. XE is a complete word processor,
requiring a great deal of code. To make it manageable, it was broken into several
source files that were compiled separately and then linked to form the load module
(.EXE file). To inspect the lpg variable, the programmer noted that the variable
was defined in the print services source file prints.c and directed TD to look
there for the variable. The syntax for this is

```
#prints#lpg
```

Because TD already knew it was debugging xe.exe, the programmer did not
have to specify that in the override syntax. Only the external source file name and
the variable name (which has global scope in prints.c) were needed to make the
request clear. Considering scope is still important when you inspect variables in

Fig. 11.6. Inspecting a variable in another source file.

```
   File   View   Run   Breakpoints   Data   Window   Options              READY
 ┌CPU 8086──┬─Module: XE  File: B:\XE.C 310────────────────────────────────3┐
 │XE#310:  sh│  }
 │  cs:31CC▶1│                        ┌Inspecting #prints#lpg═══════4┐
 │  cs:31CD B│  y=23; x=2;            │@6565:0006                    │
 │  cs:31D0 5│  sprintf( display,"Do  │int                 66 (0x42)│
 │  cs:31D1 9│▶ show_string(display)  └──────────────────────────────┘
 │  cs:31D6 5│  y=24; x=2;
 │  cs:31D7 5│  sprintf( display,"Buf<      > Col< > Mode<    >" );
 │XE#311:  y=│  show_string(display);
 │  cs:31D8 C│  y=25; x=2;
 │  cs:31DE C│  show_string("Msg/Cmd: ===>");
 │XE#312:  sp│
 │  cs:31E4 1│  tcb = NULL;
 ├Variables──│  if ( FALSE == create_tcb() ) { clrscrn(); gotoxy(1,1); exit(0)
 │DGROUP@    │
 │PADA@      │  y=tm; x=lm; gotoxy(x,y);
 │PADD@      │  load_doc(); showdoc();
 │PCMP@      │  paint(); getn();
 │PSBA@      │  showmem(TRUE); showcol(); showmode(); showistat();
 │PSBP@      │
 │PSUB@      │  ch = 32;
 │_CAPS      │  *key_buf = '\0';
 └───────────┴─────────────────────────────────────────────────────────────┘
 F2-Bkpt F3-Close F4-Here F5-Zoom F6-Next F7-Trace F8-Step F9-Run F10-Menu▓
```

other source files. The `lpg` variable, for example, was *not* in the current or local scope, from the *debugger's* point of view, when the `Inspect` command was issued, yet TD allowed the request and located the variable. Why? Because `lpg` was declared at the top of its entire block (the `prints.c` source file), placing it in the category of a global variable. Global variables are not allocated from the stack and therefore have a continued existence even when their local scope is not active.

In all this discussion of scope for inspecting variables, you may have noticed that the scope of a particular variable depends on how you look at it. In a sense, scope is relative. Following are a couple of observations about the scope of `lpg`.

❏ It has *local* scope from the point of view of `xe.c` as a whole—it is local to the `prints` source file. Thus `lpg` is invisible to modules other than `prints.c`, since it is not declared as `extern` anywhere.

❏ It has *global* scope from the point of view of the `prints.c` source file itself—it is declared at the beginning of that block, making it globally available to that entire block.

Representation of Simple Variables

It also is important to understand how TD represents the variables it displays in its Inspector windows. TD can inspect both simple and complex data structures—they do not all have to be elementary items.

What does TD tell you in an Inspector window display? Figure 11.7 shows TD displaying an Inspector window for the simple variable scrseg. It has placed the Inspector window box as close as possible to the variable reference in the source code—directly beneath it, in this case.

```
    File   View   Run  Breakpoints   Data   Window   Options              READY
┌CPU 8086──┌Module: XEHELP  File: B:\XEHELP.C 187───────────────────────────3┐
│XEHELP#188:│    oldptr = getvect(5);
│  cs:06F6►8│    setvect(5, xehelp);
│  cs:06F7 E│  }
│XEHELP#189:│
│  cs:06FA B│  main(argc,argv)
│  cs:06FD 8│   int argc;
│  cs:06FF 2│   char *argv[];
│  cs:0703 A│   {
│  cs:0706 8│    if ( argc == 2 ) strcpy(path,argv[1]);
│  cs:0708 A│      else strcpy( path,"B:\\" );
│  cs:070B 8│    gettextinfo(&s_d);
│XEHELP#190:│    if ( NULL == ( screen_save =
├Variables──┤      farmalloc( (s_d.screenheight+s_d.screenwidth)*2 ) )
│DGROUP@    │      ) return;
│PADD@      │    *fname = '\0';
│PCMP@      │    scrseg = 0xB800; scrofs = 0;
│PSUB@    ►  ┌Inspecting scrseg══════════╗4┐
│SCOPY@      │@5A8A:017D                 ║  = _SP;
│_8087       │unsigned int    47104 (0xB800)║
│_FPUTN      └═══════════════════════════╝n Statistics:\n" );
│_IOERROR   │    printf( "    CS=%04X DS=%04X SS=%04X SP=%04X BP=%04X\n",_CS,_DS
└───────────┴─────────────────────────────────────────────────────────────────┘
F2-Bkpt F3-Close F4-Here F5-Zoom F6-Next F7-Trace F8-Step F9-Run F10-Menu▓
```

What does an Inspector window tell about simple variables? Look closely at the following representation of the Inspector window from figure 11.7:

```
Inspecting scrseg
@5A8A:017D
unsigned int   47104 (0xB800)
```

Five items are presented for inspection.

❑ The symbol being inspected

❑ The TD window number

❑ The 80x86 RAM address of the variable

❑ The variable type

❑ The contents of the variable

The only confusing element in the display is the distinction between the *address* of the variable and the *contents* of the variable.

If you are a relative newcomer to the art and science of programming, note that the address of the variable is the location in RAM where the item is kept, whereas the contents of the variable are actually what is stored at that location. For items like the integer being inspected here, that distinction is obvious and trivial. For other types, such as pointer variables, the difference between the two concepts is very important and sometimes difficult to keep up with.

C features a small set of elementary data types, although there are variations and embellishments on each type. The elementary types are char, int, and float. The various modifiers (long, unsigned, double, and so on) modify how the items are handled internally, but they all display as simple variables in an Inspector window.

Representation of Compound Variables

TD can also inspect *complex data objects*—strings, arrays, and structures—recognizing that these are not elementary items and building the display accordingly. A complex data object, or *composite variable*, is just a group of very tightly related *simple variables*, or elementary items.

For example, Turbo C supports a built-in video function, gettextinfo(), which places varied information about the video-display state into a structure defined by struct text_info. The returned structure contains 11 integer type variables; because they are related, they are less meaningful apart from each other. Of what use is the screen height unless the width is also known? Or the X coordinate as a position on the screen when the Y coordinate is missing? Figure 11.8 shows the initial display of this structure.

Fig. 11.8. Inspecting a complex data object.

```
   File    View   Run   Breakpoints   Data   Window   Options              READY
┌CPU 8086──┌Module: XEHELP  File: B:\XEHELP.C 182─────────────────────────3┐
│XEHELP#188:     oldptr = getvect(5);
│  cs:06F6►0     setvect(5, xehelp);
│  cs:06F7 E   }
│XEHELP#189:
│  cs:06FA B   main(argc,argv)
│  cs:06FD 8     int argc;
│  cs:06FF 2     char *argv[];
│  cs:0703 A   {
│  cs:0706 8     if ( argc == 2 ) strcpy(path,argv[1]);
│  cs:0708 A       else strcpy( path,"B:\\" );
│  cs:070B 8     gettextinfo(&s_d);
│XEHELP#190:     if ( NULL == ┌Inspecting s_d═══════════4┐
│┌Variables─        farmalloc(│@5A8A:00DF              dth)*2 ) )
││DGROUP@           ) return; │winleft    '\x01' 1 (0x01)│
││PADD@         *fname = '\0' │wintop     '\x01' 1 (0x01)│
││PCMP@         scrseg = 0xB8 │winright     'P' 80 (0x50)│
││PSUB@    ►    install();    │winbottom  '\x19' 25 (0x19)│
││SCOPY@        mypsp = _psp; └────────────────────────────┘
││__8087        set_up();     │unsigned char
││__FPUTN       printf( "XEHE └────────────────────────────\n" );
││__IOERROR     printf( "   CS=%04X DS=%04X SS=%04X SP=%04X BP=%04X\n",_CS,_DS
```

F2-Bkpt F3-Close F4-Here F5-Zoom F6-Next F7-Trace F8-Step F9-Run F10-Menu

The display of a complex data object is similar to that of a simple variable. The display contains the symbol name, window number, starting address of the object, and a display of the contents. It differs in that the contents of not one, but the first few elements in the structure, are displayed. You can move up and down in the list of elementary items using the arrow keys or the PgUp and PgDn keys, because the list may be too large to display all at one time.

A powerful and useful feature of C structures is that they may contain objects *which are themselves structures* or other complex objects. As TD would descend into a function with `Trace Into`, you can direct TD to descend into a complex data object for more detailed analysis.

In order to see clearly what this facility can do for you, look at the program `phones.c` in listing 11.1. Its purpose is to illustrate the use of structures in simulating some (but not all) of the features of object-oriented programming techniques. Specifically, `phones.c` creates a "telephone" object which can place "calls" and record them in an associated call log. Phone calls are sent to the screen and recorded in the log automatically when a call request is made.

Note that when you compile this program, you will get four warning messages about "suspect pointers." This happens because assignments of values to `void` pointers are made: Turbo C cannot determine whether the pointer assignment is correct. These warning messages are acceptable.

Listing 11.1

```
#include <stdlib.h>
#include <stdio.h>

#include "b:phones.h"

telephones phone;    /* INSTANTIATE THE OBJECT */

main()
{
  phone.init_telephone = init_telephone; /* EXTRA WORK TO START  */
  INITOBJ(phone);                         /* IT ALL UP.           */

/* Reference the object */

  MSGOBJ(phone,"Hello,world!");
  MSGOBJ(phone,"I'm here.");
  MSGOBJ(phone,"I'm a hidden object.");
  MSGOBJ(phone,"Are you my user?");

  RPTOBJ(phone);
}
```

Most of the program's internals are hidden in the `phones.h` header file:

```
#define MAXCALLS 10
#define INITOBJ(a)  (*a.init_telephone)(&a)
#define MSGOBJ(a,b) (*a.call_out)( &a,b )
#define RPTOBJ(a)   (*a.report)( &a )

          /* BASIC DEFINITION OF OBJECT "CLASS" */
typedef struct {
  int max_msg;     /*   Here are hidden data items */
  int num_msg;
  char *call_log[MAXCALLS];

          /* And here are the methods */

  void (*init_telephone)(void *);
  void (*call_out)(void *, char *);
  void (*log_call)(void *, char *);
  void (*report)(void *);
} telephones;

void init_telephone(telephones *);
void call_out(telephones *, char *);
void log_call(telephones *, char *);
void report(telephones *);

void init_telephone(telephones *anyphone)
{
  anyphone->call_out = call_out;
  anyphone->log_call = log_call;
  anyphone->report   = report;
  anyphone->max_msg  = MAXCALLS;
  anyphone->num_msg  = 0;
}

void call_out(telephones *anyphone, char *msg)
{
  log_call(anyphone, msg);
  printf( "%s\n",msg );
}

void log_call(telephones *anyphone, char *msg)
{
  if ( anyphone->num_msg >= anyphone->max_msg ) return;
  if ( NULL == ( anyphone->call_log[anyphone->num_msg]
    = malloc(strlen(msg)+1)) ) return;
  strcpy(anyphone->call_log[anyphone->num_msg++],msg);
}

void report(telephones *anyphone)
{
  int i;

  printf( "\n\nSession Call Message Log:\n" );
  printf( "-------------------------\n" );
  for ( i=0; i<anyphone->num_msg; i++ )
    printf( "%s\n",anyphone->call_log[i] );
}
```

The call log is defined as an array of pointers to string within the `telephones` type definition. In just a moment, we will take a look at the call log shown in figure 11.9.

Each outgoing call is sent first to the screen and is recorded also in the call log. When all calls have been made, the session call message log is printed using the built-in `printf()` function. Here is the appearance of the screen after `phones.c` has run:

```
Hello,world!
I'm here.
I'm a hidden object.
Are you my user?

Session Call Message Log:
-------------------------
Hello,world!
I'm here.
I'm a hidden object.
Are you my user?
```

Now let us look more closely at how the call log is put together, using an Inspector window to descend into a complex object.

To descend into a complex object, use the cursor-movement keys to position the highlight on the item you want to examine in detail. Then simply press Enter. Figure 11.9 shows the result of the operation.

Fig. 11.9. *Descending into a complex Inspector window display.*

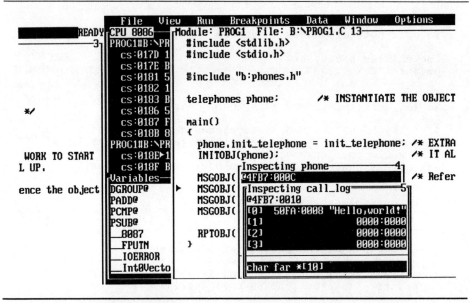

The result, as you can see, is another Inspector window overlaying the first one, containing a display of the contained composite item.

Evaluating Expressions during Debugging

You can get even fancier than the preceding techniques by evaluating C expressions during a debugging session. Sometimes this is necessary to predict what the program may do next, before you continue tracing into an area where you suspect serious problems.

The debugger considers an *expression* to be anything that uses correct C syntax and returns a value of some kind. The expression can be as simple as a variable name or as complex as you need it to be. The following are all valid expressions you could specify to TD:

```
y                          (if y is a variable name)
if( a<14 && (0 == stricmp(my_name,"Joe") )
my_function(a,b,c,d)
intdos(&reg,&reg)
```

Scope is once more an issue here. If the variable name is not available in the local scope, the command will fail; however, the scope-override syntax is available here.

Invoke the `Evaluate/Modify` command to evaluate an expression. You can do this by pulling down the `Data` menu (just as for `Inspect`), using the cursor keys to move the highlight to `Evaluate/Modify` (or just type **E**), and pressing Enter. TD prompts you for the expression to evaluate. Figure 11.10 shows how to write an expression involving a variable outside the current or local scope.

Changing Values Using Expressions with Side Effects

As you debug a program, you may wonder what would happen if you could change the value of, say, a loop control variable. If you could experiment like that, it would be possible to test a fix for a problem quickly, without having to edit and recompile the program until you were sure that the fix would work properly.

You can do this by evaluating an expression with *side effects*. An expression with side effects is one that, when evaluated, actually modifies a variable's contents. Borland was thoughtful enough to design TD so that the assignment operator (=) is valid in an expression to be evaluated. The ++, --, and similar operators can also have side effects.

Suppose that you wrote a program with a loop that controlled the main processing flow, something like this:

```
while( !endjob ) {
    ... /* main loop statements */
}
```

Fig. 11.10. *Evaluating an expression with scope override.*

```
       File    View   Run   Breakpoints   Data   Window   Options            PROMPT
 ┌CPU 8086──┌Module: XEHELP   File: B┌──────────────────────────────────┐─────3┐
 XEHELP#188:│    oldptr = getvect(5) │ Inspect...                        │
   cs:06F6▶0│    setvect(5, xehelp); │ Evaluate/modify... Ctrl-F4        │
   cs:06F7 E│  }             ┌Evaluate/Result/New Value─────────────────┐
 XEHELP#189:│                │( #xprintf#extra + 160 + 2 ) /4            │
   cs:06FA B│  main(argc,argv│                                          │
   cs:06FD 8│    int argc;   │                                          │
   cs:06FF 2│    char *argv[]│                                          │
   cs:0703 A│  {             └──────────────────────────────────────────┘
   cs:0706 8│    if ( argc ==┘
   cs:0708 A│      else strcpy( path,"B:\\" );
   cs:070B 8│    gettextinfo(&s_d);
 XEHELP#190:│    if ( NULL == ( screen_save =
 ┌Variables─│        farmalloc( (s_d.screenheight+s_d.screenwidth)*2 ) )
 DGROUP@    │      ) return;
 PADD@      │    *fname = '\0';
 PCMP@      │    scrseg = 0xB800; scrofs = 0;
 PSUB@    ▶ │    install();
 SCOPY@     │    mypsp = _psp; myss = _SS; mysp = _SP;
 _8087      │    set_up();
 _FPUTN     │    printf( "XEHELP TSR Installation Statistics:\n" );
 _IOERROR   │    printf( "    CS=%04X DS=%04X SS=%04X SP=%04X BP=%04X\n",_CS,_DS

 F1-Help ,┘-Select Esc-Abort█
```

and suppose further that you had forgotten to write any code that set endjob to
TRUE. Execution never exits the loop, and the program therefore never ends. You
are stuck in a continuous loop.

Once you start up TD, trace a while, and inspect endjob a few times, you
finally realize that this variable *never* gets updated. The solution is simple: just use
Evaluate/Modify, evaluate the expression endjob = 1;, and then resume
tracing.

A series of TD screens can illustrate how this works in a complete program.
Figure 11.11 shows the sample program branch.c ready to execute under the
debugger. The only purpose of branch.c is to illustrate how to evaluate expressions with side effects.

To understand the flow of sample screens, note the following features about
branch.c:

❑ Program flow is determined completely by the variable whichway, which is
initialized to FALSE in its declaration statement.

❑ If you do not intervene in branch's execution, b_function() will always
execute.

❑ The C value for a false condition is int 0, and for a true condition, int 1.

In figure 11.12, an Inspector window is displayed. The value of whichway is 0,
or FALSE. At this point, b_function() executes if tracing continues.

Fig. 11.11. *The branch.c sample program.*

```
    File   View   Run   Breakpoints   Data   Window   Options              READY
┌CPU 8086──┌Module: BRANCH  File: B:\BRANCH.C 1════════════════════════════3┐
│_main: main││ #include <stdlib.h>                                          │
│  cs:003C▶5││ #include <stdio.h>                                           │
│  cs:003D 8││                                                              │
│  cs:003F 1││ #define FALSE 0                                              │
│  cs:0040 B││ #define TRUE  1                                              │
│  cs:0043 8││ int whichway = FALSE;                                        │
│BRANCH#20: ││                                                              │
│  cs:0045 8││ void a_function( void )                                      │
│  cs:004A 7││ {                                                            │
│  cs:004C 0││    printf( "\n  WHICHWAY was set to TRUE ! \n" );            │
│  cs:004D E││ }                                                            │
│  cs:0050 E││                                                              │
├Variables──││ void b_function( void )                                      │
│DGROUP@    ││ {                                                            │
│PADD@      ││    printf( "\n  WHICHWAY was set to FALSE ! \n" );           │
│PCMP@      ││ }                                                            │
│PSUB@      ││                                                              │
│__8087     ││▶main()                                                       │
│__FPUTN    ││ {                                                            │
│__IOERROR  ││    if ( whichway ) a_function(); else b_function();          │
│__Int0Vecto││ }                                                            │
└───────────└──────────────────────────────────────────────────────────────┘
 F2-Bkpt F3-Close F4-Here F5-Zoom F6-Next F7-Trace F8-Step F9-Run F10-Menu▪
```

Fig. 11.12. *Inspecting the* whichway *control variable.*

```
    File   View   Run   Breakpoints   Data   Window   Options              READY
┌CPU 8086──┌Module: BRANCH  File: B:\BRANCH.C 20═══════════════════════════3┐
│_main: main││ #include <stdlib.h>    ┌Inspecting whichway═══════════4┐     │
│  cs:003C 5││ #include <stdio.h>     │@4AA7:000C                     │     │
│  cs:003D 8││                        │int                    0 (0x0) │     │
│  cs:003F 1││ #define FALSE 0        └───────────────────────────────┘     │
│  cs:0040 B││ #define TRUE  1                                              │
│  cs:0043 8││ int whichway = FALSE;                                        │
│BRANCH#20: ││                                                              │
│  cs:0045▶8││ void a_function( void )                                      │
│  cs:004A 7││ {                                                            │
│  cs:004C 0││    printf( "\n  WHICHWAY was set to TRUE ! \n" );            │
│  cs:004D E││ }                                                            │
│  cs:0050 E││                                                              │
├Variables──││ void b_function( void )                                      │
│DGROUP@    ││ {                                                            │
│PADD@      ││    printf( "\n  WHICHWAY was set to FALSE ! \n" );           │
│PCMP@      ││ }                                                            │
│PSUB@      ││                                                              │
│__8087     ││ main()                                                       │
│__FPUTN    ││ {                                                            │
│__IOERROR  ││▶   if ( whichway ) a_function(); else b_function();          │
│__Int0Vecto││ }                                                            │
└───────────└──────────────────────────────────────────────────────────────┘
 F2-Bkpt F3-Close F4-Here F5-Zoom F6-Next F7-Trace F8-Step F9-Run F10-Menu▪
```

To cause a_function() to execute instead, the value of whichway must be 1, not 0. An expression with the side effect of modifying this variable will do the trick, as shown in figure 11.13.

Fig. 11.13. *Modifying the* whichway *variable.*

```
   File   View   Run   Breakpoints   Data   Window   Options        PROMPT
┌CPU 8086──┬Module: BRANCH  File: B┌─────────────────────────────────┐─3┐
│_main: main│ #include <stdlib.h>  │  Inspect...                     │  ║
│  cs:003C 5│ #include <stdio.h>   │  Evaluate/modify... Ctrl-F4     │  ║
│  cs:003D 8│                      └┌─Evaluate/Result/New Value──────┐║
│  cs:003F 1│ #define FALSE         │whichway = 1;                   │║
│  cs:0040 B│ #define TRUE          │                                │║
│  cs:0043 8│ int whichway =        │int 1 (0x1)                     │║
│BRANCH#20: │                       │                                │║
│  cs:0045▶8│ void a_functio        │Cannot be changed               │║
│  cs:004A 7│ {                     └────────────────────────────────┘║
│  cs:004C 0│    printf( "\n  WHICHWAY was set to TRUE ! \n" );       ║
│  cs:004D E│ }                                                       ║
│  cs:0050 E│                                                         ║
├Variables─│ void b_function( void )                                  ║
│DGROUP@    │ {                                                       ║
│PADD@      │    printf( "\n  WHICHWAY was set to FALSE ! \n" );      ║
│PCMP@      │ }                                                       ║
│PSUB@      │                                                         ║
│_8087      │ main()                                                  ║
│_FPUTN     │ {                                                       ║
│_IOERROR  ▶│    if ( whichway ) a_function(); else b_function();     ║
│_Int0Vecto │ }                                                       ║
└F1-Help .┘-Select Esc-Abort▓─────────────────────────────────────────┘
```

The Evaluate/Result/New Value box appears as a result of evaluating the expression. It is divided into three parts. The Evaluate section shows the expression that was evaluated. The Result section shows the resulting state or contents of the variable that was modified. The New Value section contains the mysterious message Cannot be changed. This does not mean that anything is wrong, but just that the right side of the assignment is a constant value and therefore cannot be changed.

As you continue tracing after evaluating the expression, you can see that the flow of execution was in fact altered. Figure 11.14 shows the current-position indicator poised to begin execution of a_function(), just as intended.

Using a Watches Window

Besides instructing TD to inspect the value of a variable or the contents of a complex object, you can tell TD to monitor the contents of any number of variables at the same time. This has a couple of advantages. You can see the status of this information in its own window (which can display continuously if you leave that

Fig. 11.14. New execution flow after Evaluate.

```
    File    View    Run   Breakpoints   Data   Window   Options              READY
┌CPU 8086──┌Module: BRANCH  File: B:\BRANCH.C 8══════════════════════════3┐
│_a_function│  #include <stdlib.h>
│  cs:000C▶5│  #include <stdio.h>
│  cs:000D 8│
│  cs:000F 1│  #define FALSE 0
│  cs:0010 B│  #define TRUE  1
│  cs:0013 8│  int whichway = FALSE;
│BRANCH#10:
│  cs:0015 1▶ void a_function( void )
│  cs:0016 B│  {
│  cs:0019 5│    printf( "\n  WHICHWAY was set to TRUE ! \n" );
│  cs:001A 9│  }
│  cs:001F 5│
│─Variables─│  void b_function( void )
│DGROUP@    │  {
│PADD@      │    printf( "\n  WHICHWAY was set to FALSE ! \n" );
│PCMP@      │  }
│PSUB@
│_8087      │  main()
│_FPUTN     │  {
│_IOERROR   │    if ( whichway ) a_function(); else b_function();
│_Int0Vecto │  }
└───────────└────────────────────────────────────────────────────────────┘
  F2-Bkpt F3-Close F4-Here F5-Zoom F6-Next F7-Trace F8-Step F9-Run F10-Menu▓
```

window active), and you do not have to interrupt the execution of the program to update the display—it is updated automatically whenever you make changes to one of the variables being examined.

To perform this function, you need to open a *Watches window*. Although you can request TD to watch a variable by selecting a choice from the Data menu, the best way is to go to the View menu, as shown in figure 11.15, to open the Watches window itself (Data/Watch adds a watch to the active list, but does not open the window).

When you request Watches from the View menu, the Watches window is created and displayed, as shown in figure 11.16. As just mentioned, you can leave this window active all the time. If you do, it is advisable to go to the Window menu, select Move, and drag the Watches window to one corner of the display so that the window does not block all the other displayed actions during debugging.

Now that you have displayed the Watches window, what do you do with it? Press Alt-F10 to pop up the local menu for the Watches window. This menu presents options that are perhaps as powerful as any other TD feature. Figure 11.17 shows this menu.

Fig. 11.15. Selecting Watches from the View menu.

```
   File    View    Run    Breakpoints    Data    Window    Options                    MENU
┌CPU 8086┌─────────────────────────┐B:\PRINTS.C 489══════════════════════════3┐
│PRINTS#4│ Breakpoints             │etn();
│  cs:16C│ Stack                   │' && *(edbuf+1) == '*' ) route_mrkup();
│  cs:16D│ Log                     │save(1); else lsave(-1);
│  cs:16D│ Watches                 │         {                    /* PROCESS RESTART
│  cs:16D│ Variables               │
│  cs:16D│ Module...        Alt-F3 │'/' && *(edbuf+1) == '*' ) {
│  cs:16D│ File...                 │; lsave(-1);
│  cs:16D│ CPU                     │1); restart = FALSE; }
│  cs:16E│ Dump                    │
│PRINTS#4│ Registers               │                              /* PRINT FILE L
│  cs:16E│ Numeric processor       │
│  cs:16E│ User screen      Alt-F5 │eaders);
│┌Variable│                        │oto xearly;
│ DGROUP@ │ Another                │num<=lprt && k<1; lnum++ ) {  /* PRINT PAGE L
│ PADA@   │                        │    ) {
│ PADD@   └────────────────────────┘     ch = getch(); if ( ch == 0 ) ch = getch(); goto xearly;
│ PCMP@   │              }
│ PSBA@   │              getn();
│ PSBP@  ▶│              if ( *edbuf == '/' && *(edbuf+1) == '*' ) {
│ PSUB@   │                 route_mrkup(); lnum--; lsave(-1); continue;
│_CAPS    │              }
└─────────┴──────────────────────────────────────────────────────────────────┘
F1-Help Esc-Abort
```

Fig. 11.16. An empty Watches window.

```
   File    View    Run    Breakpoints    Data    Window    Options                   READY
┌CPU 8086──┌Module: PRINTS  File: B:\PRINTS.C 489═══════════════════════════════3┐
│PRINTS#489:│      pnum = 1;
│  cs:16CD▶B│      restart= FALSE; getn();
│  cs:16D0 8│      if ( *edbuf == '/' && *(edbuf+1) == '*' ) route_mrkup();
│  cs:16D2┌Watches════════════════════════════════════════4┐
│  cs:16D8│                                                 │* PROCESS RESTART
│  cs:16DA│                                                 │
│  cs:16DD│                                                 │{
│  cs:16DF│                                                 │
│  cs:16E5│                                                 │
│PRINTS#49└─────────────────────────────────────────────────┘
│  cs:16E7 0│      while ( k<1 ) {                            /* PRINT FILE L
│  cs:16E8 E│         write_headers(headers);
│┌Variables─│      if ( !PRTOK ) goto xearly;
│ DGROUP@   │      for ( lnum=1; lnum<=lprt && k<1; lnum++ ) { /* PRINT PAGE L
│ PADA@     │         if ( kbhit() ) {
│ PADD@     │            ch = getch(); if ( ch == 0 ) ch = getch(); goto xearly;
│ PCMP@     │         }
│ PSBA@     │         getn();
│ PSBP@    ▶│         if ( *edbuf == '/' && *(edbuf+1) == '*' ) {
│ PSUB@     │            route_mrkup(); lnum--; lsave(-1); continue;
│_CAPS      │         }
└───────────┴─────────────────────────────────────────────────────────────────┘
F2-Bkpt F3-Close F4-Here F5-Zoom F6-Next F7-Trace F8-Step F9-Run F10-Menu
```

Fig. 11.17. The Watches window local menu.

```
    File   View   Run   Breakpoints   Data   Window   Options            MENU
  ┌CPU 8086──┌Module: PRINTS   File: B:\PRINTS.C 489─────────────────────────3┐
  │PRINTS#489:     pnum = 1;
  │  cs:16CD►B     restart= FALSE; getn();
  │  cs:16D0 8     if ( *edbuf == '/' && *(edbuf+1) == '*' ) route_mrkup();
  │  cs:16D2┌Watches═══════════════════════════════════════════4┐
  │  cs:16D8│                                                   │/* PROCESS RESTART
  │  cs:16DA│                                                   │
  │  cs:16DD│   Watch                                           │  {
  │  cs:16DF│   Edit...                                         │
  │  cs:16E5│   Remove                                          │
  │PRINTS#49│   Delete all                                      │
  │  cs:16E7│ ┌──────────┐ k<1 ) {                     /* PRINT FILE L
  │  cs:16E8│ │ Inspect  │ headers(headers);
  ├Variables─│ │ Change   │ PRTOK ) goto xearly;
  │DGROUP@   │ └──────────┘ lnum=1; lnum<=lprt && k<1; lnum++ ) {  /* PRINT PAGE L
  │PADA@            if ( kbhit() ) {
  │PADD@               ch = getch(); if ( ch == 0 ) ch = getch(); goto xearly;
  │PCMP@            }
  │PSBA@            getn();
  │PSBP@     ►      if ( *edbuf == '/' && *(edbuf+1) == '*' ) {
  │PSUB@               route_mrkup(); lnum--; lsave(-1); continue;
  │_CAPS            }
  └──────────────────────────────────────────────────────────────
  F1-Help Esc-Abort
```

Because the `Watch` and `Delete all` options do not refer to one specific entry in the Watches window, it does not matter where the highlight is when you select them. The `Edit`, `Remove`, `Inspect`, and `Change` options do refer to one entry; you must move the highlight to the entry you want to affect before selecting them.

Because these options are so powerful, it is worthwhile to describe each of them as they appear in the menu. Of course, before you pop up the `Watches` local menu, you must stop execution of the program (using breakpoints, the F7 key, or other means).

`Watch`	Select this option to add a new watch. You are prompted for the symbol name to add to the list of entries to be watched. This is the one time you may enter the name of a variable that is not yet valid. It begins to display the variable's contents when the variable does become valid.
`Edit`	Use this option to edit and update the highlighted entry or—if the highlight is beyond the end of the list—to add a new one. You can also highlight an existing expression and press Enter to edit it.
`Remove`	This option discards the highlighted entry from the list of active watches. Alternatively, highlight an entry and press Del to remove it.

Delete All   This option cleans up the display by discarding all watch entries and restoring an empty Watches window.

Inspect   A compound variable occupies only one line in the Watches window, regardless of the number of elementary items that make up the complex object. At certain points in the debugging process, you may want to use Inspect for the highlighted entry in the Watches window, so that you can break out the detailed structure.

Change   This option is the lazy way to evaluate an expression with side effects. When you highlight an entry in the Watches list and select the Change option, you can enter an expression (any valid C expression, as in Evaluate/ Modify). This expression is evaluated, and the results *replace the contents of the active Watches variable.* If necessary (and if possible), any required type conversions are performed before a new value is assigned to the variable.

Figure 11.18 shows a populated Watches window. One item is displayed on each line. The symbol name is given at the far left, followed by the data type, then by a display of the contents of the variable. Notice that the integer values are given in decimal and hexadecimal here, as they were in the Inspector window. A string value is displayed as a quoted string such as you would code in a source file. This is a much handier way to see it than the Inspector window's format.

Fig. 11.18. An active Watches window.

Using the Variables Window

When you request the Turbo Debugger to load an .EXE file to be debugged, TD not only creates a Module window to display the associated source code, it also creates a Variables window, like the one shown in figure 11.19. Unless you name it specifically, this is called TD window 2, and you can navigate directly to it by pressing Alt-2.

Fig. 11.19. *The Turbo Debugger Variables window.*

```
   File    View    Run    Breakpoints    Data    Window    Options          READY
 ┌CPU 8086──┌Module: PRINTS  File: B:\PRINTS.C 489──────────────────────────3┐
 │PRINTS#489:│    pnum = 1;
 │ cs:16CD▶B│    restart= FALSE; getn();
 │ cs:16D0 8│    if ( *edbuf == '/' && *(edbuf+1) == '*' ) route_mrkup();
 │ cs:16D2 │Watches──────────────────────────────────────────4
 │ cs:16D8 │edbuf    char [121] "#include <stdlib.h>\0\n#includ│/* PROCESS RESTART
 │ cs:16DA │pnum                          int 1 (0x1)          │
 │ cs:16DD │lnum                          int 1 (0x1)          │{
 │ cs:16DF │
 │ cs:16E5 │
 │PRINTS#49│
 │ cs:16E7 0│    while ( k<l ) {                                 /* PRINT FILE L
 │ cs:16E8 E│        write_headers(headers);
 ┌Variables══════════════════════════════════════════════════════2┐
 │_atoi                    ????│ch                'e' 101 (0x65)│PRINT PAGE L
 │_atol              @63FB:0008│oldk  893D:0006 "#include <stdli│
 │_b                     0 (0x0)│token   "NUL\0T\0We\0e\x9Fd\xF5e\│oto xearly;
 │_blnk                  " \0"│tp                   65F5:0FA4 "NUL"│
 │_bm                  21 (0x15)│sp                   6500:017B ""│
 │_buf_size    131072L (0x20000)│oldy                 2 (0x2)│
 │_bufbot            @5E7A:03F7│oldx                 2 (0x2)│
 │_buftop            @5E7A:02B1│ttype                4 (0x4)│
 └────────────────────────────────────────────────────────────────┘
  F2-Bkpt F3-Close F4-Here F5-Zoom F6-Next F7-Trace F8-Step F9-Run F10-Menu▒
```

Similar to the breakpoints entry list and detail panes discussed in Chapter 10, the Variables window has two panes. The left pane is the *Global pane*, which displays all the *global symbols* for the module as a whole. The right pane is the *Static pane*, which displays all the *static* symbols in the current source file, together with all the *local symbols* in the current function (the function in which the current position is located).

The Variables window is controlled by the Tab, arrow, and paging keys. Pressing Shift-Tab causes the highlight to switch back and forth between the two panes. The up- and down-arrow keys cause the list to be scrolled up or down, respectively, one line at a time. The PgUp and PgDn keys scroll the window up and down a whole window at a time.

Both panes of the Variables window pop up a local menu when you press Alt-F10, like other TD display windows. In both cases, the local menu presents two options: Inspect and Change. Highlight the list entry and select Inspect or Change just as you do in the Watches local menu. The same effects are produced.

The Watches window gives a viewport into just those elements you want to see during debugging, and does it dynamically even when you press F9 to run the program. The Variables window, by contrast, gives you a viewport into *all* the variables available to TD without a scope override. If you need to check on a large number of items during debugging and do not mind paging around in this window, the Variables window is the one to use. It is very handy also if your data-viewing requirements change frequently during the debugging session. It may be easier to scroll this window than to edit and update a Watches window, and it is certainly easier than using multiple discrete Inspect commands.

Using the CPU Window

The CPU window is created at TD start-up time and is always present unless you specifically close it with F3. The CPU window is shown in figure 11.20.

Fig. 11.20. The Turbo Debugger CPU window.

```
  File   View   Run   Breakpoints   Data   Window   Options              READY
┌CPU 8086───────────────────────────────────────────┐─1────────────────3──┐
│PRINTS#489:  if ( *edbuf == '/' && *(edbuf+1)│ax 000B │c=0│                 │
│  cs:16CD▶B80065        mov     ax,6500       │bx 00AC │z=0│                 │
│  cs:16D0 8EC0          mov     es,ax         │cx 1B04 │s=0│_mrkup();        │
│  cs:16D2 26803EF7002F  cmp     es:byte ptr [ │dx 893E │o=0│                 │
│  cs:16D8 7521          jne     PRINTS#492 (1 │si 0002 │p=0│PROCESS RESTART  │
│  cs:16DA B80065        mov     ax,6500       │di 0002 │a=0│                 │
│  cs:16DD 8EC0          mov     es,ax         │bp 0FD4 │i=1│                 │
│  cs:16DF 26803EF8002A  cmp     es:byte ptr [ │sp 0F94 │d=0│                 │
│  cs:16E5 7514          jne     PRINTS#492 (1 │ds 6565 │   │                 │
│PRINTS#490:  route_mrkup(); lnum--; lsave(-1) │es 6500 │   │                 │
│  cs:16E7 0E            push    cs            │ss 65F5 │   │/* PRINT FILE L  │
│  cs:16E8 E8C0FA        call    _route_mrkup  │cs 6062 │   │                 │
│  cs:16EB FF0E1800      dec     word ptr [_ln │ip 16CD │   │                 │
│                                              │        │─2─│PRINT PAGE L     │
├──────────────────────────────────────────────┤        │5) li            │
│5A84:0000 CD 20 00 A0 00 9A F0 FF = á ü≡      │ss:0F9A 0004│e\ oto xearly;  │
│5A84:0008 0D F0 60 03 3E 2F 2D 03 .≡`,>/-,    │ss:0F98 0002│L"              │
│5A84:0010 3E 2F 2F 02 6D 34 80 1A >//,m4⌐.    │ss:0F96 0002│""              │
│5A84:0018 01 01 01 00 02 07 FF FF ,,, ..      │ss:0F94▶6500│                 │
├──────────────────────────────────────────────┤            │2)             │
│_bufbot            @5E7A:03F7│oldx              2 (0x2)                       │
│_buftop            @5E7A:02B1│ttype             4 (0x4)                       │
└──────────────────────────────────────────────────────────────────────────┘
  F2-Bkpt F3-Close F4-Here F5-Zoom F6-Next F7-Trace F8-Step F9-Run F10-Menu⬛
```

The CPU window contains five panes. At the upper left corner of the window the *Code pane* is displayed. This pane contains the Assembler code for the program, interspersed with C source code above its associated set of machine instructions. As you recall from Chapter 10, this is the pane used during Instruction Trace.

As you move clockwise around the display, the *Register pane* appears next. The Register pane shows all the CPU registers and, in a narrow strip on the right edge, a pane showing breakout of the CPU flag states. The flag states are always either 0 or 1, because a CPU flag is a single bit wide.

The next box contains the *Stack pane*. Turbo C uses the stack to store CPU linkage information, to pass parameters to a function, and to store automatic variables when a function is created. The Stack pane display has a different appearance from the Stack *window*, which is created from the View menu, and is discussed under "Analyzing Parameters Passed to Functions."

Before you use the Stack pane in debugging, note the following features of the 80x86 stack and the way Turbo C uses it.

First, the stack is (at most) 64K bytes long and is addressed by the SS (stack segment) register. You can see the value of SS in the Register pane of this window. Turbo C generally uses the entire 64K bytes.

The SS register points to the top of the stack at its low address end. Access to individual items in the stack is through combining the segment address (SS) with an offset to the item in SP (stack pointer). Further, when you treat stack entries as data items, the BP (base pointer) register is loaded with an offset relative to SS (usually from SP). This is how Turbo C gains addressability to parameters passed to a function. Because the 80x86 stack is technically a last-in, first-out stack (LIFO), SP usually has a high offset value (such as 0xFFEE). Items are pushed onto the stack beginning at the bottom (high-address end), and SP is *decremented* to point to the next available slot.

There is, of course, a moral to this story. Do not attempt to use the Stack pane unless you *really* know what you are doing. It is a different story with the Stack window, but more on that later.

The last pane in the CPU window is the *Data pane*. Press Ctrl-G to set the address of memory to display, anywhere in RAM. However, when you load an .EXE file for debugging, the address is initially set to display the Program Segment Prefix (PSP) for the module. You can learn more about the PSP and how to use it from the *DOS Technical Reference Manual* and from advanced books on IBM PC programming.

Using the Registers Window

An example of the Registers window is shown in figure 11.21. This is obviously an approximation of the Register pane in the CPU window without some of its information.

The Registers window is occasionally useful precisely because it is small and compact. It can be moved to one side out of the way, leaving the Module window visible. You could use this window

- to debug programs that directly modify the machine registers via the pseudovariables _AX, _BX, and so on.

- to debug large memory model programs that frequently reload segment registers.

Fig. 11.21. *The TD Registers window.*

```
  File  View  Run  Breakpoints  Data  Window  Options          READY
CPU 8086──┌Module: PRINTS  File: B:\PRINTS.C 489─────────────────┐3┐
PRINTS#489:│    pnum = 1;
  cs:16CD▶B│    restart= FALSE; getn();
  cs:16D0 8│    if ( *edbuf == '/' && *(edbuf+1) == '*' ) route_mrkup();
  cs:16D2 2│    if ( !restart ) lsave(1); else lsave(-1);
  cs:16D8 7│    while ( restart ) {                    /* PROCESS RESTART
  cs:16DA B│      getn();
  cs:16DD 8│      if ( *edbuf == '/' && *(edbuf+1) == '*' ) {
  cs:16DF┌Registers──────5┐rkup(); lsave(-1);
  cs:16E5│  ax 000B   c=0│lsave(1); restart = FALSE; }
PRINTS#49│  bx 00AC   z=0│
  cs:16E7│  cx 1B04   s=0│  ) {                              /* PRINT FILE L
  cs:16E8│  dx 893E   o=0│ders(headers);
  cs:16EB│  si 0002   p=0│OK ) goto xearly;
         │  di 0002   a=0│m=1; lnum<=lprt && k<1; lnum++ ) {  /* PRINT PAGE L
5A84:0000│  bp 0FD4   i=1│hit() ) {
5A84:0008│  sp 0F94   d=0│getch(); if ( ch == 0 ) ch = getch(); goto xearly;
5A84:0010│  ds 6565      │
5A84:0018│  es 6500      │
         │  ss 65F5      │dbuf == '/' && *(edbuf+1) == '*' ) {
_bufbot  │  cs 6062      │_mrkup(); lnum--; lsave(-1); continue;
_buftop  │  ip 16CD      │
```

F2-Bkpt F3-Close F4-Here F5-Zoom F6-Next F7-Trace F8-Step F9-Run F10-Menu●

❑ to debug complex conditional logic using a combination of register contents and CPU flag states.

Boundary Value Analysis

The casual programmer approaches data debugging and analysis in a casual way. The serious programmer, however, realizes that *data* is one of the tools of the trade and should be regarded seriously and carefully.

There is an old saying that to one who has only a hammer, every problem is a nail. If the only debugging philosophy you have is to ask, "What happens next?" you have a hammer—when you need a wrench.

Data analysis asks the question, "Why did it happen just that way?" To answer that question, you need to understand that there is more than one use for data.

Generally, you can distinguish two kinds of data by the way the data is used. A *data* variable is one that contains simple information: how much FICA was withheld, for example. A *state* variable also contains information, but the information pertains to controlling program flow, or more generally, controlling events within the CPU.

A moment's reflection will show that sometimes these categories overlap. Annual wages is certainly a data variable, but the magnitude of the wages determines what tax bracket is used to calculate taxes.

Determining the Possible Range of Values

A prerequisite step to analyzing the behavior of a program using a given data set is to determine the *possible range of values* for each item and type. This result must then be weighed against the *allowed* range of values (see "Data Range Checking") in order to reach a firm conclusion about the program's actual behavior.

The first consideration is the constraint on value that is imposed by your computer and the compiler. Turbo C's data types have minimum and maximum values that closely parallel the 80x86 architecture. Table 11.2 shows these values.

Table 11.2. *Maximum and Minimum Values of Data Types*

Data Type	Minimum Value	Maximum Value
int	− 32768	+ 32767
unsigned int	0	65535
long	− 21474836448	2147483647
unsigned long	0	4294967295
char	− 128	127
unsigned char	0	255
enum	− 32768	32767
float	3.4E − 38	3.4E + 38
double	1.7E − 308	1.7E + 308
long double	3.4E − 4932	3.4E + 4932

It is necessary to know these values because in many cases (for the integer types especially), *wrap around* is arithmetically possible. For example, if a loop control variable is also being used inside the loop as an index to an array, indexing will be unreliable if the value of the loop control variable wraps around. Consider the following short code sample:

```
for ( i=5; table [i]!=0; i++ )
    printf( "Array value is %d\n", table1[i] );
```

The problem with this `for` loop is that indexing begins with 5, is incremented to the maximum positive number, wraps to the maximum negative number, and proceeds until the table entry is zero—which it may never be. This is not usually what the programmer intended.

Although this is perhaps a trivial and silly example, programmers inadvertently commit this type of error all too often. The example also leads directly to the second step in analyzing anticipated program behavior.

Once the theoretically possible range of values is known (that is, the range acceptable by the compiler), the program logic must be scrutinized to determine what range of values the *program design* can accommodate.

The analogy to driving a car applies again. Just like steering the car, if you do not control it, *it will be uncontrolled.* You must take charge of the program and deliberately write code that correctly responds to both valid *and invalid* data.

Finding Upper and Lower Limits, and One Beyond

Data range limitations come in two flavors: *mathematical* and *functional*. The subject of functional limitations is covered shortly in "Data Range Checking." For the time being, consider how the mathematical behavior of numbers affects program behavior.

The sample loop shown in the preceding example demonstrates the behavior of numbers as used in computers—the value of the loop counter wrapped around from positive to negative, leading to unpredictable results during indexing of an array. In other words, the loop violated *boundary value extremes.*

An inherent aspect of arithmetic is that there are *discontinuities* between groups and ranges of numbers. Boundaries on the valid range of values exist for a given mathematical operation. Another inherent aspect of mathematics is that a given arithmetic operation has (at least potentially) not one, but three different behaviors.

❑ Normal behavior within the valid range of values

❑ Uncertain behavior at the boundary value extremes (analysis is required to determine what will happen at these extremes)

❑ Abnormal behavior outside the valid range of values

Being unaware of other types of logic behavior, the novice programmer frequently falls into the trap of designing a program with only the first type in mind. You can use the Turbo Debugger to unit-test functions (keeping a particularly close eye on looping structures) with the following rules of thumb in mind:

❑ Use `Evaluate/Modify`, a Watches window, or a Variables window local menu to force the value of the control variable being analyzed into its normal range (if it is not already) as you step or trace through the logic. Observe whether the control variable is well behaved in this range of values.

❑ Change the value to either an upper or lower boundary value, and use `Trace` line by line. Does the logic successfully handle this condition? If not, in what way did it diverge from expected behavior? At this point, you may use `Evaluate/Modify` to determine what it will take to regain control of logic flow.

❏ Change the control variable to a value just outside the allowed range. If the lower limit for an integer value is 0, for example, use `Change` to make it −1. Make the same observations and ask the same questions as before. Then repeat the process after you set the value just beyond the upper limit.

Automated Validation of Data

Fortunately, not all data-validation procedures have to be manual, like the ones previously described. It is far more desirable to insert error-handling routines so that a single instance of invalid data does not bring the whole show to a halt. In this way, the *only* manual intervention required is to make occasional corrections and resubmit work to the program. At the very least, such routines will remove the necessity of rewriting the program whenever something unexpected happens.

What Turbo C Can Do

Turbo C has a number of built-in functions you can use to validate data as it is presented to the running program. They fall into the broad categories of I/O, process control, classification, conversion, manipulation, and diagnostic functions.

I/O Functions

The best time to validate input data is when the user first introduces it in your application. This means that if you can perform at least some of the checking during initial input, you have drastically reduced the possibility of an error later.

Two input functions—`scanf()` and `sscanf()`—can perform much of this initial checking without requiring a great deal of coding on your part.

The `scanf()` function accepts as input a C string from `stdin` and scans it. This function looks for data items to convert into internal format according to a format string (see the *Turbo C Reference Guide* for details). The `scanf()` function returns an integer value indicating how many items were successfully scanned, converted, and stored (but the function does not report items scanned but not stored). The `sscanf()` function differs from the first function only in that it scans a string that is already in memory.

These functions are a good way to input data to your application. You can quickly determine at least whether the items presented are of the right type before you proceed to actual range checking.

Process Control Functions

The process control functions provide some assistance when an error *does* occur. The simplest of these is `abort()`. Using this function is just a shorthand way of calling `exit(3)` to terminate the program immediately.

A much more sophisticated way to handle errors is a *signal-handler* function, which you write and install using the `signal()` function. A signal handler can be one of the following types:

SIGABRT Abnormal termination processing. Caused by request (see the description of the `raise()` function). This signal handler can then terminate the program by calling `abort()`.

SIGFPE   Arithmetic-error handler. Handles floating-point, divide-by-zero, and overflow errors.

SIGILL   Illegal operation-code handler. Invoked when the CPU tries to execute a machine instruction but does not recognize the instruction code. The 8088, 8086, NEC V20, and NEC V30 CPUs do not support an exception-condition interrupt for this event.

SIGINT   Ctrl-Break or Ctrl-C interrupt-condition handler

SIGSEGV Segment violation (illegal access) handler

SIGTERM Normal termination clean-up routine. Caused by `raise()`. The handler routine can perform normal clean up, such as closing files and freeing storage, and terminate the program by calling `exit()` or `_exit()`.

A related function is `raise()`. This function can force the activation of any of these signal types, except for SIGILL and SIGSEGV on 8088 or 8086 processors. In addition, SIGABRT and SIGTERM are signalled *only* by `raise()`.

The `signal()` and `raise()` functions are powerful routines and are not particularly difficult to implement. You should, however, understand them thoroughly before you attempt to use them.

Classification Macros

The Classification macros are composed of the `is...` family. Table 11.3 shows the macros included in this family.

Table 11.3. *Turbo C Classification Macros*

Macro	*Description*
`isalnum()`	Checks for alphanumeric character
`isalpha()`	Checks for alphabetic character
`isascii()`	Checks for true ASCII (0–127) character
`iscntrl()`	Checks for control character
`isdigit()`	Checks for numeric code

Macro	Description
isgraph()	Checks for printable character, but for not space
islower()	Checks for lowercase
isprint()	Checks for printable character, including space
ispunct()	Checks for punctuation
isspace()	Checks for a space
isupper()	Checks for uppercase
isxdigit()	Checks for hexadecimal digit, either upper- or lowercase

Input to the is... functions is always a single character, defined as an integer (these are equivalent, up to a point). If the character matches the requested type condition, TRUE (int 1) is returned; otherwise, FALSE (int 0) is returned.

Conversion Functions

As an alternative to type checking and conversion of several items at a time with scanf(), you can check and convert single items with the conversion functions. Table 11.4 summarizes these functions.

Table 11.4. *Turbo C Format Conversion Functions*

Function	Description
atof()	Convert string to float
atoi()	Convert string to integer
atol()	Convert string to long integer
ecvt()	Convert float to string (specify total number of digits)
fcvt()	Convert float to string (specify digits to right of decimal point)
gcvt()	Convert float to string (convert to Fortran-style F-format if possible)
itoa()	Convert integer to string
ltoa()	Convert long integer to string
strtod()	Convert string to double float
strtol()	Convert string to long integer
strtoul()	Convert string to unsigned long
toascii()	Convert character to ASCII (turns off high-order bit)
tolower()	Convert upper- to lowercase
toupper()	Convert lower- to uppercase
ultoa()	Convert unsigned long to string

This set of functions provides just about complete control over the internal format of data and type of data. Use these functions frequently in portions of your program where the validity of a data item is doubtful. Of course, one of the side benefits is that if an item is correct, the function converts it nonetheless, so that it is ready for immediate use after checking.

Manipulation Functions

Manipulation functions include the `str...` family. The string comparison functions are especially useful, because they can be used to validate text input data.

For more powerful analysis of text input data, whether or not it is eventually converted to a numeric format, use the `strtok()` function. Listing 11.2 illustrates its use.

Listing 11.2

```
/* token.c program */
#include stdio.h
#include string.h

main()
{
    char *message = "Hello. I am a C program!";
    char *token;

    token = strtok(message, ". !");
    while( token != NULL ) {
        printf("%s\n",token);
        token = strtok(NULL,". !");
    }
}
```

When `token.c` runs, it produces the following output on the display screen:

```
Hello
I
am
a
C
Program
```

How did it do that? It was easy to scan the message string using the `strtok()` function. To completely scan a string, `strtok()` requires an initial call with a parameter pointing to the string and a series of repeated calls with a NULL pointer to continue through the string.

The `strtok()` function considers every character that is *not* found in the separator list (the second string parameter) to be part of a valid token. A word of caution is in order here. You may want to pass a copy of the original string to `strtok()`, because it places a \0 character immediately after every token it finds.

As each token is broken out, you can apply the classification and/or conversion routines to finish the type-validation process.

Using `strtok()` you gain complete and almost totally flexible control over input strings. Just about the only way you can get more power from an input-checking function is to write your own lexical scanner.

Diagnostic Functions

The last group of functions that can help you automate the validation of incoming data streams is the diagnostic group. This group contains three functions: `assert()`, `matherr()`, and `perror()`.

The macro `assert( int expression )` expands to an `if` statement. The macro evaluates the `expression` parameter, and if it is not TRUE, the macro aborts the program. This function can be used when you test for conditions considered fatal to proper program execution. Usually, you should use other, less destructive means of handling errors.

The `matherr()` function provides a user hook into the exception-handling routines of the Turbo C math library; it overrides the default (supplied) `matherr()` function. You can use this routine to verify or change input parameters to math functions when domain and range errors are detected by the compiler-generated code. Code this routine to return an integer TRUE or FALSE (1 or 0), depending on whether the routine was able to resolve the problem. Read the function description carefully in the *Turbo C Reference Guide* before implementing your custom function.

The `perror(const char *s)` statement prints to `stderr` your error message string s followed by a colon and a system-error message string. The system-error messages correspond to the return codes from DOS system requests. This function enables you to verify visually whether the DOS error was caused by an improper parameter or some other condition.

What Turbo C Cannot Do

It is obvious that Turbo C provides many of the tools you need to maintain a clean data environment. You can detect, scan, check, and convert by types any kind of data you encounter. There are few languages this rich in data-handling capabilities.

What Turbo C *cannot* do is implement all the power available, nor can it tell you whether the data is *correct* or even what the correct type of input data should be. You must take the time and trouble to write routines that do this—and you should be aware that this is where a great deal of a program's size comes from. It takes focused attention and discipline to write clean code. But that is what makes a good programmer good.

Data Range Checking

At this point you have control over the format and type of data coming into your program. It remains for you to ensure that this data is *correct* or contains the proper information. You have to go beyond addressing the mathematical limitations on data to the *functional* limitations. Data range checking is the means to that end.

Basically, you determine the range of allowed values for a variable. How you do that depends entirely on what you are trying to do. Once you determine what the limits are, however, you certainly can code them into your program.

Another aspect of the problem is what to do when you find an error. How do you handle range errors? In programming, as in engineering, the best method usually is the simplest one that gets the job done. But be sure that the method does *enough*. No error handling is better than inadequate error handling. If the method is inadequate, it is more likely to mislead than to help.

The following function, getmon() illustrates simple methods for range error detection, error handling, and in this case, recovery:

```
char *getmon(int monum)
{
    static char *moname[] = {
                            "January",
                            "February",
                            "March",
                            "April",
                            "May",
                            "June",
                            "July",
                            "August",
                            "September",
                            "October",
                            "November",
                            "December",
                            "INVALID MONTH"
                        };

    if ( monum>0 && monum<13 ) return(moname[monum-1]);
        else return(moname[12]);
}
```

The getmon() function receives an integer parameter that is supposed to correspond to a valid month number (range 1–12). If it does correspond, the parameter is adjusted to be used as an index, and a month name string is returned to the caller. If the parameter does not correspond to a valid month number, an error message string is returned. All of this is accomplished with a simple two-line if statement.

Other error detection and recovery procedures may be more or less complex, but they all follow the same idea. It is advisable to separate detection and recovery aspects into different functions, if the conditions are much more complex than they are here.

Hard-Coded Data versus Code-Independent Data

The `if` statement in the sample function just given is an example of a *hard-coded error recovery routine*. The most direct and most easily implemented method is simply to write the routines right in the code. It is possible to do this and still achieve a dependable and flexible program. It is possible, however, to write a program that is dependable and yet more flexible using the concept of code-independent data.

In its simplest form, code independence revolves around the refusal to write *constant* data into the program. Using a constant for comparing values to permissible ranges requires changing and recompiling the program if the criteria for range checking change. This is clearly a time-consuming and tedious part of the programmer's job. Would it not be better, especially in a large and complex program, to store those criteria somewhere else and just load them at runtime? The answer depends on the nature of the application, but in many cases the answer is "Yes!"

Which data items you locate outside the program depends on your preferences. Consider that there is a sense in which it is impossible for the code to be entirely independent of its associated data. Still, the notion of removing some constants from the code is a good rule of thumb. Here are some examples of items that could be stored in a table or a file:

- ❏ Date ranges for time-dependent applications
- ❏ Bracket values for placing items in subgroups (tax tables are a good example of this)
- ❏ Upper and lower valid limits for any kind of numerical input
- ❏ Physical constants and conversion units for scientific programs

The list of what *can* be done is exhausted only by the range of applications you write code for and by your imagination and judgment.

Metadata Concepts and Techniques

The constant information serving as validity criteria is technically called *metadata*. Metadata is just information about information. Having a conscious appreciation for the concept can help you create powerful programs. Metadata can also include environmental information (display type, size of RAM, and so on) and flow-control information (actions to perform given certain data values).

As you may recall from the discussion of compound variables, Turbo C provides a structure type `text_info`, which contains information about the video environment. This structure is an example of a *control block*, or a structure containing related items of control information. There is nothing very mysterious about control blocks. The point is that you should learn to think in terms of providing them in your complex applications.

In many cases, one control block is not enough; you may need several (or many) control blocks of the same kind. When this is the case, you can arrange them into tables, files, or linked lists. A linked list is probably the best way to keep track of multiple or complex control blocks, because an item in a table can be identified mainly by its position in the table, whereas an entry in a linked list can contain much more information, and hence more identifying information. There is a trade-off in speed and flexibility between the methods that may force the decision in favor of tables, but a linked list is preferred when flexibility is the greater need.

Designing Test-Case Data

Even if you take all the care and consideration in the world during the design of your program, it usually is not a good idea to just dump real data into it and trust that everything will work. The new program needs to be "burned in" with test data.

There are many ways of generating test-case data. You can select a subset of records from an existing file or database, you can carefully tailor test records that will stress the program's ability to handle boundary value extremes, or you can just generate it with a random-number generator. Most of the time, all of these methods go into developing a test case.

How Much Is Enough? Too Much?

Before you develop a test case, decide how to size it. If the program is a file-update module, how many records should you select (or generate) to test with the program?

There is no single response to this question, because the answer always depends to some extent on the nature of your application. Only you know the program well enough to decide. There are, however, some rules of thumb that data-processing professionals use to develop a test case.

- ❏ The theory of probability and statistics tells us that a sample set numbering less than 30 items does not yield a satisfactory confidence level in the results. Always assume that you need 30 records (or items) as a minimum.

- ❏ Beyond that, assume a minimum of 10 percent of the total universe of possible selections. If you have a file containing 1,000 records, select at least 100 and try to ensure that the selected records fairly represent the entire spectrum of possible values and conditions.

- ❏ Once you meet the minimum requirements, it is generally pointless to select more than 20 percent (some say 30 percent) of the sample universe. Beyond that, data tends to become repetitive.

Allowing for Boundary Value Extremes

If you have done your job as an analyst well—existing data, from which you draw the test case, is clean. Data values are uniformly in the allowed ranges, with no type errors. This creates a problem—your data is *too* good!

Because the purpose of testing your program is to stretch it to its limits, you must go out of your way to ensure that test case samples in fact contain bad data and data that stretches or violates boundary value extremes.

Again, there is no single way to generate this part of the test data. You, the programmer, are the only one who knows the code well enough to design a "stress test" for it. If you do not bulletproof your code, users will pierce its armor later.

Designing Manageable Data Structures

You can head off many problems that confront less-experienced programmers by designing your program with *manageable data structures* to begin with. In this context, "structure" can mean anything from a simple integer to C structures that contain other C structures. What counts is that they fit the application properly.

Local versus Global Variable Definitions

Programmers generally tend to go to one extreme or the other; some place all variable definitions at the top of the source file, whereas other designers make all definitions local within functions. Generally, in fact, neither solution is optimal.

Before you start tacking variables wherever you happen to be editing at that moment, stop and consider one question: "What will need access to this variable?"

If you answer that functions in another source file will require access or that several functions in this source will also, then by all means make the variable global. But if such is not the case, consider carefully whether to make it local to one function.

For local variables, a second question arises: "Should this be an automatic variable or a static variable?" Remember that local variables are by default automatic variables and that they are allocated from the stack. This takes time. If slow performance does not prohibit it, local variables are probably superior.

If performance prohibits using automatic variables or if the contents of the variable must still be in place on successive calls to the function, static variables are necessary. The trade-off is that static variables are allocated in the data segment at compile time and are a permanent part of the object code. If data space is at a premium, you may not want such permanence. Then, define them once globally rather than multiple times locally.

Field Structuring

Field structuring is the process not only of designing individual fields (variables), but also of designing the way in which fields exist together in composite objects (records, tables, etc.). Two problems tend to crop up in this area.

First, my experience indicates that forgetting to do this in the formal design phases is very easy. Frequently, because it is left as a last minute hurry-up patch to the design, you have to go back (perhaps more than once) and plug a new field into the code, with understandably sloppy results.

Second, an inadequate field structure can impose performance penalties on a program. Suppose, for example, that your program must perform frequent table or file look-ups. If similar parts of the key fields are grouped together, one comparison often is sufficient to identify the entry or record. If not, many comparisons at different locations within the object may be needed. Clearly, this will take more time.

Structuring groups of fields is another area in which it pays to become consciously analytical in your thinking.

Data Fields

Structuring the way data fields (variables) are placed together in groups can be important when, for example, the structure is a file record. Their size, their order of appearance, and their number of repetitive fields (arrays) are all items you must weigh.

Of particular importance to the programmer who maintains the program and data structures is the order of appearance of fields. A haphazard conglomeration of fields can be confusing and lead to mistakes, both in design and in debugging. Try to order them so that your fields make sense.

Numeric Data

The primary constraints on designing numeric fields are their intended use and the allowed range of values. In general, make numeric fields as small as possible, but large enough to meet outside requirements.

After the range of values has dictated the minimum field size, turn next to the intended use of the field. A wrong decision here can directly affect the performance of the program. For example, do not use a floating-point number when an integer will do; do not use a long integer when a short one will do. Increases in either size or complexity of the number's structure mean more CPU time to process the data.

Text Data

Text is text, right? Not necessarily. Text is composed of characters, whether they are arranged in C strings or just in a large blob. Characters can be either signed (the default) or unsigned. Unsigned characters can have the full range of ASCII values (0 through 255) and can interpret correctly, for example, the IBM extended ASCII graphics characters.

A second issue is whether to store text on disk as "classical" strings (terminated with carriage returns and line feeds), as binary data, or as C strings with \0 termination. Pick the method that allows the text to be moved in and out of the program and with the least conversion in format.

Controlling Variable Proliferation

Hardly a programmer alive has not experienced the phenomenon of variables that expanded geometrically. After writing and debugging a large program, you very likely will realize that the variable definitions in various parts of the program contain unused variables, indicative of those times and places where you changed your mind about how to do something. The best treatment for this ailment is preventive: stay organized as you write the program! When that fails (and it will), take the time to review the variable definitions, weeding out the junk.

Decide before you start writing what your variables will be and code them at the very beginning. Then resist the temptation to add new variables on the fly.

Handling Large Amounts of Data

File-oriented programs usually do not consume large blocks of RAM, whereas text-oriented programs do. Let's look at several situations in which you must decide what to store in RAM at a given time.

Tables versus Files

Some applications fall into a gray area where you have trouble deciding whether to handle data in a table or in a file. This can occur when the amount of data is moderate, rather than very large or very small. Table 11.5 offers tips on which route to take.

Table 11.5. *File and Table Characteristics*

Concern	Data-Handling Device
Very large amounts of data	Files
Fast access	Tables
Easy-to-add entries	Files or Tables
Easy-to-insert entries	Tables
Easy-to-reorganize/sort data	Tables

This is not an exhaustive list, but it does give an adequate overview of characteristics to consider when you select your means of data handling.

Designing File Layouts

Beyond the requirements already described for structuring data fields, you must devise workable file layouts for large amounts of data. Try the following strategies as you develop a suitable layout:

❑ Write it all down. Many programmers (even professionals) fail to document layouts.

❑ For random-access files that will be accessed by key values, group all the key fields together at the beginning of the record. This is not physically required on the IBM PC, but it reduces access time. Other operating systems may require such structuring.

❑ Design the record so that key fields are never updated. Updates destroy their addressability. The only valid update involving record keys is to add or delete the whole record.

❑ Position all repetitive information (arrays or "field buckets") at the end of the record. This makes field updates much easier.

❑ Do not store an item as a field in a record that can be easily calculated. Such extravagances may eat up all available space in larger files.

Record and Block Buffers

Handling large amounts of data stored in disk files can involve some fairly severe performance problems. Failure to manage the data correctly can result in a sluggish, infuriating program.

The principal solution to limits on I/O performance is to *buffer* I/O operations. A *buffer* is a block of storage set aside to hold many file records at a time. A *block* of records is read into it or written from the buffer at once.

The secret pitfall behind I/O is *setup time*. The setup time required for an I/O operation comes from two places: first, from the operating system, which must set up system-control information as well as prepare the I/O device; second, from the I/O device itself.

Setup time is especially apparent for disk operations. When the disk receives an I/O request, it decodes it, moves the read/write head into the proper position (seek time), and waits for the requested record to rotate under the head (rotational delay). For disks with more than one recording surface, there is also a fairly small wait while the correct read/write head is switched electronically to the active state (latency).

The only way to enhance I/O performance is to reduce this overhead—and the only way to do that is to access the disk as seldom as possible. How? Ask for several consecutive records at once, thereby incurring the overhead only once.

Suppose that your program reads and writes a file that has fixed-length records 100 bytes long and that it needs to read the file rapidly. In this case, the larger the buffer, the better. Because a 100,000-byte buffer is possible in today's PCs, assume that figure. With only one request to the operating system, 1,000 records at a time can be physically read from the disk. Because many PC files have fewer than 1,000 records all together, there would be only one I/O request during the whole run. Naturally, the program must check the buffer to see whether a record is available there, and if not, read in another block.

A word of warning here. It is not always true that the larger the I/O buffer, the better the performance. Programs that update random files in an unpredictable fashion (perform unsorted input transactions) do better with a moderate-sized buffer. You can begin with a buffer equal to 10 records and fine tune the size from there.

Using Turbo Debugger with Files

Earlier in the chapter, I mentioned several Turbo C built-in functions (the diagnostic group of functions) that assist you in pinning down system-oriented errors, including DOS errors for I/O requests.

The Turbo Debugger offers another, more direct method of solving file problems when those problems are related to file contents, rather than request parameters. This is the File window (see fig. 11.22), available from the View menu.

This figure shows the file contents displayed in both hexadecimal and ASCII translation. For really serious file problems, this is the mode you most likely will use.

You can—if the file is of the correct type—pop up the File window local menu by pressing Alt-F10. Then select Display As to display the file as ASCII characters only. To select between hexadecimal and ASCII formats, move the highlight over the option you want and press Enter; the Display As value will toggle to the other value.

To move around in the file as you are debugging, use the Go To and Search (for an argument) options. Before you use these options, narrow down the problem's possible location in the file. Otherwise, you may flounder around in this window for some time before you are oriented.

Large-scale Text Buffers

A common problem with large amounts of text occurs when the text needs more RAM space than can be made available in the near C heap or when you need to guarantee that the near heap is not used for the allocation.

Fig. 11.22. *The Turbo C File window.*

```
    File   View   Run   Breakpoints   Data   Window   Options              READY
┌CPU 8086──┬Module: XE  File: B:\XE.C 313─────────────────────────────────────3┐
│XE#313:  sh│    gotoxy(2,22); writechs(196,2,78);   /* bottom bar */
│  cs:31F6▶1│    gotoxy(80,22); writechs(189,2,1);   /* bottom right corner */
│  cs:31F7 B│    for ( x=1,y=2; y<22; y++) {
│  cs:31FA 5│       gotoxy(x,y); writechs(186,2,1);
│  cs:31FB 9│    }
│  cs:3200 5│    for ( x=80,y=2; y<22; y++) {
│  cs:3201 ┌File b:xe.c══════════════════════════════════4┐
│XE#314:   │00000: 23 69 6e 63 6c 75 64 65   #include
│  cs:3202 │00008: 20 3c 73 74 64 6c 69 62    <stdlib
│  cs:3208 │00010: 2e 68 3e 0d 0a 23 69 6e   .h>..#in
│XE#315:   │00018: 63 6c 75 64 65 20 3c 73   clude <s
│  cs:320E │00020: 74 64 69 6f 2e 68 3e 0d   tdio.h>.
│Variables │00028: 0a 23 69 6e 63 6c 75 64   .#includ
│DGROUP@   │00030: 65 20 3c 63 6f 6e 69 6f   e <conio              >" );
│PADA@     └──────────────────────────────────────────────┘
│PADD@         y=25; x=2;
│PCMP@         show_string("Msg/Cmd: ===>");
│PSBA@
│PSBP@         tcb = NULL;
│PSUB@         if ( FALSE == create_tcb() ) { clrscrn(); gotoxy(1,1); exit(0)
│_CAPS     
└──────────────────────────────────────────────────────────────────────────────
```

F2-Bkpt F3-Close F4-Here F5-Zoom F6-Next F7-Trace F8-Step F9-Run F10-Menu

---

To circumvent this problem, Borland provides the `farmalloc()` function, which acquires storage from the *far* heap—the area of RAM beyond the end of the program.

A note for you assembly language programmers—this compiler, unlike some others, performs a SETBLOCK DOS call at start-up time and resizes its total memory allocation to just the amount it needs. You do not have to shrink the initial allocation, therefore, before you use `farmalloc()` or another means of allocating DOS storage. Borland provides the start-up code in C0.ASM, if you are interested in seeing exactly how this is done.

Using the Memory Dump Window

When dealing with large scale buffers, you may want to poke around inside the buffers to see their actual contents. You can do this with the Dump window, also available from the `View` menu. Figure 11.23 shows the Dump window displaying a large-scale text buffer.

The Dump window is just like the Dump pane of the CPU window. You can use `Go To` to access any valid address in RAM from the window's local menu. In this example, the Variables window was used to look up the pointer value to the beginning of the text buffer residing in the far heap, and the Dump window positioned to it. In this, as in other windows, you can use the navigation keys to move around in the window.

Fig. 11.23. *The Turbo Debugger Dump window.*

```
    File   View   Run  Breakpoints  Data   Window   Options              READY
┌CPU 8086──┐┌Module: XE  File: B:\XE.C 328──────────────────────────────────3┐
│XE#328:  if│                                                                 │
│  cs:3298►1│    y=tm; x=lm; gotoxy(x,y);                                      │
│  cs:3299 B│    load_doc(); showdoc();                                       │
│  cs:329C 5│    paint(); getn();                                             │
│  cs:329D 9│    showmem(TRUE); showcol(); showmode(); showistat();           │
│  cs:32A2 5│                                                                 │
│  cs:32A3 5│    ch = 32;                                                     │
│  cs:32A4 8│    *key_buf = '\0';                                             │
│  cs:32A8┌Dump═══════════════════════════════════════════4┐                 │
│  cs:32AC│6BFD:0008 23 69 6E 63 6C 75 64 65  #include     │n(edbuf)+lm;      │
│  cs:32AE│6BFD:0010 20 3C 73 74 64 6C 69 62   <stdlib     │);               │
│  cs:32B0│6BFD:0018 2E 68 3E 0D 0A 23 69 6E  .h>..#in     │                  │
┌Variables│6BFD:0020 63 6C 75 64 65 20 3C 73  clude <s     │─────────────2┐  │
│_gotoxy   └─────────────────────────────────────────────┘  1 (0x5AFB)   │  │
│_handle               0 (0x0)│r              12029 (0x2EFD)              │  │
│_hdrlines  {{"\0\0\0\0\0\0\0\0│oldy            4109 (0x100D)  r+=2;       │  │
│_headers              6 (0x6)│oldx              29 (0x1D)                │  │
│_holdit          0000:0000   │argv          65F5:1004  ;                 │  │
│_i  6BFD:0008 "#include <stdlib.│argc            1 (0x1)  ;               │  │
│_incr_blks       @5AFB:0001                                              │  │
│_init_banners    @6062:01EF                                              │  │
└──────────────────────────────────────────────────────────────────────────┘
  F2-Bkpt F3-Close F4-Here F5-Zoom F6-Next F7-Trace F8-Step F9-Run F10-Menu
```

Analyzing Parameters Passed to Functions

Finding a problem with a parameter passed to a function is one of the more difficult debugging exercises, because the parameters are passed in the system stack, where they probably are least visible.

Details on Address and Value Parameters

As Turbo C scans the parameter list in a function call, it pushes parameters onto the stack (from right to left as you view it). Each parameter does not necessarily make it to the stack in its original form, however. Strings and arrays are not placed in the stack directly—only their addresses are.

This is the difference between address and value parameters. In addition to that, 80x86 system architecture dictates that they be pushed onto the stack with the least significant digits at the lowest storage address. A four-byte pointer, for example, is pushed onto the stack as two (reversed) back-words, if you will excuse the terminology.

Clearly, analyzing passed parameters in the stack would be confusing if you viewed them in the CPU window's Stack pane. The TD Stack window, however, puts parameters in a little different light. Figure 11.24 shows the format of the Stack window's display.

Fig. 11.24. *The Stack window with three levels of function calls.*

```
   File   View   Run   Breakpoints   Data   Window   Options            READY
┌CPU 8086──┬Module: VID  File: B:\VID.C 103──────────────────────────3┐
│_show_strin│    sp += ofs;
│  cs:04F8┌Stack═══════════════════════════════5┐nt-- ) *sp = *str++;
│  cs:04F9│_show_string(6500:00F7)
│  cs:04FB│_get_line(6500:00F7,2,2,77,0,0)
│  cs:04FC│_main(1,65F5:1004)
│  cs:04FF│
│VID#106: │
│  cs:0501│                                      *(y-1),anystring,strlen(anystring)
│  cs:0504└──────────────────────────────────────┘
│  cs:0507│6│
│  cs:050C│6│   void paint()
│  cs:050D│6│   {
│Variables│6│      int q,oldx,oldy;
│_gotoxy  └─│      char huge *savek;
│_handle     │
│_hdrlines   │      oldy = y;
│_headers    │      oldx = x;
│_holdit     │      q = (y-1)*160+(lm-1)*2;
│_i  6BFD:00 │      x = lm;
│_incr_blks  │      savek = n = k;
│_init_banne │      while ( (y<bm+1) && (n<l) )
```

F2-Bkpt F3-Close F4-Here F5-Zoom F6-Next F7-Trace F8-Step F9-Run F10-Menu

---

This form definitely is more readable. Notice that pointers are displayed in *xxxx:xxxx* hexadecimal format, and integers are displayed in decimal notation. The most recent function call is shown physically on top of the stack, following its logical order. The execution path is visible at a glance. If you view this together with the Module window displays, you have it all before you. Make sure that you compiled with the IDE's default Options/Compiler/Code Generation/Standard Stack Frame on. Or make sure that you did not use the –k– command-line option (ON by default unless you disable it). You have to work at it, but it is possible. If one or more functions that *should* appear in Stack Window don't, this is the reason. By the way, if you have any assembly language routines in your program, they will *not* be there.

Common Sources of Data Errors

The rest of this chapter is a cookbook compendium of the most common sources of data errors as the programmer sees them—whether an error was generated arithmetically, or bad data was picked up accidentally.

Failure to Initialize Automatic Variables

Once the current location is within a called function, you might think that the function's local variables are ready to go. Although they have in fact been allocated from the stack, they are not yet defined. The program must initialize them before they are valid.

This can be an easy omission to make in your program if you are accustomed to using global variables frequently, because global variables are initialized to zero at compile time.

Reference to Automatic Variables That No Longer Exist

You may be tempted to return from a function the *address* of one of its local variables. The compiler will let you do this, because the variable actually does exist at the time the return() is executed.

But the calling function is now left with the address of something that used to be on the stack. It is possible—indeed, likely—that that area of the stack has been reused since then. The contents of the locations are completely unpredictable, and so is the future behavior of the program.

Confusion of Operators

Many of C's logical (boolean) and action operators are similar in appearance. The *logical* operators = =, &&, | |, and so forth can be used by if without changing the value of the variables tested. The *action* operators =, &, |, and so on, *do* change their contents. The situation is made more confusing by the fact that C allows the action operators inside conditional expressions (one of the features that makes such compact code possible in C).

Confusion about Operator Precedence

Some operators have higher *precedence* than others; their operands are before other operators. The classic example of this is the compact way of opening a stream, illustrated in the following example:

```
#include <stdio.h>
#include <string.h>

main()
{
  FILE *myfile;

  if ( (myfile = fopen("b:fopen.c","r") ) == NULL )
     abort();
  printf("%p\n",myfile);
}
```

The inner parentheses surrounding the pointer assignment are necessary because == has higher precedence than = does. Let's see what would happen if you forgot those parentheses and coded instead:

```
if ( myfile = fopen("b:fopen.c","r") == NULL )
    abort();
printf("%p\n",myfile);
```

First, fopen() will be performed. Next, the returned file pointer is compared to NULL. If the file opened correctly, the valid pointer will not be equal to NULL—the comparison returns FALSE or zero. Finally, the zero value is assigned to the myfile pointer. As the printf() will plainly show, the value of myfile is now 0000:0000. When you later attempt to access the file, whatever is in low storage will be overwritten when Turbo C attempts to update file-control information—thereby destroying the system interrupt vectors.

Knowing and keeping track of operator precedence is important. Table 11.6 summarizes the levels of precedence, with the highest at the top of the list.

Table 11.6. *C Operator Precedence*

Operator Symbol	Purpose
( ) [ ] -> .	Associative/Grouping
! ~ ++ -- - (type) * & sizeof	Unary
* / %	Arithmetic
+ -	Arithmetic
<< >>	Shift
< <= > >=	Comparison/Relational
== !=	Comparison/Relational
&	Bitwise logical
^	Bitwise logical
|	Bitwise logical
&&	Logical operator
||	Logical operator
?:	Ternary operator/Conditional
= += -= etc.	Assignment
,	Multiple expressions separator

Pointer Problems

Pointers are the method of indirect reference to variables. The contents of a pointer is *an address*, not the data pointed to. Confusion about this can lead to a couple of interesting situations.

First, you can forget to initialize the pointer. Using the pointer without initialization means that the variable you thought you changed could literally be *anywhere* in RAM—usually in a sensitive system area. A system crash may result.

Second, you can damage the contents of a pointer by doing arithmetic on it without knowing how the pointer is constructed. Far pointers, for example, are not kept normalized the way huge pointers are. Their contents may well be invalid if you tinker much with them. Far pointers do not always compare as correctly as do huge pointers, again because of a lack of normalization.

Third, you can get thoroughly lost as you attempt mixed-model programming. If your code uses both near and far pointers, and you inadvertently use the wrong kind, the location actually referenced is once more completely unpredictable.

Arithmetic Errors

Arithmetic errors can be somewhat subtle, and hence difficult to locate. Most common errors of this type can be prevented with a little forewarning. The most commonly committed errors fall into three groups, discussed in the following sections.

Signed and Unsigned Types

You need to be careful not to confuse what can be done with signed and unsigned variables. You can assign an unsigned value to a signed variable, for instance, but you may suddenly discover an unexpected negative value.

Another thing that can bite you sharply is value wrap-around. Adding 1 to the maximum positive signed integer suddenly yields the maximum negative integer (because the high-order bit becomes involved). Similarly, adding 1 to the maximum unsigned integer yields 0.

Mixed Field Lengths

You can freely assign long to short and short to long variables, but you should be prepared for unexpected results if you have not observed maximum value constraints.

For example, assigning a long integer with a value of $+65536$ (0x10000) to a short integer will result in 0 (because the most significant word does not fit and is truncated).

Another source of error is that, when you assign short into long signed variables, Turbo C preserves the sign by extending it.

Failure To Account for Mathematical Anomalies

This chapter has already discussed the idea of discontinuity in analyzing boundary value conditions. Failing to account for boundaries can cause one of two frequent errors: a runaway loop or a divide-by-zero exception.

A less-understood situation arises from floating-point arithmetic. Floating-point numbers are inherently less precise than integers (which are exact). Be careful about selecting short or double floating-point types, depending on the required precision.

Furthermore, most people tend to mentally round intermediate results in arithmetic and to write this mistake into their programs. *Do not round* with float types. Round only when you are completely finished with a calculation. Floating-point rounding errors can propagate so quickly that they can totally destroy the validity of the answer.

Scope Errors

Much has been said about scope in this chapter, but it never hurts to say a little more. A scope error that gets by the compiler causes serious errors that can be mystifying.

Two kinds of scope error affect your code here. *Reference to a variable not in the local scope* can occur when you "borrow" global data names for use in the local scope but forget to actually code the names in the local function. Reference to such a variable then causes the *global* version to be modified without your knowledge. The real problem is that the program probably will crash somewhere other than in the function that caused it. This error can be very difficult to find, even with all the resources of the Turbo Debugger at hand.

Just the opposite effect of this error occurs if you define variables with the *same name in different scopes*. You may think you have updated a global variable, but in fact you have only modified a local variable—which disappeared when the function terminated.

Summary

This chapter covered a large number of topics under the following four main headings:

❏ Data validation

❏ Designing test-case data

❏ Designing manageable data structures

❏ Common sources of data errors

When we momentarily turn our attention away from program logic to examine data validation, we immediately discovere that logic and the data it uses are intimately connected. The data drives the logic, implying that the logic must be tailored not merely to handle data, but to control it.

Turbo Debugger is a powerful tool for examining live data and verifying that program logic is in fact dealing with it correctly. TD allows you not only to examine any variable in detail and to evaluate expressions, but also to change data values on the fly by using expressions with side effects.

Expressions with side effects also allow you to check program behavior thoroughly when data values are at or beyond the extreme boundaries of their permissible range. This is extremely important, since many program errors occur under just these conditions.

You also can, and should, automate data validation by writing validation routines into your programs. Automated data validation is more tedious than difficult to program. Yet this feature is one of the hallmarks of professional-quality code—it can make or break the user friendliness and overall usability of a program.

Next you saw that the proper design of test-case data is a critical part of the process of integrating program logic with data handling capabilities. The basic rules of thumb are

❏ Always provide at least 30 test items/records.

❏ You need not provide more than 20 to 30 percent of the production-level quantity of data.

❏ Be sure to specifically include test cases involving boundary value extremes.

As early as the initial design phase of program development, designing manageable data structures is also an important consideration. You should be aware particularly of variable scope, efficient field structuring, controlling variable proliferation, methods for handling large amounts of data, and the ways in which Turbo C controls variables internally.

Finally, common sources of data errors were discussed. All of the errors discussed here can be programmer induced—by not having a clear grasp of Turbo C characteristics rather by a simple failure to provide validation logic. The seven important things to watch out for are

❏ automatic variable initialization

❏ incorrect reference to automatic variables (when they no longer exist)

❏ confusion of operators

❏ confusion about operator precedence

❏ pointer problems

❏ arithmetic errors

❏ scope errors

These are all C-related problems, and may take different forms with other languages or have no counterpart at all.

Data validation depends on a knowledge of basic computer science, on a detailed knowledge of both the particular application and the programming and debugging tools being used, and a good deal on the intelligent use of common sense. Hopefully, this chapter has helped you master these things.

Part IV

Programming Projects

William M.
Brown

CHAPTER **12**

Producing Graphs and Graphics

This chapter focuses on a sample program that accepts data from the screen. By displaying a simple data-entry screen, the program offers the user a means to enter data directly into fields. This data will be used to create and display a bar graph. Here are several key features of the sample program:

❏ It saves and restores the text screen. When you run this program, it returns the text screen to its condition prior to program execution.

❏ It determines the graphics device and adjusts to common screen dimensions (640 × 200).

❏ It uses text-mode functions to implement a simple data-entry function (`getValue`). This function displays a prompt at specified screen coordinates and then displays a highlighted field for data entry.

❏ It loads and registers the graphics devices and fonts. In this way you create a single executable file that runs without supporting graphics device files (*.BGI) and graphics font files (*.CHR). This executable will support all available graphics devices that support the 640 × 200 mode.

❏ A single make file creates this program and the graphic device and font library.

This chapter also demonstrates how to create .OBJ files from the supplied .BGI and .CHR files, by using the Turbo C utility `BGIOBG`.

Defining Requirements

To produce a graphics application (or any other application), the first task is to determine the requirements of the program. For this program the requirements are reading parameters from a data-entry screen and generating a three-dimensional bar graph using Turbo C graphic functions.

371

As you can see, these requirements are pretty weak and do not explain

❏ how many bars to draw.

❏ what parameters are to be read.

❏ whether to print the graph.

❏ whether color or shading patterns should be used.

❏ whether titles or legends are needed.

❏ what graphics devices this program will be used on.

These questions and others you may think of should be answered before you start the application design and implementation. But for now, practice turning this list of requirements into a full-fledged design.

Designing the Program

To design this program, use pseudocode; it is similar to but much easier to read than C code. Use the top-down method of design for this program. The pseudocode is as follows:

```
Begin Graphics Program

Use function saveScreen to save the text mode screen
If saveScreen function returns error then
     print "Could not save screen." message
     exit program

Use function regGraphics to load device drivers and fonts
If regGraphics function returns error then
     exit program

Use function getValues to obtain parameters from screen

Use function initGraphics to initialize graphics subsystem

Use function drawBars to display 3-D bar graph on screen

Use Turbo C function getch to wait for a character
(To end program, clear 3-D bar graph and restore
original text screen)

Use function closegraph to close the graphics subsystem

Use function restoreScreen to restore the text mode screen

Use function exit to return an error code of 0 to DOS and exit the program
```

The functions used in the graphics program should be designed and implemented in parallel. If you document your C program code well, the code can become a part of your design document. (Sometimes—especially for smaller programs—that's all there is!) Always create a detailed design before you start coding, regardless of whether your fellow programmers do.

Implementing the Program

Several Turbo C utilities assist you in development of Turbo C programs. Using these utilities, you can reduce drastically the amount of time it takes to compile, link, and debug your code.

Make Files

The tools in this graphics program are MAKE and BIGOBJ (the Turbo C command-line compiler and Turbo Linker also come into play). Listing 12.1 contains the sample make file used for the graphics program. A make file specifies files (source, object, etc.) that are needed in order to construct the complete program, files that are dependents, and what is to be done in order to make files (object, executable, etc.) if a dependent changes. Take a closer look at this make file.

Listing 12.1

```
# BAR3D.MAK, this is the make file for the bar3d demonstration program.
# Created: 1/23/89
#
# To execute this makefile, type in the following command:
#
#     make -fbar3d.mak
#
# All commands invoked in this make file assume that they are in either the
# current directory or the DOS path. If they aren't, they must be changed to
# indicate the proper directory.
#
# Directory locations, change these if your Turbo C environment is different.
#
DRIDIR  = c:\tc
FONDIR  = c:\tc
LIB     = c:\tc\lib

#
# Drivers and fonts available. Using bgiobj will create these obj files.
#
DRIVERS = $(DRIDIR)\att.obj  $(DRIDIR)\cga.obj     $(DRIDIR)\egavga.obj \
          $(DRIDIR)\herc.obj $(DRIDIR)\ibm8514.obj $(DRIDIR)\pc3270.obj
FONTS   = $(FONDIR)\goth.obj $(FONDIR)\litt.obj    $(FONDIR)\sans.obj \
          $(FONDIR)\trip.obj

#
# Make the bar3d.exe program. Link using small data model.
#
```

Listing 12.1 continues

Listing 12.1 continued

```
bar3d.exe:    $(LIB)\ourgrap.lib bar3d.obj
    @tlink $(LIB)\c0s bar3d, bar3d, bar3d,\
        $(LIB)\ourgrap $(LIB)\graphics $(LIB)\emu $(LIB)\maths $(LIB)\cs

#
# Using TLIB, build our own private library. Place this library in the
# directory defined by the macro $(LIB). Note: if directory names are changed,
# update the OURGRAP.RSP file.
#
$(LIB)\ourgrap.lib:    $(DRIVERS) $(FONTS)
    @echo Creating driver/font library, please wait...
    @tlib $(LIB)\ourgrap @ourgrap.rsp, ourgrap.lst

#
# Make bgi modules if the source has changed. These files are located in the
# directory defined by the macro $(DRIDIR).
#
$(DRIDIR)\att.obj:         $(DRIDIR)\att.bgi
$(DRIDIR)\cga.obj:         $(DRIDIR)\cga.bgi
$(DRIDIR)\egavga.obj:      $(DRIDIR)\egavga.bgi
$(DRIDIR)\herc.obj:        $(DRIDIR)\herc.bgi
$(DRIDIR)\ibm8514.obj:     $(DRIDIR)\ibm8514.bgi
$(DRIDIR)\pc3270.obj:      $(DRIDIR)\pc3270.bgi

#
# Make chr modules if the source has changed. These files are located in the
# directory defined by the macro $(FONDIR).
#
$(FONDIR)\goth.obj:        $(FONDIR)\goth.chr
$(FONDIR)\litt.obj:        $(FONDIR)\litt.chr
$(FONDIR)\sans.obj:        $(FONDIR)\sans.chr
$(FONDIR)\trip.obj:        $(FONDIR)\trip.chr

#
# Make C programs used in this program.
#
bar3d.obj:   bar3d.c

#
# Standard inference rule to make Obj files from BGI and CHR files. Because the /F
# switch in bgiobj is used, a segment name other than _TEXT (the default)
# is used. This will remove the Segment exceeds 64K (or similar error) when
# linking all the drivers and fonts.
#
# The destination ($*.obj) is specified in this call so that both the source
# and destination will have the same prefix. If this option is not used, the
# destination file will have an F appended to the prefix. This caused the
# dependency checking of the makefile to fail (eg. attf.obj: att.bgi).
#
# Bgi -> Obj files.
#
.bgi.obj:
    @bgiobj /F $* $*.obj
```

```
#
# Chr -> Obj files.
#
.chr.obj:
    @bgiobj /F $* $*.obj
#
# Standard inference rule to make Obj files from C files. #
.c.obj:
    @tcc -w -ms -c -v -f- $*
```

You can use comments in a make file by placing the pound-sign character (#) as the first character on the comment line. The lines with DRIVERS, FONTS, and LIB are make macros, a shorthand way of representing the string of text to the right of the equal sign (=).

The *bar3d.exe* File

The first target file you see here is bar3d.exe:; its dependents are ourgrap.lib and bar3d.obj. If either of the dependents is newer (time and date) than the target, the actions below that target line are to be executed. The action for this target is to link the modules using tlink. and to create the program bar3d.exe.

The *ourgrap.lib* File

The next target is ourgrap.lib:; its dependents are represented by the macros DRIVERS and FONTS. If any of the files listed in the macros are newer than the target (ourgrap.lib), the action below the target line is executed. In this case, tclib.exe, Turbo C's utility that creates libraries, is executed. The tclib.exe program manages libraries of object modules. A single library may contain one or more object modules. In this sample program, a library is created to hold the object modules for the device drivers and fonts. If another graphics program were written that needed to link in these object modules, it could use this library also.

Other Object Code Files

Several targets exist that do not have actions (such as att.obj). These targets use *standard inference rules* (also know as *implicit rules*) that appear toward the end of the make file. An example would be that if the file att.bgi is newer than att.obj, make would look for a target implicit rule in the format of .bgi.obj and execute the actions for that rule. Implicit rules are used if no explicit rule is given for a target, or if no commands exist for that target.

Make files can be powerful and are extremely helpful when you are dealing with several modules or C programs. This example created a library using this make file, then linked that library into a graphics demonstration program. It is not likely that the .BGI or .CHR files would change (except with a new release of Turbo C) or that the library would have to be created more than once.

Input File for Module Names

Instead of supplying a list of modules you want to include in a library, you can create an input file and use the at-sign character (@) to indicate which module names will come from an input file. The file `ourgrap.rsp`, shown in listing 12.2, is used to supply the library utility TLIB with the names of the modules to be loaded into the library file `ourgrap.lib`. You can use this feature also with `tlink.exe`, supplying all of its arguments in a response file and using the at-sign character to prefix the name of the response file.

Listing 12.2

```
Graphics Demonstration Program--LIB Graphics Response File

-+c:\tc\att.obj -+c:\tc\cga.obj -+c:\tc\egavga.obj -+c:\tc\herc.obj &
-+c:\tc\ibm8514.obj -+c:\tc\pc3270.obj -+c:\tc\goth.obj -+c:\tc\litt.obj &
-+c:\tc\sans.obj -+c:\tc\trip.obj
```

The Source Code

The source code for the graphics program is provided in listing 12.3. The comments in this program make many of the functions self-explanatory. Now take a closer look at the code.

Listing 12.3

```
Graphics Demonstration Program
/***********************************************************************
 *                                                                     *
 *      Program:   graphics.c                                          *
 *                                                                     *
 *      Purpose:   Simple graphics bar-graph demonstration program.    *
 *                                                                     *
 *      History:   Date        Person      Change Description          *
 *                 --------     ---------   --------------------------- *
 *                 2/14/89      WMB         Created.                    *
 ***********************************************************************/

/* Include header files we will use. */
#include <graphics.h>
#include <stdio.h>
#include <stdlib.h>
```

```c
#include <string.h>
#include <process.h>
#include <fcntl.h>
#include <alloc.h>
#include <conio.h>
#include <io.h>
#include <ctype.h>

/* Macros used in this program. */
#define   FALSE          0
#define   TRUE           !FALSE
#define   CHARATTR       2
#define   NDRIVERS(n)    (sizeof(n) / sizeof(DRIVER))
#define   MAXTICS        8
#define   MAXBARS        16
#define   ID             "SAMPLE BARGRAPH PROGRAM"
#define   VERSION        "1.0A"

/* A structure we will use to save the screen information. */
typedef  struct   _screenTag
    {
    struct    text_info    saveText;
    char                   *textBuffer;
    int                    textSize;
    } SCREEN, *SCRPTR;

/* A structure we will use to save driver information. */
typedef  struct   _driverTag
    {
    void  far *driver;
    char *Msg;
    } DRIVER, *DRVPTR;

/* graphics device drivers and fonts that are linked in from the library
   created by the make file (using TLIB.EXE). The utility BGIOBJ, using the
   /F switch, creates the name appending a _far to the driver and font names.
*/

DRIVER   allDrivers[] =                    /* Graphic drivers. */
    {    {CGA_driver_far,       "CGA"},
    {EGAVGA_driver_far,   "EGA or VGA"},
    {IBM8514_driver_far,  "IBM 8514"},
    {Herc_driver_far,     "Hercules"},
    {ATT_driver_far,      "AT&T"},
    {PC3270_driver_far,   "IBM PC3270"}
    };
```

Listing 12.3 continues

Listing 12.3 continued

```
DRIVER    allFonts[] =                          /* Fonts. */
    {
    {triplex_font_far,    "Triplex"},
    {small_font_far,      "Small"},
    {sansserif_font_far,  "Sansserif"},
    {gothic_font_far,     "Gothic"}
    };

int       maxColors;                  /* Max colors. */
int       maxX;                       /* Max X positions. */
int       maxY;                       /* Max Y positions. */
int       barH[MAXBARS];              /* Will hold values for Bars. */
SCREEN    scrSave;                    /* Structure to save screen into. */

/*********************************************************************
 *      Function:   saveScreen                                       *
 *                                                                   *
 *      Purpose:    Will save current text screen into an array.     *
 *                                                                   *
 *      Returns:    TRUE if successful, FALSE if something wrong.     *
 *                                                                   *
 *      Args.:      Pointer to screen structure.                     *
 *                                                                   *
 *      History:    Date      Person      Change Description         *
 *                  --------   ----------   ----------------------------  *
 *                  2/14/89    WMB         Created.                  *
 *********************************************************************/
int    saveScreen(SCRPTR scr)
{

    /* Get current text mode configuration and save screen. */
    gettextinfo(&(scr->saveText));

    /* Calculate size of buffer and allocate. */
    scr->textSize = scr->saveText.screenheight *
                    scr->saveText.screenwidth *
                            CHARATTR;

    /* Allocate storage for text buffer. */
    if((scr->textBuffer = malloc(scr->textSize)) == NULL)
        return(FALSE);

    /* Save screen. */
    if(gettext(scr->saveText.winleft, scr->saveText.wintop,
            scr->saveText.winright, scr->saveText.winbottom,
               scr->textBuffer) == 0)
        return(FALSE);

    /* All done. */
    return(TRUE);
}
```

```
/*****************************************************************************
 *      Function:  restoreScreen                                             *
 *                                                                           *
 *      Purpose:   Will restore current text screen into an array.           *
 *                                                                           *
 *      Returns:   N/A                                                       *
 *                                                                           *
 *      Args.:     Pointer to screen structure.                              *
 *                                                                           *
 *      History:   Date         Person      Change Description               *
 *                 --------      ----------  ------------------------------   *
 *                 2/14/89       WMB         Created.                         *
 *****************************************************************************/
void   restoreScreen(SCRPTR scr)
{

   /* Restore screen attribute and text. */
   textattr(scr->saveText.attribute);
   puttext(scr->saveText.winleft, scr->saveText.wintop,
       scr->saveText.winright, scr->saveText.winbottom,
          scr->textBuffer);

   /* Free memory that was allocated and set pointer to NULL. */
   free(scr->textBuffer);
   scr->textBuffer = NULL;

   /* Put the cursor back where it was. */
   gotoxy(scr->saveText.curx, scr->saveText.cury);
}

/*****************************************************************************
 *      Function:  regGraphics                                               *
 *                                                                           *
 *      Purpose:   Will register drivers and fonts which are included at     *
 *                 run-time. The function registerfarbgidriver() is used to  *
 *                 register the bgi drivers so that they will be linked in to*
 *                 this program. The function registerfarbgifont() is used to*
 *                 register the chr font files so that they will be linked in*
 *                 to this program. This will allow the device and font files*
 *                 to be included in a single executable.                    *
 *                                                                           *
 *      Returns:   TRUE if successful, FALSE if error occurs.                *
 *                                                                           *
 *      Args.:     N/A                                                       *
 *                                                                           *
 *      History:   Date         Person      Change Description               *
 *                 --------      ----------  ------------------------------   *
 *                 2/14/89       WMB         Created.                         *
 *****************************************************************************/
```

Listing 12.3 continues

Listing 12.3 continued

```c
int    regGraphics(void)
{
   int    drv;                                  /* Index into driver. */

   /* Register all possible drivers that might be used. */
   for(drv = 0; drv < NDRIVERS(allDrivers); drv++)
      {
      if(registerfarbgidriver(allDrivers[drv].driver) < 0)
         {
         fprintf(stderr, "Failed to load %s graphics driver.\n",
            allDrivers[drv].Msg);
         return(FALSE);
         }
      }

   /* Register all possible fonts that might be used. */
   for(drv = 0; drv < NDRIVERS(allFonts); drv++)
      {
      if(registerfarbgifont(allFonts[drv].driver) < 0)
         {
         fprintf(stderr, "Failed to load %s font.\n",
            allFonts[drv].Msg);
         return(FALSE);
         }
      }

   /* Everything ok. */
   return(TRUE);
}

/***************************************************************************
 *    Function:  initGraphics                                              *
 *                                                                         *
 *    Purpose:   This will initialize the graphics system to  a common     *
 *               setting.                                                  *
 *                                                                         *
 *    Returns:   TRUE if successful, FALSE if error occurs.                *
 *                                                                         *
 *    Args.:     N/A                                                       *
 *                                                                         *
 *    History:   Date         Person       Change Description             *
 *               --------      ---------    ----------------------------   *
 *               2/14/89       WMB          Created.                       *
 ***************************************************************************/
int    initGraphics(void)
{
   int    grapDriver;             /* Driver that we detected. */
   int    grapMode;               /* Mode to put it into. */
   int    grapError;              /* Any errors? */
```

```
/* Detect what hardware we have out there. */
detectgraph(&grapDriver, &grapMode);

/* Override mode, this program assumes a 640 x 200 area. */
switch(grapDriver)
    {
    case  CGA:
        grapMode = CGAHI;
        break;

    case  MCGA:
        grapMode = MCGAMED;
        break;

    case  EGA:
        grapMode = EGALO;
        break;

    case  EGA64:
        grapMode = EGA64LO;
        break;

    case  ATT400:
        grapMode = ATT400MED;
        break;

    case  VGA:
        grapMode = VGALO;
        break;

    case  EGAMONO:
    case  IBM8514:
    case  HERCMONO:
    case  PC3270:
        fprintf(stderr, "This graphics adapter not supported.\n");
        grapDriver = -1;
        break;
    }

/* Check to see that everything is ok. */
if(grapDriver < 0)
    {
    fprintf(stderr, "No Graphics Display Adapter detected.\n");
    return(FALSE);
    }

/* Bring up the graphics system. */
initgraph(&grapDriver, &grapMode, "");
if((grapError = graphresult()) < 0)
    {
    fprintf(stderr, "initgraph error: %s.\n", grapherrormsg(grapError));
    return(FALSE);
    }
```

Listing 12.3 continues

Listing 12.3 *continued*

```
    /* Get specific information about our environment. */
    maxColors = getmaxcolor() + 1;          /* Maximum colors. */
    maxX = getmaxx();                        /* Size of screen. */
    maxY = getmaxy();
    /* Done. */
    return(TRUE);

}

/***************************************************************************
 *       Function:   drawBars                                              *
 *                                                                         *
 *       Purpose:    This will draw the grid and bar graph.                *
 *                                                                         *
 *       Returns:    N/A                                                   *
 *                                                                         *
 *       Args.:      N/A                                                   *
 *                                                                         *
 *       History:    Date        Person      Change Description            *
 *                   --------     ----------  ---------------------------- *
 *                   2/14/89      WMB         Created.                     *
 ***************************************************************************/
void  drawGrid(char *title, int vTicks, int hTicks)
{
    int    height;                          /* Height of text. */
    int    width;                           /* Width of text. */
    int    xTicks;                          /* Ticks on the X line. */
    int    yTicks;                          /* Ticks on the Y line. */
    int    i;
    int    temp;
    char   szBuf[5];

    /* Draw border around screen. */
    setcolor(maxColors - 1);
    setlinestyle(SOLID_LINE, 0, NORM_WIDTH);
    setviewport(0, 0, maxX, maxY, 1);       /* Open viewport to full screen. */
    rectangle(0, 0, maxX, maxY);

    /* Draw title. */
    settextstyle(TRIPLEX_FONT, HORIZ_DIR, 2);
    settextjustify(CENTER_TEXT, CENTER_TEXT);
    height = textheight("H");
    outtextxy(maxX / 2, height / 2, title);

    /* Draw grid. */
    settextstyle(DEFAULT_FONT, HORIZ_DIR, 1);
    width  = textwidth("H");
    height = textheight("H");
    temp   = width * MAXTICS;

    line(temp, height * 2, temp, maxY - height);
    line(temp, maxY - height, maxX - temp, maxY - height);
```

```
    /* Draw ticks. */
    xTicks = (maxX - (temp * 2)) / hTicks;
    yTicks = (maxY - (height * 4)) / vTicks;
    for(i = 1; i <= hTicks; i++)
        {
        setfillstyle(SOLID_FILL, i);
        line(temp + (xTicks * i), maxY - height, temp + (xTicks * i),
            maxY - (height / 2));
        bar3d(temp + (xTicks * (i - 1)), (maxY - height) - (yTicks * barH[i - 1]),
            temp + (xTicks * i), maxY - height, 15, 1);
        }

    for(i = 1; i <= vTicks; i++)
        {
        line(temp, (maxY - height) - (yTicks * i), temp - width,
          (maxY - height) - (yTicks * i));
        itoa(i, szBuf, 10);
        outtextxy(temp - (width * (strlen(szBuf) + 1)),
            (maxY - height) - (yTicks * i), szBuf);
        }

}

/****************************************************************************
 *      Function:   getValue                                                *
 *                                                                          *
 *      Purpose:    This will obtain a value and return it into an array.   *
 *                                                                          *
 *      Returns:    N/A                                                     *
 *                                                                          *
 *      Args.:      N/A                                                     *
 *                                                                          *
 *      History:    Date        Person      Change Description              *
 *                  --------     ----------   ------------------------------ *
 *                  2/14/89      WMB         Created.                        *
 ****************************************************************************/
void  getValue(int nCol, int nRow, char *szPrompt, char *szValue, int nLen)
{
    int     nValCol;
    int     i;
    int     nTempLen;
    int     moreChars;
    int     ch;

    /* Goto position and display prompt. */
    gotoxy(nCol, nRow);
    cputs(szPrompt);
    nValCol = nCol + strlen(szPrompt) + 1;

    /* Display field. */
    gotoxy(nValCol, nRow);
```

Listing 12.3 continues

Listing 12.3 *continued*

```c
textattr(CYAN + (BLUE<<4));
for(i = 0; i < nLen; i++)
   putch(' ');

gotoxy(nValCol, nRow);

/* Obtain value. */
nTempLen = 0;
moreChars = TRUE;
memset(szValue, 0, sizeof(szValue));

while(moreChars)
   {
   ch = getch();
   if(!isalnum(ch) && ch != ' ')
      {
      if(ch == '\b' && nTempLen > 0)
         {
         nTempLen--;
         szValue[nTempLen] = 0;
         putch(ch);
         putch(' ');
         putch(ch);
         continue;
         }
      else if(ch == '\r')
         break;
      putch('\007');
      continue;
      }
   putch(ch);
   szValue[nTempLen++] = ch;
   if(nTempLen == nLen)
      break;
   }
   textattr(scrSave.saveText.attribute);
}

/*****************************************************************************
 *       Function:  getValues                                               *
 *                                                                          *
 *       Purpose:  This will obtain values needed from the user.            *
 *                                                                          *
 *       Returns:  N/A                                                      *
 *                                                                          *
 *       Args.:    N/A                                                      *
 *                                                                          *
 *       History:     Date        Person      Change Description            *
 *                   --------     ----------  ------------------------------*
 *                   2/14/89      WMB         Created.                      *
 *****************************************************************************/
```

```
void  getValues(char *szTitle, int titleLen, int *vTicks, int *hTicks)
{
    int    i;
    char   szVal[10];
    char   szBar[31];

    /* Clear the screen, printer header. */
    clrscr();
    i = (80 - (strlen(ID) + strlen(VERSION) + 3)) / 2;
    cprintf("%*.*s%s [%s]", i, i, " ", ID, VERSION);

    getValue(5, 3, "Enter in maximum number of vertical ticks:", szVal, 2);
    *vTicks = atoi(szVal);

    getValue(15, 4, "Enter in maximum number of bars:", szVal, 2);
    *hTicks = atoi(szVal);

    memset(szTitle, 0, titleLen);
    getValue(21, 5, "What is the graph's title:", szTitle, titleLen);

    for(i = 0; i < *hTicks; i++)
        {
        sprintf(szBar, "What is the value for bar #%2d:", i + 1);
        getValue(17, 6 + i, szBar, szVal, 2);
        barH[i] = atoi(szVal);
        }

    cputs("\r\n\r\n..Press any key to display graph..");
    getch();

}

/*******************************************************************
 *      Function:  main                                            *
 *                                                                 *
 *      Purpose:   Main function for dump program.                 *
 *                                                                 *
 *      Returns:   Exit 0 if successful, Exit 1 if an error occurs.*
 *                                                                 *
 *      Args.:     argc        count of command line arguments     *
 *                 argv        array of pointers to command line args.*
 *                                                                 *
 *      History:   Date        Person     Change Description       *
 *                 --------     ---------  -----------------------  *
 *                 2/14/89      WMB        Created.                 *
 *******************************************************************/
void  main(void)
{
    int     vTicks;
    int     hTicks;
    char    szTitle[25];
```

Listing 12.3 continues

Listing 12.3 *continued*

```
        /* Save the current screen. */
        if(!saveScreen(&scrSave))
          {
          printf("Could not save the screen.\n");
          exit(1);
          }

        /* Register the drivers and fonts. */
        if(!regGraphics())
           exit(1);                          /* regGraphics prints message. */

        /* Get values from the user. */
        getValues(szTitle, sizeof(szTitle), &vTicks, &hTicks);

        /* Initialize the graphics subsystem. */
        if(!initGraphics())
           exit(1);                          /* initGraphics prints message. */

        /* Display graph and wait for any key. */
        drawGrid(szTitle, vTicks, hTicks);

        /* Close the graphics system and return the screen. */
        getch();
        closegraph();
        restoreScreen(&scrSave);
        exit(0);
}
```

The purpose of the first part of this program is to include the include files and to define the macros, several structures, and global storage.

Program Structures

The SCREEN structure is defined to hold the information regarding the text screen. This structure is used by the functions saveScreen and restoreScreen.

The DRIVER structure is defined to hold information about the device drivers and font files. It holds a far pointer and an optional error message that prints if the driver cannot be loaded.

The allDrivers structure contains code for all the graphics device drivers Borland provides with Turbo C. The function regGraphics uses this structure to load the drivers.

The allFonts structure contains all the fonts Borland provides with Turbo C. The function regGraphics uses this structure to load the fonts.

Program Variables and Functions

The global variables `maxColors`, `maxX`, and `maxY` store information about the maximum colors, maximum columns, and maximum rows, respectively. The global variable `barH` holds the value for each bar; the size of this variable is based on the macro `MAXBARS`.

The first two functions, `saveScreen()` and `restoreScreen()`, save and restore the text screen. Additional information on these functions can be found in Chapter 14, "Reading and Processing a Binary File."

The next function registers graphics device drivers and fonts. This function, which is called `regGraphics()`, first traverses the `allDrivers()` structure and registers the graphics device driver using the Turbo C function `registerfarbgidriver()`. The second action of `regGraphics()` is to register the fonts using the Turbo C function `registerfarbgifont()`. If any errors occur, an error message is printed and a error return code is returned to the `main` function.

The function `initGraphics()` uses a Turbo C function to initialize the graphics subsystem and switch the screen to graphics mode. The function `detectgraph()` determines the type of device being used. To keep this program simple, a common size (640 × 200) screen is selected. If a device does not support the common size, an error message is printed and an error code returned. If the program did not override the size of the screen, the highest resolution available would be selected. After the mode is set, a call to `initgraph` switches the screen to graphics mode. The `initgraph()` function makes calls to determine the maximum number of colors, maximum columns, and maximum rows this device supports and places these values into global variables for use later.

The next function, `drawBars()`, uses data the user supplies to produce three-dimensional bar graphs by calling the Turbo C function `bar3d()`. This function also draws a border, displays a title line, and draws the X and Y axes. Finally, the function draws the vertical ticks next to the Y axis.

The function `getValue` implements a simple data-entry function that displays a prompt, displays a field using different color attributes, and accepts data from the user. The data is returned in the string `szValue` and has a maximum length of `nLen`.

The function `getValues()` obtains the maximum number of vertical and horizontal ticks, as well as an optional title and the value for each bar. To do this, `getValues()` uses the data-entry function `getValue()` and converts user input to a number where applicable.

The `main()` function uses the other functions to implement the graphics demonstration program. This function begins by saving the screen with `saveScreen`.

It then registers graphicsdevice drivers and fonts using the function regGraphics(). Next, getValues() is called to get the title, vertical ticks, horizontal ticks, and the values for the bars. Several local variables are passed to getValues(). The main() function then calls initGraphics to place the screen into a common graphics mode. The function drawBars() uses the local variables and global variables to draw the bar graph, incorporating different colored bars if the graphics device supports multiple colors in that graphics mode. Finally, the graphics system is closed and the text-mode screen restored after the user presses any key. An exit code of 0 is sent to DOS, indicating a successful operation.

Program Output

Executing the graphics program displays a screen for entering parameters for the bar graph program. (This was the first part of the program requirements.) An example of the data-entry screen display is shown in figure 12.1.

Fig. 12.1. *Sample entries in graphics program data-entry screen.*

```
Graphics Demonstration Program--Data-Entry Screen

                      EXAMPLE BARGRAPH PROGRAM [1.0A]
    Enter the maximum number of vertical ticks: 10
         Enter the maximum number of bars: 10
            What is the graph's title? SALES FORECAST 1989
        What is the value for bar # 1? 3
        What is the value for bar # 2? 4
        What is the value for bar # 3? 3
        What is the value for bar # 4? 2
        What is the value for bar # 5? 1
        What is the value for bar # 6? 2
        What is the value for bar # 7? 4
        What is the value for bar # 8? 5
        What is the value for bar # 9? 10
        What is the value for bar #10? 9

  ..Press any key to display graph..
```

After a user enters the parameters and presses any key, the three-dimensional bar graph in figure 12.2 is displayed. This satisfies the original program requirements.

Fig. 12.2. Graphics demonstration program output.

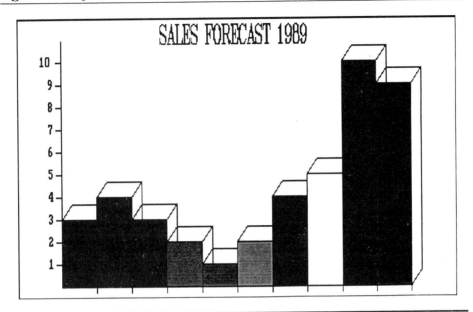

Summary

The graphics program developed and run in this chapter shows you how to read parameters from the screen in order to generate a bar graph. The chapter also shows you how to convert the .BGI and .CHR files and link them in to create a single executable file that does not require additional supporting files.

Although this program is simple, it does demonstrate several advanced features of Turbo C graphics and the Turbo C MAKE file utility.

William M.
Brown

CHAPTER 13

Reading a Mail Merge File

This chapter traces how to write a program that merges a file of names and addresses with a document file that resembles a standard letter. The program can be adapted to fit any situation in which you merge as many as seven fields from one file into another, such as for printing envelopes.

This programming example follows the first three steps of a typical software-development life cycle: requirements analysis, design, and implementation. Some unit testing is done by providing sample data and checking for the proper results.

Analyzing Requirements

The first phase of writing the mail-merge program (or any other program) is to determine exactly what it is required to do. To do this, write a requirements analysis. For a mail-merge program, this is a brief analysis of the merge functions to be performed. In order to write a requirements analysis, you may need to interview users of the program and determine their specific needs. With the mail-merge program, the requirements can be summarized as follows: Read two ASCII text files and write the result to a third text file.

The first text file is the mailing list; for every line in this file, a mail-merge letter is produced. Each line in this file is in ASCII "text" file format—ending with a carriage return/line feed, with the fields separated by commas. Each line of the mail-merge list file has the following format:

```
first name,last name,address 1,address 2,city,state,zip code
```

The second file is the mail-merge letter. This file should contain text with keyword entries that are replaced by their corresponding fields in the mailing-list file. Table 13.1 shows the keywords used to reference fields in the mailing-list file.

391

Table 13.1. *Keywords and Reference Fields in Mailing-List File*

Keyword	Field
‹F1›	first name
‹F2›	last name
‹F3›	address 1
‹F4›	address 2
‹F5›	city
‹F6›	state
‹F7›	zip code

The third file is the output file. For every record in the mailing-list file, a mail-merged letter is created and placed in the output file. Then, before sending the output file to the spooler for printing, the program checks whether the DOS print spooler is active.

The program prompts the user for the names of the files if they are missing from the command line. If a file (except the output file) is missing or has an incorrect name, the program prints an appropriate error message and then aborts. If the output file exists, the program prompts the user to decide whether it should be removed. If the user decides not to remove the output file, the program aborts.

The contents of the fields are written into the mail-merged letter, and the text is not reformatted. Missing fields contain a single space in the mail-merge list file.

Designing the Program

In the next phase of writing the mail-merge program, you use the requirements analysis and write a design document or design outline. This design document should provide enough information for a programmer to implement the application and meet all of the requirements specified in the requirements analysis.

For the mail-merge program, the design document is a brief outline of the program's functionality, broken into specific functions that will be implemented as functions in a Turbo C program. Because this program is small, it can be stored in a single C file called merge.c. The sample design document follows:

1. Open Files

    A. Check command line for each file name and ask user for list file name if not on command line.

    B. Open list file for reading; check it for errors. If errors occur, print message and then abort program.

    C. Ask user for letter file name.

    D. Open letter file for reading; check it for errors. If errors occur, print message and then abort program.

    E. Ask user for output file name.

    F. Check whether output file exists.

        a. If output file exists, ask user whether existing file should be overwritten.

        b. Remove existing output file if user has requested this action.

        c. If the existing output file is not to be removed, abort mail-merge program.

    G. Open output file for writing; check for errors.

2. Process Files

    A. Read each line in mailing list file (and do Step 2. B on each) until end-of-file is reached.

    B. Parse line and fill in field buffers. Note: if field buffers have inappropriate format, this program may produce unexpected results.

    C. Rewind letter file and write form feed to output file.

    D. Read each line in the letter file and replace keywords with field contents.

    E. Write each line from letter file (keywords replaced) to output file.

3. Close Files

    A. Close each open file.

4. Print Output File

    A. If print spooler is active (in other words, if DOS PRINT has already been installed), print output file.

    B. If the print spooler is inactive, do not print output file.

After you have written the design outline, compare it with the requirements, making sure that all of the requirements have been addressed in the design outline. It is much easier to catch design problems at this stage than at the implementation and testing stages.

Now it is time to develop the actual Turbo C program to implement the mail-merge application. This program should follow the design outline as closely as possible.

Implementing the Application

The actual mail-merge program consists of one source-code file, merge.c, and one support file, makefile. This file will be used to create the executable image. You invoke the MAKE utility by simply typing in the command **make** at the DOS prompt. Listing 13.1 shows the contents of this file.

Listing 13.1

```
# MAKEFILE, this is the make file for the mail-merge sample
# program.
# Created: 1/23/89
#
     merge.exe:    merge.c
  tcc -ms -f -v merge
```

The MAKE utility checks to see whether the file merge.c is newer than merge.exe. If it is newer, the Turbo C compiler is executed in stand-alone mode with the arguments -ml -f merge.

The Turbo C source code for the mail-merge program is in Listing 13.2. This program is broken into several functions that closely resemble the major steps in the design document.

Listing 13.2

```
/*****************************************************************************
 *       Program:   merge.c                                                  *
 *                                                                           *
 *       Purpose:   Simple mail merge program.                               *
 *                                                                           *
 *       History:   Date       Person      Change Description               *
 *                  --------    ----------  ------------------------------   *
 *                  1/23/89     WMB         Created.                          *
 *****************************************************************************/

/* include header files that we will use */
#include <stdio.h>
#include <stdlib.h>
#include <string.h>
#include <process.h>
#include <dos.h>
#include <dir.h>

/* macros used in this program */
/*#define  SPAWNPRINT*/        /* remove the comments from the define
                                  statement if you want to print the
                                  file by spawning the DOS print spooler. */
```

```
#define   FALSE       0
#define   TRUE        !FALSE
#define   MAXLINE     140
#define   MAXFIELDS   7
#define   DELIMIT     ",\n"
#define   SPOOLERINT  0x2F
#define   MINUS       '-'

/* storage for file names */
char   listFile[MAXPATH];
char   letrFile[MAXPATH];
char   outpFile[MAXPATH];
/* pointers for fields */
char   *fields[MAXFIELDS];

/* multiplexor packet for print.com */
typedef struct _packTag
    {
    unsigned char level;
    long fileName;
    } PACKET;

/* pointers to streams */
FILE   *listFS = NULL;
FILE   *letrFS = NULL;
FILE   *outpFS = NULL;

/************************************************************************
 *      Function:   usage                                               *
 *                                                                      *
 *      Purpose:  Print usage information.                              *
 *                                                                      *
 *      Returns:  N/A                                                   *
 *                                                                      *
 *      Args.:    N/A                                                   *
 *                                                                      *
 *      History:      Date        Person    Change Description          *
 *                    --------    --------   ---------------------------- *
 *                    1/23/89     WMB        Created.                    *
 ************************************************************************/
void  usage(void)
{
   printf("Usage:\n\n");
   printf("\tMERGE [-L letter_file] [-N list_file] [-O output_file]\n\n");
   printf("Where:\n\n");
   printf("\tletter_file is the name of the letter template to be merged\n");
   printf("\tlist_file   is the name of file containing the names\n");
   printf("\toutput_file is the name of the output file\n\n");
   printf("You must omit the [] characters when using these commands. These\n");
   printf("brackets are used to denote that these are optional commands.\n");
}
```

Listing 13.2 continues

Listing 13.2 *continued*

```
/***************************************************************************
 *      Function:  closeFiles                                             *
 *                                                                        *
 *      Purpose:  Close all files that are opened.                        *
 *                                                                        *
 *      Returns:  N/A                                                     *
 *                                                                        *
 *      Args.:    N/A                                                     *
 *                                                                        *
 *      History:  Date        Person      Change Description              *
 *                --------     ---------   ----------------------------    *
 *                1/23/89      WMB         Created.                        *
 ***************************************************************************/
void  closeFiles(void)
{
   /* close all file streams that are not NULL pointers */
   if(listFS != NULL)
       fclose(listFS);
   if(letrFS != NULL)
       fclose(letrFS);
   if(outpFS != NULL)
       fclose(outpFS);
}

/***************************************************************************
 *      Function:  openFiles                                              *
 *                                                                        *
 *      Purpose:  Open all the files that are needed for this program.    *
 *                                                                        *
 *      Returns:  TRUE if successful, FALSE is something wrong.           *
 *                                                                        *
 *      Args.:    N/A                                                     *
 *                                                                        *
 *      History:  Date        Person      Change Description              *
 *                --------     ---------   ----------------------------    *
 *                1/23/89      WMB         Created.                        *
 ***************************************************************************/
int   openFiles(void)
{
   int   ch;                           /* Character read */

   /* open list file; obtain its name from the user. This
      file must exist */
   if(listFile[0] == 0)
       {
       printf("Mail merge list   file: ");
       gets(listFile);
       }

   /* open file */
   if((listFS = fopen(listFile, "r")) == NULL)
```

```
      {
      printf("\nERROR: Could not open list file [%s].\n", listFile);
      perror("MS-DOS Error");
      return(FALSE);
      }
 /* open letter file; obtain its name from the user. This
    file must exist */
if(letrFile[0] == 0)
      {
      printf("Mail merge letter file: ");
      gets(letrFile);
      }

/* open file */
if((letrFS = fopen(letrFile, "r")) == NULL)
      {
      printf("\nERROR: Could not open letter file [%s].\n", letrFile);
      perror("MS-DOS Error");
      closeFiles();                    /* Close the list file */
      return(FALSE);
      }

/* open output file; obtain its name from the user. This
   file must not exist */
if(outpFile[0] == 0)
      {
      printf("Mail merge output file: ");
      gets(outpFile);
      }

/* check to see if file exists */
if(!access(outpFile, 0))
      {
      /* ask if we should remove it */
      do
          {
          printf("Output file [%s] exists, remove it (Y/N)? ", outpFile);
          ch = toupper(getche());
          putchar('\n');
          }
      while(ch != 'Y' && ch != 'N');

      /* get out if answer is No */
      if(ch == 'N')
          {
          closeFiles();
          return(FALSE);
          }
```

Listing 13.2 continues

Listing 13.2 continued

```
         /* remove it */
         if(remove(outpFile))
            {
            printf("\nERROR: Could not remove output file [%s].\n", outpFile);
            perror("MS-DOS Error");        return(FALSE);
            }
         }

   /* open file */
   if((outpFS = fopen(outpFile, "w")) == NULL)
      {
      printf("\nERROR: Could not open output file [%s].\n", outpFile);
      perror("MS-DOS Error");
      closeFiles();                     /* Close the list and letter file */
      return(FALSE);
      }

   /* everything is okay */
   return(TRUE);
}

/*****************************************************************************
*      Function:   processLetter                                            *
*                                                                           *
*      Purpose:    Process the letter using the fields from mail list.      *
*                                                                           *
*      Returns:    TRUE if successful, FALSE if something wrong.            *
*                                                                           *
*      Args.:      N/A                                                      *
*                                                                           *
*      History:    Date        Person     Change Description               *
*                  --------     ----------  ------------------------------- *
*                  1/23/89      WMB        Created.                          *
*****************************************************************************/
int    processLetter(void)
{
   char   inputLine[MAXLINE];
   char   tailLine[MAXLINE];
   char   fieldName[4];
   char   *tailPtr = NULL;
   char   *strPtr  = NULL;
   int    i;

   /* make sure that we are at the top of the letter file */
   fseek(letrFS, 0L, SEEK_SET);

   /* put a form feed into output file */
   fputc('\f', outpFS);

   while(fgets(inputLine, sizeof(inputLine), letrFS) != NULL)
      {
      /* check to see if a field is in this line */
```

```
        for(i = 1; i <= MAXFIELDS; i++)              {
            /* make field names */
            sprintf(fieldName, "<F%d>", i);
            if((strPtr = strstr(inputLine, fieldName)) == NULL)
                continue;

            /* found a field, let's transfer new contents */
            tailPtr = strPtr;

            /* skip past keyword */
            tailPtr += 4;

            /* make a new line, inserting field */
            strcpy(tailLine, tailPtr);
            strcpy(strPtr, fields[i - 1]);
            strcat(inputLine, tailLine);
            }

        /* write line to output file */
        if(fprintf(outpFS, "%s", inputLine) == EOF)
            return(FALSE);
        }

    /* everything is okay */
    return(TRUE);
}

/******************************************************************************
 *      Function:   processMailingList                                        *
 *                                                                            *
 *      Purpose:    Process the mailing list and send fields to letter.       *
 *                                                                            *
 *      Returns:    TRUE if successful, FALSE if something wrong.             *
 *                                                                            *
 *      Args.:      N/A                                                       *
 *                                                                            *
 *      History:    Date        Person    Change Description                  *
 *                  --------     ---------  ---------------------------        *
 *                  1/23/89      WMB        Created.                          *
 ******************************************************************************/
int    processMailingList(void)
{
    char   inputLine[MAXLINE];
    char   *inPtr;
    int    i;
    int    retcod = TRUE;

    /* for every line in the list file create a letter file */
    while(fgets(inputLine, sizeof(inputLine), listFS) != NULL)        {
        /* parse the input line, and place the values into the fields */
        inPtr = inputLine;
        for(i = 0; i < MAXFIELDS; i++)
```

Listing 13.2 continues

Listing 13.2 *continued*

```
            {
            fields[i] = strtok(inPtr, DELIMIT);
            inPtr = NULL;
            }

        /* process the letter file */
        if(!processLetter())
            {
            retcod = FALSE;
            break;
            }
        }

    /* everything is okay */
    return(retcod);
}

/****************************************************************************
 *      Function:  printSpoolerActive                                       *
 *                                                                          *
 *      Purpose:  Using INT 2FH check to see if spooler active.             *
 *                                                                          *
 *      Returns:  TRUE if spooler active, FALSE if it's not.                *
 *                                                                          *
 *      Args.:    N/A                                                       *
 *                                                                          *
 *      Notes: The interrupt 2FH is the multiplex interrupt. This interrupt *
 *             is used so that a transient program can communicate with a   *
 *             resident one. Microsoft uses the multiplex interrupt for DOS *
 *             TSR's PRINT, ASSIGN, SUBST, MODE, etc. It may work in DOS    *
 *             2.x even though it is undocumented.                          *
 *                                                                          *
 *      History:    Date        Person      Change Description              *
 *                  --------     ---------   ------------------------------  *
 *                  1/23/89      WMB         Created.                       *
 ****************************************************************************/
int    printSpoolerActive(void)
{

    /* determine status of spooler using the PRINT multiplexor (_AH = 0x01) */
    _AH = 0x01;                        /* function: spooler */
    _AL = 0x00;                        /* sub-function: status */

    /* get installed state for multiplex handler specified in _AH */
    geninterrupt(SPOOLERINT);    if(_AL != 0xFF)          /* spooler running? */
        {
        printf("\nERROR: Print spooler is not running or installed.\n");
        return(FALSE);
        }

    /* Everything is okay */
    return(TRUE);
}
```

```
/****************************************************************
 * Function:  main                                             *
 *                                                             *
 * Purpose:  Main function for merge program.                 *
 *                                                             *
 * Returns:  Exit 0 if successful, Exit 1 if an error occurs. *
 *                                                             *
 * Args.:    argc  count of command-line arguments            *
 *           argv  array of pointers to command-line args.    *
 *                                                             *
 * History:    Date     Person    Change Description          *
 *           --------  ----------  --------------------        *
 *           1/23/89   WMB         Created.                    *
 ****************************************************************/
void  main(int argc, char *argv[])
{
    int     i;
    PACKET  packet;  /* used by the multiplexor interrupt to print the file */

    /* place 0's into the file name arrays */
    memset(listFile, 0, sizeof(listFile));
    memset(letrFile, 0, sizeof(letrFile));
    memset(outpFile, 0, sizeof(outpFile));

    /* check for command-line options. */
    for(i = 1; i < argc; i++)
        {
        if(argv[i][0] != MINUS) /* arguments are preceded by - character */
            continue;
        switch(argv[i][1])
            {
            case 'n':
            case 'N':
                strcpy(listFile, argv[i + 1]);
                break;

            case 'o':
            case 'O':
                strcpy(outpFile, argv[i + 1]);                break;

            case 'l':
            case 'L':
                strcpy(letrFile, argv[i + 1]);
                break;

            default:
                usage();
                exit(1);
            }
        }
```

Listing 13.2 continues

Listing 13.2 *continued*

```
    /* Open the files */
    if(!openFiles())
        exit(1);

        /* Merge the list file with the letter file */
    if(!processMailingList())
        {
        closeFiles();
        exit(1);
        }

    /* Close the files */
    closeFiles();

    /* Print the output file */
    if(printSpoolerActive())
        {
#ifdef SPAWNPRINT
        if(spawnlp(P_WAIT, "print", "print", outpFile, NULL) == -1)
            {
            printf("\nERROR: Could not print output file [%s].\n", outpFile);
            exit(1);
            }
#else
        packet.level = 0;   /* this is required */
        packet.fileName = (long)outpFile;  /* name of file to print */
        _DS = FP_SEG(&packet); /* load segment into _DS */
        _DX = FP_OFF(&packet); /* load offset into _DX */
        _AH = 0x01; /* function: spooler */
        _AL = 0x01; /* sub-function: submit file */
        geninterrupt(SPOOLERINT);
#endif
        }

    /* Exit back to dos */              exit(0);
}
```

This program was designed in a top-down fashion. The first section defines the global variables and macros, and lists the include (header) files. The next module of the program declares the functions. The main function module appears at the end of the program. You will notice a hierarchy in the way the functions were defined and how they are called. If you program this way, the functions themselves become function prototypes. This works only when the functions are contained and called within the same source-code file.

The first function, `closeFiles()`, closes all the open files in the mail-merge program. This function determines that a file is opened by checking whether the file pointer is NULL. No arguments are passed to this function, and no return status is sent to the calling function.

The next function, openFiles(), opens all of the files the application requires. The first file opened is the mailing-list file; it is opened for read mode only. The next file, the letter file, also is opened for read mode only. The last file opened is the output file. This file is treated differently because it is opened for write mode only. If this file exists, permission is requested to remove it before a new output file is created. Any errors occurring in the openFiles() function are reported, and a status code of FALSE is returned to the calling function (the main in this case). No arguments are passed to this function.

The openFiles() module is followed by the function processLetter(). This function reads the letter file, replaces keywords with field contents, and then writes the data to the output file. Each line in the letter file is checked for MAXFIELDS, and the fields are replaced in the order 1 through 7. The function calls strstr(), which returns a pointer to the the keyword's starting position within the buffer.

The program skips over the keyword by incrementing this pointer by four bytes, and the information from this point to the end of the string is saved in a local buffer (tailLine). The keyword is replaced with the contents of the appropriate field buffer; then the tailLine buffer is concatenated to the original string. After this line has been processed for all field keywords, it is written to the output file. This function also writes an ASCII (0xC) form feed at the beginning of each letter in the output file. This function always returns TRUE. No arguments are passed to this function.

The next function, processMailingList(), reads each line in the list file. The string is tokenized, using the comma and new-line characters as delimiters. Each token is expected to be a field. The pointer returned is placed in the global array *fields. After all of the fields have been processed, processMailingList() calls processLetter(). After every line in the list file has been processed (end-of-file has been reached), this function returns TRUE. If an error occurred in the processLetter() function (not in this version), this error causes processMailingList() to return a FALSE indication to the calling function. No arguments are passed to this function.

The final function that precedes the main module is printSpoolerActive(). This function determines whether the print spooler is available and ready to accept requests. If the print spooler is not available and you try to print a letter using the print command, the resident portion of the print program will be loaded after your program, resulting in memory fragmentation. If the spooler is active, a TRUE indication is returned to the calling function. No arguments are passed to this function.

The main entry point of any C program is the main() function. This function begins by calling the openFiles() function. If an error occurs in openFiles(), main() will exit with a status of 1. Next, this module calls processMailing-List(). If an error occurs while processMailingList() executes, the files are closed and main( ) again exits with a status of 1. After processing of main( ) is completed, closeFiles( ) executes. The print spooler is checked to determine whether it is active and, if it is, the output file is printed. The main( ) function exits with a status of 0 if everything goes according to plan (yes, sometimes it does).

Now that the program is coded, try running some test data. The following list of data and the letter in figure 13.1 can be used to test the mail-merge program. The second and third lines of data contain a missing field (denoted by , ,). Use this data to test what happens when the program encounters blank fields. Figure 13.1 is the letter with which the data is merged. Notice that one field is embedded in a sentence. This program should also be tested with several other data sets to determine its limitations.

Fig. 13.1. Sample letter file.

```
John,Doe,1120 Mockingbird Lane,Suite 102,Somewhere,MI,48067
Jane,Doe,19755 Lois Lane, ,Thisplace,DE,00120
J.Q.,Public,1505 Our House Lane, ,That Place,FA,32450

January 23, 1989

<F1> <F2>
<F3>
<F4>
<F5>, <F6> <F7>

This is a sample letter that will be merged with a sample
mailing list. As you know, <F1>, I have very little to say in
this
letter.

Thanks for your assistance.



William M. Brown
```

When the program is executed it asks for the list file, the letter file, and the output file. Given these parameters, the program tries to merge the two files and write the results to an output file. If the list and letter files are not of the correct format, the program still executes, but the old adage, "Garbage in—Garbage out," applies. Figure 13.2 shows a sample session using the test files.

Fig. 13.2. Sample session with merge.exe.

```
Mail merge list file: list.txt
Mail merge letter file: letter.txt
Mail merge output file: merge.out
```

or

```
      merge -L letter.txt -N list.txt -O merge.out
```

After the program executes, the printer produces the information shown in figure 13.3 if PRINT has been installed. Otherwise you will get a message that the print spooler is not running or installed. In any case, create `merge.out` (unless you have a disk error).

Fig. 13.3. Sample output file.

```
January 23, 1989

John Doe
1120 Mockingbird Lane
Suite 102
Somewhere, MI 48067
```

This is a sample letter that will be merged with a sample mailing list. As you know, John, I have very little to say in this letter.

Thanks for your assistance.

William M. Brown

```
January 23, 1989

Jane Doe
19755 Lois Lane

Thisplace, DE 00120
```

This is a sample letter that will be merged with a sample mailing list. As you know, Jane, I have very little to say in this letter.

Thanks for your assistance.

William M. Brown

Fig. 13.3 continues

Fig. 13.3 *continued*

```
January 23, 1989

J.Q. Public
1505 Our House Lane

That Place, FA 32450

This is a sample letter that will be merged with a sample
mailing list. As you know, J.Q., I have very little to say in
this letter.

Thanks for your assistance.



William M. Brown
```

Summary

Although the merge.c program in listing 13.2 is simple in design and implementation, you can adapt and implement the code in many ways to suit your style, techniques, and application.

The merge.c program is not a complete mail-merge system; rather, it serves as a template for a mail-merge system. Because macros were used, the merge.c program can be enhanced to include additional fields simply by increasing the macro MAXFIELDS. The line length can be expanded by increasing the value of MAXLINE. You can use different delimiters for fields by changing DELIMIT. An improved version would add features such as "left justify the output."

William M.
Brown

<u>CHAPTER</u>

14

Reading and Processing a Binary File

This chapter illustrates how to design and implement a program to read binary files. The difference between text files and binary files is the way you open them and what translation occurs when you read them. The best way to describe a binary file is "what-you-see-is-what-you-get"—when you read a character in a binary file you can be confident that that character is not being translated.

When you open a file in text mode, the following translation occurs behind the scenes: for every carriage return (\r) encountered in the text file, a carriage return/line-feed pair (\r\n) is returned. The Ctrl-Z character (1A hex) is treated as the end-of-file mark. When you open a file in binary mode, no translation occurs.

Turbo C provides several ways to open files and inform the compiler what mode to open the file with. One approach is to set the global variable _fmode (see Chapter 5). Another way is to use the O_BINARY value for the open() function. The default mode for both open() and _fmode is text.

Normally, the first step in program development is writing a requirements analysis, but with this program the requirements have already been written by the user. The requirements for this program are

❏ The program should read binary files and display the contents of the file in both hexadecimal and character format (if printable).

❏ It must be able to handle very large files.

❏ It must have options for scrolling up and down inside this file and for going to the top and bottom of the file.

Requirements may assume various forms and shapes. Although some users provide complete descriptions, others leave much to be desired. If insufficient information is available from an analysis, it is up to you to find the necessary information to fill in the gaps. You can obtain this information by interviewing the users and by doing research. Once enough information has been obtained, you can start the design process.

Designing the Program

In many cases you can write your design in plain English statements, or you can mix pseudocode (something that looks like C) and C code to produce a design document. The method you use depends on your style and what is acceptable to you (or your boss or client). Ensure that the intended user looks at and approves your design. This will save you time in the long run and may prevent the ever-famous user complaint, "That's what I asked for, but not what I want." The design for this program is written in simple English, and it works as follows:

1. Get the file name by looking at the first command-line argument given to the program. If no argument is given, prompt the user for the file name. Place the file name in a global variable for later use.

2. Open the file for reading with the binary mode flag set so that no translation occurs as the file is read. If an error occurs, print an informative message and the DOS error message, then exit with a code of *1* to indicate that an error occurred.

3. Position the file pointer to the bottom of the file and obtain the number of bytes in the file. Place this number in a global variable for use later. Initialize the position variable to *0* (top-of-file) and the end-of-file variable to FALSE (to indicate that the current position is not at end-of-file).

4. Start main loop processing. This loop continues until the user asks to exit.

    4A. The file in the main loop is processed as follows. Position the file pointer based on the contents of the position variable (first time is ▢). Read the contents into a global array. The number of bytes requested will be the maximum size of the array. The actual number of bytes read is saved in the global variable. If the actual number does not equal the expected number, the end-of-file flag is set to TRUE.

    4B. Clear the screen and display title lines. The contents of the array are dumped to the screen in both hexadecimal and character format. If the character is nonprintable, display a period. Included in each line is that line's starting location within the file, 16 bytes of the file in hex, and the same 16 bytes in character format.

    4C. Print the available commands and wait for the user to enter a command from the keyboard. Process the following commands for whatever key was pressed:

X   then exit the main loop

B   then position the file pointer to the end of the file and set the end-of-file flag to TRUE

T   then position the file pointer to the top of the file; if the end-of-file flag was TRUE, set it to FALSE

+   then position the file pointer to the next record in the file (a *record* is defined as the size of the array)

−   then position the file pointer to the previous record in the file

5. Perform Steps 4A through 4C until the Exit-the-main-loop command is executed in Step 4C.

6. When the main loop has been terminated by the `exit()` function, close the file and exit with a code of 0.

7. When the design has been completed (and approved, if necessary), start on the implementation.

Implementing the Program

Listing 14.1 gives the source code for this program. You will notice a couple of extra functions and some small variations in the design of this program. This happens because this program has evolved through implementation and testing, and the design document was not kept up to date. This often occurs unless you spend time updating your design as you implement it.

Listing 14.1

```
/************************************************************
 * Program:  dump.c                                        *
 *                                                         *
 * Purpose:  Simple binary file listing program.           *
 *                                                         *
 * History:     Date      Person      Change Description    *
 *           --------    --------    ------------------     *
 *           1/23/89      WMB         Created.               *
 *           3/13/89      WMB         Fixed minor bug.       *
 ************************************************************/

/* include header files that program will use */
#include <stdio.h>
#include <stdlib.h>
#include <string.h>
```

Listing 14.1 continues

Listing 14.1 continued

```
#include <process.h>
#include <dos.h>
#include <dir.h>
#include <fcntl.h>
#include <alloc.h>
#include <conio.h>
#include <io.h>

/* macros used in this program */
#define   FALSE        0
#define   TRUE         !FALSE
#define   MAXARRAY     256
#define   OFFSET       16
#define   ID           "BINARY FILE LISTER"
#define   VERSION      "1.0A"
#define   CRLF         "\r\n"
#define   BEEP         "\007"

/* character + attribute */
#define   CHARATTR     2
#define   MESSAGE      "+) Next  -) Previous  B) Bottom  T) Top X) Exit "

/* a structure to save the screen information */
typedef  struct    _screenTag
   {
   struct   text_info    saveText;
   char                  *textBuffer;
   int                   textSize;
   } SCREEN, *SCRPTR;

/* globals used in this program */
unsigned char array[MAXARRAY];          /* holds partial contents of file */
char     fileName[MAXPATH];             /* file name */
long     fileSize;                      /* file size in bytes */
int      eofFlag;                       /* TRUE if end-of-file */
long     curPos;                        /* current position in file */
int      fHandle;                       /* file handle */

/**********************************************************************
 * Function:  saveScreen                                              *
 *                                                                    *
 * Purpose:   Save current text screen into a dynamically allocated   *
 *            array using the Turbo C function gettext(). This array  *
 *            is a component of the SCREEN structure.                 *
 *                                                                    *
 * Returns:   TRUE if successful, FALSE if screen not saved.          *
 *                                                                    *
 * Args.:     Pointer to screen structure.                           *
 *                                                                    *
 * History:   Date      Person      Change Description                *
 *            --------   ---------   --------------------             *
 *            1/23/89   WMB         Created.                          *
 **********************************************************************/
```

```
int    saveScreen(SCRPTR scr)
{

    /* get current text mode configuration and save screen */
    gettextinfo(&(scr->saveText));
    /* calculate size of buffer and allocate */
    scr->textSize = scr->saveText.screenheight *
                    scr->saveText.screenwidth  *
        CHARATTR;

    /* allocate storage for text buffer */
    if((scr->textBuffer = malloc(scr->textSize)) == NULL)
        return(FALSE);

    /* Save screen using Turbo C gettext() function. This function
       stores the contents of an on-screen rectangle into the
       scr->textBuffer buffer. */
    if(gettext(scr->saveText.winleft, scr->saveText.wintop,
            scr->saveText.winright, scr->saveText.winbottom,
            scr->textBuffer) == 0)
        return(FALSE);

    /* done */
    return(TRUE);
}

/***********************************************************
 * Function:   restoreScreen                               *
 *                                                         *
 * Purpose:  Restore current text screen into an array.    *
 *                                                         *
 * Returns:  N/A                                           *
 *                                                         *
 * Args.:    Pointer to screen structure.                  *
 *                                                         *
 * History:    Date      Person      Change Description     *
 *           --------    ---------   ------------------     *
 *           1/23/89     WMB         Created.               *
 ***********************************************************/
void   restoreScreen(SCRPTR scr)
{

    /* restore screen attribute and text */
    textattr(scr->saveText.attribute);
    puttext(scr->saveText.winleft, scr->saveText.wintop,
            scr->saveText.winright, scr->saveText.winbottom,
            scr->textBuffer);

    /* free memory that was allocated and set pointer to NULL */
    free(scr->textBuffer);
    scr->textBuffer = NULL;
```

Listing 14.1 continues

Listing 14.1 continued

```
    /* put the cursor back where it was */
    gotoxy(scr->saveText.curx, scr->saveText.cury);
}

/***********************************************************************
 * Function:  displayArray                                            *
 *                                                                    *
 * Purpose:  Display array in both hex and character format.          *
 *                                                                    *
 * Returns:  N/A                                                      *
 *                                                                    *
 * Args.:    lLoc    starting location for this array (in file)       *
 *           nRead   number of bytes read <= MAXARRAY                 *
 *                                                                    *
 * History:    Date    Person     Change Description                  *
 *           --------  ---------   --------------------               *
 *           1/23/89   WMB         Created.                           *
 ***********************************************************************/
void    displayArray(long lLoc, int nRead)
{
    int            indx;                 /* temporary index variable */
    int            indx1;                /* temporary index variable */
    unsigned char  ch;                   /* to store the character */

    /* update display and print header */
    clrscr();
    cprintf("%s [%s] - File name: %s  Length: %ld (bytes)", ID, VERSION,
        fileName, fileSize);

    gotoxy(1, 3);
    cputs("Loc.     0  1  2  3  4  5  6  7   8  9  A  B  C  D  E  F ");
    cputs("0123456789ABCDEF");

    gotoxy(1, 4);
    cputs("-------  ------------------------------------------------ ");
    cputs("--------------");

    gotoxy(1, 5);

    /* display the matrix of bytes */
    for(indx = 0; indx < nRead; indx += OFFSET)
        {
        /* display position in file */
        cprintf("%-07ld ", lLoc + (long)indx);

        /* display the first 8 bytes */

        for(indx1 = 0; indx1 < OFFSET / 2; indx1++)
            {
            ch = array[indx + indx1];
            cprintf("%02X ", ch);
            }
        printf("- ");
```

```
          /* display the second 8 bytes */
          for(indx1 = OFFSET / 2; indx1 < OFFSET; indx1++)
              {
              ch = array[indx + indx1];
              cprintf("%02X ", ch);
              }

          /* display printable characters */
          for(indx1 = 0; indx1 < OFFSET; indx1++)
              {
              ch = array[indx + indx1];
              if(ch >= ' ' && ch <= '~')
                  cprintf("%1.1c", ch);
              else
                  cputs(".");      /* you get this for
                                       nonprintable characters. */
              }
          cputs(CRLF);
          }

   /* display message if end of file reached */
   if(eofFlag)
       cputs("** END OF FILE **\n");

   /* display message if beginning of file */
   if(lLoc == 0L)
       cputs("** BEGINNING OF FILE **\n");

   /* display commands */
   cputs(CRLF);
   cputs(MESSAGE);

}

/**********************************************************************
 * Function:  getCommand                                              *
 *                                                                    *
 * Purpose:  Get a character user and execute a command.              *
 *                                                                    *
 * Returns:  TRUE if the exit command was requested, FALSE if not.    *
 *                                                                    *
 * Args.:    N/A                                                      *
 *                                                                    *
 * History:    Date      Person     Change Description                *
 *           _____   _____   _____              *
 *           1/23/89    WMB          Created.                         *
 **********************************************************************/
int   getCommand(void)
{
    int   retcod = FALSE;  /* return code */
    int   ch;
```

Listing 14.1 continues

Listing 14.1 continued

```
Again:                    /* goto label. */
switch((ch = getch())) /* don't echo character, yet */
    {
    case '+':              /* next page */
        /* if not at end-of-file, read next page */
        if(!eofFlag)
            curPos += MAXARRAY;
        break;

    case '-':              /* previous page */
        curPos -= MAXARRAY;

        /* if at the top of file, reset the counter to 0 */
        if(curPos < 0L)
            curPos = 0L;
        break;

    case 'B':              /* bottom of file */
    case 'b':
        /* seek to the bottom minus a full record */
        curPos = lseek(fHandle, (long)-MAXARRAY, SEEK_END);
        eofFlag = TRUE;
        break;

    case 'T':              /* top of file */
    case 't':
        curPos = lseek(fHandle, 0L, SEEK_SET);
        break;

    case 'X':              /* eXit program */
    case 'x':
        retcod = TRUE;
        break;

    default:               /* anything else, beep */
        cputs(BEEP);
        ch = -1;
        break;
    }

/* invalid character entered? */
if(ch == -1)
    goto Again;
else
    cprintf("%c", ch);

/* provide proper return code */
 return(retcod);
}
```

```
/****************************************************************
 * Function:  main                                             *
 *                                                             *
 * Purpose:   Main function for dump program.                  *
 *                                                             *
 * Returns:   Exit 0 if successful, Exit 1 if an error occurs. *
 *                                                             *
 * Args.:     argc  count of command-line arguments            *
 *            argv  array of pointers to command-line args.    *
 *                                                             *
 * History:    Date     Person      Change Description         *
 *            --------  ----------  --------------------        *
 *            1/23/89   WMB         Created.                    *
 ****************************************************************/
void  main(int argc, char *argv[])
{
    int     getOut;    /* gets out of while look if TRUE */
    int     nRead;     /* number of actual bytes read */
    SCREEN  scrSave;   /* structure to save screen into */

    /* save the current screen */
    if(!saveScreen(&scrSave))
        {
        printf("Could not save the screen.\n");
        exit(1);
        }

    /* get file name from argument if an argument is to be found */
    if(argc > 1)
        strcpy(fileName, argv[1]);
    else
        {
        cputs("Enter file name: ");
        gets(fileName);
        }

    /* open file for reading */
    if((fHandle = open(fileName, O_RDONLY | O_BINARY)) == -1)
        {
        cprintf("Could not open file %s for reading!%s", fileName, CRLF);
        perror("MS-DOS Error");
        exit(1);
        }

     /* get file size */
    fileSize = lseek(fHandle, 0L, SEEK_END);

    /* initialize variables to use in the main loop. */
    curPos  = 0L;
    getOut  = FALSE;
    eofFlag = FALSE;
```

Listing 14.1 continues

Listing 14.1 continued

```
    /* main loop to read and display */
    while(!getOut)
        {
        /* initialize the array */
        memset(array, 0, MAXARRAY);

        /* read the file */
        lseek(fHandle, curPos, SEEK_SET);
        if((nRead = read(fHandle, array, MAXARRAY)) < MAXARRAY)
            eofFlag = TRUE;

        /* display the matrix */
        displayArray(curPos, nRead);
        eofFlag = FALSE;

        /* wait for command */
        getOut = getCommand();
        }
    /* close file, restore screen and exit */
    close(fHandle);
    restoreScreen(&scrSave);
    exit(0);
}
```

The first part of this program is devoted to inserting include files, defining macros, and setting up a structure and global storage. For convenience, I have included several include files in this program (thereby slowing down the compile time). Instead of having all these include files, you may want to define the function prototypes and constants that are required for this program. The dump.c program can be modified to display more or fewer than 256 bytes by changing the macro MAXARRAY. The program's identification and version names both are stored in the macros ID and VERSION. When more commands are added to the command processor, you can change the command-line prompt by changing the macro MESSAGE.

The SCREEN structure type holds the information regarding the text screen and is used by the functions saveScreen() and restoreScreen(), which take a pointer to this type as the argument to each.

The global string of characters (named array) stores the current record and contains up to MAXARRAY bytes. The fileName array stores the file name that was requested by the user. The variable fileSize holds the size of fileName in bytes. The variable eofFlag is set to TRUE when the end-of-file has been reached, curPos holds the current position in the file, and fHandle is the file's handle, set by the open() function.

The first function in the dump.c program is saveScreen(). This function saves the current text screen so that when the program terminates, the text screen is returned to its original state. In order to store the text-screen image, save-Screen() first gets the current text-information state by calling gettextinfo() and then fills the structure saveText. Next, the size of the text screen is calculated by multiplying the screen's height by its width. An attempt (which may fail) is made to allocate memory dynamically by using the function malloc() with enough room to store all of the characters and their attributes. The area of memory pointed to by a pointer is then filled with text by calling gettext(). If any errors occur in this function, the value FALSE is returned. A pointer to a structure of type SCREEN is the only argument needed by the saveScreen() function.

The function restoreScreen() is responsible for restoring the text screen after a successful saveScreen() function has been called. This is accomplished by first using the function textattr() to set the text attribute to the attribute in the screen structure. After the attribute has been restored, the text is restored by using puttext(), and the memory that was used for the text array is returned to Turbo C by calling free(). The final task for restoreScreen() is to return the cursor to its previous location by calling gotoxy(). A pointer to a structure of type SCREEN is the only argument needed by restoreScreen().

Following restoreScreen(), you will find the function displayArray(), which displays the contents of the array in two different formats. First, this function clears the screen using clrscr(); then the function displays a header. In this header is the program's ID and VERSION; also, a title banner is printed for convenience. The array is printed based on the actual number of bytes read; 16 (OFFSET) bytes are printed on a line.

The first item printed on a line is the data's location within the file. Next, the contents of the array are printed, using a hexadecimal format. The contents of the array are then printed in a character format, with each nonprintable character printed as the period (.) character. After all of the lines have been printed, the message ** END OF FILE** or ** BEGINNING OF FILE ** is printed, depending on the value of lLoc and the global variable eofFlag. Finally, the contents of the macro MESSAGE are printed and the function returns. This function requires the location (lLoc) and number of bytes (nRead) as arguments.

The next function, getCommand(), reads a character using the function getche() and performs a command based on that character. If you press the + key, the current position (curPos) is incremented by MAXARRAY if you are not at the end-of-file. Pressing the − key decrements the current position (curPos) by MAXARRAY; if this results in a negative number, the current position is set to 0. Pressing **B** (or **b**) causes an immediate seek to the end of the file minus MAXARRAY and sets the end of file flag to TRUE. If you press **T** (or **t**), a seek to the top of file is performed; if the end-of-file flag is TRUE, it is switched to FALSE. Pressing **X** (or **x**) sends an exit code to the main function. Any other key causes the computer to beep. The getCommand() function returns TRUE if the **X** (or **x**) key is pressed.

The final function is main(). This function begins by saving the screen with saveScreen(). Then, by determining whether the variable argc is greater than 1, the main() function checks whether a file name is being passed on the command line.

If the file name is not on the command line (argc = 1), the user is prompted to enter a file name. In either case, a file name is placed in the global array fileName. The open() function is called with the file name, and the flags for reading, writing, and binary mode are set.

Next, lseek() obtains the file size in bytes by seeking to the bottom of the file. Several local and global variables are initialized before the main processing loop begins. The main processing loop is executed until the variable getOut is TRUE. This variable is set by the getCommand() function when the user presses either **X** or **x**. The loop first initializes the array to all 0s. This clears the array and removes any leftover characters from the previous read() (if not the first time through the loop). After an lseek into the file, starting from the top until curPos, a read copies the file into the array up to MAXARRAY bytes. In this programming example the unbuffered file I/O functions were used; the buffered I/O functions (fread, fseek) could have been used.

After this, the function displayArray() is called to display the data and command line. Finally the function getCommand() is called to await commands from the user. Again, this loop continues until the exit() function is requested by the user. After the loop terminates, the file is closed and the screen is returned to its original state. An exit code of 0 is sent to MS-DOS when this program terminates.

This program uses the exit() function to communicate to MS-DOS whether the program terminated normally or if an error occurs. You can test this error condition by using IF ERRORLEVEL in a batch file or, if this program is spawned as a child process, by using the spawn() function to test the exit code.

Now that the program is written, you compile and link it. Assuming that you called this program dump.c, you generate an executable called dump.exe by entering the following command:

```
tcc -w -v -ms -f- dump
```

Now execute the dump program by typing the following command:

```
dump dump.exe
```

Executing this command displays the information shown in figure 14.1. To return to the DOS prompt, press **X**.

***Fig. 14.1.** Sample output from binary file listing program.*

```
BINARY FILE LISTER [1.0A] - File name: dump.exe  Length: 15760 (bytes)

Loc    0  1  2  3  4  5  6  7    8  9  A  B  C  D  E  F  0123456789ABCDEF
----   ---------------------------------------------------  ----------------
0      4D 5A 90 01 1F 00 E3 00 - 40 00 2D 00 FF FF B7 03  MZ......@.-.....
16     E6 00 00 00 00 00 00 00 - 22 00 00 00 01 00 FB 20  ........".......
32     72 6A 15 01 00 00 01 00 - 00 00 D6 00 00 00 DB 00  rj.............
48     00 00 05 01 00 00 0B 01 - 00 00 C5 01 00 00 02 04  ...............
64     4F 00 F6 03 4F 00 E7 03 - 4F 00 CB 03 4F 00 C0 03  0...0...0...0...
80     4F 00 95 03 4F 00 7A 03 - 4F 00 58 03 4F 00 CF 02  0...0.z.0.X.0...
96     4F 00 BF 02 4F 00 B3 02 - 4F 00 A7 02 4F 00 93 02  0...0...0...0...
112    4F 00 75 02 4F 00 63 02 - 4F 00 54 02 4F 00 20 02  0.u.0.c.0.T.0. .
128    4F 00 FE 01 4F 00 EB 01 - 4F 00 C9 01 4F 00 AD 01  0...0...0...0...
144    4F 00 9E 01 4F 00 92 01 - 4F 00 86 01 4F 00 77 01  0...0...0...0.w.
160    4F 00 6B 01 4F 00 5F 01 - 4F 00 4F 01 4F 00 2E 01  0.k.0._.0.0.0...
176    4F 00 1D 01 4F 00 F3 00 - 4F 00 E1 00 4F 00 A9 00  0...0...0...0...
192    4F 00 86 00 4F 00 3B 00 - 4F 00 10 00 4F 00 07 05  0...0...0...0...
208    4F 00 F3 04 4F 00 B8 04 - 4F 00 A3 04 4F 00 8C 04  0...0...0...0...
224    4F 00 5B 04 4F 00 49 04 - 4F 00 3E 04 4F 00 31 04  0.[.0.I.0.>.0.1.
240    4F 00 12 04 4F 00 C4 02 - 1A 03 C0 02 1A 03 BC 02  0...0...........
** BEGINNING OF FILE **

+) Next   -) Previous   B) Bottom   T) Top   X) Exit
```

Summary

The dump.c program (listing 14.1) shows how to read a binary file and display its contents. The program also shows how to save and restore the text screen. Although this was not a stated requirement, it does add a little sparkle to the program and generally is a good idea.

With the use of macros in this program, changing portions of the program's appearance and functionality is done by changing macros and enhancing the functions. You can add more functionality by simply expanding the MESSAGE macro and implementing the new commands in the getCommand() function. Some possible enhancements to this program include the ability to edit and print binary files. And, if the file to be read does not exist, why not say so and give the user the option of entering an new file name or quitting?

ASCII Codes and the Extended Character Set

This appendix had two parts: a table showing ASCII codes, and a table showing the Extended Character Set available on IBM PCs and compatible computers. Codes for the characters are given in decimal, hexadecimal, octal, and binary notation.

ASCII Codes

Control characters (codes 0 through 31) are identified by their names and by their control-key equivalents.

Decimal	Hex	Octal	Binary	ASCII	
0	00	000	00000000	^@	NUL
1	01	001	00000001	^A	SOH
2	02	002	00000010	^B	STX
3	03	003	00000011	^C	ETX
4	04	004	00000100	^D	EOT
5	05	005	00000101	^E	ENQ
6	06	006	00000110	^F	ACK
7	07	007	00000111	^G	BEL
8	08	010	00001000	^H	BS
9	09	011	00001001	^I	HT
10	0A	012	00001010	^J	LF
11	0B	013	00001011	^K	VT
12	0C	014	00001100	^L	FF
13	0D	015	00001101	^M	CR
14	0E	016	00001110	^N	SO
15	0F	017	00001111	^O	SI
16	10	020	00010000	^P	DLE
17	11	021	00010001	^Q	DC1
18	12	022	00010010	^R	DC2
19	13	023	00010011	^S	DC3
20	14	024	00010100	^T	DC4
21	15	025	00010101	^U	NAK
22	16	026	00010110	^V	SYN
23	17	027	00010111	^W	ETB
24	18	030	00011000	^X	CAN
25	19	031	00011001	^Y	EM
26	1A	032	00011010	^Z	SUB
27	1B	033	00011011	^[	ESC
28	1C	034	00011100	^\	FS
29	1D	035	00011101	^]	GS
30	1E	036	00011110	^^	RS
31	1F	037	00011111	^_	US
32	20	040	00100000	(space)	
33	21	041	00100001	!	
34	22	042	00100010	"	
35	23	043	00100011	#	

Decimal	Hex	Octal	Binary	ASCII
36	24	044	00100100	$
37	25	045	00100101	%
38	26	046	00100110	&
39	27	047	00100111	'
40	28	050	00101000	(
41	29	051	00101001	)
42	2A	052	00101010	*
43	2B	053	00101011	+
44	2C	054	00101100	,
45	2D	055	00101101	-
46	2E	056	00101110	.
47	2F	057	00101111	/
48	30	060	00110000	0
49	31	061	00110001	1
50	32	062	00110010	2
51	33	063	00110011	3
52	34	064	00110100	4
53	35	065	00110101	5
54	36	066	00110110	6
55	37	067	00110111	7
56	38	070	00111000	8
57	39	071	00111001	9
58	3A	072	00111010	:
59	3B	073	00111011	;
60	3C	074	00111100	<
61	3D	075	00111101	=
62	3E	076	00111110	>
63	3F	077	00111111	?
64	40	100	01000000	@
65	41	101	01000001	A
66	42	102	01000010	B
67	43	103	01000011	C
68	44	104	01000100	D
69	45	105	01000101	E
70	46	106	01000110	F
71	47	107	01000111	G
72	48	110	01001000	H
73	49	111	01001001	I
74	4A	112	01001010	J
75	4B	113	01001011	K
76	4C	114	01001100	L

Decimal	Hex	Octal	Binary	ASCII
77	4D	115	01001101	M
78	4E	116	01001110	N
79	4F	117	01001111	O
80	50	120	01010000	P
81	51	121	01010001	Q
82	52	122	01010010	R
83	53	123	01010011	S
84	54	124	01010100	T
85	55	125	01010101	U
86	56	126	01010110	V
87	57	127	01010111	W
88	58	130	01011000	X
89	59	131	01011001	Y
90	5A	132	01011010	Z
91	5B	133	01011011	[
92	5C	134	01011100	\
93	5D	135	01011101	]
94	5E	136	01011110	^
95	5F	137	01011111	_
96	60	140	01100000	`
97	61	141	01100001	a
98	62	142	01100010	b
99	63	143	01100011	c
100	64	144	01100100	d
101	65	145	01100101	e
102	66	146	01100110	f
103	67	147	01100111	g
104	68	150	01101000	h
105	69	151	01101001	i
106	6A	152	01101010	j
107	6B	153	01101011	k
108	6C	154	01101100	l
109	6D	155	01101101	m
110	6E	156	01101110	n
111	6F	157	01101111	o
112	70	160	01110000	p
113	71	161	01110001	q
114	72	162	01110010	r
115	73	163	01110011	s
116	74	164	01110100	t
117	75	165	01110101	u
118	76	166	01110110	v

Decimal	Hex	Octal	Binary	ASCII
119	77	167	01110111	w
120	78	170	01111000	x
121	79	171	01111001	y
122	7A	172	01111010	z
123	7B	173	01111011	{
124	7C	174	01111100	|
125	7D	175	01111101	}
126	7E	176	01111110	~
127	7F	177	01111111	DEL

Extended Character Set

These characters are available only on IBM PCs and compatible computers.

Decimal	Hex	Octal	Binary	ASCII
128	80	200	10000000	ç
129	81	201	10000001	ü
130	82	202	10000010	é
131	83	203	10000011	â
132	84	204	10000100	ä
133	85	205	10000101	à
134	86	206	10000110	å
135	87	207	10000111	ç
136	88	210	10001000	ê
137	89	211	10001001	ë
138	8A	212	10001010	è
139	8B	213	10001011	ï
140	8C	214	10001100	î
141	8D	215	10001101	ì
142	8E	216	10001110	Ä
143	8F	217	10001111	Å
144	90	220	10010000	É
145	91	221	10010001	æ
146	92	222	10010010	Æ
147	93	223	10010011	ô
148	94	224	10010100	ö
149	95	225	10010101	ò
150	96	226	10010110	û
151	97	227	10010111	ù
152	98	230	10011000	ÿ
153	99	231	10011001	Ö
154	9A	232	10011010	Ü
155	9B	233	10011011	¢
156	9C	234	10011100	£
157	9D	235	10011101	¥
158	9E	236	10011110	₧
159	9F	237	10011111	ƒ
160	A0	240	10100000	á
161	A1	241	10100001	í
162	A2	242	10100010	ó
163	A3	243	10100011	ú
164	A4	244	10100100	ñ

Decimal	Hex	Octal	Binary	ASCII
165	A5	245	10100101	Ñ
166	A6	246	10100110	a
167	A7	247	10100111	o
168	A8	250	10101000	¿
169	A9	251	10101001	⌐
170	AA	252	10101010	¬
171	AB	253	10101011	½
172	AC	254	10101100	¼
173	AD	255	10101101	¡
174	AE	256	10101110	«
175	AF	257	10101111	»
176	B0	260	10110000	░
177	B1	261	10110001	▒
178	B2	262	10110010	▓
179	B3	263	10110011	│
180	B4	264	10110100	┤
181	B5	265	10110101	╡
182	B6	266	10110110	╢
183	B7	267	10110111	╖
184	B8	270	10111000	╕
185	B9	271	10111001	╣
186	BA	272	10111010	║
187	BB	273	10111011	╗
188	BC	274	10111100	╝
189	BD	275	10111101	╜
190	BE	276	10111110	╛
191	BF	277	10111111	┐
192	C0	300	11000000	└
193	C1	301	11000001	┴
194	C2	302	11000010	┬
195	C3	303	11000011	├
196	C4	304	11000100	─
197	C5	305	11000101	┼
198	C6	306	11000110	╞
199	C7	307	11000111	╟
200	C8	310	11001000	╚
201	C9	311	11001001	╔
202	CA	312	11001010	╩
203	CB	313	11001011	╦
204	CC	314	11001100	╠
205	CD	315	11001101	=

Decimal	Hex	Octal	Binary	ASCII
206	CE	316	11001110	╬
207	CF	317	11001111	╧
208	D0	320	11010000	╨
209	D1	321	11010001	╤
210	D2	322	11010010	╥
211	D3	323	11010011	╙
212	D4	324	11010100	╘
213	D5	325	11010101	╒
214	D6	326	11010110	╓
215	D7	327	11010111	╫
216	D8	330	11011000	╪
217	D9	331	11011001	┘
218	DA	332	11011010	┌
219	DB	333	11011011	█
220	DC	334	11011100	▄
221	DD	335	11011101	▌
222	DE	336	11011110	▐
223	DF	337	11011111	▀
224	E0	340	11100000	α
225	E1	341	11100001	β
226	E2	342	11100010	Γ
227	E3	343	11100011	π
228	E4	344	11100100	Σ
229	E5	345	11100101	σ
230	E6	346	11100110	μ
231	E7	347	11100111	τ
232	E8	350	11101000	Φ
233	E9	351	11101001	θ
234	EA	352	11101010	Ω
235	EB	353	11101011	δ
236	EC	354	11101100	∞
237	ED	355	11101101	ϕ
238	EE	356	11101110	$\in$
239	EF	357	11101111	$\cap$
240	F0	360	11110000	$\equiv$
241	F1	361	11110001	$\pm$
242	F2	362	11110010	$\geq$
243	F3	363	11110011	$\leq$
244	F4	364	11110100	$\lceil$
245	F5	365	11110101	$\rfloor$
246	F6	366	11110110	$\div$
247	F7	367	11110111	$\approx$

Decimal	Hex	Octal	Binary	ASCII
248	F8	370	11111000	°
249	F9	371	11111001	•
250	FA	372	11111010	·
251	FB	373	11111011	√
252	FC	374	11111100	n
253	FD	375	11111101	2
254	FE	376	11111110	■
255	FF	377	11111111	

Index

8087, 80287, 80387 math coprocessors, 135-136, 145
8087 math coprocessor, instructions, 234

A

ACBP alignment information, 207
algorithms, formulating, 11
ANSI C Standard
  buffered I/O supported by, 28
  portability of programs developed in
    accordance with, 18, 238
  standard C library defined by, 60
ANSI extensions, 274
argument lists in C functions, variable-length, 83
array contents in hexadecimal format, 417
ASCII character set, extended, 294
assembly language. *See also* Turbo Assembler
  emit function to use inline hex codes to
    insert, 215
  C routines called from, 192-194
  inline assembly
    calling C functions containing, 157-159
    comments in, 154
    combining assembly language statements
      directly in C program, 149
    compiling a C program containing,
      150-152
    converted to separate object modules,
      189-190
    function arguments used by, 160-169,
      171-174
    labels in, 154-155
    problems with local data, 169-171
    referencing data in, 156-174
    returning function values with, 159-160
    semicolons in, 153-154

stand-alone compiler (tcc.exe) used for, 232
statements, using, 149-156
structure of statements for, 152-153
separate object modules linked with those
  from Turbo C compiler, 149, 178-194
  data items shared among, 183-184
audience-targeting problem, 274
autodependency checking, 213

B

Basic Input/Output Services (BIOS)
  determining whether to send output to,
    134-135
  interrupts. *See* BIOS interrupts
baud rate requirements, 8-9
benchmark software, 255-262
  array of structures for, 261
  limits of precision for functions in, 259
  memory allocation in, 256
  testlog( ), 255-256
binary file sample, 408-419
  displayArray( ) function in, 417-418
  getCommand( ) function in, 417-418
  restoreScreen( ) function in, 416
  sample output, 419
  saveScreen( ) function in, 416-418
BIOS function calls, bios.h functions in, 65-66
BIOS interrupts, 65
  11h, 159
  16h, 94
black box concept, 50, 276
block
  defined, 320-321
  file, 68
  of records, 358

Borland Graphic Interface (BGI)
    device drivers for, 1
    functions, 73
BOUND instructions, 141
boundary value analysis, 344-347, 355
brace placement styles, 38-41
breakpoint(s)
    automating program analysis with, 306-314
    Changed Data Condition, 313-314
    defined, 306
    detail pane, 308
    list, 307
    locations and external identifiers, 309-312
    types
        conditional, 307-308
        hardware, 265
        simple, 306-307
buffers
    block and record, 358-359
    defined, 28, 358
    keyboard
        determining whether keypress is stored
            in, 94
        queues used by, 23-24
    large-scale text, 359-360
    local, 403
    memory, 28
    video, 78-79
bugs
    determining the type of, 247-248
    fatal and nonfatal, 227
    fixing, 249-250
    locating, 248-249
    recognizing the existence of, 246-247

C

CAD/CAM application design, 11
calling convention, Turbo C, 156
case map, 105
CCP preprocessor, 203-204
Changed Data, 307

child process
    to communicate with parent's memory,
        141-144
    defined, 79-80
    execution while parent process waits, 270
code generators, 10
coding, 2, 7, 33-57
    defined, 33
    samples
        binary file, 409-419
        mail merge application, 394-402
    style, 33-42
command-line arguments
    file name in first, 408
    variables for reading, 131-133
commands, Turbo C Editor, 43
commands, Turbo Debugger
    Evaluate/Modify, 333
    Inspect, 318-320, 324, 326, 333
comment blocks, 35-36
comment headers, 35
comments
    defined, 36
    nesting
        compiler option for, 239
        not recommended for C, 37
communication capabilities, program
   requirements for, 8-9
compile
    via assembly option, 150
    maximum error checking for the first, 200
compiler, Turbo C
    command-line tcc.exe, 231-242
        -S option to generate an assembly
            language program directly from C
            source text, 184, 187, 206
        advantages and disadvantages of, 231
        code generation options, 232, 234
        compile via assembly option, 150
        compiler options, 232, 234-238
        environment options, 232-233
        error message options, 232, 235-238
        for inline assembly code, 232

form for invoking, 232
linker options, 233, 240-241
macro options, 232, 238
make files used only with, 199-200, 204, 212-213, 216-223
memory-model options, 232, 238
optimization options, 232, 239
output redirection with, 231
run-time library source code used with, 232
segment naming options, 232, 239
source code options, 233, 239-240
error handling in, 26-27
integrated tc.exe, 49
asm statements generate error messages with, 150
built-in syntax checking with, 200-201
project files used only with, 199, 212-214, 231
options, 201
translator, 178
type, checking errors by the, 60
compiling
defined, 199
with FORTRAN compiler, 204
with Microsoft C compiler, 204
conditional compilation, 204, 239
configuration management, 228-229
constant(s)
data, 353
macros as, 54
context-sensitive help, 13, 16-17
control block, 353
coprocessors, predefined global variables for detecting, 135-136
country information, 104-106
critical-error handler, 112-113
curves, program to calculate polar-coordinate, 145-147

D

data
constant, 353
correctness of, 351
files versus tables for, 357-358
handling large amounts of, 357-361
live, Turbo Debugger ability to look at, 318-320
logic driven by, 317-318
numeric, field structuring for, 356
range checking, 352-354
test-case, 354-355
text, field structuring for, 356-357
data abstraction, header files add to understanding of, 62
data access, 52-53
time, 30
testing, 255-262, 267
data corruption, 247
data dictionaries in program design, 14
data parsing, 68
data security, 17
data segment (DS)
auxiliary, 129
near heap part of, 63
data structures, 21-23, 63
designing manageable, 355-362
first-in, first-out (FIFO), 23
last-in, first-out (LIFO), 22, 343
data types
bytes pushed on stack for different, 166
registers used to return function value according to, 159-160
data validation, 21, 67, 317-368
automated, 347-354
formalized, 276
methods, 317
database
record deletion in, 29
relational, 19
data-entry screen, 371

debugging. *See also* Turbo Debugger (TD)
  differences between testing and, 226-227, 246-250
  environment, selecting the most useful, 277-278
  errors fixed during, 226
  evaluating expressions during, 333
  hardware, 265-266
  information deleted from final code, 235
  logical structures, 289-316
  macro, assert, 65
  options, 278
  as part of programming, 34
  philosophy, 250
  program internals, 277
  remote, 262-264
  routines, 226
  statements placed at far left margin to stand out, 42
  strategies, 245-287
  tips for simplifying, 273-277
  tools, 278-286
delimiters, pair matching, 43-44
design, program, 2, 7
  abstraction, structure, and modularization involved in, 11
  consistency important in, 16
  document, 392-393, 408
  object-oriented, 6
  samples of
    binary file, 408-409
    graphics, 371-373
    mail merge, 392-393
  strategy selection, 12-15
  structured, 15
    versus quick and dirty, 18-19
  techniques
    bottom-up, 14-15
    object-oriented, 15
    top-down, 13-14, 266, 274-275, 372, 402
device drivers
  graphics, 386

hardware debugging services implemented through, 265
  sample structure for, 386
  use of queues by, 23
directives, MAKE utility
  !elif, 221
  !else, 221
  !endif, 221
  !error, 221
  !if, 221
  !include, 221
  !undef, 221
directives, Turbo C
  .CODE, 182
  .DATA, 182
  .DATA?, 182
  .MODEL, 182
  ASSUME, 178-182
  DOSSEG, 182
  EXTRN, 183-184, 215
  GROUP, 179-182
  SEGMENT, 178
  simplified segment, 182-183
divide-by-zero handler, 140
DOS function call 37h (undocumented), 70
DOS version number, predefined global variables to detect, 135-136
double indirection, 99

E

editor. *See* Turbo C Editor
end-of-file mark, 407
error conditions
  arithmetic, 365-366
  data, causes of, 362-366
  interrupts to trap, 140-141
  logistical, 275
  predefined global variables to handle, 137-138
  range, 352-354
  scope, 366

sources of, 245
type checking, 60
error handler, DOS critical, 112-113
error handling, 26-27
functions, 83
error messages
ANSI violation, 236
common, 236-237
less common, 237-238
tcc options for, 235-238
TLINK, 210-212
exit code to MS-DOS, 418
Expression True conditions, writing, 312-314
Expression Value, 307
expressions
evaluated during debugging, 333
with side effects to change values, 333-336

F

far pointers, 29, 70
field structuring, 356-357
file(s)
access, 22, 27-28
batch, 241
checking, 213-223
command, 204, 210
configuration, 240-241
data structure, 19
dates compared by MAKE utility, 220
dependencies
autodependency feature and, 213-223
MAKE utility to check, 219
of object file on header file it contains, 212-213
encryption, 27
executable, 204
TLINK to generate, 216
format(s)
ASCII (text), 27, 391, 407
binary, 27, 407-419

determining a program's, 27
graphics library, 214
include, path for, 53-54. *See also* header files
key, 19
layouts, designing, 358
library, 213
linking, 19
mail merge, 391-406
make, 199-200, 204, 216-223
creating, 217-220
sample, 218, 373-375
map
linking and, 206-209
messages from linker during creation of, 208
paragraph alignment in, 207
publics section of, 207-208
object, 199
accessing, 213-214
format incompatibilities among compilers, 204
for sample make file, 375-376
TLINK to generate, 216
purpose of, 27
translation, 407
Turbo Debugger use with, 359
file allocation table (FAT), 69
file block, 68
file control blocks (FCBs), 69
file-handling constant, 88-89
file pointer, 28
files, Turbo C
builtins.mak, 217, 222
graphics.lib, 241
tcconfig.c, 238
TDHH386.SYS, 265
THELP.COM, 45
THELP.DOC, 45-46
turboc.cfg, 240
flag field, 29
flat file architecture, 19

floating-point libraries, 145-148
  specification not required in project files, 212
floating-point math, 61
  code generation options impact on, 234
floating-point numbers, 72
  rounding, 366
flowcharts for program design, 14-15
fonts
  sample program to load, 371
  structure containing Borland's, 386
form feed, 403
functions
  arguments accessed as memory locations in inline assembly, 165-169
  BGI, 73
  BIOS function call, 65-66
  cdecl, 235
  character conversion and classification, 67-68
  classification macro, 348-349
  conversion, 349-350
  data-entry, 387
  design of, 26-31
  diagnostic, 351
  directory manipulation, 68-69
  DOS process management, 79-82
  DOS-specific, 62, 69-71
  environmental limit, 77
  error handling, 83
  error message numbering, 71-72
  file attribute, 72
  file sharing, 82-83
  floating-point parameters, 72-73
  graphics information, 73-75
  high-speed memory, 62
  I/O, 61-62
    built-in, 347
    console, 66-67
    low-level, 75-77, 82
    unbuffered, 75
  manipulation, 350
  map for, 46

  mathematics, 77-78
  memory/buffer, 78-79
  memory-management, 62-65
  miscellaneous, 61
    standard library, 86-87
  nonlocal jump, 82
  placing, 46-49
  process control, 347-348
  screen-handling, 66
  restricting, 50
  standard definitions, 84
  string handling, 88
  text-manipulating, 66
  time, 89-90
  with Turbo Prolog modules
    declared as global predicates, 216
    preceded and followed with an underscore, 215
  type size, 77
  user-defined, arguments for, 122
  values
    passed by reference, 162-165
    passed by value, 160-162
  variable argument, 83-84
  windowing, 66
functions, Turbo C
  _chmod, 76
  _clear, 73, 87, 145
  _close, 76
  _control, 73, 87, 145
  _creat, 76
  emit, 215
  _exit, 81
  _fpreset, 73
  _getvect, 141
  _lrotl, 87
  _lrotr, 87
  _open, 76
  _read, 76
  _rotl, 87
  _rotr, 87
  _status, 73, 87, 145
  _strerror, 86, 88

_tolower, 68
_toupper, 68
_write, 77
abort, 81, 87, 347
abs, 87
absread, 70
abswrite, 70
access, 76
acos, 78
allocmem, 63, 70, 92-93, 102
arc, 73
asctime, 89
asin, 78
assert, 61, 65, 351
atan, 78
atan2, 78
atexit, 87
atof, 77-78, 87
atoi, 87
atol, 87
bar, 73
bar3d, 73, 387
bdos, 70
bdosptr, 70
bioscom, 65
biosdisk, 65
biosequip, 65
bioskey, 65, 94-98
biosmemory, 65-66
biosprint, 65-66
biostime, 65
brk, 64
bsearch, 87, 98-101, 116
cabs, 78
calloc, 63-64, 87, 256, 261
ceil, 78
cgets, 67
chdir, 69
chmod, 76
chsize, 76
circle, 73
cleardevice, 73
clearerr, 85

clearviewport, 73
clock, 90, 133
close, 76
closegraph, 73
clreol, 66
clrscr, 66, 417
compar, 116-117
coreleft, 64, 101-104
cos, 78, 147
cosh, 78
country, 70, 104-106
cprintf, 67, 215, 275
cputc, 215
cputs, 67
creat, 76
creatnew, 76
creattemp, 76
cscanf, 67
ctime, 89
ctrlbrk, 70
delay, 70, 175-176
delline, 66
detectgraph, 74, 107-109, 387
difftime, 89
disable, 70
div, 87
dosexterr, 70
dostounix, 70
drawEllipse, 18
drawpoly, 74
dup, 76
dup2, 76
ecvt, 87
ellipse, 18, 74
enable, 70
eof, 76
exec, 80
execl, 81
execle, 81
execlp, 81
execlpe, 81
execv, 81
execve, 81

execvp, 81
execvpe, 81
exit, 81, 87, 418
exp, 78
fabs, 78
farcalloc, 63-64
farcoreleft, 64, 102
farfree, 63-64
farmalloc, 63-64, 360
farrealloc, 64
fclose, 85
fcloseall, 85
fcvt, 87
fdopen, 85
feof, 85
fflush, 85
fgetc, 85
fgetchar, 85
fgetpos, 85
fgets, 85, 268, 272
filelength, 76
fileno, 85
fillellipse, 74
fillpoly, 74
findfirst, 69
findnext, 69
floodfill, 74
floor, 78
flushall, 85
fmod, 78
fnmerge, 69
fnsplit, 69
fopen, 85
fp_off, 70
fprintf, 85, 268
fp_seg, 70
fputc, 85
fputchar, 85
fputs, 85
fread, 85
free, 63, 87
freemem, 63, 70, 92
freopen, 85

frexp, 78
fscanf, 85
fseek, 85
fsetpos, 85
fstat, 88-89
ftell, 85
ftime, 89, 259
fwrite, 85
gcvt, 87
geninterrupt, 70, 141
getarccoords, 74
getaspectratio, 74
getbkcolor, 74
getc, 86, 94, 109-111
getcbrk, 70, 83
getch, 67, 109-111
getchar, 86, 109-111
getche, 67, 109-111, 417
getcurdir, 69
getcwd, 69
getdate, 70
getdefaultpalette, 74
getdfree, 70
getdisk, 69
getdrivername, 74
getdta, 70
getenv, 87
getfat, 70
getfatd, 70
getfillpattern, 74
getfillsettings, 74
getftime, 76
getgraphmode, 74
getimage, 74
getlinesettings, 74
getmaxcolor, 74
getmaxmode, 74
getmaxx, 74
getmaxy, 74
getmodename, 74
getmoderange, 74
getpalette, 74
getpalettesize, 74

getpass, 67
getpixel, 74
getpsp, 70
gets, 86
getswitchar, 70-71
gettext, 66, 417
gettextinfo, 66, 329, 417
gettextsettings, 74
gettime, 71
getverify, 71
getviewsettings, 74
getw, 86
getx, 74
gety, 74
gmtime, 89
gotoxy, 66, 417
graphdefaults, 74
grapherrormsg, 74
graphfreemem, 74
graphgetmem, 74
graphresult, 74, 109
harderr, 71, 112-116
hardresume, 112
hardretn, 71, 112
highvideo, 67
hypot, 78
imagesize, 74
initgraph, 74, 107, 387
inport, 71
inportb, 71
insline, 67
installuserdriver, 74
installuserfont, 74
int86, 71
int86x, 71
intdos, 71
intdosx, 71
intr, 71
ioctl, 76
isalnum, 68
isalpha, 68
isascii, 68
isatty, 76

iscntrl, 68
isdigit, 67-68
isgraph, 68
islower, 68
isprint, 68
ispunct, 67-68
isspace, 68
isupper, 68
isxdigit, 68
itoa, 87
kbhit, 67, 94, 110
keep, 71
labs, 87
ldexp, 78
ldiv, 87
lfind, 87, 99
line, 74
linerel, 74
lineto, 74
localtime, 90
lock, 76
log, 78
log10, 78
longjmp, 82
lowvideo, 67
lsearch, 87, 98-101, 116
lseek, 76, 418
ltoa, 87
main, 43, 46, 213, 267, 271, 291, 303, 310, 325, 387-388, 403-404, 418
malloc, 63, 87, 92, 102, 271, 417
matherr, 78, 351
max, 87
memccpy, 79
memchr, 79
memcmp, 79
memcpy, 79
memicmp, 79
memmove, 79
memset, 79
min, 87
mk_fp, 71
mkdir, 69

mktemp, 69
modf, 78
movedata, 79
moverel, 74
movetext, 67
moveto, 74
normvideo, 67
nosound, 175
open, 76, 407, 416
outport, 71
outportb, 71
outtext, 75
outtextxy, 75
parsfnm, 71
peek, 70-71
peekb, 71
perror, 86, 351
pieslice, 75
poke, 70-71
pokeb, 71
poly, 78
pow, 78
pow10, 78
printf, 83, 86, 102-103, 131, 174, 215, 268
putc, 86, 215
putch, 67
putchar, 86
putenv, 87
putimage, 75
putpixel, 75
puts, 86
puttext, 67, 417
putw, 86
qsort, 50, 55, 87, 116-118
raise, 83, 348
rand, 87, 118-120
randbrd, 71
randbwr, 71
random, 87, 118-120
randomize, 87, 118-120
read, 76, 418
realloc, 63, 87, 271
rectangle, 75

registerbgidriver, 75
registerbgifont, 75, 387
registerfarbgidriver, 75, 387
registerfarbgifont, 75
remove, 86
rename, 86
restorecrtmode, 75
rewind, 86
rmdir, 69
scanf, 83, 86, 347, 349
searchpath, 69
sector, 75
segread, 71
setactivepage, 75
setallpalette, 75
setaspectratio, 75
setbkcolor, 75
setblock, 63, 71
setbuf, 86
setcbrk, 71, 83
setcolor, 75
setdate, 71
setdisk, 69
setdta, 71
setfillpattern, 75
setfillstyle, 75
setftime, 76
setgraphbufsize, 75
setgraphmode, 75
setjmp, 82
setlinestyle, 75
setmem, 79
setmode, 76
setpalette, 75
setrgbpalette, 75
setswitchar, 71
settextjustify, 75
settextstyle, 75
settime, 71
setusercharsize, 75
setvbuf, 86
setvect, 71, 141
setverify, 71

setviewport, 75
setvisualpage, 75
setwritemode, 75
signal, 72, 83, 348
sin, 78, 147
sinh, 78
sleep, 71
sopen, 76
sound, 71, 175-176
spawn, 80-81, 83, 141
spawnl, 81
spawnle, 81
spawnlp, 81
spawnlpe, 81
spawnv, 81, 270
spawnve, 82
spawnvp, 82
spawnvpe, 82
sprintf, 86
sqrt, 78'
srand, 87, 118-120
sscanf, 86, 347
stat, 88-89
stime, 90
stpcpy, 88
strcat, 88
strchr, 88
strcmp, 88, 117
strcmpi, 88
strcpy, 88
strdup, 88
strerror, 86, 88, 93
stricmp, 88
strlen, 88, 312
strlwr, 88
strncat, 88
strncmp, 88
strncmpi, 88
strncpy, 88
strnicmp, 88
strnset, 88
strpbrk, 88
strrchr, 88

strrev, 88
strset, 88
strspn, 88
strstr, 88, 403
strtod, 87
strtok, 88, 120-122, 350-351
strtol, 87
strtoul, 87
strupr, 88
swab, 87
system, 80, 82, 87
tan, 78
tanh, 78
tell, 76
textattr, 67, 417
textbackground, 67
textcolor, 67
textheight, 75
textwidth, 75
time, 90, 119, 259
tmpfile, 86
tmpnam, 86
toascii, 68
tolower, 68
toupper, 68
tzset, 90
ultoa, 87
umask, 76
ungetc, 86
ungetch, 67
unixtodos, 71
unlink, 71, 77, 86
unlock, 77
unmovmem, 79
va_arg, 83-84, 122-125, 171
va_end, 83-84, 122-125, 171
va_list, 83, 122-125, 171
va_start, 83-84, 122-125, 171
vfprintf, 86, 124
vfscanf, 86
vprint, 84, 124
vprintf, 86
vscanf, 86

vsprint, 84, 124
vsscanf, 86
wherex, 67
wherey, 67
window, 67
write, 77

G

graphics, 371-390
  defining requirements for, 371-372
  device, 371
  output, sample, 388-389
  pseudocode to design program for, 372
  source code, 376-386
graphics adapters, 31
graphics displays, 31
graphics mode, 107, 387-388
graphs, 371-390
group defined, 179

H

hard-coded error recovery routine, 352-353
hardware breakpoint, 265
hardware timer interrupt, Int 9h, 89
hash tables, 22
hashing scheme, 9
header files, 46, 49
  ANSI C
    assert.h, 61, 65
    ctype.h, 61, 67-68
    errno.h, 61, 71-72
    float.h, 61, 72-73
    limits.h, 61, 77
    math.h, 61, 77-78
    setjmp.h, 61, 82
    signal.h, 61, 83
    stdargs.h, 61, 83-84
    stddef.h, 61, 84
    stdio.h, 61, 84-86
    stdlib.h, 61, 64, 82, 84, 86-87

string.h, 61, 68, 78, 88
    time.h, 61, 89-90
  to avoid duplications of identifiers, 53
  constants in, 54
    machine-dependent, 90
  dependency of object file on, 212-213
  global (extern) variables in, 56
  sample, 331
  selecting the correct, 60-63
  in source module to access C run-time
    library routines, 60
  statements in, 56-57
  Turbo C
    alloc.h, 62-64, 84
    bios.h, 62, 65-66
    conio.h, 62, 66-67
    dir.h, 62, 68-69
    dos.h, 62, 64, 66, 69-71
    fcntl.h, 62, 72, 82
    graphics.h, 62, 73-75
    io.h, 62, 75-77, 82
    mem.h, 62, 78-79, 88
    process.h, 62, 79-82
    share.h, 62, 82-83
    sys\stat.h, 62, 82, 88-89
    sys\timeb.h, 62, 89
    sys\types.h, 62, 89
    values.h, 62, 90
heap, 63
  length, 138-139
help file THELP.DOC, 45-46. *See also* on-line
  help
hierarchies to show program design, 15
HIPO charts, 15
hot key
  defined, 17
  THELP.COM, 45

I

identifier names
  avoiding duplicate, 53
  coding style for, 37-38

identifiers, C language
  accessing function arguments by, 165
  ANSI-only, 239
  breakpoint, 308
  external, breakpoint locations and, 309-312
  in inline assembly language code statements, 156
    referenced from, 175-177
  maximum length of, 274
  number of characters recognized in, 240
  preceded by underscore, 235
  symbol tables to track, 205
implicit rules, 375
index, 27-29
information hiding, 12, 21, 46
  for country data, 106
  debugging with, 52
  header files add to understanding of, 62
  purpose, 322
input, 8
input/output (I/O)
  buffered, functions to provide, 109
  operations, use of Accumulator register in, 128
Institute of Electronic Engineers (IEEE)
  floating-point standards, 72
instruction-path analysis, 291
Integrated Development environment (IDE)
  compiler. *See* compiler, Turbo C
  CPP used from within, 203
  programs built with BuildAll option in, 223-224
  Turbo C Editor part of, 34
interrupt handler, 141
  programming, 145
  sample programs to install custom, 141-144
interrupts
  BIOS. *See* BIOS interrupts
  defined, 141
  hardware timer, Int 9H, 89

J

Jackson structured design, 6, 15
jump(s)
  between functions, 82
  optimization to removed duplicated, 202
  two ways to cause a C program, 290

K

Kernighan and Ritchie (K&R)
  coding style for indenting and brace placement, 38-39
  specifications for syntax, 274
keys
  Alt-minus sign to complete a macro, 284
  Alt-= to define a macro, 286
  Alt-C to compile, 200
  Alt-D to access Data pull-down menu, 319
  Alt-F
    to access File global menu, 284
    to compile, 200
  Alt-F1 to move backward through help screens or return to previous place, 44
  Alt-F7 Instruction Trace, 297-300
  Alt-F8 Step Over, 300, 302
  Alt-F9 Run, 310
  Alt-F10 to pop up local menu, 308, 337, 341, 359
  Alt-O to access Options global menu, 284
  Alt-V to access View menu, 306
  Ctrl-F1 Help for functions, 45, 200
  Ctrl-I to pop up Inspector window, 304, 319
  Ctrl-K Retrieve Block, 35
  Ctrl-R Retrieve Block, 35
  F1 Help, 44-45, 200
  F2 Set-Breakpoint, 306
  F4 Execute to 'Here,' 295
  F7 Trace Into, 295, 298, 300, 310, 339
  F8 to execute one line of code, 302, 304, 310
  F9 Run, 306, 313

F10 Menu, 319
status of, 94-95
keyword, Turbo Assembler asm, 152
keywords, Turbo C
enum, 62
extern, 52, 322
if, 45
register, 202
struct, 21, 45, 62, 85
typedef, 21, 37, 54-56
union, 21, 62
while, 45

L

libraries, TLINK to generate, 216
library, routine
commercial (purchased), 20-21
custom, 20-21
graphics (GRAPHICS.LIB), 60, 73, 214
nonstandard, 91
run-time, 60, 91, 214, 232
sample graphics. 375
source code, 63
standard, 59-60, 85, 91
using, 91-125
linked lists, 22, 24-25
linker
class of memory model noted by, 30
options, 233, 240-241
using a different, 231-232
linking
map files and, 206-209
modules from other Turbo languages,
214-216
problems in, 209-212
process, 204-212
Turbo Assembler object modules with ones
from Turbo C compiler, 149, 178-194
'unresolved externals' in, 209
lint utility, 6
errors in indentation flagged by, 38

syntax checking by, 200
Turbo C's built-in features resembling, 200
logic
driven by data, 317-318
flow, 346
testing program, 290
loop statement placement on separate line from
semicolon, 42

M

machine-language code, translators to produce,
178
macros
classification, 348-349
as constants, 54
"defined" in header file, 60
keystroke, 284
MAKE utility use of, 220-221
mail merge program development example,
391-406
modules
closeFiles(), 402, 404
openFiles(), 403
printSpoolerActive(), 403
processLetter(), 403
processMailingList(), 403
sample letter file of, 404
sample output file, 405
sample session with, 405
markers, setting place, 43-44
math coprocessors, detecting presence of,
135-136
math operations, use of Accumulator register in,
128
mean time between failures (MTBF), 253
mean time to failure (MTTF), 253
memory
buffer, 28
determining the amount of available, 102
paragraphs of, 92
searching an area of, 99

stacks' use of contiguous, 24
memory models
   Compact, 29, 64, 167
     segments and types used by, 180-181
   Huge, 29, 64, 167
     segments and types used by, 181-182
   Large, 29, 64, 167
     segments and types used by, 181
     Turbo Prolog requirement of, 215
   Medium, 29, 64, 167
     segments and types used by, 180
   mixing, 30
   options, 238
   program performance affected by use of
     various, 203
   selection among
     code size a determinant in, 29-30
     data size a determinant in, 30
   Small, 29, 64, 167
     segments and types used by, 180
   Tiny, 29, 64, 167
     .COM file used as executable file by the,
      204, 210
     segments and types used by, 179
menus
   formats for, 8-9
   global, 281
   painting the screen of, 292-293
   pop-up (local), 12, 281-282
   pull-down, 12
menus, Turbo C
   Break/Watch, 278
   Breakpoints, 308, 312
   Compile, 223
   Data, 319-320, 333
   Debug, 278
   Error, 201
   File, 279, 284, 359
   Global, 319
   Integrated Environment Options, 206
   Optimization, 202
   Options, 284
   Options/Macros/Create, 285

   Run, 278
   View, 306, 337-338, 359
   Watches, 339
   Window, 337
metadata, 353-354
Microsoft C
   compiler, 204
   object file format incompatibility with Turbo
    C, 214
mixed-language programming, 149, 214-216.
   See also assembly language
   problems common to, 275-276
modes
   binary, 408
   defined, 16
   edit, 16
   file-translation, 138, 140
   function, 270
   graphics hardware operating, 73
   text, 388
   view, 16
modular program design, 11
module(s), program
   global symbols for, 341
   input file for, sample, 376
   interface problems with, 247
   placing, 46-49
multiway trees, 23

O

object modules, .BGI graphics device drivers
   converted to, 1
on-line help, 13, 16-17, 44-45
opcodes, invalid, 141
operating environment, Turbo C features to
   provide information about, 127-148
operators, Turbo C
   address-of, 127
   assignment, =, 261
   binary, space on both sides of, 42

bitwise
 AND, 68, 96
 OR, 68
confusion of, 363
I/O, 128
logical equality, = =, 261
MAKE directives used with, 222
precedence, 363-364
sizeof, 84, 261
ternary, 98
unary, no space between operand and, 41
optimization of code, 32, 202
 tcc compiler options for, 232, 239
output
 directvideo predefined global variable for
  writing, 134-135
 incorrect, 247
 integrity of file, 247
 sample program, 388-389
 unexpected, 247

P

pair-matching feature for delimiters, 43-44
paragraphs of memory, 92
 alignment of
  byte, 207
  page, 207
  word, 207
parameter passing
 analyzing parameters from, 361-362
 compiler options, 235
 inline assembly statements for direct access
  with, 172
 sequence, 166
parameters, 361-362
parent process
 defined, 79-80
 to install an interrupt handler, 141-144
 I/O redirection for, 271-273
 wait while child process executes, 270
parser(s) end of line inferred by some, 201

Pass Count, 307
path analyzers, 228
pointer(s)
 array of, 260
 to arrays, 260
 assignment
  determination of correct, 330
  nonportable, 238
 base, 167-168
 comparison, nonportable, 238
 dereferenced, 262
 frame, 168
 NULL, 271
 problems with, 365
 secondary stack, 127
 spacing between unary operator and
  operand important in work with, 41
 suspect, 330
 type cast, 263
 to a variable, 260
 void, 116
precedence, confusion about, 363-364
printer
 definitions, 27
 interrupt, 131
 spooler, 392, 405
procedure translation, 245
profilers, 31
program(s), Turbo C
 accuracy, reliability, and serviceability
  determined with system testing, 252-254
 audience, writing for the most general,
  273-274
 behavior
  bugs recognized by improper, 246
  inconsistent, 247
  'social,' 254-255
 blending modules from other languages in,
  214-216
 built in the Integrated Development
  Environment, 223-224
 changes to, 254

compiling, checking, and linking, 199-230.
See also compiler, Turbo C *and* linking
crashes, causes of, 26
defining requirements for. *See* program
requirements *and* software development,
life cycles
design. *See* design, program
implicit branching in, 290-291
indentation of, 38-41
optimization, 202
performance
considerations, 31-32
disk access affect on, 359
features to increase, 127-148
measurements, 13
portability
defined, 17-18
typedefs to aid, 55
warning options, 238
pseudovariable values change when
functions are called by, 127
single- versus multiple-file, 19
testing. *See* testing, Turbo C program
program development. *See* software
development
program requirements
communications transmission (baud rate),
8-9
customer interviews to determine, 7-9
functional, fulfillment of, 246
input editing format, 8-9
mail merge sample of analyzing, 391-392
menu design and options, 8
prototypes to define, 6, 10
record access standards, 8-9
report layout, 8
research, 245-287
specific information required for proper
implementation of, 8-9
writing up, 407
program segment prefix (PSP), 79
_psp variable containing the segment address
of, 138-140, 298-299
capturing the address of, 298-300

programs
COMMAND.COM, 79-80
MicroCalc, 272
Prokey, 43
Superkey, 43
THELP.COM, 45-46
programs, sample Turbo Assembler
A_AVG1.ASM (listing 6.17), 190-192
A_AVG2.ASM (listing 6.20), 193-194
DEMO.ASM (listing 6.15), 187-189
MEMSIZE.ASM (listing 6.12), 184-186
MEMSIZE2.ASM (listing 6.13), 186
programs, sample Turbo C
bar3d.mak (listing 12.1), 373-375
benchmrk.c (listing 9.1), 257-259, 263
blink.c (listing 6.3), 158-159
bumpup.c (listing 6.2), 157
c_avg0.c (listing 6.16), 189-191
c_avg1.c (listing 6.18), 191-192
c_avg2.c (listing 6.19), 192-194
demo.c (listing 6.14), 187
diskswap.c (listing 6.4), 161-162
dropdown.c (listing 6.5), 162-163
dump.c (listing 14.1), 409-418
flipover.c (listing 6.6), 164-165
GETINT.C (listing 2.4), 47-51
GETSTR.C (listing 2.5), 48-49
graphics.c (listing 12.3), 376-386
makefile (listing 13.1), 394
memsize.c (listing 6.1), 152-153
merge.c (listing 13.2), 392-402
MODTEST.C (listing 2.6), 48-49
MODTEST.PRJ, 49
outgrp.rsp (listing 12.2), 376
phones.c (listing 11.1), 330-332
runlog.c (listing 9.2), 268-272
song.c (listing 6.9), 175-176
token.c (listing 11.2), 350
varyasm.c (listing 6.8), 173-174
varyorig.c (listing 6.7), 171-172
prototypes, function, 6, 30, 42-43
compiler review of, 200-201
to define requirements, 10
information relayed by, 60

place markers for finding and gathering, 43-44

placement near beginning of a file, 43

to restrict knowledge of functions, 50-51

specifying, 42

to text integrated groups of functions, 252

pseudocode

comments first written as, 36

in design document, 408

in program design, 14

sample, 372

pseudorandom numbers, 118-120

pseudovariables, 65

accessing registers directly with, 127

defined, 127

names

_AH, 128, 131

_AL, 128

_AX, 128, 152

_BH, 128

_BL, 128

_BP, 130

_BX, 128

_CH, 128

_CL, 129

_CX, 128

_DH, 129

_DI, 130

_DL, 129

_DS, 129

_DX, 128, 131

_ES, 129

_SI, 130

_SP, 130

_SS, 129

rules, 127-128

types, 128-130

Q

quality assurance defined, 224

quality control defined, 224

queues, 11, 22-23

circular, 24

R

random access memory (RAM), determining whether to send output to, 134-135

random-number generator, seeding, 119

record(s)

access, 8-9

binary file, 409

buffer, 358-359

deletion, 29

fixed-length, 27-28

variable-length, 27-28

registers

accumulator (AX), 128, 156, 159-160, 299

AH for upper byte of, 128

AL for lower byte of, 128

base (BX), 128, 156

BH for upper byte of, 128

BL for lower byte of, 128

base pointer (BP), 112, 127, 130, 343

code segment (CS), 127, 129

count (CX), 128, 156

CH for upper byte of, 128

CL for lower byte of, 129

data (DX), 128, 156, 159-160

DH for upper byte of, 129

DL for lower byte of, 129

data segment (DS), 129, 156

destination index (DI), 130, 156, 169

extra segment (ES), 129, 156, 299

source index (SI), 112, 130, 156, 169

stack pointer (SP), 127, 130, 343

stack segment (SS), 127, 129, 343

Turbo C, 127

regression testers, 228

reports, determining whether to sort data in, 8

resolution, choosing the highest, 107

S

scope, 52
  backward search of symbol table facilitates concept of, 205-206
  current, 324-325
  errors, 366
  global, 324, 327
  header files add to understanding of, 62
  local, 319, 323, 327, 366
  modifier
    extern, 322
    static, 323
  override, 312-313, 320-327
    syntax, 325-327
screen blanking, 158
seed for random number generator, 119
segment
  defined, 178
  DOS, locating the end of, 300-302
  logical, 178
  names used by Turbo C, 179
  naming options of tcc.exe compiler, 232, 239
segment:offset register pairs, preserving, 155-156
SETBLOCK DOS call, 360
setup time for disk operations, 358-359
shell
  to leave a program and enter system-level commands, 80
  as user-friendly interface, 13, 80-81
side effects, 333-336
signal handler
  SIGABRT, 348
  SIGFPE, 348
    setting a signal for, 140
  SIGILL, 348
  SIGINT, 348
  SIGSEGV, 348
  SIGTERM, 348
snow on CGA adapter screens, 275

software development, 6
  goals, 10
  identification of users first step in, 7
  life cycle
    coding, 2, 7, 391. See also coding
    design, 2, 7, 11-31, 391. See also design, program
    overview, 249
    requirements analysis, 2, 5, 7-10, 391. See also program requirements
    sample mail merge file illustrating, 391-406
    "standard," 230
    testing, 2, 7. See also testing, Turbo C program
software engineering defined, 6
sort methods
  alphabetic, 117
  quicksort, 50
source code control, 229
stack(s), 11, 22
  access to arguments on the, 122, 165-169
  activity during a function call, 177
  automatic variable space allocation on, 325
  contiguous memory required by, 24
  frame, 168-169, 176, 235
  as LIFO structures, 22
  popping items from, 23
  pushing items onto, 23
  size, 138-139, 343
    exceeding, 209
standard inference rules, 375
statement, Turbo Assembler jump, 155
statements, Turbo C
  condition compilation, in header files, 57
  #define, 37, 54, 204
  #endif, 239
  #if, 56
  #ifdef, 56, 239
  #include, 53
  #pragma, 152-153
  goto, 154

if...else, 98
LOOP, 128
preprocessor, in header files, 56
tlib, 217
tlink, 217
while, 303
static storage class, 50
stderr, 85
stdin, 85, 268, 272-273, 347
stdout, 85, 268, 272-273
stdprn, 85
storage class modifiers, 52
streams, predefined, 85
stress test, 355
string(s)
   operations, use of Accumulator register in, 128
   tokenizing, 120-122
subprograms, 155
symbol table
   searching, 205-206
   to track identifies (symbols) for variables and functions, 205
   variable stored in, 157
symbols, 183-184
system values, predefined global variables for, 138-140

T

terminate-and-stay-resident (TSR) programs, hot-key combinations for, 95
test plan, 227-228
test-case generators, 228
testing, Turbo C program
   automating, 267-273
   benefits of, 224-226
   designing data for, 354-355
   differences between debugging and, 226-227, 246-250
   documentation of, 267-273
   examples of, 226-227

logic, branch, and path, 289-316
   overview of, 224
   philosophy, 250
   prototype code for incremental, 275
   strategies, 245-287
      bottom-up, 266-267, 274-275
      general, 265-266
      top-down, 266-267
   techniques for program operation, 2
   types
      beta, 277
      integration, 225-226, 251-252, 255, 267
      performance/time (benchmark), 255-262, 267
      regression, 225-226, 254-255
      system (alpha), 225-226, 252-254, 255, 267
      unit, 225-226, 250-251, 255, 267, 346
      validation (acceptance), 225-226
time, predefined global variables for, 133-134
TLINK. *See* Turbo Linker (TLINK)
token, replacing the characters from, 121
tracing, 291-298
trees
   AVL, 25
   B+, 9, 22, 25
   B*, 25
   binary, 11
      as simplest form of, 25
      as structure for data files, 19, 22
   components of, 25
Turbo Assembler, 149-195. *See also* assembly language
   avoiding case conflicts with, 177-178
   naming conventions, 174-175
   options
      /ML for case-sensitive treatment of all symbol names, 177
      /MU to convert all symbol names to uppercase, 177
      /MX for case-sensitive treatment of public and external symbols, 177-178

Turbo C program features compared with those of, 149-150
Turbo C routines called from, 215
Turbo BASIC modules incompatible with Turbo C, 214
Turbo C Editor, 34-42
  make file produced with, 217
  pair-matching feature, 43-44
  as part of integrated development environment, 34
Turbo C Professional
  assembler included in, 1
  development time accelerated with, 1
  error-checking facilities of, 200
  naming conventions, 174-175
Turbo C run-time library source code, 63
Turbo Debugger (TD)
  basic tools, 279-286
  current position in program marked with triangular bullet, 283
  descending into functions, 295
  with files, 359
  hot keys, 284
  inspection of complex data objects, 329-333
  integrated, 2, 34, 91, 227, 232
  learning the full range of, 276
  Log, 286
  macros for automation and retesting, 284-286
  RAM requirements for, 279
  selection of, 277-278
  stand-alone, 2, 34, 92, 227
  starting, 279-281
  Step Over facility of, 302-305
  Trace Into facility of, 295-298
  trace point, 307
  watch point, 92, 307
  windowing, 281-283
Turbo Linker (TLINK)
  avoiding case conflicts with, 177-178
  MAKE utility usable with, 216

options for map files
  /l for use of source code line numbers, 206
  /m for use of publics, 206
  /s for use of detailed map of the segments, 206
  /x to produce no map file, 206
  as part of Turbo C package, 204
  sample use of, 375
  warning and error messages, 209-212
Turbo Pascal modules incompatible with Turbo C, 214
Turbo Prolog
  logic handling, 214
  memory allocation in, 215
  predicates, 215
  Turbo C functions that write to screen work incorrectly with, 215
type definitions, 54-56
  NULL, 84
  ptrdiff_t, 84
  size_t, 84
  time_t, 89
typographical errors, 245

U

unconditional branch. *See* jump(s)
user interface
  behavior, poor, 247
  defining the specifics of, 8
  designing, 15-16
  major considerations of, 15
  shell for friendly, 13, 80-81
utilities, Turbo C
  BGIOBJ, 1, 373-375
  lint. *See* lint utility
  MAKE, 216
    command-line options, 217
    directives, 221-223

file dates compared by, 220
invoking, 217, 394
macros used with, 220-221
sample graphics program use of, 373-375
OBJXREF, 208-209
TDREMOTE, 263-264
TDSTRIP, 1, 203
TLIB, 376
TOUCH, 223
xehelp.c, 297-298

V

variable
proliferation, controlling, 357-361
sizes specified in inline assembly, 157
variables
automatic, 324-325
failure to initialize, 363
reference to defunct, 363
composite, 329-333
control, 335
data, 344
declaring, 56
defining, 56
global versus local, 355
DOS, 131-133
environment
COMSPEC, 80
PATH, 68
error
_doserrno, 72, 137
errno, 72, 137
_sys_errlist, 137
sys_nerr, 137
global
_8087, 135-136, 147
_argc, 131-132
_argv, 132
_doserrno, 93
_fmode, 138, 407
_heaplen, 139

_Int0Vector, 140
_Int4Vector, 140
_Int5Vector, 141
_Int6Vector, 141
_osmajor, 135-136
_osminor, 135-136
_psp, 139
_StartTime, 133
_stklen, 139
_version, 135-136
daylight, 133
directvideo, 134-135
environ, 132
extern, 56, 322
predefined, 131-141
static, 30, 37
timezone, 133
tzname, 133
inspecting
in other source files, 326-327
physical location of reference for, 319
local (auto), 30, 37
static, 106
made unavailable to other source files,
323-324
pointer, 99
representation by TD of, 327-333
scope, 322-324
state, 344
static, 325
version control, 228-229
version numbering methods, 229
version numbers of DOS, global predefined
variables to determine, 135-136
video adapters, 73
viewports, clipping outside of, 12

W

Warnier-Orr diagrams, 15
white space usage in program listings, 42

window(s)
    active, 281
    Breakpoints, 307-308, 310
    CPU, 298-300, 342-343
        Code pane, 342
        Data pane, 343
        Dump pane, 360
        Register pane, 342
        Stack pane, 343, 361
    Dump, 360-361
    File, 359
    identifying, 283
    Inspector, 304, 319, 325-326, 332-333
    Log, 286, 306-307

    Module, 283, 341, 343
        Global pane, 341
        Static pane, 341
    multiple, 282
    panes, 307
    Registers, 343-344
    Stack, 343, 361-362
    Variables, 341-342, 346
    Watches, 336-340, 346
windowing
    consistency in, 13
    Turbo Debugger, 281-283
wrap around, 345

More Computer Knowledge from Que

SELECT QUE BOOKS TO INCREASE
YOUR PERSONAL COMPUTER PRODUCTIVITY

Using Assembly Language

by Allen Wyatt

Using Assembly Language shows you how to make the most of your programs with assembly language subroutines. This book helps you understand assembly language instructions, commands, and functions—how they are used and what effects they produce. You will learn to develop and manage libraries of subroutines, successfully debug subroutines, access BIOS and DOS services, and interface assembly language with Pascal, C, and BASIC. Now you can harness assembly language's speed, versatility, flexibility, and code compaction—with Que's *Using Assembly Language*!

DOS Programmer's Reference

by Terry Dettmann

Intermediate and advanced programmers will find a wealth of information in Que's *DOS Programmer's Reference*. Designed for serious applications programmers, this "nuts and bolts" guide contains sections on DOS functions and their use; IBM-specific programs; expanded and extended memory; and the use of DOS with various languages, such as C, BASIC, and assembly language. A combination of tutorial and reference, this text helps you gain a greater understanding of what your operating system has to offer. Choose *DOS Programmer's Reference*, the definitive guide to DOS applications programming.

Using Turbo Pascal

by Michael Yester

An excellent introduction to Borland's popular Turbo Pascal Version 5.0. *Using Turbo Pascal* teaches you not only the Pascal language and protocol, but also the kind of disciplined and well-structured programming techniques that will help you become an efficient Pascal programmer. Includes a tear-out **Quick Reference Card**.

C Programming Guide, 3rd Edition

by Jack Purdum, Ph.D.

A completely new edition of a Que classic. Rewritten to reflect C's ongoing development—including the new ANSI standard—this text contains many programming tips that let readers benefit from the author's practical programming experience. Also included are a complete keyword reference guide, a host of program examples, and a tear-out quick reference card. This is the perfect guide for beginning programmers in the C language.

ORDER FROM QUE TODAY

Item	Title	Price	Quantity	Extension
107	Using Assembly Language	$24.95		
883	Using Turbo Pascal	21.95		
76	DOS Programmer's Reference	24.95		
850	C Programming Guide, 3rd Edition	24.95		

Book Subtotal _____

Shipping & Handling ($2.50 per item) _____

Indiana Residents Add 5% Sales Tax _____

GRAND TOTAL _____

Method of Payment

☐ Check   ☐ VISA   ☐ MasterCard   ☐ American Express

Card Number _____ Exp. Date _____

Cardholder's Name _____

Ship to _____

Address _____

City _____ State _____ ZIP _____

If you can't wait, call **1-800-428-5331** and order TODAY.

All prices subject to change without notice.

FOLD HERE

Place
Stamp
Here

_____
_____
_____
_____

Que Corporation
P.O. Box 90
Carmel, IN 46032